Data Visualization for Social and Policy Research

All social and policy researchers need to synthesize data into a visual representation. Producing good visualizations combines creativity and technique. This book teaches the techniques and basics to produce a variety of visualizations, allowing readers to communicate data and analyses in a creative and effective way. Visuals for tables, time series, maps, text, and networks are carefully explained and organized, showing how to choose the right plot for the type of data being analyzed and displayed. Examples are drawn from public policy, public safety, education, political tweets, and public health. The presentation proceeds step by step, starting from the basics, in the programming languages **R** and **Python** so that readers learn the coding skills while simultaneously becoming familiar with the advantages and disadvantages of each visualization. No prior knowledge of either **Python** or **R** is required. Code for all the visualizations are available from the book's web site.

JOSE MANUEL MAGALLANES REYES is a Professor of Political Science and Public Policy and Director of the Institute of Social Analytics and Strategic Intelligence at Pontificia Universidad Católica del Perú (PUCP) and a Visiting Professor at the Evans School of Public Policy at the University of Washington. He is also an Affiliated Researcher at the Center for Social Complexity at George Mason University and a Catalyst Fellow at the University of California–Berkeley Initiative for Transparency in the Social Sciences BITSS. His work has been funded by BITSS, the eScience Institute of the University of Washington, the Vice Rectorado de Investigación PUCP, the NSF, the Washington Research Fund, the Sloan Foundation, and the Moore Foundation.

"Sometimes social science students understand the value of data visualization, but they are wary of the costs of mastering high-tech approaches. Professor Magallanes is the answer to this problem. This text skillfully articulates a step-by-step guide for using two of the most powerful tools in a data scientist's toolbox: R and Python. Professor Magallanes has a talent for simplifying the complicated, and honing in on the most important components of telling stories with data. This book is an essential resource for anyone whose regular habits of making graphs involve searching for someone else's code chunks on the Internet. With this book, we can all stop Googling and start graphing."

- Jennifer Nicoll Victor, Professor of Political Science, George Mason University

"José Manuel Magallanes Reyes is back at it again with his unique approach of simultaneously introducing users to computational social science programming in both R and Python. The approach allows readers not just to 'learn a language,' but rather to learn the key conceptual ideas behind programming and computational social science. With his first volume having tackled data collection and statistical analysis, it was an absolute pleasure to see him turn his approach to the all-important subject of data visualization in this text. Having recommended his previous book to countless numbers of students, I am absolutely thrilled to now have a second volume to share as well!"

- Joshua A. Tucker, Professor of Politics and Co-Director,
Center for Social Media and Politics, New York University

"Professor Magallanes cuts directly to the heart of the matter, quickly and clearly imparting the concepts and skills that a modern social science researcher needs to communicate complex data relationships. He leads the reader through a wide variety of visualization approaches using a conversational style and systematic approach."

- Dr. Timothy Gulden, Senior Policy Researcher, RAND Corporation

"A wise professor once told me, 'If there is something you want your audience to remember, put it in a figure.' This timely volume will show you how, with copious examples drawn from extensive experience in social and policy research."

- Abraham D. Flaxman, Professor of Global Health at the Institute for
Health Metrics and Evaluation, University of Washington

"Information literacy demands that we convey data in digestible, visually appealing plots and graphs. However, even advanced quantitative researchers often lack the tools to produce effective visualizations of the data they work with. This is where Magallanes' book comes in. With his characteristic narrative – a meticulous but nimble prose, chock full of illustrative examples – Magallanes guides inexperienced and sophisticated readers alike through easy-to-grasp data visualizations. His presentation of geospatial and network data visualizations alone makes this an invaluable go-to reference for those working in R and Python."

- Guillermo Rosas, Professor of Political Science, Washington University in St. Louis

"Surviving the current deluge of social science data is only possible with novel computational analysis and machine learning techniques. Among the many approaches currently in vogue, none is more important than human visualization of data, whether in raw form, suitably plotted, or else transformed in some way meaningful to the problem at hand. Professor Magallanes' new book offers a wide range of general approaches and explicit code for developing modern data visualizations. It will be an important addition to the library of every social scientist and policy researcher contending with the flood of new data."

- Robert Axtell, Professor of Computational Social Science, Department of
Computational and Data Sciences, and Department of Economics,
George Mason University

"José Manuel Magallanes Reyes' *Data Visualization for Social and Policy Research* is an outstanding and greatly needed resource in a rapidly expanding area of academic and applied data analysis and empirical methodology. The guided instruction is accessible to novice users and soon has us producing powerful visualizations from simple univariate, bivariate, multivariate, geospatial, and social-media text data."

- Robert J. Franzese Jr., Professor and Associate Chair, Department of Political Science,
The University of Michigan, Ann Arbor; Fellow and former President,
The Society for Political Methodology

" 'A picture is worth a thousand words.' Nowhere is this more the case than when presenting data to policymakers in order to guide decision-making. In this book, José Manuel Magallanes Reyes shows us how, drawing upon his extensive background in social science, public policy, data science, analytics, and teaching visualization to undergraduate and graduate students in political science and public policy."

- Ed Lazowska, Professor, and Bill & Melinda Gates Chair Emeritus, Paul G. Allen School of
Computer Science & Engineering, Founding Director of the eScience Institute,
University of Washington

Data Visualization for Social and Policy Research

A Step-by-Step Approach Using R and Python

JOSE MANUEL MAGALLANES REYES
Pontificia Universidad Católica del Perú and
The University of Washington

CAMBRIDGE
UNIVERSITY PRESS

University Printing House, Cambridge CB2 8BS, United Kingdom

One Liberty Plaza, 20th Floor, New York, NY 10006, USA

477 Williamstown Road, Port Melbourne, VIC 3207, Australia

314-321, 3rd Floor, Plot 3, Splendor Forum, Jasola District Centre,
New Delhi – 110025, India

103 Penang Road, #05–06/07, Visioncrest Commercial, Singapore 238467

Cambridge University Press is part of the University of Cambridge.

It furthers the University's mission by disseminating knowledge in the pursuit of
education, learning, and research at the highest international levels of excellence.

www.cambridge.org
Information on this title: www.cambridge.org/9781108494335
DOI: 10.1017/9781108625425

First published 2022

Printed in the United Kingdom by TJ Books Limited, Padstow Cornwall

ISBN 978-1-108-49433-5 Hardback
ISBN 978-1-108-71438-9 Paperback

Contents

1

Introduction

This book shares my experience of teaching undergraduate and graduate students in political science and public policy how to plot findings to guide decision-making in scientific and professional settings. At both levels of education, I found students with different backgrounds in quantitative tools. To my surprise, younger generations of undergrads, which master many technological gadgets, are having a hard time dealing with analytics, and have no basic understanding of how to encode information obtained into a visual. At graduate level, on the other hand, it seems easier to teach these contents as they relate analytics to problems they have been facing. That required that I developed a particular teaching approach for not leaving anybody behind, while keeping my class interesting, so the reader should expect detailed explanations in this book.

My courses emphasize three different skills: data pre-processing (collecting and organizing), data analysis (modeling and inferencing), and producing information (visualizing and publishing). This book focuses on the last stage, and all its related procedures. In a previous work, I covered the first skill (Magallanes Reyes, 2017), which is arguably the most time-consuming; but finding a way to produce insight once the second stage is done (analysis) is an art difficult to transfer, and even more so if the tools are difficult to learn (or to buy).

However, I think that it is not the lack of visualization tools that causes trouble; it is the opposite, there is an incredible amount of methods of producing graphics that might confuse social and policy science scholars during their first steps in data science. I plan to give a step-by-step approach to the basics of producing information visually, a crucial element in today's complex society.

To be honest, I thought that writing this book would not be a difficult task, but it has taken too long to produce as it was done during the COVID-19 pandemic and, like most you, my life habits changed in many ways. But even though my work took longer than expected, I also had the chance to confirm how valuable it is to have simple plans available to help decision-making, while explaining why a decision had to be made.

Keeping that in mind, I decided to prepare a book that will not contain beautiful visuals that are difficult to interpret, but a collection of plots familiar enough to most people, but with a lot of explanations on how to make plots most audiences can understand. I will do my best to avoid offering too many choices of plots in each case; but in general, I will produce a simple plot and expand on it as long as the extra detail will not distract the reader.

1.1 Some Assumptions

This book assumes you want to learn to produce the best possible visuals. So, I assume you are already producing plots, but you are not sure if your choices are the right ones. I also assume you do not know if Python is better than R or vice versa, so I offer you both versions; however, every visual you see in the book is made using R and I just offer a Python code that will produce the same result as R.

I also assume that you believe that using the *the grammar of graphics* that R uses via the package **ggplot** (Wickham, 2016) is a well-documented option; thus, every R plot will be made using that approach and I will avoid using a different one; this will put me in trouble with Python as many great libraries do not follow that same coding approach; this will not be solved easily, so several times you will not be able to see the same coding approach.

A strong assumption is that you know some basic R or Python. I will not use complex operations at all in R, but you might find some Python code that is not easy to get understand just by reading it (so pay attention to the explanations I will give). I also assume you know how to install libraries or packages in R and Python.

Finally, I have not produced interactive plots, because I assume that if you can prepare a static plot, you can take an extra step and make it interactive. After assuming so many things, I was surprised by the amount of pages this book contains.

Why R or Python? This book will use **R** and **Python** to teach you how to prepare an informative visualization. The selection does not mean that you should avoid visualization tools that require no coding, it just means that if you have done pre-processing and modeling in those languages, you can still use them to communicate your results or findings. I am also using them because the market requests skills in both languages for the non computer scientist. If it were not for R or Python, data science would not have invaded the territory of social science. I can not imagine social science programs or government schools teaching JAVA or C++.

Python and R are also attractive as they are well documented, with lots of applications in different areas of knowledge, active communities in the web sharing code and examples; and, of course, you can use R and Python free of charge. Some other details follow:

- **R** is a high-level programming language. That is, its creators have tried to abstract it, so that some commands are in English. This means that there are low level languages that *talk* to the computer in a language closer to what a computer understands (far from direct human understanding). Because it is free-of-charge and open-source, it has allowed many scholars not only to carry out data analysis, but also to contribute to R itself with very specific functionalities, so that R now has support for almost any kind of quantitative technique. It has been said that R represents a slow learning curve at the beginning, but I found that working with R is just different, not harder. However, that depends on the coding style the user develops (messy codes are difficult to follow in any programming language). This book emphasizes a basic coding style and habits to make R instantaneously reachable.
- **Python**, is an all-purpose programming language with many more features for computational work than R, but, for the goals of this book, I will not make that difference clear for the reader. I can only say that you can not build sophisticated information systems with R, but for sure you can with Python. Python, as well as R, has a very active community of users and developers, and you can practically write any question about Python in your browser and find several answers. After reading this book you can try that, just keep in mind that those who reply are often advanced users who may use jargon that a novice user may not understand.

As for speed, regular users may not find a difference between Python and R. If you find that computing results is taking too much time, writing a better code can improve the speed, but advanced programming techniques require more preparation, and the code may become difficult to read. This book will not turn you into an advanced programmer; it will turn you into an effective user of both languages in order to deal with situations similar to the examples. It may be that your code is very good, so take into consideration that other factors also affect speed, such as the size and contents of the file, your hardware (laptop, tablet, etc.), your internet provider, your operating system version, the memory available, and so on. For the examples in this book, speed will not be an issue.

1.2 R and Python Environments

There are several ways you can use R or Python, but I have used these environments:

- **Anaconda** for **Python**.
- **RStudio** for **R**.

The code I use in the book is independent of what environment you use. Anaconda is a free **Python** distribution, which includes the most popular **Python** packages needed in this book for data analysis. That is, it is almost ready to be used without much downloading. Nevertheless, Anaconda has a simple way of adding packages that are not included. I will let you know when a package is needed. RStudio is also a coding environment that makes the R experience easier and more versatile. However, RStudio does not include R, so you will need to install **R** first. RStudio is also free-of-charge.

Both RStudio and Anaconda offer business options, which are not free. These options are needed to deploy large-scale applications. Not everything is free in the data analytics business, but the free versions are enough for all applications you need for academic and professional work.

However, they both have a way to help you install and use external programs called *packages/modules/libraries* (I will use them interchangeably). These are very useful when you need to carry out complicated tasks that need some large code, as it is likely that someone has created a package that does what you need. You do not need to know every package available, but progressively you will become familiar with packages that will save you lots of coding time.

I use RStudio because it gives me a nice interface to install any package I need. You can use the command `install.packages()` but I prefer using the RStudio window for that, as shown in Figure 1.1.

Anaconda has a window to help you install packages, as shown in Figure 1.2.

RStudio might not interact with you during installation, but Anaconda may request your permission after the four steps in Figure 1.2. In general, another window will pop up telling you what other changes will be done to proceed with the installation. While RStudio will show you "almost" every available package, Anaconda may miss several packages in the menu

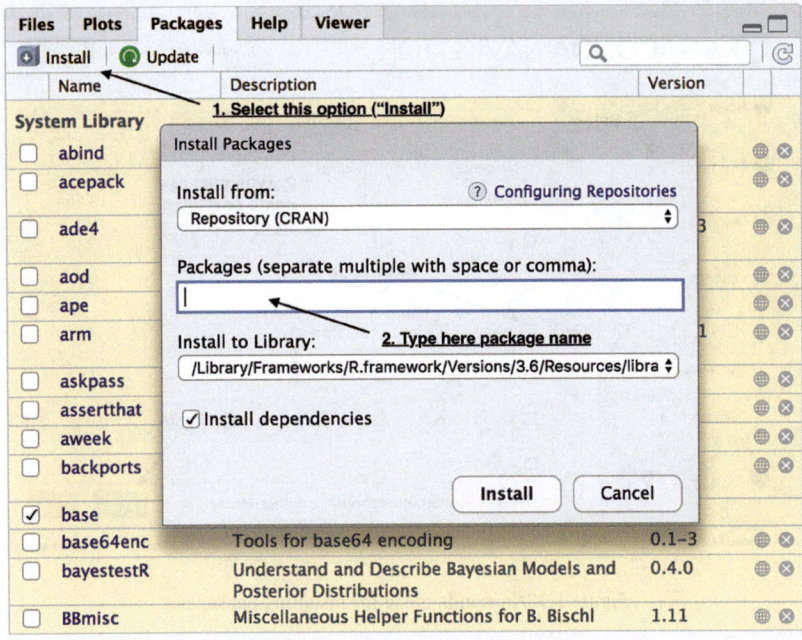

Figure 1.1 RStudio menu for installing packages

shown in Figure 1.2, in that situation you should first request *the terminal*, as shown in Figure 1.3.

Notice that in Figure 1.2 you can have the option to have "Environments". There, I have created an environment where I will install all the libraries needed for this book. In Figure 1.3 I am using my "bookVisualDS" environment, and I decided to "Open Terminal" because I need to install a library not available in Anaconda. In Figure 1.4 you can see the terminal, where you can type the commands needed to install other libraries (pip install, in this case). Notice that the installation will be done in the "bookVisualDS" environment. I highly recommend you create an environment for this book, and, if you do so, request Python 3.7 or above. After the terminal window appears, you can install a package using the command `pip install` plus the name of the package to install. I show you that in Figure 1.4.

The command *pip* is a familiar alternative, but there are more options for installing, like *conda install*. Every package recommends a particular procedure for this, and you should follow that advice.

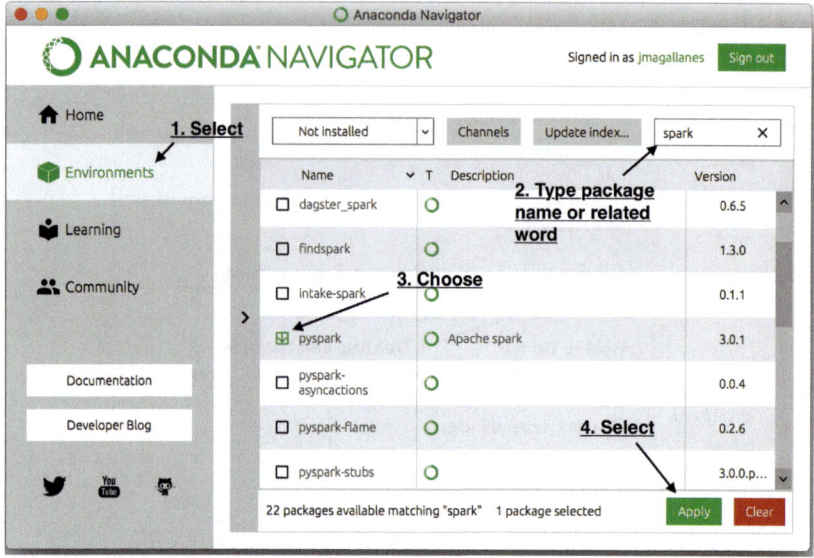

Figure 1.2 Anaconda menu for installing packages

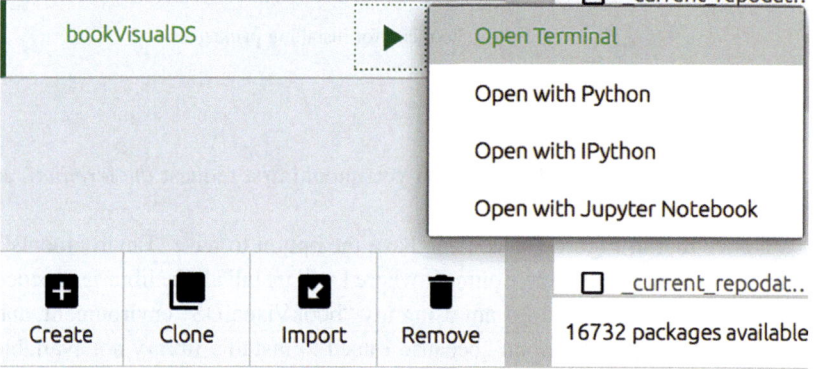

Figure 1.3 Calling the terminal from Anaconda
The call is done from an environment named bookVisualDS.

1.3 The Rest of the Book

This book is organized into three parts. The first part includes two chapters. The first, chapter one, is a review on data nature, and how the identification

Figure 1.4 Using pip for installing a package
The installation will be done only at the environment that made the call.

of data type and structure is an important previous step for producing visuals; the second chapter deals with basic concepts you should master when making plots. I recommend you pay close attention to this chapter as it mentions elements you should include in your plots, elements I may not include in every plot in the book. The second part of the book deals with data organized in tables, the most well-known structure for people familiar with spreadsheets. I have organized this part into three chapters, each one dealing with plots for one, two, or three or more variables. In each case, you will see options for numerical and categorical data. The last part will offer two chapters to briefly cover data that are not exactly tables, such as maps, and networks; the chapter on networks, the last one, will include some basic plots for text data coming from Twitter.

1.4 How to Read This Book

In this book, each section depends on something previously said; so, I recommend you read it from beginning to end because in each chapter I am assuming you read the previous chapter. Therefore, I may not explain why I do something if I have explained it before. Of course, if you know most of the material covered, you are most welcome to visit the chapter or section you believe you need, while skipping previous material. I tried to include references to previous sections as needed.

This book has been conceived for students, professors and professionals of social and policy sciences at all levels. It can be used for self-learning, and to complement any quantitative analysis course.

All the book codes and data are stored in repositories in GitHub, which I will make available upon request to my email address: jmagallanes@ pucp.edu.pe or magajm@uw.edu.

1.5 Acknowledgements

I am very grateful to Cambridge University Press for giving me the opportunity to share this new work, specially to my editor Lauren Cowles. I am also very grateful to the reviewers that had the time to comment and suggest improvements on my initial drafts.

This book has been possible due to the continuous support from the eScience Institute at the University of Washington (UW) and the Evans School of Public Policy from UW; and the support from my home institution in Peru, the Pontificia Universidad Catolica del Peru, particularly from the support given by the Department of Social Sciences, and the grant (Concurso Anual de Proyectos PUCP - ID 713/Codigo 2019-3-0026) which required me to share these techniques with the data analytics team. I have to express my particular thankfulness to Ed Lazowska, Bill Howe, Tyler McCormick, Bernease Herman, Micaela Parker, and Sarah Stone from eScience; and to Sandra Archibald, Allison Cullen, Craig Thomas, David Layton, Ann Bostrom, and Leigh Anderson from the Evans School. They have been very supportive during my stay at UW and motivated me finish this book in different ways. I am also thankful to the graduate students at the Evans School, who help me to better organize these contents with their feedback from my teaching. I also would like to thank my colleagues at George Mason University, Robert Axtell, William Kennedy, Annetta Burger, and especially Claudio Cioffi-Revilla, my PhD advisor who recently retired as an Emeritus Professor.

I also express my deepest thanks to my home institution, the Department of Social Sciences of the Pontificia Universidad Catolica del Peru, which has made great efforts to support my work in Peru and in the United States. I am particularly very thankful for that to Alejandro Diez, David Sulmont, Aldo Panfichi, Eduardo Dargent, Sinesio Lopez, and Catalina Romero. I would also like to send special thanks to the crew of my 'Grupo Interdisciplinario de Prospectiva para Políticas Públicas' – GI3P (Interdisciplinary Group on Foresigth for Public Policy) Chiara Zamora, Gabriela Rengifo, Airam Bello, Diana Heredia, Claudia Linares, Manuel Sigueñas, Nicolas Jacobs, Fresia Gómez, Sofia Ticliahuanca, Luis Torres, Yurfa Toralva, Alejandro Boyco, and Pavel Coronado.

This book was finished while I suffered the lost of my "viejitos" Alfredo, and Jorge. However, it was not all bad news: Diana, my wife, was finishing her masters dissertation; and Rafael, my son, was starting high school in Lima and improving his tennis skills. Seeing them flourish keeps me moving forward.

PART ONE

Getting Started

2

Data for Plotting

I am a firm believer in the idea that the first step before embarking into producing a plot is knowing the characteristics of the data. This may seem pretty obvious for the experienced analyst, but it may not be so for the novice, especially if this new apprentice is using default plots and lacks some formal training on basic methodological, statistical, and visual concepts. It is also important to keep in mind that some plotting functions require particular data structures as input, which are not necessarily the ones you have in hand.

In the next sections, I will provide different ways of thinking about the data in your hands, which will allow you to identify their characteristics and format, so that you can profit from these in the coming chapters.

2.1 Data-Types

When you have information about the society you are analyzing, you will definitely run into very different data types. In general, if we have a traditional spreadsheet in mind where rows are the individuals or units of study and the columns are their variables, the data type is a characteristic of the column. Considering the types managed by **R** or **Python**, let me summarize those into these groups:

- **Text**. A column where its set of values is a candidate for a *key* field: values that are not repeated because they are uniquely identifying the unit of analysis (i.e. "full name"). If it is not unique, the text or *string* or *character* values are generally turned into a categorical column. However, if the text is, for example, a "tweet" it will remain as text to extract its meaning (it will not be a categorical, and it will not be a key).
- **Categorical**. These data are produced by organizing or categorizing a variable into statuses or levels. These statuses have names to differentiate

11

one from the other, and they can represent an ordering or not. They are limited and discrete; that is, each represents one particular characteristic. Notice that categories can be represented with numbers[1].

- **Numerical**. You have numerical data when your data values are potentially unlimited. These values appear when a variable can be measured or counted. Values from counting are discrete (not allowing decimals). Measurement allows for decimal values.

- **Boolean**. Values that are used in logical operations, as they only accept two values: True and False.

- **Date**. They are simple numbers behind the scenes, but when a column has a date format it allows for particular operations that can give, for example, a result in terms of days or months.

- **Missing**. We generally consider a missing value as the cell that has no information, and most programs will recognize them like that. However, when doing surveys, there are people that do not want to give answers to a particular question (which will then produce a missing value) but you still collect the reason for that (i.e. "do not know", "not interested"). You need to be aware of this, because those answers may be present in categorical and numerical values[2].

R or **Python** will "decide" the data types by default, but this does not mean you have to rely on that default judgment. Most of the time the data types need to be formatted to the right type by the user. For example, when visiting the Wikipage of Freedom Indices[3] you see text in every column, but that text is just a label to identify the levels of a scale (Stevens, 1946). Those texts represent values that may need further mathematical treatment. You also see the text "n/a" being used to represent a missing value. Part of this data table is shown in Figure 2.1.

You will need to turn the text into the right data type. Notice that each column should represent a single data type, but the exception is that a missing value can always be present in any of them.

R and **Python** can manage the data types presented in this book very well. **R** will directly implement any of these, while **Python** will need libraries[4] beyond its basic functionality to represent those values. Let me give you further details and examples.

---

[1] You can find data where *1* represents "single"; *2* represents married, *3* represents divorced, and so on.

[2] Imagine that you have the value -9 in a variable like *age*, that may not be a typing error, but a code telling you "I refuse to give my age." To avoid such errors, you must always read the methodological section of all data you collect.

[3] https://en.wikipedia.org/wiki/List_of_freedom_indices.

[4] I will mainly use *Pandas* as the default (see McKinney, 2010).

List by country [edit]

Country	Freedom in the World 2019[10]	2019 Index of Economic Freedom[11]	2019 Press Freedom Index[3]	2018 Democracy Index[13]
Abkhazia	partly free	n/a	n/a	n/a
Afghanistan	not free	mostly unfree	difficult situation	authoritarian regime
Albania	partly free	moderately free	noticeable problems	hybrid regime
Algeria	not free	repressed	difficult situation	authoritarian regime
Andorra	free	n/a	satisfactory situation	n/a

Figure 2.1 Example of data frame with text values

Image captured from List of freedom Indices, in Wikipedia, n.d., Retrieved June 1, 2019.

2.2 Data Types in R and Python

2.2.1 Text Values

In Figure 2.1, you see five columns, where each should have a particular data type. The first column is not qualifying in any way the country, it is just naming or *identifying* the row. An identifier is unique (unless it is a composite identifier[5]), and you should set its data type as text. You are not planning to do any mathematical operation with identifiers. **R** will use the type *character (or* chr*)* for this kind of data; while **Python** will use the type *string (or* str*)* (or *object* if it is a column in a data frame as defined by *Pandas* in **Python**).

2.2.2 Categorical Values

You have categorical variables when the column represents a characteristic of the unit of analysis. In this situation, you are aware that one characteristic or attribute can be shared among many rows in your data.

---

[5] A city name can be an identifier, but sometimes you need city and county names, making a composite identifier when city names are not unique in a county. This is solved if the row has a unique code.

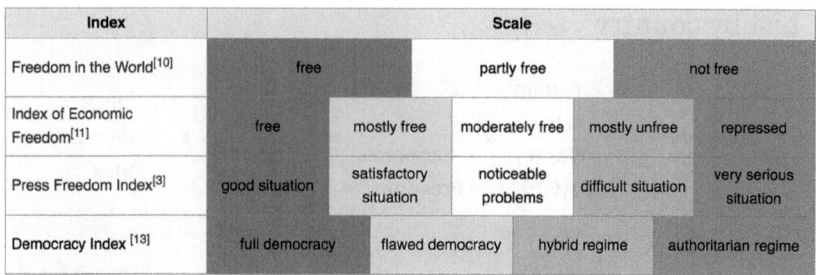

Index	Scale				
Freedom in the World[10]	free		partly free		not free
Index of Economic Freedom[11]	free	mostly free	moderately free	mostly unfree	repressed
Press Freedom Index[3]	good situation	satisfactory situation	noticeable problems	difficult situation	very serious situation
Democracy Index [13]	full democracy		flawed democracy	hybrid regime	authoritarian regime

Figure 2.2 Levels of ordinal variables

Image captured from List of freedom Indices, In Wikipedia, n.d., Retrieved June 1, 2019.

Categorical data can be of two sub-types:

- Nominal. These are attributes that do not express any kind of order other than alphabetical. They will not tell you which is the "best" or the "worst". When nominal values can only take two values, they are known as dichotomous variables. The data from Figure 2.1 has no nominal data. **R** will use the type *factor* for this kind of value; while **Python** will use the type *category* if it is a column in a data frame as defined by *Pandas* in **Python**.
- Ordinal. These are attributes that do express, as the name implies, some kind of order. They indicate a certain degree of achievement or sequence. However, as these are not numbers, you cannot compute a numerical distance among the levels. In general, the amount of levels is limited to a few values. The last four columns in Figure 2.1 represent ordinal data, whose levels are labelled with some text. **R** will use the type *ordered* for this kind of data; while **Python** will use the type *Ordered category* if it is a column in a data frame as defined by *Pandas* in **Python**.

Figure 2.2 shows the levels of each column. In this situation you see that each level has a text label, but these columns are not text type. You can also use integer numbers to represent levels, but keeping in mind they are not actually numbers. In other words, if you use the numbers from one to five to represent the levels of the *Press Freedom Index*, you cannot say that level four is two times better than level two, as that statement implies numerical distance. You can only say that four is two levels above two.

2.2.3 Numerical Values

Numbers are simpler to explain. These are values that represent order, as with the ordinals, but that also represent distance. We can divide numbers into two groups:

- Counts. As the name implies, these values arise from counting. Population is an example of count data, for instance. **R** will use the type *integer* for this kind of data; and **Python** will also use the type *integer* if it is a column in a data frame as defined by *Pandas* in **Python**.
- Measurements. When you measure something, you can expect decimal values. However, a measurement process has particular characteristics which can divide numbers into two different groups or scales:
  - Interval scale. These are values where the distance can not be expressed as a proportion, only as distance; that is, 40° Fahrenheit is not two times warmer than 20°, but it is in fact 20 units apart in that scale. Of course, you can even express that distance using decimals. Scales where zero does not represent the absence of the attribute are designated as interval values. In that situation, zero in Fahrenheit does not mean an absence of temperature, or zero in the Intelligence Quotient (IQ) does not mean the absence of intelligence. As the zero is not absolute, you will find that, as in temperature and IQ, there are alternative ways to measure that characteristic; and in each situation, the zero may have a different meaning. **R** will simply use the type *numeric* or *double* for this kind of data; while **Python** will use the type *float* if it is a column in a data frame as defined by *Pandas* in **Python**.
  - Ratio scale. You have Ratio values when the distance can also be interpreted as a proportion. A person with a height of 1.80 meters, is 1.5 times taller than a person who measures 1.20 meters, while also 60 centimeters taller. You can have alternative units to measure height, but zero has the same meaning in all of them: zero US Dollars is zero Euros, and zero Yens; and zero meters is zero feet. **R** uses the type *numeric* or *double*; while **Python** uses *float*.

2.2.4 Boolean Values

You have Boolean data types when values can be either true or false. You can use dichotomous values or even a text value for that, but programming languages support this specific data type. **R** will simply use the type *logical* for this kind of data; while **Python** will use the type *boolean* if it is a column in a data frame as defined by *Pandas* in **Python**.

2.2.5 Date Values

Date values are a particular representation of time. The computer is actually counting time, but it has a means to convert that into a date, which may be used in some particular applications that involve, for example, time differences. Both **R** and **Python** have a *date* data type.

2.2.6 Missing Values

Missing values can always be present in any column, but this is not informed as a separate data type: if a column is a number or a category, the presence of a missing value will not change the data type. Missing values need to respect how a language represents them; if you use an "x" to denote a missing value in a numeric column, that character will turn or *coerce* the column into a text data type. **R** uses *NA* to signal a missing value, and **Python** uses *None*.[6]

Here, I want to show you how **R** and **Python** can open a file and recognize a default data type. Let me use some data I collected in 2017 from the Common Core of Data from the US Department of Education.[7] I kept detailed information on public schools from the state of Washington. Let me try **R** first:

```
> #link to data
> linkRepo='https://github.com/resourcesbookvisual/data/'
> linkEDU='raw/master/eduwa.csv'
> fullLink=paste0(linkRepo,linkEDU)
> #
> #getting the data:
> #avoiding that text values are read as categorical
> eduwa=read.csv(fullLink,stringsAsFactors = FALSE)
> #
> #what you have
> str(eduwa,width = 65,strict.width='cut')
```

```
'data.frame':    2427 obs. of  24 variables:
 $ NCES.School.ID     : num  5.30e+11 5.30e+11 5.31e+11 5.30e..
 $ State.School.ID    : chr  "WA-31025-1656" "WA-06114-1646""..
 $ NCES.District.ID   : int  5304860 5302700 5309100 5300030 ..
 $ State.District.ID  : chr  "WA-31025" "WA-06114" "WA-34033"..
 $ Low.Grade          : chr  "6" "KG" "9" "PK" ...
 $ High.Grade         : chr  "8" "12" "12" "6" ...
 $ School.Name        : chr  "10th Street School" "49th Stre"..
 $ District           : chr  "Marysville School District" "E"..
```

---

[6] Notice that both **R** and **Python** also use *Inf/-Inf* to represent infinite values, and *NaN* to say a value is not a number. Pay attention to those, as you may need to decide whether they are to be considered missing when a column is the result of a computation.

[7] https://nces.ed.gov/ccd/.

```
$ County              : chr  "Snohomish" "Clark" "Thurston" "..
$ Street.Address      : chr  "7204 27th Ave NE" "14619B NE 4"..
$ City                : chr  "Marysville" "Vancouver" "Tumwa"..
$ State               : chr  "WA" "WA" "WA" "WA" ...
$ ZIP                 : int  98271 98682 98512 98520 99205 98..
$ ZIP.4.digit         : int  NA 6308 NA 5510 NA NA NA NA NA 9..
$ Phone               : chr  "(360)965-0400" "(360)604-6700""..
$ Locale.Code         : int  22 12 13 33 12 13 21 12 41 41 ...
$ LocaleType          : chr  "Suburb" "City" "City" "Town" ...
$ LocaleSub           : chr  "Suburb: Midsize" "City: Midsiz"..
$ Charter             : chr  "No" "No" "No" "No" ...
$ Title.I.School      : chr  "Yes" "No" "No" "Yes" ...
$ Title.1.School.Wide : chr  "Yes" NA NA "Yes" ...
$ Student.Teacher.Ratio: num 23.4 8.4 21.5 15.9 6.5 15.3 NA 1..
$ Free.Lunch          : int  28 53 169 292 12 411 48 102 101 ..
$ Reduced.Lunch       : int  3 9 40 10 4 23 12 22 23 0 ...
```

The data were stored in the GitHub repo of the book. I split the link to the data into two texts, 'linkRepo' and 'linkFile', and then I concatenated both into 'fullLink' (paste0 will not put any character between the texts being concatenated). This step is not needed but I like to do it so that it does not use the whole page width (you will see that I follow this strategy throughout the book). Notice that read.csv can read the data from the GitHub link directly (notice I stopped the conversion of text into categorical data, the default behavior when reading in the data). Finally, you see I use the function str to get the data type information. I have included some parameters so this function does not populate the width of the page (in most cases, the default output can be very messy).

I will translate the previous **R** code into **Python**. The coding strategy will be the same, but there will be differences: **Python** can use a + to concatenate text, and the *Pandas* function read_csv will also call the link, but will not try to convert text into categories by default. Notice that **R** does not need to activate a particular package to deal with 'data frames'; this is a native structure for **R**. On the other hand, **Python** needs you to activate *Pandas*. In both cases 'eduwa' is a data frame, but **R** will use a function (str) to recover the data type, while **Python** will call the data types an attribute (dtypes) of the data frame.

```
# link to data
linkRepo ='https://github.com/resourcesbookvisual/data/'
linkEDU ="raw/master/eduwa.csv"
fullLink= linkRepo + linkEDU

# activating Pandas and getting the data:
import pandas as pd
eduwa = pd.read_csv(fullLink)

#what you have
eduwa.dtypes
```

In both cases, you get the default data types, which may or may not correspond to what they are supposed to be.

```
NCES.School.ID              int64
State.School.ID             object
NCES.District.ID            int64
State.District.ID           object
Low.Grade                   object
High.Grade                  object
School.Name                 object
District                    object
County                      object
Street.Address              object
City                        object
State                       object
ZIP                         int64
ZIP.4-digit                 float64
Phone                       object
Locale.Code                 float64
LocaleType                  object
LocaleSub                   object
Charter                     object
Title.I.School              object
Title.1.School.Wide         object
Student.Teacher.Ratio       float64
Free.Lunch                  float64
Reduced.Lunch               float64
dtype: object
```

From what you learned in the previous subsections, you realize that both **R** and **Python** could differentiate textual from numeric values. However, numeric values are not of the same sub-type in some cases; this is not a problem at all, as integers and real numbers will go through the same processes. You can also see that the ones recognized as text are candidates to be *identifiers* or *key* columns. In this case, the first four are identifiers, as well as the the 7th, 10th, and 15th columns ('school name', 'address', and 'phone', respectively). Those variables are not to be analyzed statistically, but may be used for annotating (7th and 15th column) or for geocoding[8] (10th column). Notice that for these data, 'State' is not an identifier but is not a variable either; it is a constant and will not be analyzed statistically. A small issue would be the manual identification of categorical, ordinal or non-ordinal, values that are in fact variables and not identifiers.

2.3 Dataset Structure

It is important to be aware that there are different formats in which the data values are stored. The example data in Figure 2.1 are in a rectangular shape, but

---

[8] Use **R** or **Python** to recover a geographical coordinate.

that may not always be the case. Data formats do not affect the data type, but do affect the way you plan your visuals. And, more important, some functions are good for some formats but fail if the format is not the right one.

2.3.1 Tables

Tables are by far the most common format you will encounter. This will be very familiar to most of you as it is the basic structure a spreadsheet represents. In this situation, the values are in the intersection of a row and a column, and the column represents a particular data type. Rows may or not be the unit of analysis, as it depends whether the table has a *wide* or *long* format. All table types are well managed in **R** and **Python**.

Wide Format

Wide formats are the most familiar table structures. In this situation, one row gives us all the information of the unit of analysis.

Long Format

Long formats[9] are less common than wide formats, but are still very familiar for analysts used to panel data. In this format, there will be a row for every value measured or observed, then the unit of analysis may be distributed in more than one row; that is, it will be a sub-table. This may produce a more concise table.

Data in wide format can be turned into long format, and vice versa. Figure 2.3 shows you the analogy.

Notice that in Figure 2.3, the missing value that was present in the wide format, need not be present in the long one. As mentioned, in the long format each age has its own row, and most units of analysis are a sub table (except for the last case).

2.3.2 Non-Table Formats

Most of what analysts do makes use of tables; but non-table formats exist and are also becoming very important. In the next subsections, I will show these data structures.

---

[9] Wickham (2014a) prefers to called this data "stacked", which will represent a *tidy* format.

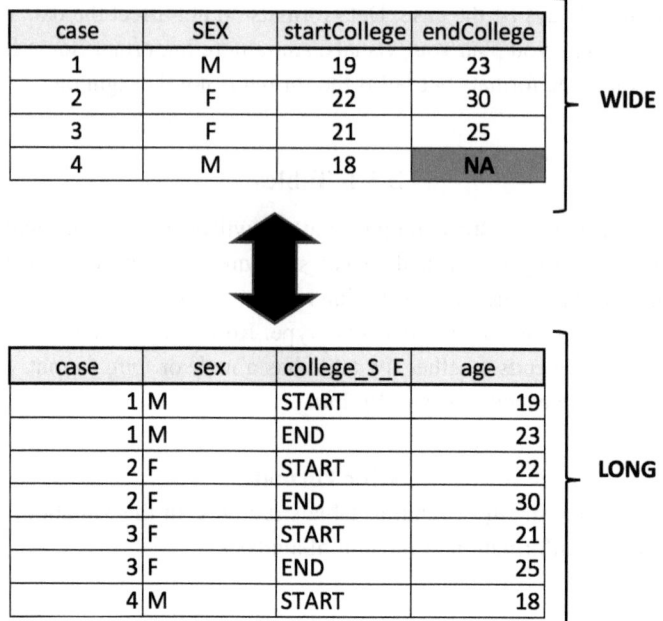

Figure 2.3 Wide and long formats

Networks

Imagine we want to show if five neighboring countries ever invaded one another. We can have a plot like the one in Figure 2.4 for this invented situation.

This imaginary plot can be stored in a spreadsheet like an **adjacency matrix**, as shown in Figure 2.5.

An adjacency matrix will have the same elements as row names and column names, and the intersection will signal if there is a link between them. In this example, the diagonal will not be populated, because I am not assuming that a country can invade itself (there may be other networks when a self-loop is possible). That same information can come in other structures. An **adjacency list**, as shown in Figure 2.6, is a structure where the first element to the left is the source, and every element to the right is a target. The **edge list** is a collection of pairs, where the first element indicates the *source* and the second the *target*. The edge list for our network is shown in Figure 2.7.

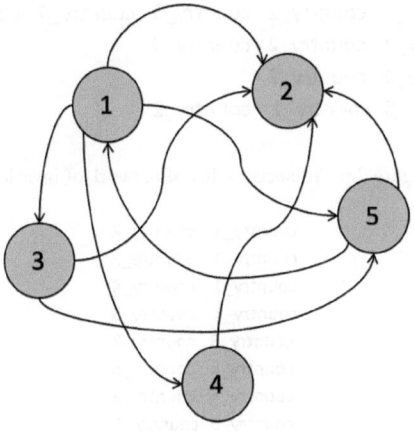

Figure 2.4 Network of invasions

Imaginary network representing a country that ever invaded another one.

	country_1	country_2	country_3	country_4	country_5
country_1		1	1	1	0
country_2	0		0	0	0
country_3	0	1		0	1
country_4	0	1	0		0
country_5	1	1	0	0	

Figure 2.5 Adjacency matrix of network of invasions

```
country_1  country_2  country_3  country_4  country_5
country_3  country_2  country_5
country_4  country_2
country_5  country_1  country_2
```

Figure 2.6 Adjancency list of network of invasions

```
country_1  country_2
country_1  country_3
country_1  country_4
country_1  country_5
country_3  country_2
country_3  country_5
country_4  country_2
country_5  country_1
country_5  country_2
```

Figure 2.7 Edge list of network of invasions

These structures can be stored in tables, so **Python** and **R** can be used without problem. Of course, dictionaries are always an alternative to tables. This structure comes next.

Dictionaries

You may be interested in a simple way of storing information about people. As it is a simple task, you want to populate a table with the data you collect from those people. However, even in this simple situations you may be limited by the table.

If you happen to have an online form, you need to plan the form structure that people will see and fill out. Asking for language spoken, for instance, will need a cell filling out; but this is uncomfortable for a person that speaks natively more than one language, and who uses the table. It may also be important for you to know that the person speaks more than one language. If you use a table, you will need to have several columns for languages spoken, but it will be difficult to anticipate how many columns you need (and many empty cells, that will be interpreted as missing values, could appear). In this situation, a dictionary is a great alternative. Our imaginary example is represented in Figure 2.8.

The dictionary is a structure that allows for a particular key (i.e. 'language', 'country', etc.) to have a collection of values assigned to it. This is what the lower part represents in Figure 2.8. According to Seeger (2009), dictionaries are the base data structure of the NoSQL model, which is precisely working to

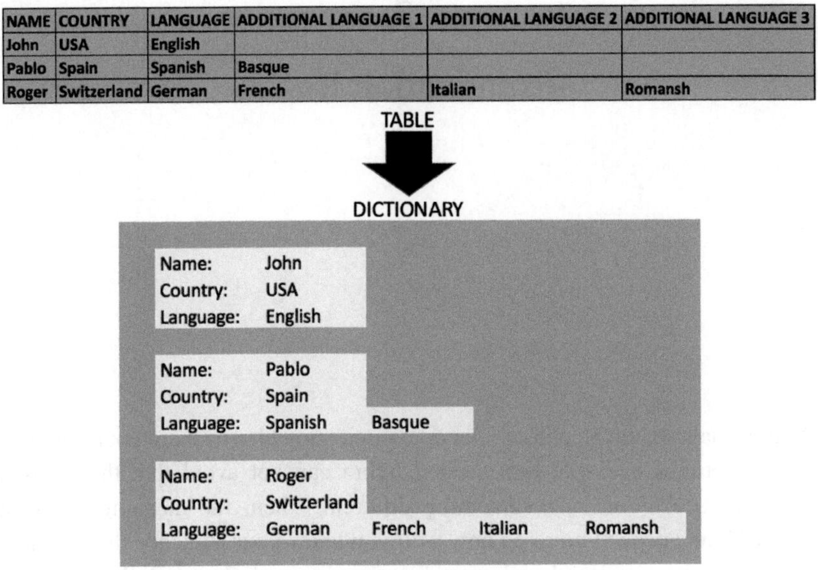

NAME	COUNTRY	LANGUAGE	ADDITIONAL LANGUAGE 1	ADDITIONAL LANGUAGE 2	ADDITIONAL LANGUAGE 3
John	USA	English			
Pablo	Spain	Spanish	Basque		
Roger	Switzerland	German	French	Italian	Romansh

TABLE

DICTIONARY

Name:	John
Country:	USA
Language:	English

Name:	Pablo
Country:	Spain
Language:	Spanish	Basque

Name:	Roger
Country:	Switzerland
Language:	German	French	Italian	Romansh

Figure 2.8 Converting data frame to dictionary

promote strategies that overcome the limitations of tables. If you run into open data portals you will for sure deal with this format, as the results are obtained in JSON format. Most information coming from social media applications like Twitter use dictionaries. Every *tweet* is represented by a complex dictionary.

Finally, complex formats such as maps, generally represented using *shape-files*, have a competitor in dictionaries, as they can be implemented more efficiently using these: the GeoJSON and TopoJSON formats.

A dictionary is not a native structure in **R**, but it is in **Python**. **R** generally uses lists to represent a dictionary. Collecting and formatting all these different data types and dataset formats has been widely discussed in Magallanes Reyes (2017).

3

Visualization Basics

Your visuals should be part of your communication plan to share your findings, but sometimes even the best crafted figure can not avoid that the reading audience seeks and sees something different. Then, the meaning of "best crafted" may depend more on how well you know your audience than on how good you are at using the plotting functionalities of **R** and **Python** (or any other software for that matter). I have come to the conclusion that the simpler the better, and that is what I am planing to share next.

In this chapter, I will give some general recommendations on making your visuals, while helping you become familiar with **R** or **Python** plotting functions and philosophy. I will introduce all of this using data present in tables (data frames), just focusing on the data types mentioned in Section 2.1. When dealing with tabular data, you can suspect that you might produce a visualization for each column, and then for a couple of them simultaneously, and then for three or more. In this chapter, the examples will simply use univariate exploration; which is common for searching for problems or verifying outcomes; not for giving explanations.

3.1 Elements of Information Visualization

3.1.1 Components

The components of most visuals are well known, but I just want to make sure you have this clear, as often you may find visuals that do not include what should be included. Also, consider the kind of product you are making: unless there is such a thing as "free style", you should follow a particular academic style.

24

Title

Important academic styles, such as the one from the American Psychological Association (2010), or APA, recommend that titles go below the image (while *tables* should have them on top). For APA, you are expected to explain the image shown, as well as assign a number to it.

However, if you were to put a title on the top space within the plotting area you may consider using this to make a point:

- a *question* answered by the plot
- a *guide* for the reader to understand the purpose of your plot
- It can *suggest* a possible conclusion.

Titles that achieve those goals are not that easy to produce. You need to rewrite them many times, until you find a good combination of words that can be read and understood fast enough before the audience loses connection. It is also good to keep in mind that you must never give your audience a cacophonous version (a "tongue twister"). If you need, make use of subtitles with a smaller font size, to explain period and location, or similar information worth stating. Let me use the *Democracy Index for 2019* (The Economist Intelligence Unit, 2019). Let's call the data:

```
> linkRepo="https://github.com/resourcesbookvisual/data/"
> linkDemo="raw/master/demo.rda" # "R data" file!
> load(url(paste0(linkRepo,linkDemo)))
```

These examples will use *ggplot2* functions(Wickham, 2016), or simply *ggplot*, whose approach is to build layers of information to improve a visual layer after layer:

```
> # call plotting library
> library(ggplot2)
> # produce info: inform dataset, and variables to use
> info=ggplot(data=demo,aes(x=Continent))
```

That code just called the library which needs to be previously installed. Then, I created the **info** object. This object represents the input: the data frame, and the variables to use. The variables to plot are defined in **aes**thetics. Each variable will later be represented in some way. The next step is to add *geometry object* being used:

```
> # add a particular geometry object with the info and create plot
> titles1=info + geom_bar()
```

```
> # show it:
> titles1
```

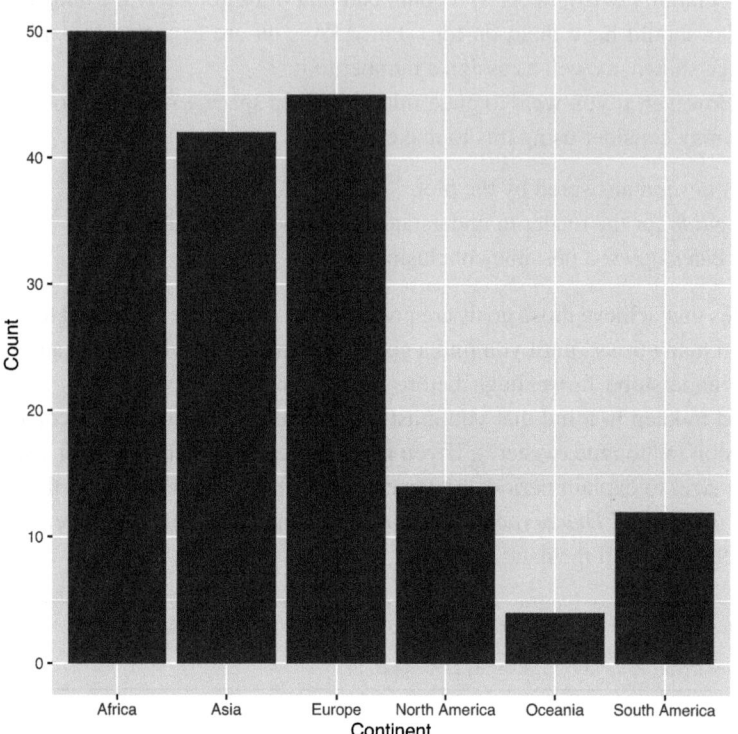

Figure 3.1 Default plot
Data from Index of Democracy, in Wikipedia, n.d., Retrieved June 1, 2019.

I have added a layer to the object `info`. Generally, the first layer represents the type of plot, in this case the variable in `aesthetics` from the `info` object will be represented by bars. The resulting plot is stored into the `titles1` object.

The default plot, as shown in Figure 3.1, does not have a title as *ggplot* does not produce one by default (a barplot using basic plotting functions in **R**, without using *ggplot*, puts the name of the variable as the default title). Let's write a title and a subtitle:

```
> # Titles to be used:
> the_Title="A NICE TITLE"
> the_SubTitle="A nice subtitle"
> # adding the titles:
> titles2=titles1 + ggtitle(label = the_Title,
+                           subtitle = the_SubTitle)
```

```
> # result
> titles2
```

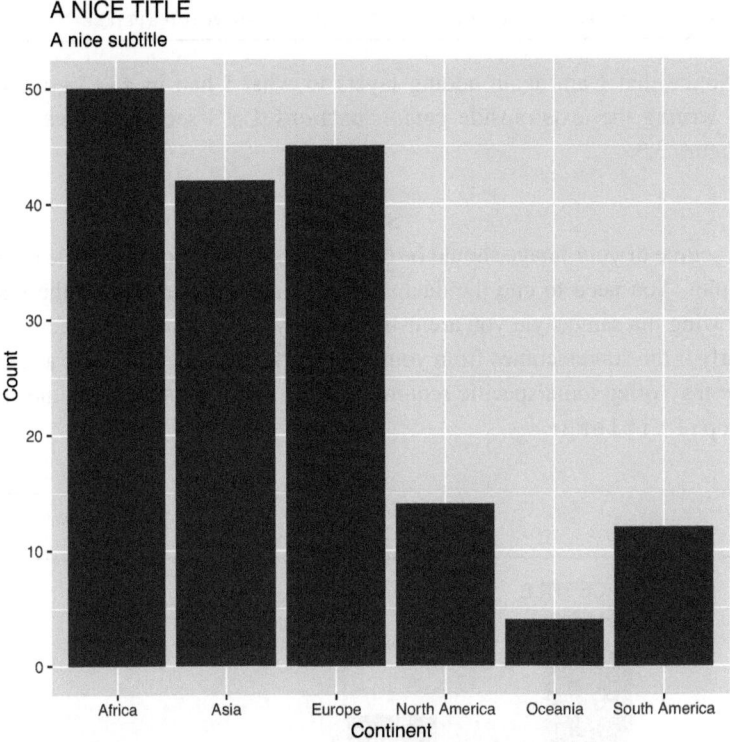

Figure 3.2 Adding titles
Data from Index of Democracy, in Wikipedia, n.d., Retrieved June 1, 2019.

Notice that I prefer writing the text outside the code. I consider that this practice enhances readability and reusability: you can use this code again with other variables, just changing the text. Besides, the changes you will make to the text will be not be close to the functions, which will reduce the possibility of your erasing something important by mistake. You can see the result in Figure 3.2.

Figure 3.2 offers you default axes titles, which most of the time you need to change. Make sure they are clearly stated, specially if they represent some unit of measurement. If you are using a plot in a meeting, you do not want the decision maker or any one in the audience constantly interrupting your presentation with questions that reveal they found basic imperfections in your work. Let's add the axes titles:

```
> # Axes to be used:
> horizontalTitle="Continents present in the study"
> verticalTitle="Number of countries studied"
> # adding the axes titles:
> titles3=titles2 + xlab(horizontalTitle) + ylab(verticalTitle)
```

Notice that I am again adding layers to what I had in `titles2`; I am also writing the texts outside *ggplot* functions. Let's see the newest version in Figure 3.3:

Source

The source of your image should be clearly stated. You should include it below the plot. You need to cite the data source, or any other author of the image, following the same style you are using for all your citations. You should state clearly if the source comes from your own work. Again, a particular academic style may offer some specific requirement for this. Let me add another layer on top of `titles3`:

```
> # result
> titles3
```

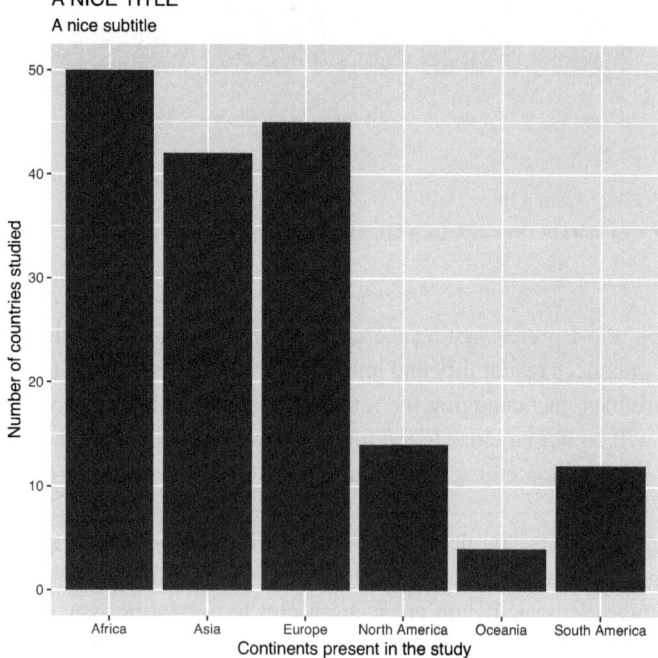

Figure 3.3 Axes titles
Data from Index of Democracy, in Wikipedia, n.d., Retrieved June 1, 2019.

```
> # Source to be used:
> theSource="Source: Democracy Index at Wikipedia"
> # adding the source:
> source=titles3 + labs(caption = theSource)
```

Now, the `source` object will have a plot with its source, as shown in Figure 3.4.

Annotations

Annotations help readers focus on some section of your plot. There can be one or more, and they can be a combination of text messages, reference lines, and reference polygons.

Annotations need location information: identify the coordinates from the previous plot. You have to manually locate an annotation using the coordinate system of your current plot (the range of values of your data). Notice that the horizontal is showing the levels of the nominal variable, but not numbers.

```
> # result
> source
```

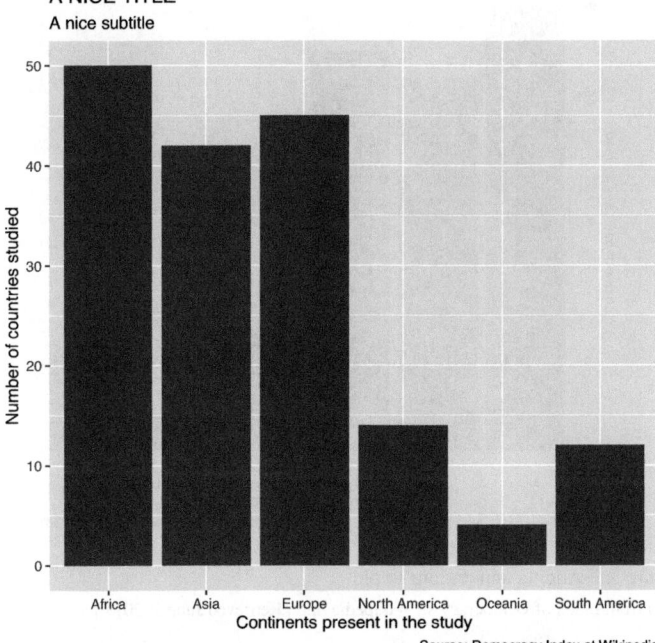

Figure 3.4 Adding source to plot

Data from Index of Democracy, in Wikipedia, n.d., Retrieved June 1, 2019.

Then the possible values in the horizontal represent a number based on how many levels your nominal variable has. Let me prepare my extra layer for an annotation:

```
> # data to input to \emph{ggplot} layer:
> theCoordinates=list(X=5,Y=10)
> theMessage="So few?!"
> # adding annotation layer
> annot=source + annotate("text",
+                          x = theCoordinates$X,
+                          y = theCoordinates$Y,
+                          label = theMessage)
```

I chose **5** for the horizontal, as the limit of this axis are one and six (six bars). I chose **10** for the vertical, which is a possible value in that axis. The last version can be seen in Figure 3.5.

```
> # result
> annot
```

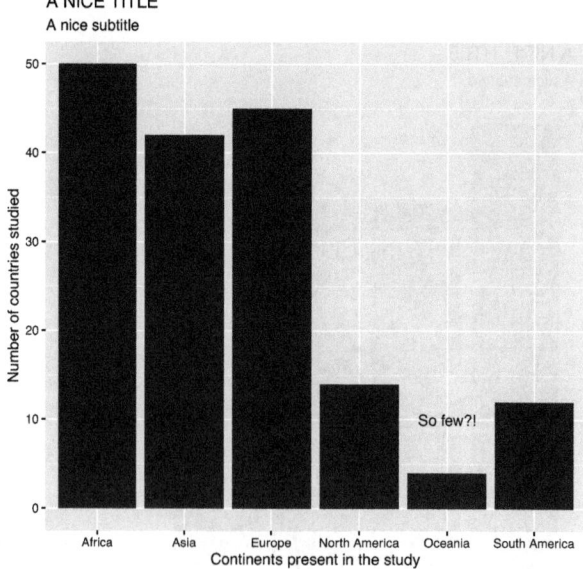

Figure 3.5 Adding annotations to plot
Data from Index of Democracy, in Wikipedia, n.d., Retrieved June 1, 2019.

You must avoid cluttering your plot with annotations. If you believe several annotations are needed, then it might be possible you chose the wrong plot in the first place.

Legend

Legends are a traditional element that are generally used to explain the symbols used in the plot. Legends are part of the plotting area. Let me illustrate the relationship between a couple of numerical variables:

```
> info=ggplot(demo, aes(x=Culture, y=Functioning,shape=Continent))
> leyenda=info + geom_point()
> # result
> leyenda
```

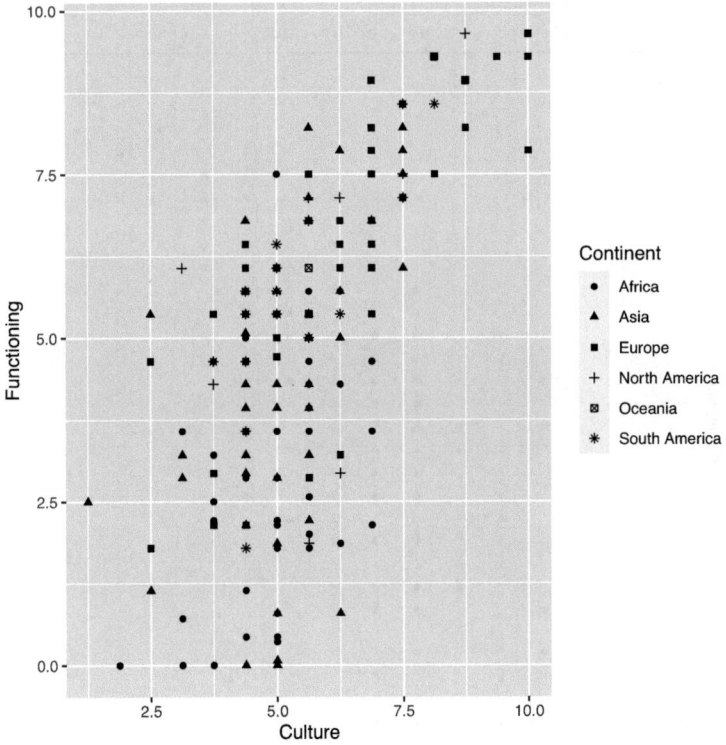

Figure 3.6 Plotting with legend

Data from Index of Democracy, in Wikipedia, n.d., Retrieved June 1, 2019.

From Figure 3.6, you can notice the following:

- The **aes** defined the coordinates of the points with x and y values, but shape caused the presence of the legend (you did not request a legend in the code).
- The plot and the legend share the same area; now you have less room for your main message.
- The shape of the dot is not a square anymore, so the legend affected the quality of the plot, by default.

If your aesthetics included color and size besides shape, you will get multiple legends. You can decide which legend stays by using the command guides (see Figure 3.7):

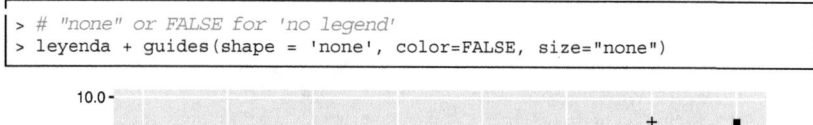

```
> # "none" or FALSE for 'no legend'
> leyenda + guides(shape = 'none', color=FALSE, size="none")
```

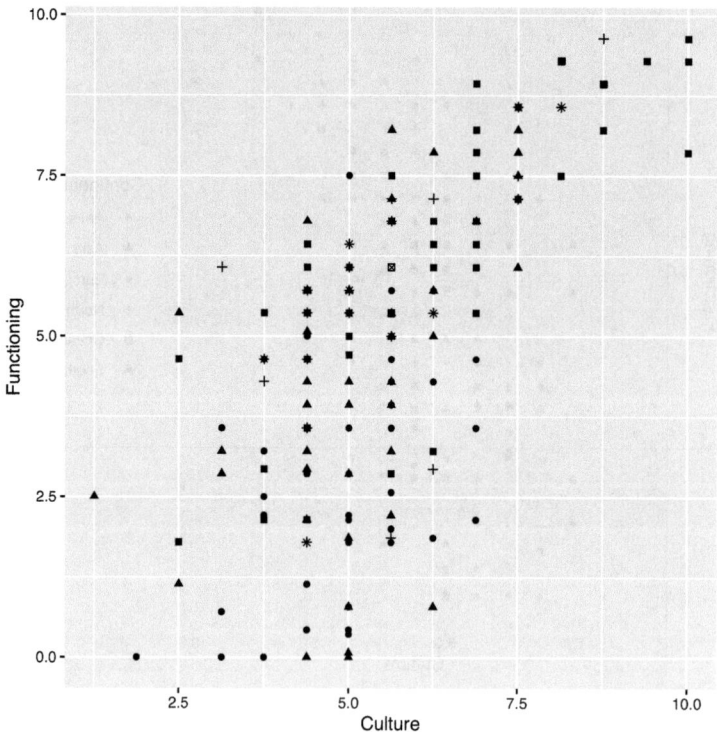

Figure 3.7 Plotting with no legend using guides
Data from Index of Democracy, in Wikipedia, n.d., Retrieved June 1, 2019.

3.1.2 Objects

Every visual is composed of a set of objects that will encode the information you are trying to share. In *ggplot* jargon, they are known as the `geoms`. Now, I can classify objects by their dimensionality:

- **Dots** are theoretically an adimensional object (no width, no height), so they can represent **location**. In Figure 3.6, each dot location was determined by the value of the axes: *culture* on the horizontal, and *government functioning* on the vertical. You can change the default shape using Figure 3.8.

You can then use a value from Figure 3.8 in `geom_point`:

```
> geom_point(shape=18)
```

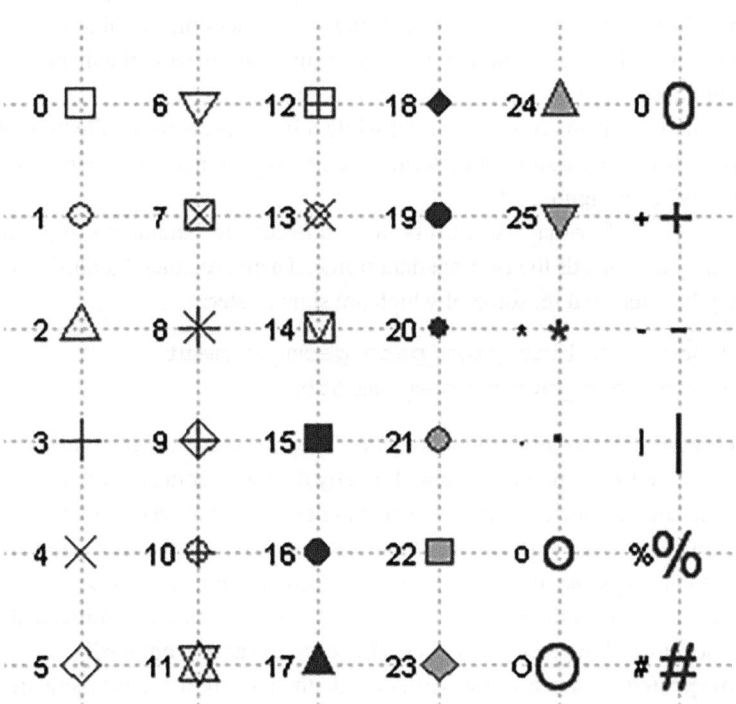

Figure 3.8 The different shapes of points in **R**

The number or symbol to the left determines the shape to be used. The image source is from the Quick-R website (Kabacoff, 2017), Retrieved May 1, 2019.

In this case, `shape` is not an aesthetics, now the shape is fixed and not depending on a variable. Keep in mind that dots are good for location, a property suitable for numerical and categorical data which is fastly interpreted by average humans (Mackinlay, 1986).

- **Lines** are unidimensional objects. They mainly represent **distance**, so they are a clear option for **numerical** values; if they are to be used for categorical values, make sure the audience will not interpret them as distance values. They can also serve to:

  _ represent direction (with or without arrow tips) and slope
  _ represent linear relationships
  _ represent angles (two lines needed).

  Let me add a line to Figure 3.6 with `geom_smooth`.

  I have used a line in Figure 3.9 to encode a linear relationship captured from the cloud of points. The slope informs a positive relationship when read from left to right. Notice you can change thickness to improve default visibility (using `size`), but avoid doing so for encoding variable values. I have also set the `se` argument to `FALSE`, in order to avoid the display of confidence intervals around the line.

  A particular line type is a curve: while a line represents a collection of points following a straight pattern, the curve represents dots moving more "freely" (see Figure 3.10).

  I have used `geom_smooth` because it needs few parameters to produce a line, and it needs the original data frame. There are other "geoms" you may be interested in, some of which are shown later:

  _ Lines: `geom_line`, `geom_path`, `geom_segment`.
  _ Curves: `geom_curve`, `geom_smooth`.

- **Polygons** are two-dimensional objects. They are made out of combining at least three line segments. You will mostly deal with some common quadrilaterals (such as squares or rectangles), or common closed curves (i.e. a circle or an ellipse); but when plotting maps you will run into very irregular polygons. In general, you will need polygons to represent **area** or size. Size is a continuous value, so it is a possible option for **numerical** values instead of categorical ones. However, **areas are not easily interpreted**, or much less easy to decode than location, unless there are huge differences.

```
> info=ggplot(demo, aes(x=Culture, y=Functioning))
> dots1=info + geom_point(shape="*", size=4)
> lines1=dots1 + geom_smooth(method = lm,se=FALSE,colour="black")
> # result
> lines1
```

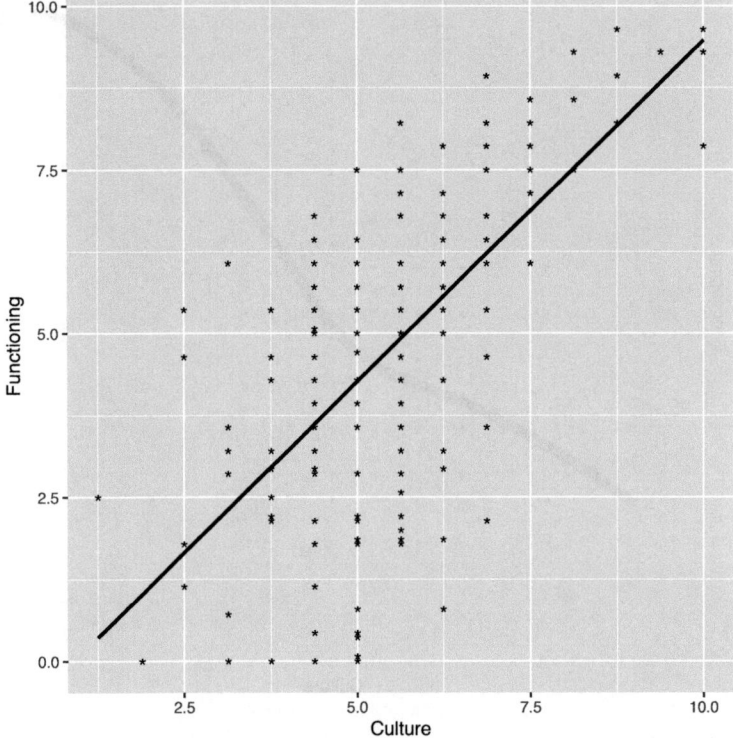

Figure 3.9 Using lines

The line is computed using the simple regression (lm method). Data from Index of
Democracy, in Wikipedia, n.d., Retrieved June 1, 2019.

Figure 3.5 uses bars, a polygon whose height represents counts, so
strictly speaking the area property has not been used. Let me modify
Figure 3.6 to represent a size variable, as shown in Figure 3.11.

You can see that the default sizes offered are not that discernible with the
exception of the extreme values.

```
> lines2=dots1 + geom_smooth(se=FALSE,size=3,colour="black")
> # result
> lines2
```

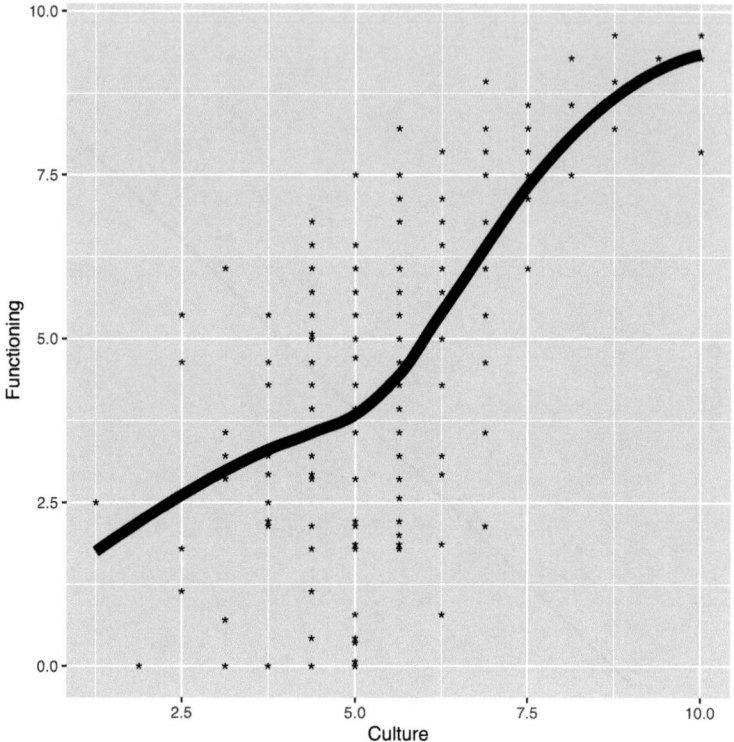

Figure 3.10 Using curves

The line is computed using a local polynomial regression (Fox and Weisberg, 2019), the
default method for geom_smooth. Data from Index of Democracy, in Wikipedia, n.d.,
Retrieved June 1, 2019.

3.1.3 Color

My first advice will be to think in black and white, or gray scale. Considering
the possibility of a multicultural audience, you need to keep calm and use
color wisely, as color may be the first cause to confusion due to cultural factors
(Kroulek, 2016). Then, consider the following when using colors:

- Nominal values. In this case, you use colors to differentiate elements. Avoid
  any color combination that may induce the reader to see ordering or

```
> info=ggplot(demo, aes(x=Culture, y=Functioning,size=Regime))
> polyg1=info + geom_point(shape=23)
> # result
> polyg1
```

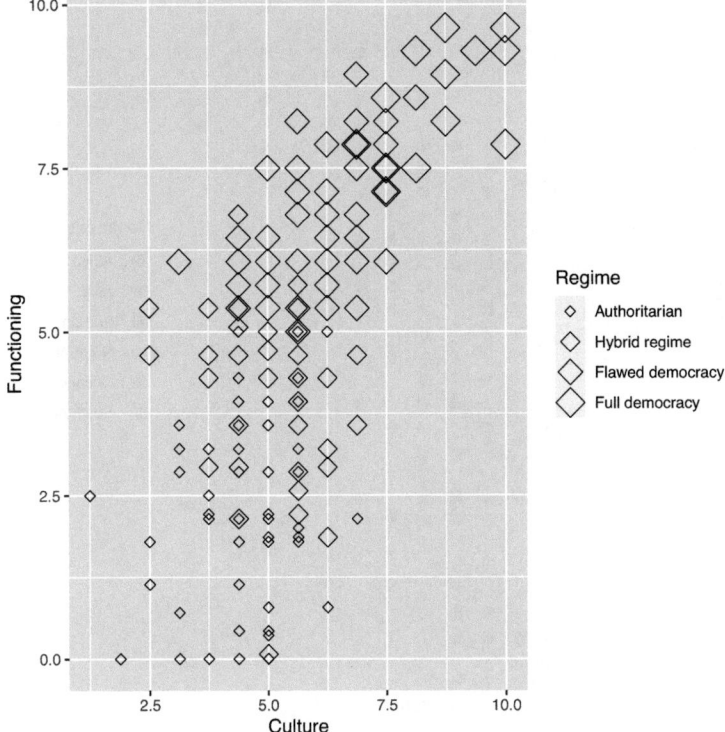

Figure 3.11 Using polygons

Here, the bigger the rhombi sizes the more democratic the country. Data from Index of Democracy, in Wikipedia, n.d., Retrieved June 1, 2019.

intensity. Let me use the `color` aesthetics to produce object `colorNom1`(see the output in Figure 3.12):

Using basic colors, or *hues*, (such as blue, red, green) is the best option; you can also use any other set of hues or 'qualitative schemes' (Brewer, 1999), which differentiate nominal values. Notice that there are schemes available in case of colorblindness for the nominal case, as offered by Brewer (2009)[1].

[1] http://colorbrewer2.org

```
> info=ggplot(demo, aes(x=Culture, y=Functioning,colour=Continent))
> colorNom1=info+geom_point(size=3)
> colorNom1
```

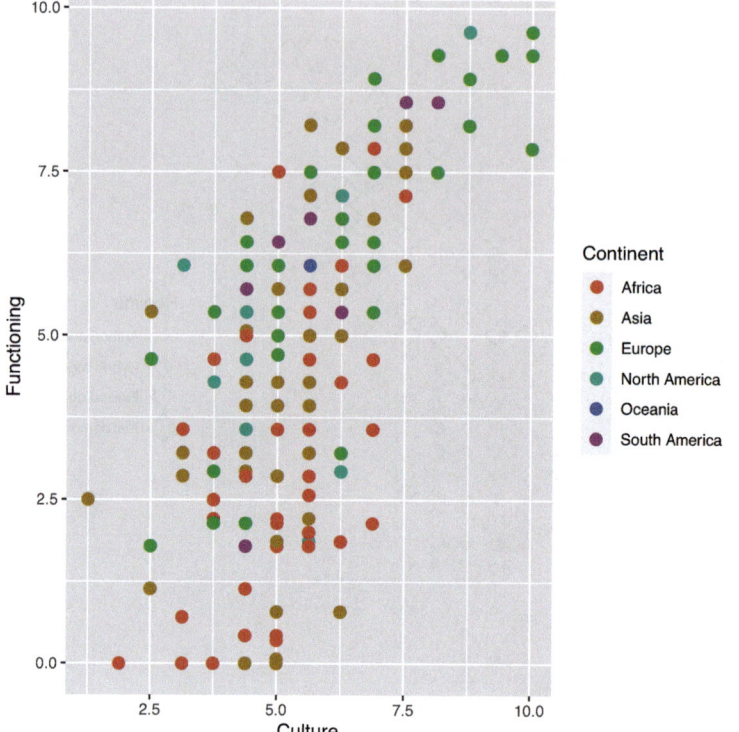

Figure 3.12 Color and nominal data
The colors must not reflect order. Color chosen by default. Data from Index of Democracy,
in Wikipedia, n.d., Retrieved June 1, 2019.

- Ordinal values. In this case you do need to show some ordering. In general,
  you can use one *hue*, and play with different levels of lightness or
  illumination, for example, from light orange to dark orange. This is also
  called a sequential scheme in Brewer (1999). If using just black and white
  for polygons, you can opt for different gray levels. For sure, if you have
  many ordinal levels, the color of each level may become difficult to
  differentiate. Let me use values in Regime as ordinal values in the *color*
  aesthetic to create the object colorOrd1; as I am not customizing the
  color, *ggplot* will use a multi-hue sequence (see the result in Figure 3.13).

```
> info=ggplot(demo, aes(x=Culture, y=Functioning,
+                       color=as.ordered(Regime)))
> colorOrd1=info+geom_point()
> colorOrd1
```

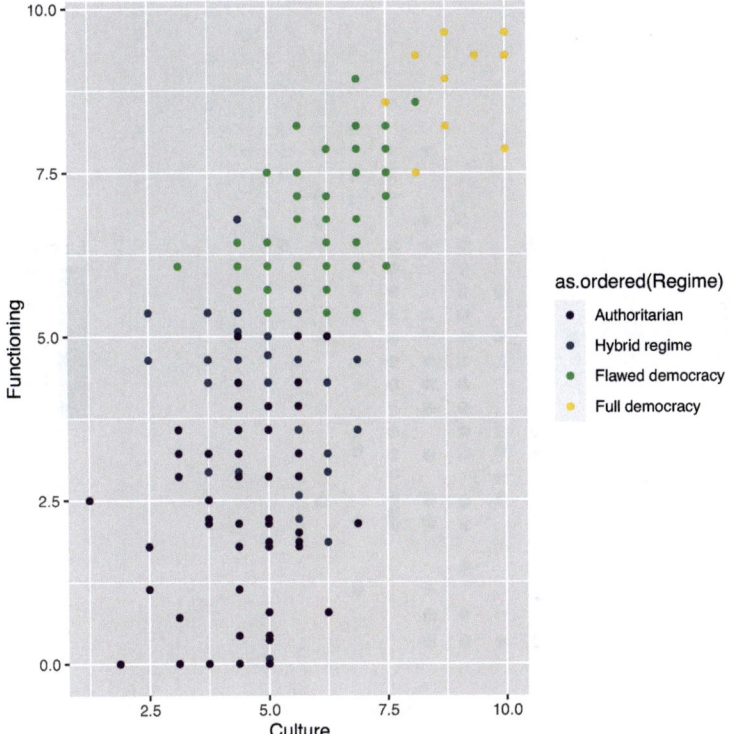

Figure 3.13 Color and ordinal data

The argument `colour` needed a numeric value to show ordering. A multi-hue sequential palette is chosen by default. Data from Index of Democracy, in Wikipedia, n.d., Retrieved June 1, 2019.

- Numeric values. Let me use the numerical variable `Electoral` from the data we have been using in this chapter (The Economist Intelligence Unit, 2019) to create object `colorNum1`. When you use numerical values in the color aesthetic you will get Figure 3.13, where you see a continuous shade of a particular hue, whose lightness depends on the maximum and minimum value of the variable.

Sometimes you may need to organize your numeric values into intervals which are in fact interpreted as ordinal values, and, in that situation, you can make use

```
> info=ggplot(demo, aes(x=Culture, y=Functioning,colour=Electoral))
> colorNum1=info+geom_point(size=3)
> colorNum1
```

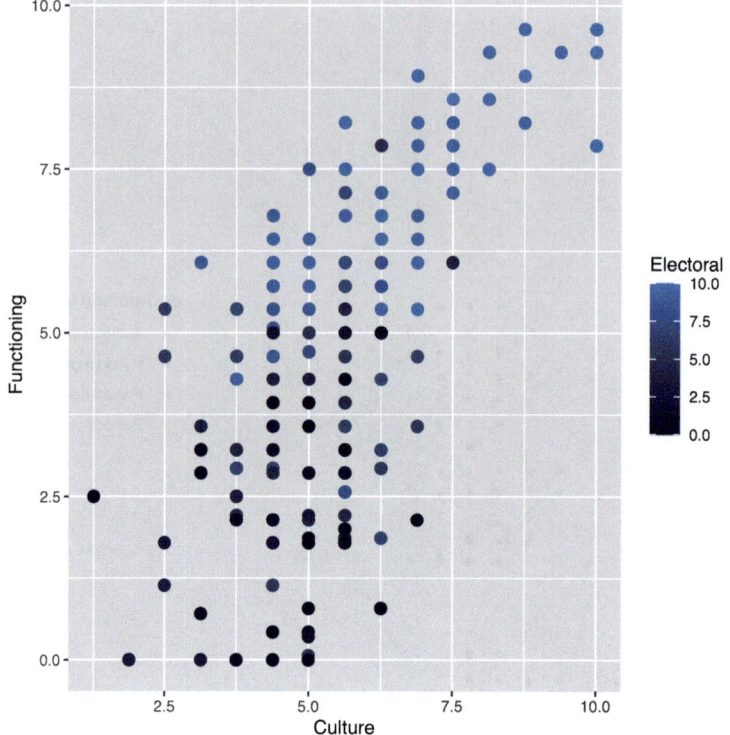

Figure 3.14 Color and numerical data
Color chosen by default. Data from Index of Democracy, in Wikipedia, n.d., Retrieved June
1, 2019.

of the sequential scheme. Also, as numeric values can have zero and negative
values, the intervals can combine two hues into a diverging scheme, as noted
by Brewer (1999) (see Figure 3.19).

3.2 Beyond Default

I have kept the defaults on the previous plots, only using some function
arguments when strictly needed; I did that to save me time and make your
learning easier. However, as you suspect, I could have done a better job, but

that demands more work too. In this section, I will show you how to change some defaults while giving you more work.

3.2.1 The Brewer Palettes

Since finding an effective set of colors can be time-consuming, Geographer Cynthia Brewer organized a portal to help us choose palettes (Brewer, 2009).

Figure 3.15 shows you how to choose a qualitative palette: `Set1`. Let's **add** the suggested palette to change Figure 3.12 into Figure 3.16.

Figure 3.16 just added `scale_colour_brewer` to Figure 3.12 to change colors that represent variable *Continent*; however, Figure 3.15 also tells you that this palette may not be colorblind safe (notice the question mark on the eye icon), and that it is not photocopy safe (notice the X-mark); but, if you needed less colors this may change. From Figure 3.15, you should first select how many colors you need; then the nature of the palette (qualitative for nominal, and the others for ordinal or numerical). Alternatively, you can request the palette covers some properties (colorblind safe, etc.).

Figure 3.13 shows a sequence of colors, but I had to turn the ordinal variable into a number. If I use a sequential Brewer palette, I can keep the original data type.

Figure 3.17 follows the same strategy as Figure 3.16; however, the lighter colors are difficult to see. The smart move here will be to color the border of the dots. That little change requires:

- In `geom_point`:
  - Use a `shape` greater than **20** (these have borders).
- In `aes`:
  - Change the aesthetics from `colour` to `fill`.
- Use `scale_fill_brewer` instead of `scale_color_brewer`.

See the result of those changes in Figure 3.18.

Finally, let me redo Figure 3.14. If we use a diverging scheme, the middle value of the variable will be the lightest color (see Figure 3.19).

Figure 3.19 and Figure 3.17 color the objects using a similar strategy, using the `fill` argument (not color); however, to have more control over the numerical data, I used a different function from **ggplot**: `scale_fill_gradient2` instead. This function is specific for divergent schemes[2].

---

[2] Do not confuse this function with `scale_fill_gradient`, which helps produce sequential color schemes, and which can actually be an alternative to the function `scale_fill_brewer` that I used to make Figure 3.18.

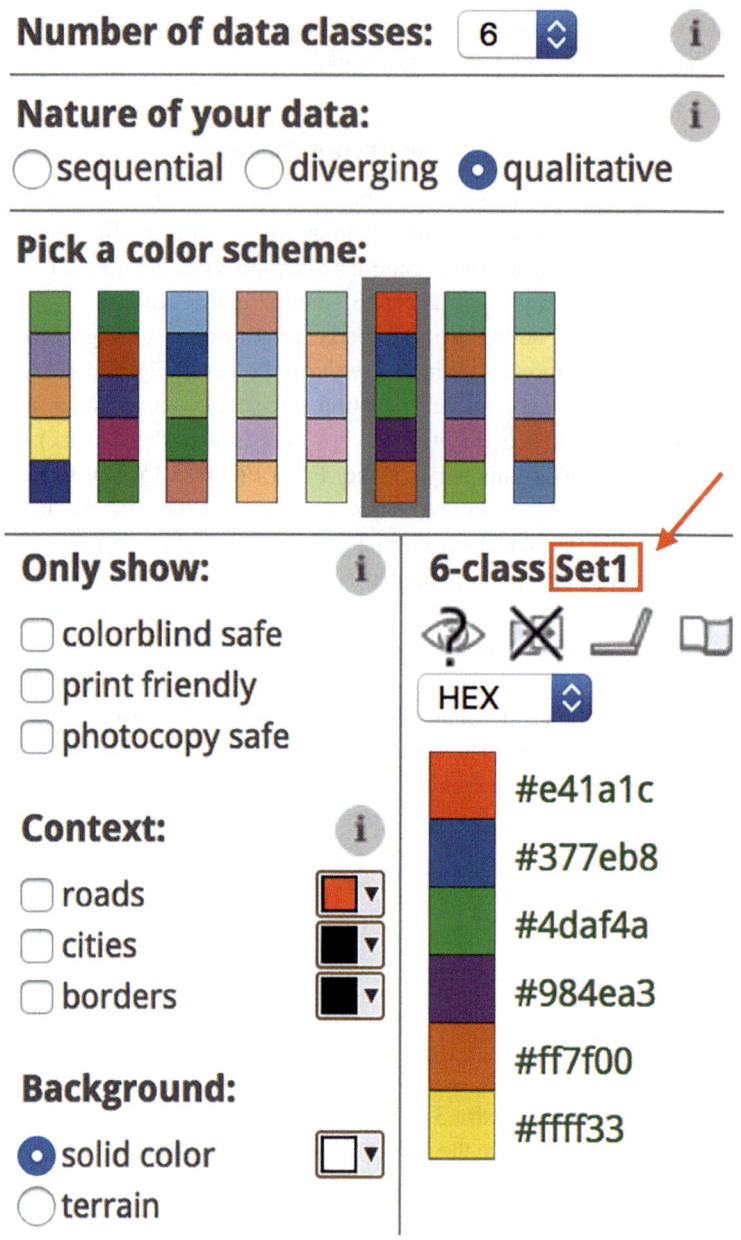

Figure 3.15 Brewer color selection
The arrow signals palette name. Image captured from ColorBrewer website (Brewer, 2009).

```
> colorNom2=colorNom1 + scale_colour_brewer(palette = "Set1")
> #result:
> colorNom2
```

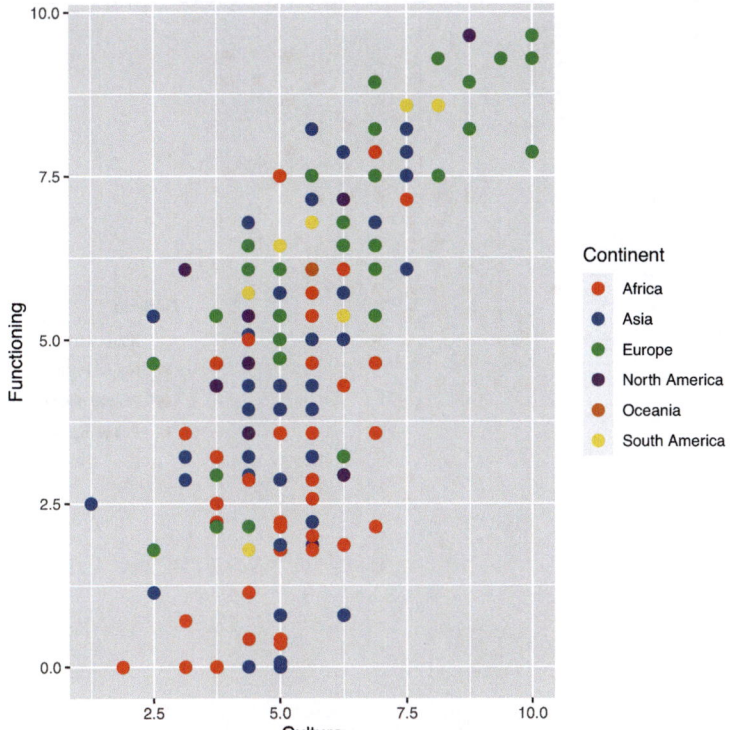

Figure 3.16 Brewer palette for nominal data

Color chosen is **Set1** (Brewer, 2009). Data from Index of Democracy, in Wikipedia, n.d., Retrieved June 1, 2019.

There is this function `scale_fill_distiller`, which I could have used to accomplished something similar, as it accepts the scheme **PuOr** as an argument for the **palette** argument. You can try this code:

```
> info4=ggplot(demo, aes(x=Culture, y=Functioning,fill=Electoral))
> colorNum=info4+geom_point(size=3, shape=21)
> # no midpoint
> colorNum + scale_fill_distiller(palette = "PuOr", direction = -1)
```

After runing the code, you will get a similar plot to Figure 3.19; however, `scale_fill_distiller` does not allow for the selection of a middle value, it just picks the actual value in the middle. On the other hand,

```
> info2=ggplot(demo, aes(x=Culture, y=Functioning,colour=Regime))
> colorOrd2=info2+geom_point(size=3)
> # direction -1 will show the scheme in the inverse order.
> colorOrd2 + scale_color_brewer(palette = "OrRd", direction = 1)
```

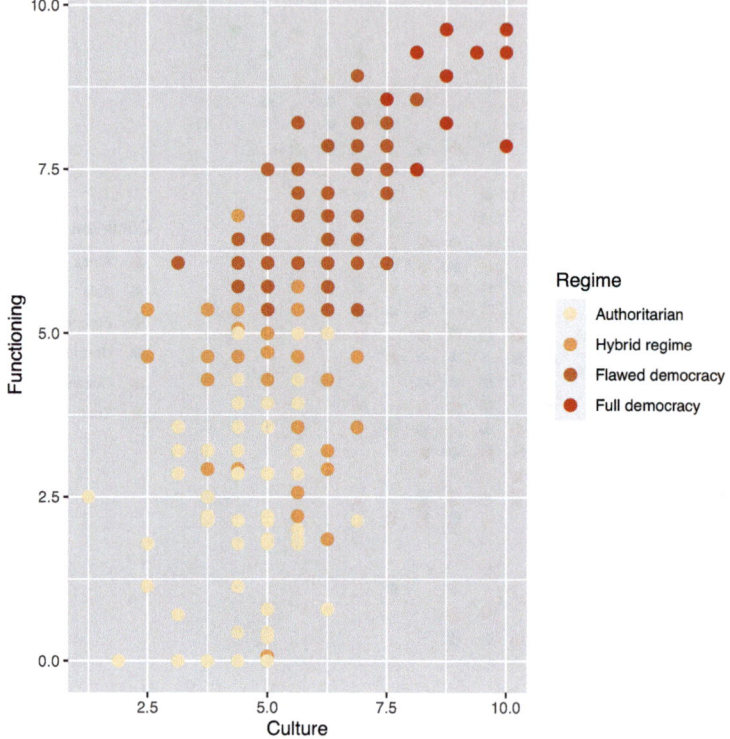

Figure 3.17 Brewer palette for ordinal data

The colors must reflect order. Brewer palette chosen is **OrRd**. Notice this scheme is colorblind safe, print friendly, and photocopy safe (Brewer, 2009). Data from Index of Democracy, in Wikipedia, n.d., Retrieved June 1, 2019.

even though `scale_fill_gradient2` does not have the argument for `palette`, it does allow you to select the middle value of the palette (and its color using `mid`). The downside of `scale_fill_gradient2`, however, is that you need to manually provide the *hues* for the `low` and `high` arguments. In this case, since I wanted to use the **PuOr** palette, I had to visit Brewer's web-page (Brewer, 2009) and select a diverging scheme, so that I could see the the first and last *hues* from the palette; in this case, I just copied the hexadecimal

```
> # fill in aes
> info3=ggplot(demo, aes(x=Culture, y=Functioning,fill=Regime))
> # shape > 20
> colorOrd3=info3+geom_point(size=3, shape=21)
> # differnt function
> colorOrd3 + scale_fill_brewer(palette = "OrRd")
```

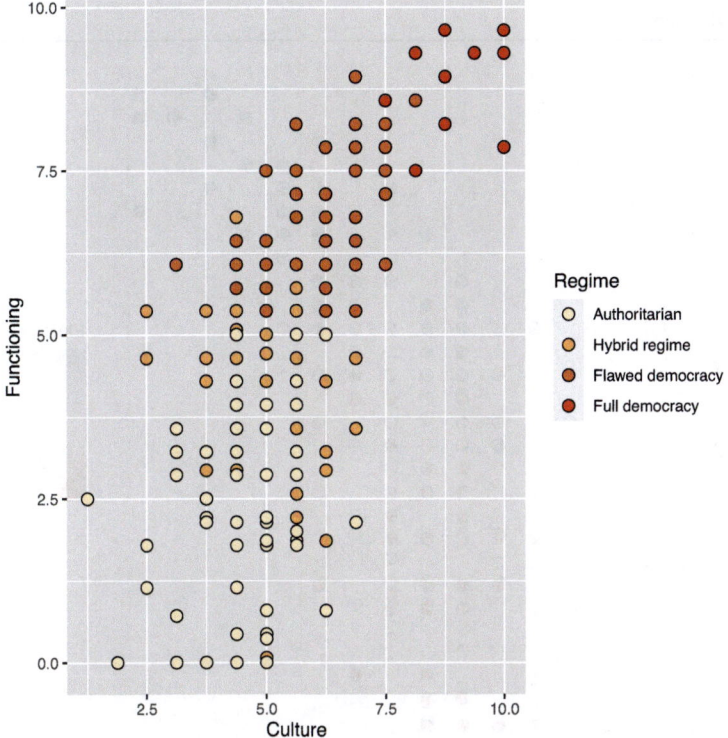

Figure 3.18 Fixing color for ordinal data

Code for Figure 3.17 was changed to improve the visibility of objects. Color chosen from Brewer **OrRd** (Brewer, 2009). Data from Index of Democracy, in Wikipedia, n.d., Retrieved June 1, 2019.

values and paste them into the code. In `scale_fill_distiller` you can also set the `direction` of the colors, but in `scale_fill_gradient2` you simply assign the colors of the limits.

You must understand that the use of color is not for decorating your images, it is for information. If you are not under control, your readers may get a message different from the one you intend for them.

```
> info4=ggplot(demo, aes(x=Culture, y=Functioning,fill=Electoral))
> colorNum=info4+geom_point(size=3, shape=21)
> # new function with midpoint
> colorNum2=colorNum + scale_fill_gradient2(midpoint = 5,
+                                            mid= 'white',
+                                            low = '#e66101',
+                                            high = '#5e3c99')
> # result
> colorNum2
```

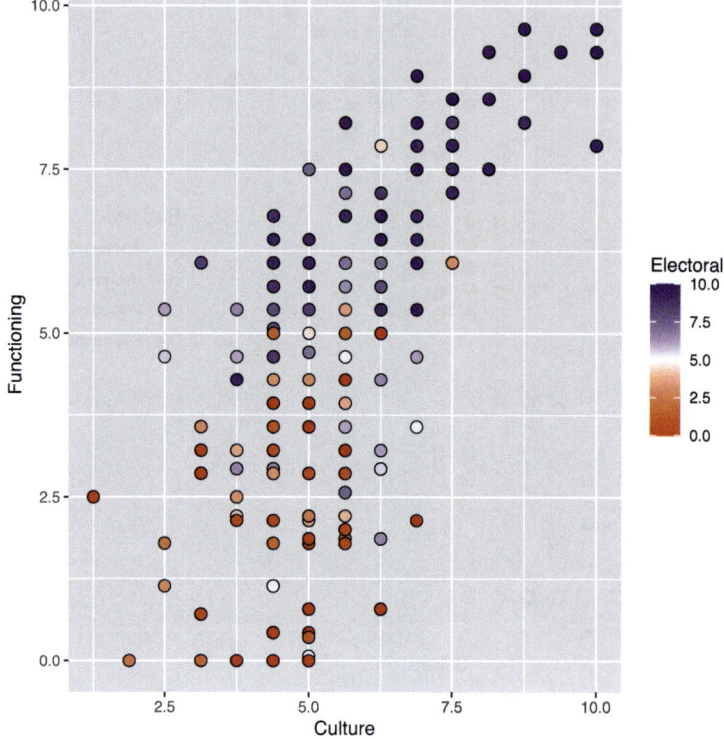

Figure 3.19 Color and numerical data

The colors must reflect order. The `low` and `high` colors are chosen from Brewer palette **PuOr** (Brewer, 2009). Data from Index of Democracy, in Wikipedia, n.d., Retrieved June 1, 2019.

3.2.2 The Background

Most plots have default backgrounds. In the previous examples, you have seen the default background for **ggplot**, which has a light grey plotting zone and a grid. The option for background should maximize "data–ink ratio",

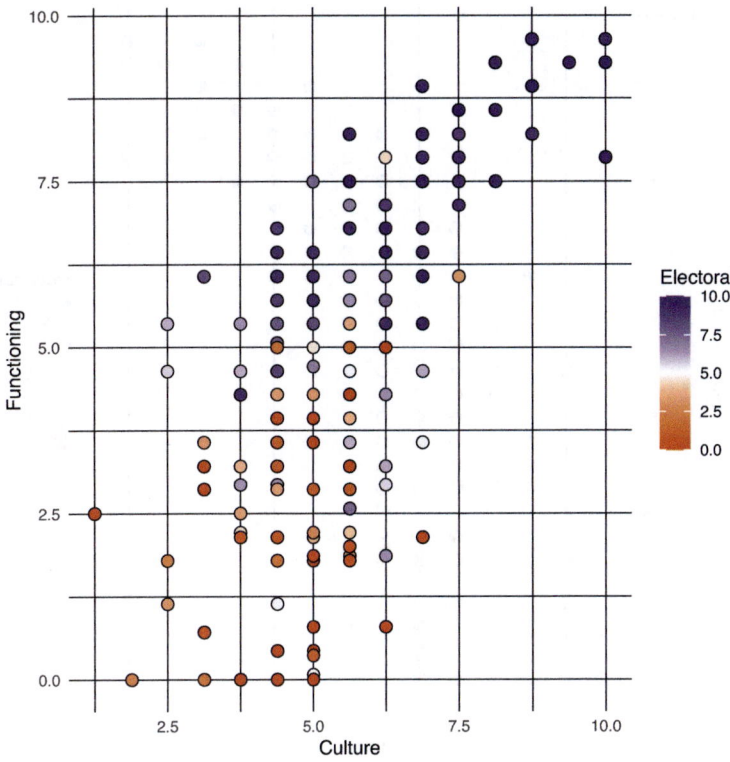

Figure 3.20 Minimal theme
Using **ggplot**'s theme_minimal (Wickham et al., 2019a) to try maximizing data-ink ratio.
Data from Index of Democracy, in Wikipedia, n.d., Retrieved June 1, 2019.

according to Tufte (2001). Now, this code can be an option for the Figure 3.19 background:

```
> colorBack1a=colorNum2 + theme_minimal()
```

The object colorNum2 was holding Figure 3.19, so I just added theme_minimal to get Figure 3.20. Do you consider that respects Tufte's advice?

Using theme_minimal turned the gray background from Figure 3.19 into a white one, while turning the white grid lines into black ones. It also got rid of the axes lines. Notice that the grid lines are of two types: the primary, or the major, and the secondary, or the minor. Also notice that major grid lines are thicker than minor ones. Will Tufte be happy with this version? The presence

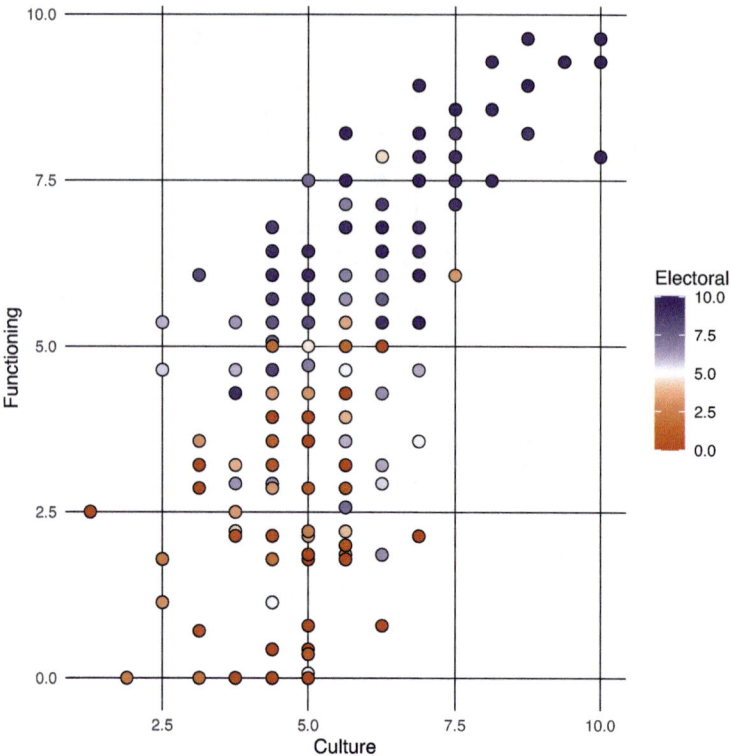

Figure 3.21 Minimal theme without minor grid

Using **ggplot**'s `theme_ minimal` (Wickham et al., 2019a) to try maximizing data-ink ratio. This plot gets rid of minor grid lines by adding a `theme` layer and modifying the `panel.grid.minor` argument with the value `element_blank()`. Data from Index of Democracy, in Wikipedia, n.d., Retrieved June 1, 2019.

of grid lines might disturb Tufte's followers, as in this case they are more an annotation than actual information. Let me show you how to get rid of the minor grid lines:

```
> colorBack1a + theme(panel.grid.minor =    element_blank())
```

That code will produce Figure 3.21. The use of an extra `theme` layer is recommended when you want to change details of the theme at work. In this case, you are changing the properties of the minor grid lines.

If you still want no grid lines at all, you can keep using `theme`, but a better option will be to use `theme_classic`. This theme offers no grid lines, and

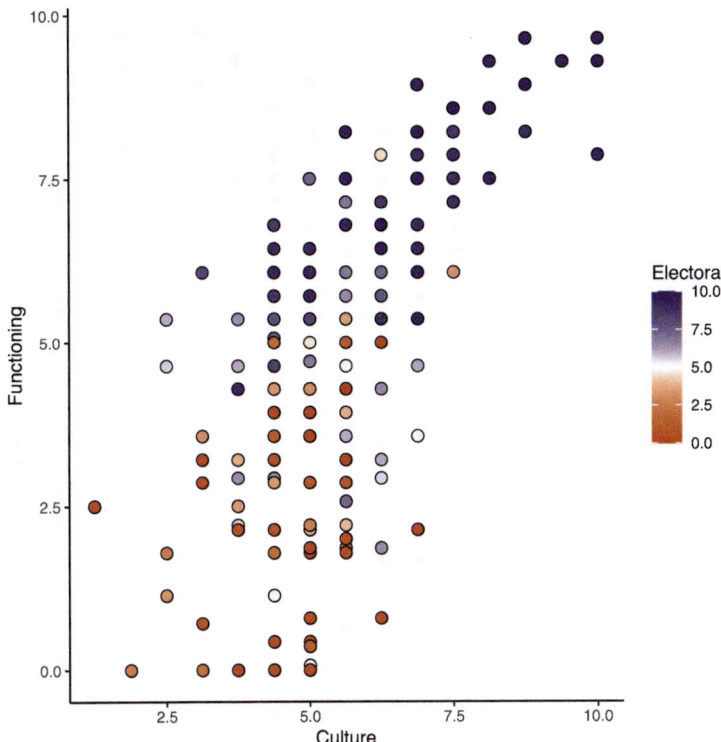

Figure 3.22 Classic theme

Using **ggplot**'s `theme_classic` (Wickham et al., 2019a) to try maximizing data-ink ratio.
Data from Index of Democracy, in Wikipedia, n.d., Retrieved June 1, 2019.

no grey background; however, it will make axes lines come back. The code is simply:

```
> colorBack1b=colorNum2 + theme_classic()
```

The new object `colorBack1b` is holding the latest plot, which you can see in Figure 3.22.

If you want a plot using `theme_classic` but without the axes lines you again use `theme`. You just need to set its `axis.line` argument with the property `element_blank()`, like this:

```
> colorBack1b + theme(axis.line = element_blank())
```

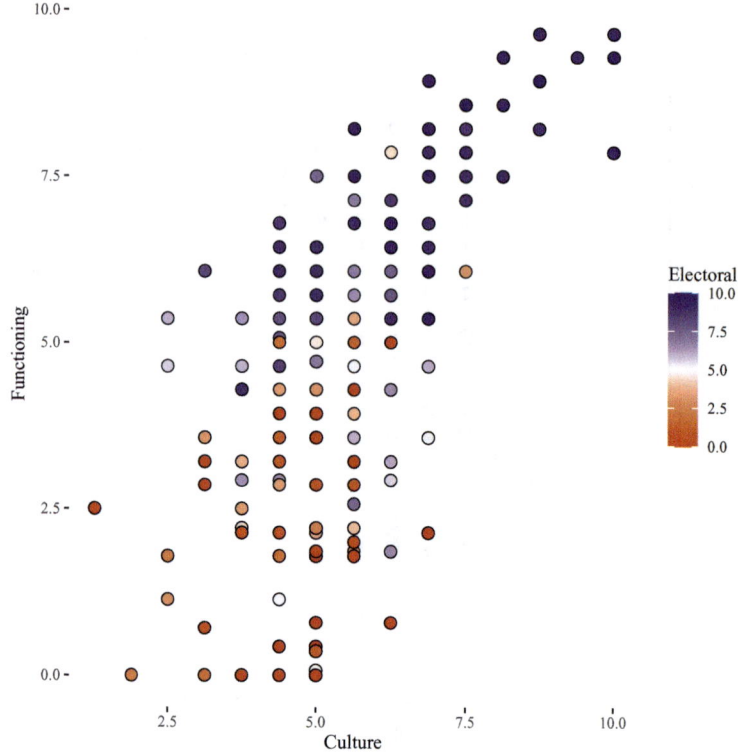

Figure 3.23 Tufte's theme

Using ggthemes's `theme_tufte` (Arnold et al., 2019) to try maximizing "data–ink ratio".
Data from Index of Democracy, in Wikipedia, n.d., Retrieved June 1, 2019.

You may consider installing a particular package named **ggthemes** (Arnold et al., 2019) which has several themes that can be used in any *ggplot* object just by adding it like any other **ggplot** function. This package offers a theme named **tufte**:

```
> library(ggthemes)
> colorBack2a = colorNum2 + theme_tufte()
```

Now, the object `colorBack2a` has the looks Tufte required, according to **ggthemes** (Arnold et al., 2019). This new plot object is shown in Figure 3.23.

As mentioned, the package *ggthemes* offers several other themes that resemble the default themes in Stata, Tableau and others (*The Economist*, *Wall Street*, etc.).

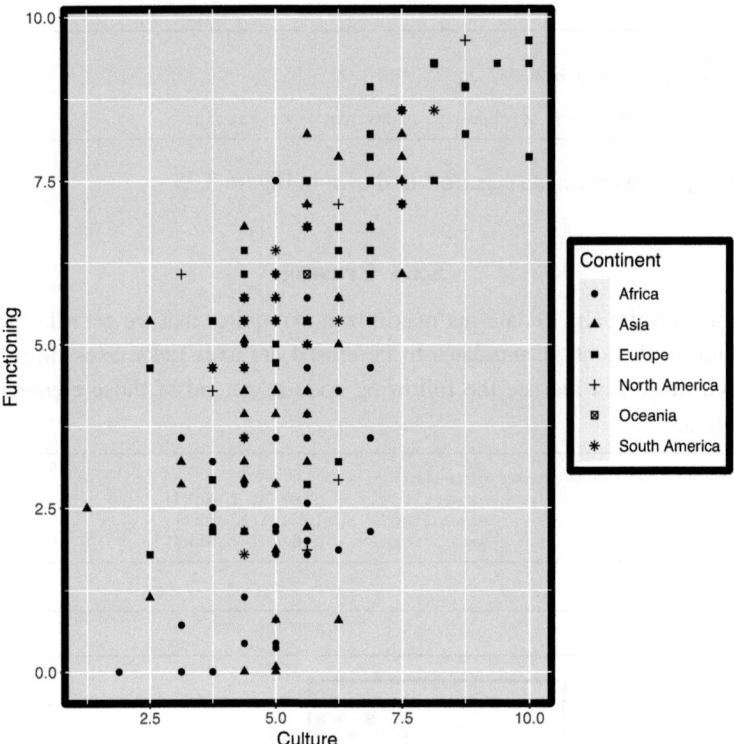

Figure 3.24 Default margins highlighted

Borders have been thickened. Data from Index of Democracy, in The Economist Intelligence Unit, 2019.

3.2.3 Margins

The plot and the legend have margins, and they are within other margins. Let me use this code to alter the object leyenda to highlight the margins in Figure 3.6:

```
> # changes to border lines:
> newBorders=element_rect(colour = "black",size = 2)
> # highlighting borders :
> margins1= leyenda + theme(panel.background = newBorders,
+                           plot.background = newBorders,
+                           legend.background = newBorders)
```

In general, you should respect default margin setups. However, **ggplot**'s theme gave you the power to change these in Figure 3.24.

Next, let me alter the default margin values using:

```
> # new info:
> newMargins=margin(3, 3, 3, 3, "cm") #top, right,bottom, left
> #changing:
> margins2= margins1 + theme(plot.margin = newMargins)
```

The plot in object `margins2` is shown in Figure 3.25.

3.2.4 Erasing

Keeping our loyalty to data-ink maximization requires that we get rid of some
redundant elements. Candidates to be erased are axes ticks, axes titles, and
legend titles. Let me use the following code to get rid of those elements in
Figure 3.4:

```
> erase1= source + theme_classic() +
+                   theme(axis.title.x = element_blank(),
+                         axis.line.x = element_blank(),
+                         axis.ticks.x = element_blank())
```

```
> margins2
```

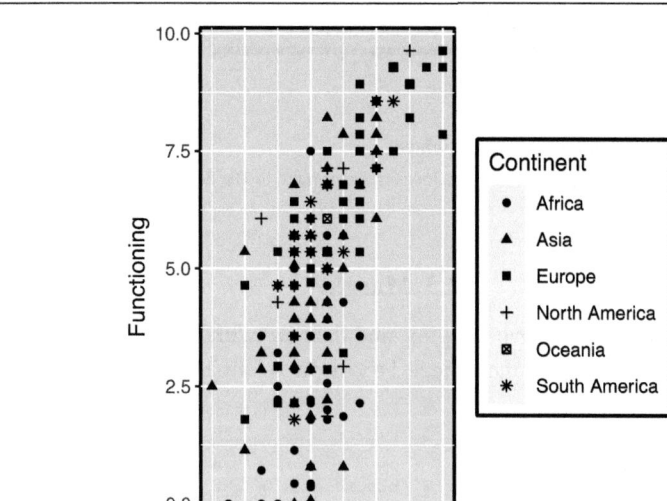

Figure 3.25 Altering margins
The main plot suffers more the consequences of altering margins, but not the legend.
Consider that altering margins in one plot may considerably differentiate this from the other
ones in your work. Data from Index of Democracy, in Wikipedia, n.d., Retrieved June 1,
2019.

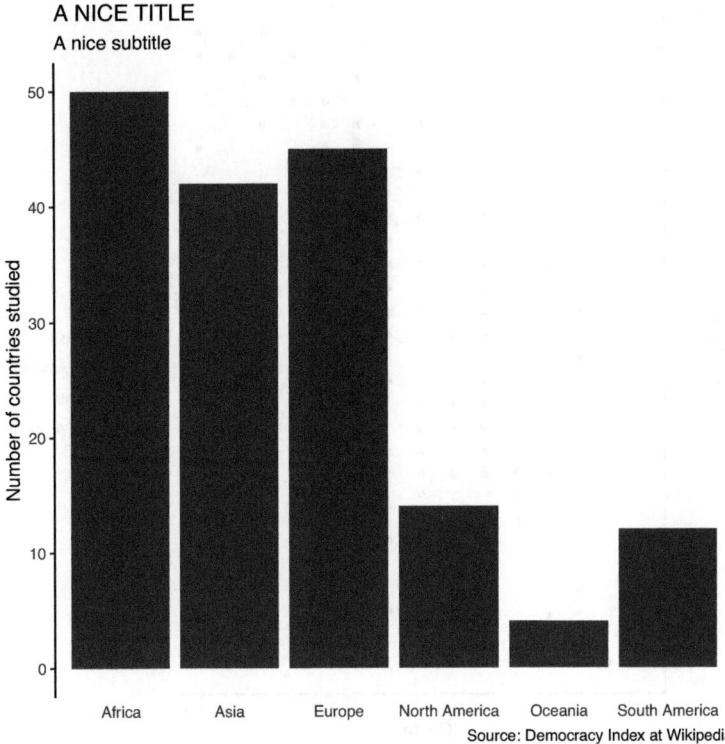

Figure 3.26 Erasing text elements in plot

The plot is erasing several elements using element_blank. The theme used is theme_classic. Data from Index of Democracy, in Wikipedia, n.d., Retrieved June 1, 2019.

You can see object erase1 in Figure 3.26.

The categorical nature of the data helps you support your decision to erase the axis line (it is not a continuity), and erase the tick marks (it is redundant if a label is present to clearly differentiate one bar from the other). Also, since the bars represent a small and complete set of elements (the continents), the axis title becomes redundant.

The theme element can help you get rid of legend titles as well. Let me do that in Figure 3.6:

```
> erase2 = leyenda + theme_classic() +
+                    theme(legend.title = element_blank())
```

Object erase2 is shown in Figure 3.27

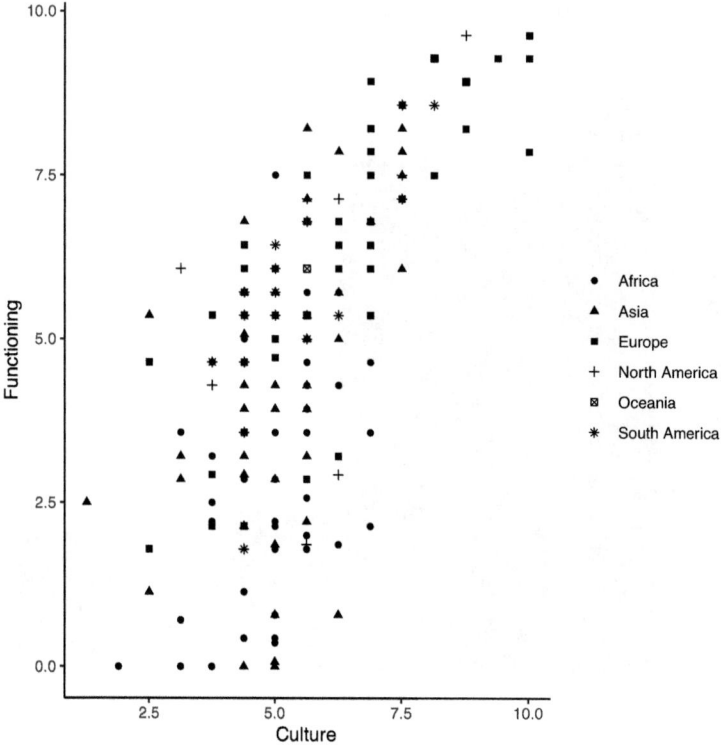

Figure 3.27 Erasing text elements in legend

The plot is erasing the legend title using `element_blank`. The theme used is `theme_classic`. Data from Index of Democracy, in Wikipedia, n.d., Retrieved June 1, 2019.

Notice the fact I put `theme_classic` before the `theme` element in Figures 3.26 and 3.27. If it goes after, the changes in `theme` will have no effect.

3.2.5 Alignment

Let's modify the title, subtitle, source caption and axis titles alignment from Figure 3.26. This necessitates writing a value from zero to one in the argument `hjust` (zero is on the far left in the horizontal or the bottom on the vertical).

```
> ali1= erase1 + theme(plot.title = element_text(hjust = 0.5),
+                      plot.subtitle = element_text(hjust = 0.5),
+                      plot.caption = element_text(hjust = 0),
+                      axis.title.y = element_text(hjust = 1))
```

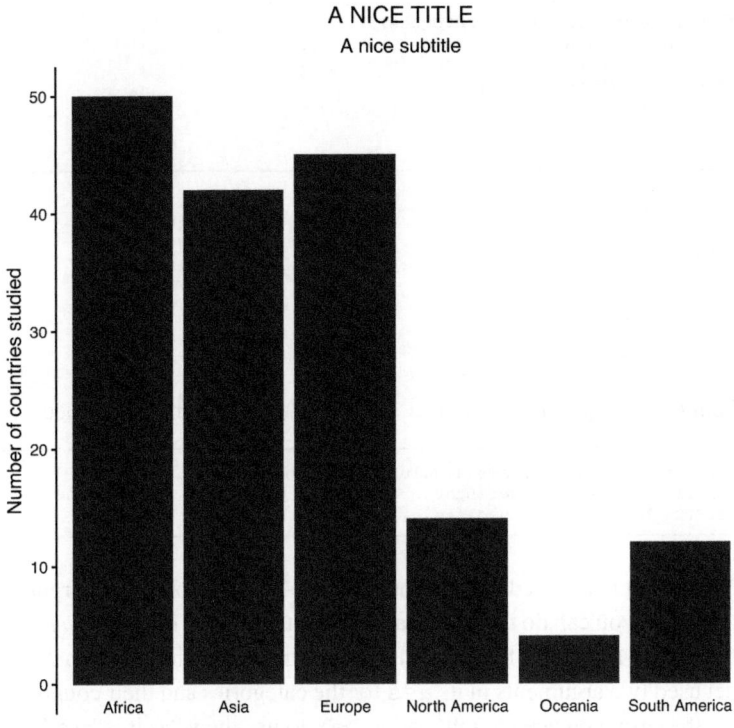

Source: Democracy Index at Wikipedia

Figure 3.28 Altering text alignment

The theme used is `theme_classic`. This plot corrected the categorical labels position from Figure 3.26. Data from Index of Democracy, in Wikipedia, n.d., Retrieved June 1, 2019.

```
> # categorical labels alignment correction!!
> ali1= ali1 + theme(axis.text.x = element_text(vjust = 7))
```

Notice I used `vjust` to realign vertically the categorical labels, which remained far from their bars in Figure 3.26 after erasing (see Figure 3.28).

3.2.6 Repositioning

Changing the default position of some elements may improve understanding or take more advantage of the plotting space. Let me first prepare a **frequency table** as a data frame for the variable *Continent* we have previously used:

```
> ValuesAndCounts=table(demo$Continent)
> values=names(ValuesAndCounts)
```

```
> counts=as.vector(ValuesAndCounts)
> FT=data.frame(Values=values,Counts=counts)
> # ordering FreqTable by ascending counts
> FT=FT[order(FT$Counts),]
> row.names(FT)=NULL # resetting row names
> # here it is:
> print(FT, row.names = F)
```

```
          Values Counts
          Oceania     4
   South America    12
   North America    14
            Asia    42
          Europe    45

          Africa    50
```

I am ready to plot the FT object. Let's start by using the basic code:

```
> info=ggplot(data=FT, aes(x=Values,y=Counts))
> barFT1= info + geom_bar(stat = 'identity')
> barFT2= barFT1 + theme_classic()
```

Notice that I produced the barplot in Figure 3.1 using only the **x** argument in **aes** element; you can do that with data frames that do not represent *summaries*. Our current FT data is a frequency table (a summary of the data), so the info object used two arguments in its aes for the categories and their counts. When that is the case, you need to tell geom_bar to use the **y** "as it is"; so I set **stat** to **"identity"**. The object barFT1 will produce the same as Figure 3.1. Then, I added the theme_classic element we have been using, and saved it all in barFT2.

Next, I will do some modifications to the theme_classic. Based on previous default changes (remember that the last line is moving the continent label upwards) I produced the object barFT3, which will look like Figure 3.28.

```
> barFT3 = barFT2 + theme(axis.title.x = element_blank(),
+                         axis.line.x = element_blank(),
+                         axis.ticks.x = element_blank(),
+                         axis.ticks.y = element_blank(),
+                         axis.text.x = element_text(vjust = 5))
```

After object barFT3 is created, I can try some repositioning. My first try will be changing the column order in Figure 3.28. For that, I will use scale_x_discrete, whose limits argument will be set using the Continents ordered according to the our FT data frame:

```
> barFT4 = barFT3 + scale_x_discrete(limits=FT$Values)
```

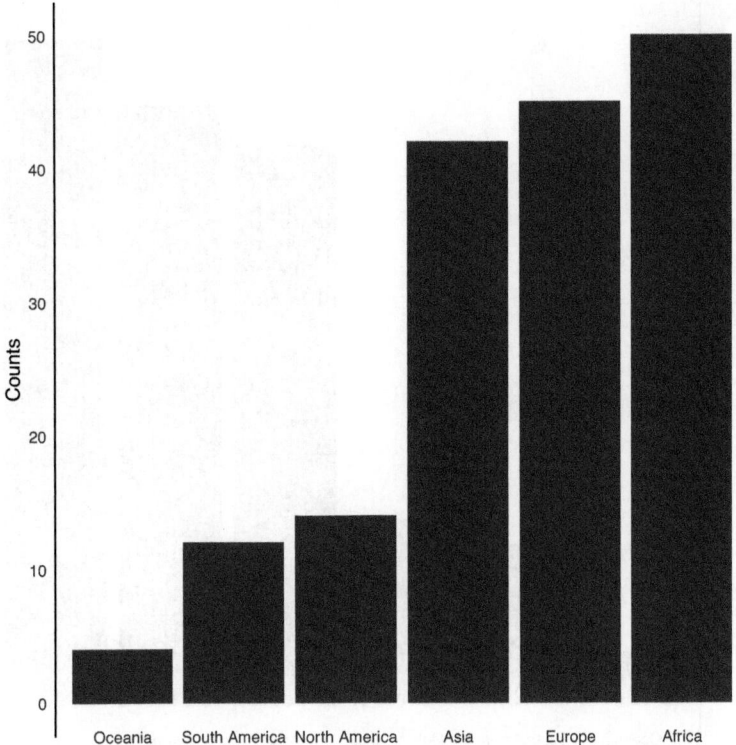

Figure 3.29 Changing order of bars

The theme used is theme_classic. This plot uses an ordered frequency table as data input. Data from Index of Democracy, in Wikipedia, n.d., Retrieved June 1, 2019.

The modified barplot proposal is saved in object barFT4, and is shown in Figure 3.29.

What about annotating the bars in Figure 3.29, while dropping the y-axis values? We could use the Counts in the data frame as an aes in geom_text:

```
> barFT4 + geom_text(aes(label=Counts),
+                    vjust=1.6, # manual alignment
+                    color="white", size=3.5) +
+          theme(axis.text.y = element_blank())
```

Let's see the result from the code above in Figure 3.30.

My second try will be an alternative to Figure 3.30, using a vertical grid for the count values:

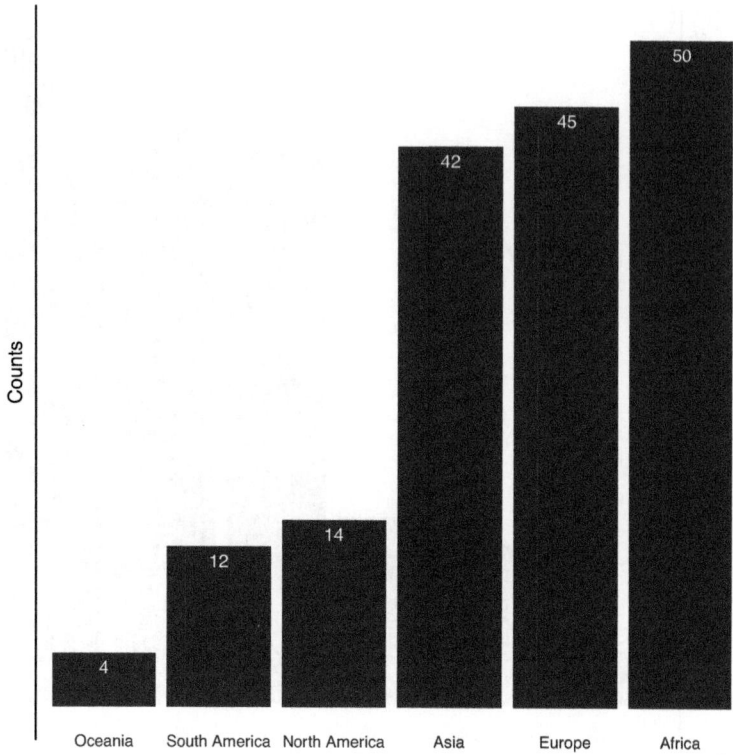

Figure 3.30 Position of horizontal bar with annotations

The theme used is theme_classic. Each bar was annotated, so redundant y-values were
erased. Data from Index of Democracy, in Wikipedia, n.d., Retrieved June 1, 2019.

```
> barFT4 + theme(panel.grid.major.y = element_line(color = "grey60")) +
+          scale_y_discrete(limits=FT$Counts)
```

Using theme, I requested a vertical grid with a dark grey color;
and then, I instructed where the grid lines had to be, this time using
scale_y_discrete. This alternative version can be seen in Figure 3.31.

Moving elements around gets easy as you become more and more familiar
with the **ggplot** functions. However, that does not solve the problem. The more
possibilities you have, the less clear becomes what the right combination to
choose is; and even worse, it could complicate things by solving an unintended
negative effect after you change a default[3].

---

[3] Remember that this happened in Section 3.2.4 when I erased the x-axis line, which caused the
categorical labels be too far from the bars, and which was corrected later in Section 3.2.5.

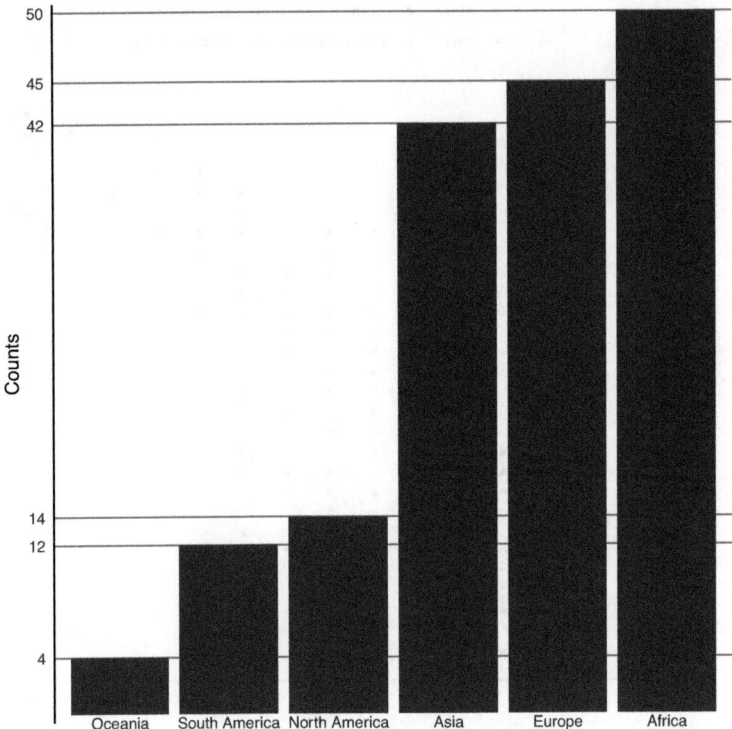

Figure 3.31 Position of vertical grid

The theme used is theme_classic. The grid serves to annotate frequency table plot. Data from Index of Democracy, in Wikipedia, n.d., Retrieved June 1, 2019.

Let me show you a similar situation when repositioning the legend. This should not be hard at all:

```
> repo1 = erase2 + theme(legend.position="top")
> # you can try "bottom", too.
```

Object repo1 is a new version of Figure 3.27, which is shown in Figure 3.32, but if you want to make changes, you still have some further steps to follow.

For instance, in this (and all the previous plots), you may require that:

- One **measurement unit** in either axis has the same length.
- The legend should occupy less space.

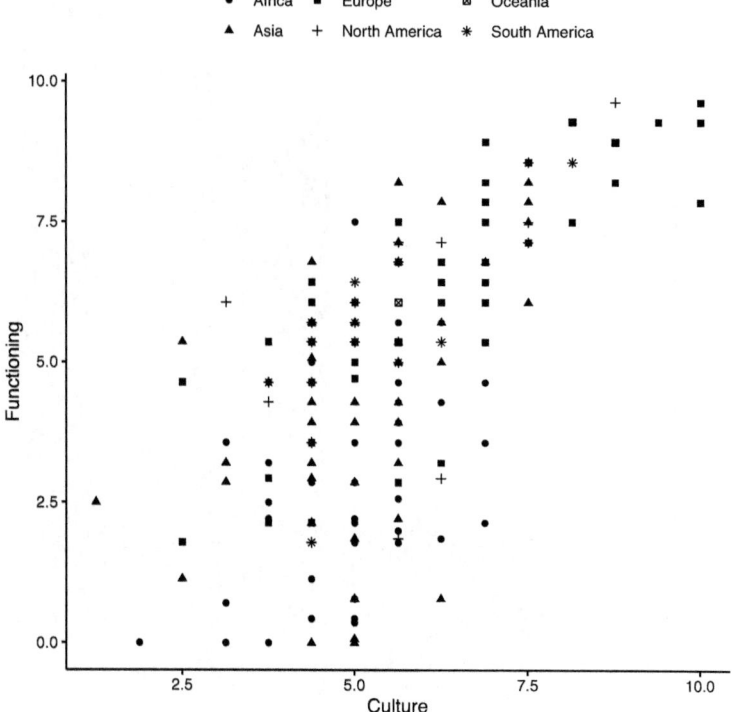

Figure 3.32 Position of legend

The theme used is theme_classic from Figure 3.27. Data from Index of Democracy, in Wikipedia, n.d., Retrieved June 1, 2019.

Let's test this code, and see the result in Figure 3.33. Notice that the changes needed functions other than theme this time; and realize I used the argument shape because the legend represents shapes in the input aes from Figure 3.6.

```
> repo2 = repo1 +
+           # One unit same length in both axes
+           coord_fixed(ratio=1) +
+           # less space
+           guides(shape=guide_legend(nrow = 1))
```

When you see the output, you may consider that the legend occupies a smaller space, but you do not like that the legend elements are too far from each other; then, you can plan another change with this code:

```
> repo2 + theme(#legend elements no too far from each other
+               legend.key.width = unit(0, 'lines'),
+               # frame the legend
```

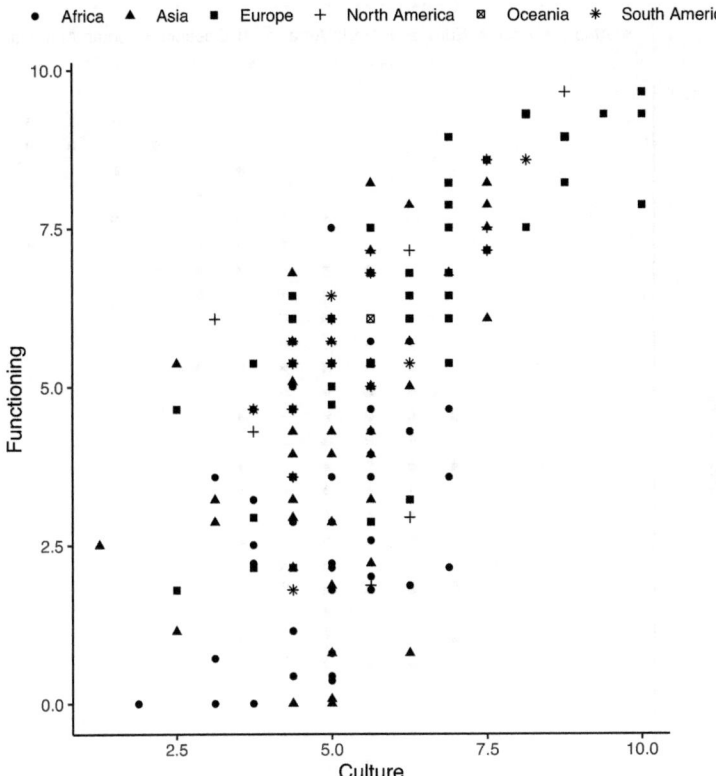

Figure 3.33 Position of legend (II)

Legend occupies just one row. By default, legend elements are a little far from each other in this case. The theme used is `theme_classic` from Figure 3.27. Data from Index of Democracy, in Wikipedia, n.d., Retrieved June 1, 2019.

```
+              legend.background = element_rect(size=0.5,
+                                               linetype="solid",
+                                               colour ="grey"))
```

Figure 3.34 is the resulting plot after using the previous code.

3.3 Python's Grammar of Graphics

Python has its own grammar of graphics thanks to the library **plotnine** created by Kibirige (2019). Let me call a data file following the same approach I used in the code on page 25:

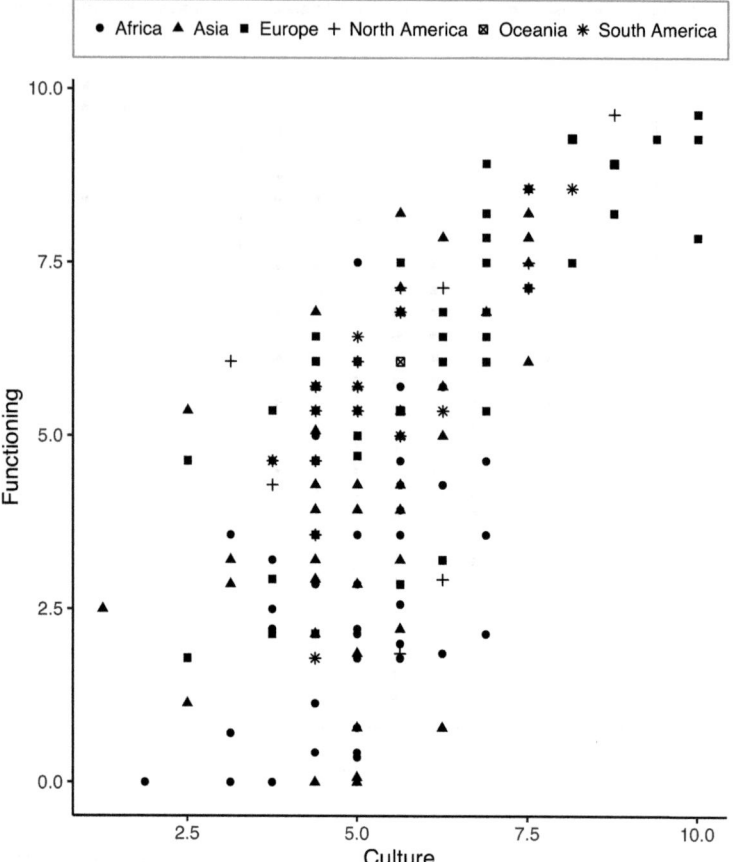

Figure 3.34 Position of legend (III)

Legend is in one row, elments are closer to each other, and the whole legend is in a frame.
The theme used is theme_classic from Figure 3.27. Data from Index of Democracy, in
Wikipedia, n.d., Retrieved June 1, 2019.

```
import pickle
from urllib.request import urlopen
linkRepo='https://github.com/resourcesbookvisual/data/'
linkDemo="raw/master/demo.pkl" # 'pickle' file!

demo = pickle.load(urlopen(linkRepo+linkDemo))
```

This time I opened a **pickle** file format. Like my example in **R**, a pickle
file can keep the information on the data types (numeric, nominal, ordinal).
The load function from pickle returns a **Pandas** data frame. Remember that

data frames are not a native structure in **Python**, so you need to have **Pandas** pre-installed.

Let me recreate the plots I showed you in this chapter using the *plotnine* library in **Python**, in all cases, I am using `theme_classic`:

- The next code recreates Figure 3.9 from page 35. Notice that *plotnine* is extremely similar to **R**'s **ggplot**. The main difference is that, in the `aes` section, you must write the name of the variables in quotations. Also, the argument for `method` has to be in quotations. Pay attention to the capitalization of `False` (or `True`), as **R** uses all letters in capitals (or just the first letter capitalized). Keep in mind that the symbols needed for dots depend on another set of values[4].

```
from plotnine import *

info=ggplot(demo, aes(x='Culture', y='Functioning'))
dots1=info + geom_point(shape="*", size=2)
lines1=dots1 + geom_smooth(method = "lm",se=False,colour="black")
lines1 + theme_classic()
```

- Making some basic changes to the previous code, I recreate Figure 3.10 from page 36. Notice that the code is the same as in R.

```
lines2=dots1 + geom_smooth(se=False,colour="black")
lines2 + theme_classic()
```

- This time, I recreate Figure 3.11 from page 37. Notice that the code is the same as in **R**, just using a valid symbol for dots.

```
info=ggplot(demo,aes(x='Culture',y='Functioning',size='Regime'))
polyg1 = info + geom_point(shape ="x")
polyg1 + theme_classic()
```

- This code will produce Figure 3.12 from page 38. Besides the use of quotations, notice that `scale_colour_brewer` requires that you specify the `type` argument[5]. Pay attention to the line breaks. **R** will keep reading code even after a line break, as long as the plus symbol (+) is at the end of the line; that is not the case in **Python**: you need to add the backslash symbol (\) after +. Of course, as you can see, you do not need to do that when you have a line break inside a function (first two lines in the code below).

```
info=ggplot(demo,aes(x='Culture',y='Functioning',
                     colour='Continent'))
colorNom1=info+geom_point(size=3)
colorNom1 + scale_colour_brewer(type='qual',palette = "Set1") + \
            theme_classic()
```

---

[4] Visit `https://matplotlib.org/3.1.1/api/markers_api.html` to see the available symbols.
[5] The options are 'seq', 'div' and 'qual', being the first one the default.

- This code will produce Figure 3.18 from page 45.

```
info2=ggplot(demo,aes(x='Culture',y='Functioning',fill='Regime'))
colorOrd3 = info2 + geom_point(size=3,shape='o')
colorOrd3 + scale_fill_brewer(palette = "OrRd") + theme_classic()
```

- This code will produce Figure 3.19 from page 46.

```
info4=ggplot(demo,aes(x='Culture',y='Functioning',
                      fill='Electoral'))
colorNum=info4 + geom_point(size=3, shape='o')
colorNum + scale_fill_gradient2(midpoint = 5,
                      mid= 'white',
                      low = '#e66101',
                      high = '#5e3c99')
```

- I worked very hard on a bar plot to show you how to make changes, let me show you the main steps I will follow in **Python**:

  1. Create a frequency table:

```
import pandas as pd

FT = pd.value_counts(demo.Continent,ascending=True).reset_index()
FT.columns = ['Values','Counts']
```

  2. Create text for titles and annotations:

```
# Titles to be used:
the_Title="A NICE TITLE"
the_SubTitle="A nice subtitle"
TheTopTitles=the_Title+'\n'+the_SubTitle  # adaptation
horizontalTitle="Continents present in the study"
verticalTitle="Number of countries studied"
# data for annotation
theCoordinates={'X':1,'Y':7} #dict instead of list
theMessage="So few?!"
```

  Plotnine does not have functionality to show a subtitle, yet; so, I combined both in the title using line break (\n). Notice that the object `theCoordinates` uses a *dictionary* to store the coordinates of the annotation (I used a list in **R**).

  3. Set up information for bar plot while changing defaults:

```
titles2= titles1 + xlab(horizontalTitle) + ylab(verticalTitle)

annot1= titles2 + annotate("text",
                      x = theCoordinates['X'], #reading dict
                      y = theCoordinates['Y'],
                      label = theMessage)
align1= annot1 + theme(plot_title = element_text(ha = "center"),
                      axis_title_y = element_text(ha = "top"))

barFT1= align1 + geom_bar(stat = 'identity')
barFT2= barFT1 + theme_classic()
barFT3= barFT2 + theme(axis_title_x = element_blank(),
                      axis_title_y = element_text(ha = "center"),
                      axis_ticks_major_x = element_blank(),
```

```
                           axis_ticks_major_y = element_blank(),
                           axis_text_x = element_text(va = 'top',
                                                        size=6),
                           plot_title = element_text(ha = "center"),
                           axis_line_x = element_blank())

barFT4 = barFT3 + scale_x_discrete(limits=FT.Values)
```

Notice some difference from R's **ggplot** in the code above:

- While some arguments in **ggplot** use a dot
  (i.e. `axis.title.x`), *plotnine* will use an underscore (_) instead.
- The arguments that control horizontal or vertical alignment
  are written as `hjust` or `vjust` in *ggplot*, while they are `ha` or
  `va`, respectively, in *plotnine*; besides, the arguments allowed in **ggplot**
  are numeric, while you need to write a specific location in *plotnine*[6].

4. Now, producing Figure 3.30 from page 58.

```
barFT4 + geom_text(aes(label='Counts'),
                   va='top',
                   color="white", size=8) + \
                   theme(axis_text_y = element_blank())
```

5. Now, producing Figure 3.31 from page 59.

```
barFT4 + theme(panel_grid_major_y=element_line(color="grey")) +\
         scale_y_continuous(breaks=FT.Counts)
```

- Let's code the **Python** version of Figure 3.34 on 62:

```
info=ggplot(demo, aes(x='Culture', y='Functioning',
                      shape='Continent'))
leyenda=info + geom_point()
erase2=leyenda + theme_classic() + \
                 theme(legend_title=element_blank())
repo1=erase2 + theme(legend_position="top")
repo2=repo1 + coord_fixed(ratio=1) + \
              guides(shape=guide_legend(nrow=1))
repo2 + theme(legend_key_width = 0,
              legend_background = element_rect(size=0.5,
                                               linetype="solid",
                                               colour ="grey"))
```

Calling *matplotlib*

As *plotnine* does not have a subtitle and caption, let me finally invoke the main
plotting library in **Python** : *matplotlib* (Caswell et al., 2019). Since *plotnine*
uses *matplotlib*, we simply turn our *plotnine* visual into a *matplotlib* object:

---

[6] These can be 'center', 'left', or 'right' for ha; or 'center', 'top', 'bottom', or 'baseline' in va.

```
## plotnine

info=ggplot(demo, aes(x='Culture', y='Functioning',
                      shape='Continent'))
leyenda=info + geom_point()
erase2=leyenda + theme_classic() + \
                theme(legend_title=element_blank())
repo2=erase2 + coord_fixed(ratio=1)
repo2=repo2 + theme(legend_key_width = 0,
                legend_background = element_rect(size=0.5,
                                                 linetype="solid",
                                                 colour ="grey"))

# HELP from matplotlib
import matplotlib.pyplot as plt
fig = repo2.draw()
# x=0,y=0 is lower left corner; x=1,y=1 is upper right
fig.text(x=0.7,y=0.01,s="The Caption with matplotlib")
# suptitle for TITLE
plt.suptitle(the_Title, y=0.95, fontsize=18)
# title for subTITLE
plt.title(the_SubTitle, fontsize=10)
```

Matplotlib is a huge plotting library, and all you needed here, as you just saw, is to find a way to get a *matplotlib* `fig`. After that, you can apply the missing functionalities.

PART TWO

Visualizing Tabular Data

4

Insights from ONE Variable

Any phenomenon, event, organization or the like that we study always has several if not lots of characteristics. In this chapter, I will pay attention to visuals that are used to represent one variable. I assume you have a basic knowledge of statistics, as several statistical measures are related to univariate exploration; however, I will include basic comments on what is appropriate to use in each situation.

4.1 Information from ONE Variable

If your data has one column it does not mean it is poor information, maybe it is a summary variable representing several dimensions, and which was computed via some process. So, *one* column can represent:

- **Raw values**: These are direct measurements that may need further processing to represent some insightful information. A raw value is a count of newborns.
- **Indicators**: These are processed raw values computed via some mathematical operations. Familiar indicators are presented as some sort of ratio or rate. The ratio of dead newborns by total newborns in a specific year for a particular location is an indicator.
- **Indexes**: These are aggregated or composite indicators (Babbie, 2013). The democracy index (The Economist Intelligence Unit, 2019) we used in the previous chapter is a clear example of a value that tries to aggregate several indicators; notice that these indicators were indexes themselves, then an index can have sub-indexes. In economics, indexes also represent a measure of change related to a base value (Dorin et al., 2020).

As any of the options above[1] can be in one column, please reflect on what you have. In this book, we often use indicators or indexes; and you must be aware that the raw values you may have in your data table might often need further processing. For a further discussion on this, please refer to OECD et al. (2008) and Magallanes Reyes (2017).

4.2 Categorical I: Visualizing Gaps

You think of gaps when you have a threshold, a value that represents a particular boundary from which some values represent something qualitatively different than the others. Then, once categorical data are organized into a frequency table, you can see which category count or percent is beyond or above a certain threshold value.

For this example, let me use the data from 2017 on public schools from the US Department of Education presented on page 16. Let me open that file again:

```
> #link to data
> linkRepo='https://github.com/resourcesbookvisual/data/'
> linkEDU='raw/master/eduwa.csv'
> fullLink=paste0(linkRepo,linkEDU)
> #getting the data:
> eduwa=read.csv(fullLink,stringsAsFactors = FALSE)
```

The data frame `eduwa` has a column *LocaleType*, a nominal variable (see page 14) that tells you the location of a school. I should start by preparing its frequency table as a data frame, this time I will include the percent values:

```
> ValuesAndCounts=table(eduwa$LocaleType,useNA = "ifany")
> values=names(ValuesAndCounts)
> counts=as.vector(ValuesAndCounts)
> FTloc=data.frame(Location=values,Count=counts)
> FTloc$Percent=100*round(counts/sum(counts),4)
> # ordering FreqTable by ascending counts
> FTloc=FTloc[order(FTloc$Count),]
> row.names(FTloc)=NULL # resetting row names
> # here it is:
> print(FTloc, row.names = F)
```

Location	Count	Percent
<NA>	72	2.97
Town	338	13.93
Rural	505	20.81
City	714	29.42
Suburb	798	32.88

---

[1] The options presented will be consistent throughout the book, but I am aware this distinction may not always be clear or discussed elsewhere.

The previous frequency table included missing values as locations, because some schools had not been categorized (I forced that using if any). However, you may want to name that category level:

```
> # adding a level:
> levels(FTloc$Location) = c(levels(FTloc$Location),'Uncategorized')
> # using that level for the 'NA' value:
> FTloc$Location[is.na(FTloc$Location)]='Uncategorized'
```

Notice that the column Location in **R** was created as a categorical one, then I needed to add a new level before replacing the missing value. In *Pandas*, later, that column will be considered as text, so its replacing will require one step less.

At this point, I need to decide the threshold value. For this example, let's use 25 percent, the value that represents the uniform share if you have four alternatives (remember we have four location types). Then, a gap value is simply the difference. Let me add that column to my FT1loc object:

```
> # new column with gap value
> FTloc$Gap=round(FTloc$Percent-25,0)
```

Let me also create a *flag* (Above_Equal_Share), which will tell me if a value is negative or positive:

```
> # new column with True if gap is positive (False otherwise)
> FTloc$Above_Equal_Share=FTloc$Gap>0
```

The **Python** code that will create a frequency table as a *Pandas* data frame in a similar fashion can be:

```python
import pandas as pd

#link to data
linkRepo='https://github.com/resourcesbookvisual/data/'
linkFile='raw/master/eduwa.csv'
fullLink=linkRepo+linkFile
eduwa=pd.read_csv(fullLink)
#
# Frequency table
FTloc = pd.value_counts(eduwa.LocaleType,
                        ascending=True,
                        dropna=False).reset_index()
FTloc.columns = ['Location','Count']
# adding column
FTloc['Percent']=100*(FTloc.Count/FTloc.Count.sum()).round(4)
#
FTloc['Location'].fillna('Uncategorized', inplace=True)
# new column with gap value
FTloc['Gap']=(FTloc.Percent-25).round(0)
# new column with True if gap is positive (False otherwise)
FTloc['Above_Equal_Share']=FTloc.Gap>0
```

Let's make a barplot with `FTloc`, generally a safe choice for categorical data. Let me show you step by step:

1. Prepare the text for the titles (I will not use axes titles):

```
> texts=list(TITLE="Distance from even distribution",
+            sTITLE="Location of Schools in WA State (2018)",
+            SOURCE="Source: US Department of Education")
```

2. By default, *ggplot* will plot the categorical levels alphabetically, so you need the bars ordered by count:

```
> rePOSITION=FTloc$Location
```

3. Prepare the base layer. I use for y the values in `Gap`, which are positive and negative. I use `label` argument to later annotate bars with `geom_label`.

```
> library(ggplot2)
> info1=ggplot(data=FTloc, aes(x=Location,y=Gap,label=Gap))
```

4. Choose the geometry element needed:

```
> barFT1= info1 + geom_bar(stat = 'identity',width = 0.5)
```

5. Set the basic style:

```
> barFT1= barFT1 + theme_classic()
```

6. Change alignment defaults (notice that while *ggplot* requires coding for centering titles, **Python** will use center aligment by default):

```
> barFT1= barFT1 + theme(plot.title= element_text(hjust= 0.5),
+                        plot.subtitle= element_text(hjust= 0.5),
+                        plot.caption= element_text(hjust= 0))
```

7. Get rid of elements to maximize "data–ink ratio":

```
> barFT1= barFT1 + theme(axis.ticks= element_blank(),
+                        axis.text.y= element_blank(),
+                        axis.title.y= element_blank(),
+                        axis.title.x= element_blank(),
+                        axis.line.y= element_blank(),
+                        axis.line.x= element_blank())
```

8. Add titles using the list `texts` from step 1. above:

```
> barFT1= barFT1+ labs(title=texts$TITLE,
+                      subtitle = texts$sTITLE,
+                      caption = texts$SOURCE)
```

9. Reposition the bars:

```
> barFT1= barFT1 + scale_x_discrete(limits=rePOSITION)
```

10. Add the threshold line:

```
> barFT1=barFT1 + geom_hline(aes(yintercept=0))
```

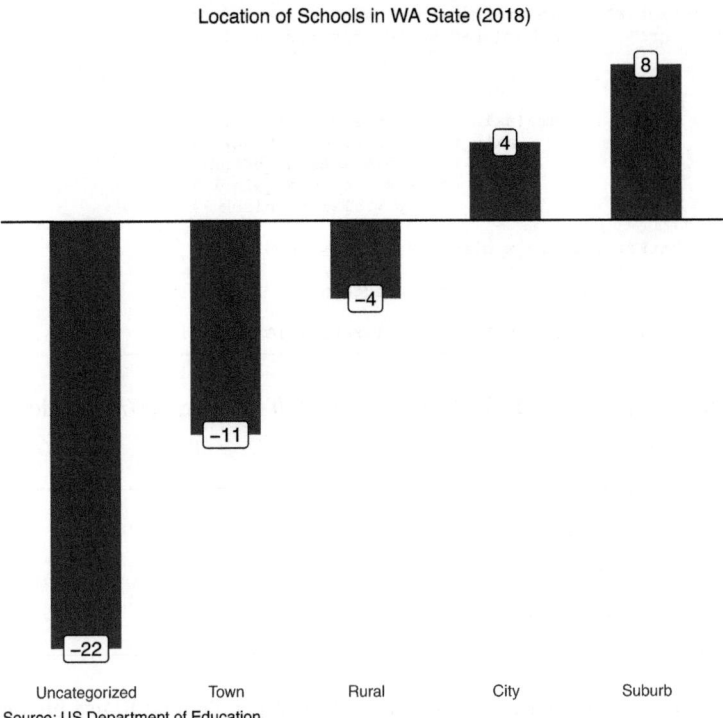

Figure 4.1 The barplot for gaps

Each bar represents the distance to the threshold.

Source: The Common Core of Data from the US Department of Education, available at
https://nces.ed.gov/ccd/.

11. Annotate the bars. Remember that the `aes` for `geom_label` was
    defined in the object `info` in step 3. above. The final version is displayed
    in Figure 4.1.

```
> #text in bars
> barFT1=barFT1 + geom_label()
```

As expected, since the `y` represent `Gap`, the bars show positive and negative
direction.

Using **Python**'s *plotnine*, I can obtain Figure 4.1 with this code:

```
texts={'TITLE':"Distance from even distribution",
       'sTITLE':"Location of Schools in WA State (2018)",
       'SOURCE':"Source: US Department of Education"}

rePOSITION=FTloc.Location

from plotnine import *
```

```
info1=ggplot(FTloc,aes(x='Location',y='Gap',label='Gap'))
barFT1= info1 + geom_bar(stat = 'identity',width=0.4)
# theme
barFT1= barFT1 + theme_classic()
#erasing
barFT1= barFT1 + theme(axis_ticks= element_blank(),
                       axis_text_y = element_blank(),
                       axis_title_y = element_blank(),
                       axis_title_x = element_blank(),
                       axis_line_y = element_blank())
#repositioning
barFT1= barFT1 + scale_x_discrete(limits=rePOSITION)
#threshold
barFT1=barFT1 + geom_hline(aes(yintercept=0))
#text in bars
barFT1=barFT1 + geom_label(aes(label=rePOSITION),
```

The code above needs the help of *matplotlib* (Hunter, 2007) for adding the text titles and caption:

```
# text with matplotlib
import matplotlib.pyplot as plt

fig = barFT1.draw()
fig.text(x=0.1,y=-0.02,s=texts['SOURCE'])
plt.suptitle(texts['TITLE'], y=0.97, fontsize=14)
plt.title(texts['sTITLE'], fontsize=10)
```

Do we have an alternative to barplots? Most people tend to use **pie charts** with categorical data, but this should not be the default option, as proposed by Hickey (2013). However, if you are looking for an alternative for categorical data consider the **Lollipop plot**. The lollipop, as proposed by Cleveland and McGill (1984), can replace the barplot. The position of head of the lollipop, a dot, will represent the value, and the stick (or stem) will highlight that value as a distance (as the bar does). Let me show you what you need to adapt from the **R** code from page 72.

- Step 1 and 2 are the same.
- Adapt step 3:

```
> # changes in aes:
> info2 = ggplot(FTloc, aes(x=Location,
+                           y=Gap,
+                           color=Above_Equal_Share, #new
+                           label=Gap))
```

- Change geom in step 4: We actually need two geoms (point and segment). Notice the structure of geom_segment. I recommend to add the dot layer after the stick, if not, when you use text for the dot, the stick will cover the value.

```
> # one for the lollipop stick
> loll= info2 + geom_segment(aes(y = 0, #from
+                                 yend = Gap, #to
+                                 x = Location,#from
+                                 xend = Location),#to
+                                 color = "gray")
> # one for the lollipop head (just a dot)
> loll= loll + geom_point(size=10)
```

- Step five and six are the same
- I will improve here the fact that in Figure 4.1 the category labels are far from the bars. So, in step 7, you will get rid of the categorical labels in the x-axis. The visual after this step will have no x-axis labels.

```
> # NO X-AXIS
> loll = loll + theme(axis.ticks= element_blank(),
+                     axis.text.y = element_blank(),
+                     axis.title.y = element_blank(),
+                     axis.line.y = element_blank(),
+                     # no more x-axis elements
+                     axis.text.x = element_blank(),
+                     axis.line.x = element_blank(),
+                     axis.title.x = element_blank())
```

- Steps eight and nine remain unchanged.
- I will change the default type of line in step ten:

```
> # annotating threshold
> loll = loll + geom_hline(yintercept=0,
+                          linetype = "dashed")
```

- Step eleven will have major changes. I will need two labels, one for the values of Gap, and one for the label of the location the bar represents (remember that I erased the x-axis elements). The former does not need to set aes, so the aesthetic label will be *inherited*. In the latter, I do need to tell what is the aesthetic to plot. Notice that geom_label will generate a legend element by default, so I am preventing that (you can try not preventing it, and see what happens).

```
> # for 'Gap' values.
> loll = loll + geom_text(show.legend = FALSE,color='white',size=4)
> # for 'Location' values.
> loll = loll + geom_label(aes(label=rePOSITION),
+                          color='black',size=3,
+                          y=0,show.legend = FALSE)
```

- A new step will be to use a *geom* that uses the aesthetics color I requested at the ggplot's aes. In this case, I request gray colors. Since the color depends on the values of Above_Equal_Share, it will have two gray levels: I reverted the gray scale so that FALSE receives the lightest gray.

```
> #coloring
> loll = loll + scale_color_grey(start=0.6,end=0.2)
```

- The final and new step will be the legend positions. The element
  scale_color_grey will generate a legend, I am allowing it to reinforce
  the concept of gaps. However, the default position will shrink the plotting
  area (see that discussion on Section 3.2.6); then, I will move the legend to a
  different location. In this case, I will use the plotting area coordinates,
  where (0,0) represents the lower left corner, and (1,1) is the top right corner.
  Finally, I frame the legend.

```
> # legend position and frame
> loll = loll + theme(legend.position = c(0.8,0.4),
+          legend.background = element_rect(linetype="solid",
+                                            colour ="grey"))
```

Of course, if you believe the color legend is not needed, you simply write:

```
> #  IF YOU PREFER NO LEGEND:
> loll = loll + guides(color=FALSE)
```

I will use the color legend this time.

As you are following a *grammar of graphics* approach, you realize several
points by now after the examples:

- Order of layers matter.
- *ggplot* in **R** will align title and subtitles to the left, and caption to the right.
  Plotnine in **Python** centers the titles by default.
- The plotting area has the same coordinate system, from (0,0) to (1,1).
- The size of elements is managed in the same way in both **R** and Python.
- The text size is not understood in the same way in **R** and Python. The value
  you use to increase or decrease text is different in each case, so you should
  try manually different sizes (**R** needs smaller values than Python).

Keep in mind all those differences, as I will not be giving that much detail
later on this same issues in the book. With that in mind, see the result from the
previous code in Figure 4.2.

Notice that the transformation from bars in Figure 4.1 to lollipops in Figure
4.2 was worth the effort. However, bars are a strong point as they are very
familiar to most people with or without a statistical background. So having
this as a default for categorical data is generally a good choice. Also, consider
the possibility of removing the legend, as most details are already clear.

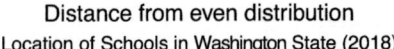

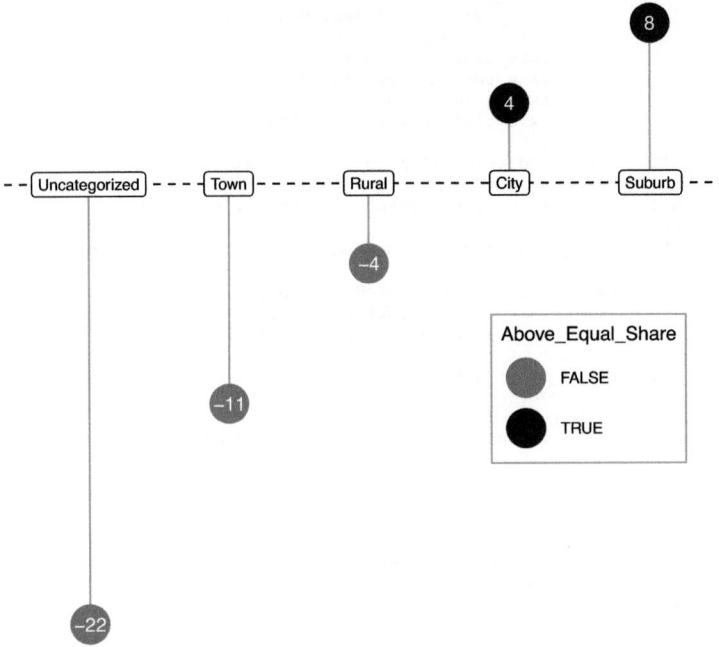

Source: US Department of Education

Figure 4.2 Lollipop to represent gaps

The lollipop can be used to easily show distance to threshold. Each dot represents the gap to
a uniform distribution of schools per location type in Washington State. See code to realize
how to put legend inside plotting area.

Source: The Common Core of Data from the US Department of Education, available at
https://nces.ed.gov/ccd/.

The adaptation to the previous code using Plotnine to re create a **Python**
version of Figure 4.2, and with the now usual help of Matplotlib, can be created
using the next code (notice all the differences):

```python
# changes in aes:
info2 = ggplot(FTloc, aes(x='Location',
                          y='Gap',
                          color='Above_Equal_Share',
                          label='Gap'))
# one for the lollipop stick
loll=info2 + geom_segment(aes(x = 'Location',xend = 'Location',
                              y = 0,yend = 'Gap'),#here
                          color = "lightgray")
# one for the lollipop head (just a dot)
loll = loll + geom_point(size=10)
# NO CHANGES (no realignment needed in Plotine)
```

```
loll = loll + theme_classic()
# NO X-AXIS
loll = loll + theme(axis_ticks= element_blank(),
                    axis_text_y = element_blank(),
                    axis_title_y = element_blank(),
                    axis_line_y = element_blank(),
                    axis_text_x = element_blank(),
                    axis_line_x = element_blank(),
                    axis_title_x = element_blank())
# NO CHANGES (title later)
loll = loll + scale_x_discrete(limits=rePOSITION)
# annotating threshold
loll = loll + geom_hline(yintercept=0, linetype = "dashed")
# for 'Gap' values
loll = loll + geom_text(show_legend = False,color='white',size=8)
# for 'Location' values.
loll = loll + geom_label(aes(label=rePOSITION),
                         color='black',size=9,
                         y=0, show_legend = False)
# coloring
loll = loll + scale_color_gray(0.6,0.2)
# legend position and frame
loll = loll + theme(legend_position = (0.8,0.4),
                    legend_background = element_rect(linetype="solid",
                                                     colour ="grey"))
# text with matplotlib
import matplotlib.pyplot as plt

fig = loll.draw()
fig.text(x=0.1,y=-0.02,s=texts['SOURCE'])
plt.suptitle(texts['TITLE'], y=0.97, fontsize=14)
plt.title(texts['sTITLE'], fontsize=10)
```

4.3 Categorical II: Visualizing Representativity

Representativity is of interest when you want to know how much a particular
population is present among others. Let me open a dataset with the residence
and party of each member of the Washington House of Representatives for the
66th Legislature (Washington State Legislature, 2019). I can find the amount
of representatives from the party or from the residence of the member. Let
me try *Residence*, a nominal variable, so that I can get to see which cities are
represented.

```
> linkREPS='raw/master/reps.csv'
> fullLink=paste0(linkRepo,linkREPS)
> reps=read.csv(fullLink, stringsAsFactors = F)
```

As before, I should start by preparing its frequency table as a data frame:

```
> ValuesAndCounts=table(reps$Residence,useNA = "ifany")
> values=names(ValuesAndCounts); counts=as.vector(ValuesAndCounts)
> FTrep=data.frame(Residence=values,Legislators=counts)
> FTrep=FTrep[order(FTrep$Legislators),]; row.names(FTrep)=NULL
```

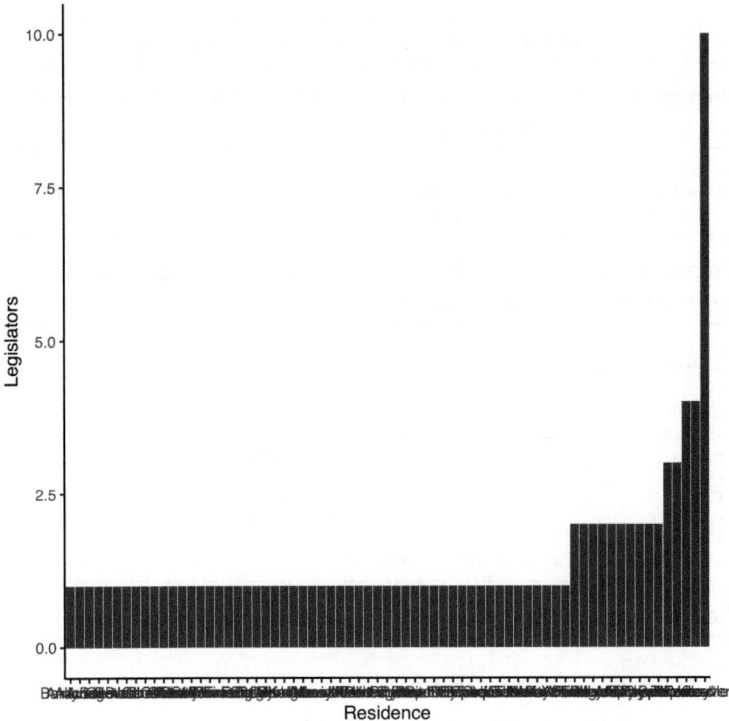

Figure 4.3 Bars for representivity

Using bars to show how sixty-nine cities are represented. The plot has not gone through major editing.

Source: Washington House of Representatives for (66th Legislature) (Washington State Legislature, 2019).

Let me make a basic barplot of the object `FTrep`:

```
> info3=  ggplot(FTrep,aes(x=Residence,y=Legislators)) + theme_classic()
> barFT2= info3+geom_bar(stat='identity')
> barFT2=barFT2 + scale_x_discrete(limits=FTrep$Residence)
```

The State House has sixty-nine cities represented in the 66th legislature (Washington has 212 cities according to the 2010 census (Wikimedia Foundation, 2019)), so you have this many bars in Figure 4.3. It has been shown that this many bars can cause annoying distractions to readers, a phenonenon called *The Moiré Effect* (Saveljev et al., 2018). So when too many bars are present, we need to find a better solution. This better way is the lollipop. Let's do it step by step:

1. Prepare texts for titles and caption:

```
> # text for titles
> texts_2=list(TITLE="Cities represented by Legislators",
```

```
+               sTITLE="WA State House of Representative (2019-2021)",
+               SOURCE="Source: Washington State Legislature.")
```

2. Prepare text for tick labels. I am saving these values so I can alter the labels of ticks in each axis later.

```
> # text for tick labels
> rePOSITION_2=FTrep$Residence
> CountToShow=FTrep$Legislators
```

3. Prepare a lollipop using `FTrep` object. I will not use the `label` aesthetics here, but I will use it later.

```
> #base
> info4 = ggplot(FTrep, aes(x=Residence,
+                           y=Legislators))
> # Lollipop stick
> lol2= info4 + geom_segment(aes(y = 0,
+                           yend = Legislators,
+                           x = Residence,
+                           xend = Residence),
+                           color = "black")
> # Lollipop head
> lol2= lol2 + geom_point(size=1.5)
```

4. Add the usual classic theme, the titles and align the titles text.

```
> # theme:
> lol2 = lol2 + theme_classic()
> # titles:
> lol2 = lol2 + labs(title=texts_2$TITLE,
+                   subtitle = texts_2$sTITLE,
+                   caption = texts_2$SOURCE)
> # adjustments: alignment
> lol2 = lol2 + theme(plot.title= element_text(hjust= 0.5),
+                   plot.subtitle= element_text(hjust= 0.5),
+                   plot.caption= element_text(hjust= 0))
```

5. Here, you can make the repositioning of lollipops:

```
> # repositioning
> lol2 = lol2 + scale_x_discrete(limits=rePOSITION_2)
```

6. You have by now a lollipop that will resemble Figure 4.3. So a good improvement will be to flip the plot:

```
> #flipping
> lol2 = lol2 + coord_flip()
```

7. After the plot is flipped, be careful with horizontal and vertical controls. Most of what used to be the horizontal axis is now the vertical one, and vice versa. Let's get rid of the elements in the vertical:

```
> # Vertical axis changes
> lol2 = lol2 + theme(axis.title.y=element_blank(),
+                   axis.text.y=element_blank(),
+                   axis.ticks.y=element_blank(),
+                   axis.line.y = element_blank())
```

8. On the horizantal axis, I will customize the ticks with the CountToShow object I created in step 2; I will also get rid of the horizontal line, and customize the lines of the major grid (the ones for the ticks I requested):

```
> # Horizontal axis changes
> lol2 = lol2 + scale_y_discrete(limits=CountToShow)
> lol2 = lol2 + theme(axis.line.x = element_blank())
> lol2 = lol2 + theme(panel.grid.major.x =
+                         element_line(color = "grey60",
+                                      linetype = "dashed"))
```

9. I erased the tick labels because I will write the city name next to the lollipop head. Notice I will add the label aesthetics. I could have done this in the step 3. above, but I just wanted to show how to add an aesthetics in a particular element, instead of having the element inherit it.

```
> # annotations: text near dot
> lol2 = lol2 + geom_text(aes(label=Residence),# its own aes
+                         hjust = 0,# left justified
+                         nudge_y = 0.1,#move a little to the right
+                         size=2)
```

Notice that nudge_y will move to the right instead of pushing it towards the top (what the logic of the function suggests). This is a case where flipping did not change orientation.

Figure 4.4 is a major improvement from Figure 4.3, and required some more detail than Figure 4.2. Notice I had to do some work on the text of both axes. This was needed on the horizontal axis because if you do not write the name of the city next to the dot, it will be very uncomfortable to read as a tick text on the vertical axis. I also decided to use the same approach I followed for Figure 3.31, so that the grid can serve to signal the value of each dot, and so I have room for the city name.

In order to re create Figure 4.4 in **Python**, I first need to create the frequency table:

```
linkRepo='https://github.com/resourcesbookvisual/data/'
linkREPS='raw/master/reps.csv'
fullLink=linkRepo+linkREPS
reps=pd.read_csv(fullLink)
# Frequency table
FTrep = pd.value_counts(reps.Residence,
                        ascending=True,
                        dropna=False).reset_index()
FTrep.columns = ['Residence','Legislators']
```

Then, this code will re-create Figure 4.4:

```
# text for titles
texts_2={'TITLE':"Cities represented by Legislators",
         'sTITLE':"WA State House of Representative (2019-2021)",
         'SOURCE':"Source: Washington State Legislature."}
# text for tick labels
```

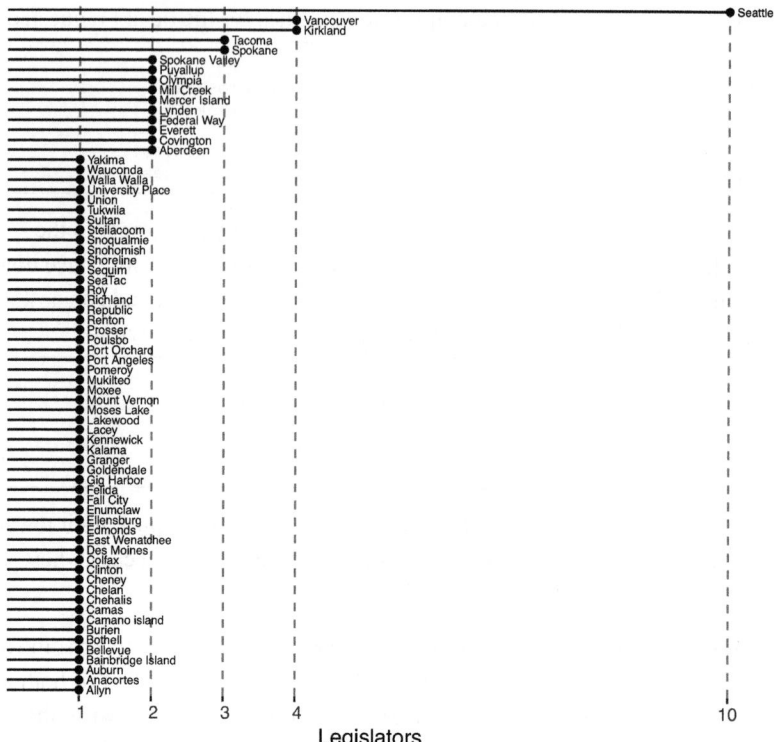

Cities represented by Legislators

WA State House of Representative (2019–2021)

Legislators

Source: Washington State Legislature.

Figure 4.4 Lollipop for representivity

Using Lollipop plot to show how sixty nine cities are represented. The plot has been flipped and gone through major editing.

Source: Washington House of Representatives for (66th Legislature) (Washington State Legislature, 2019).

```
rePOSITION_2=FTrep.Residence
CountToShow=FTrep.Legislators
#base
info4 = ggplot(FTrep, aes(x='Residence',
                          y='Legislators'))
# Lollipop stick
lol2= info4 + geom_segment(aes(y = 0,
                               yend = 'Legislators',
                               x = 'Residence',
                               xend = 'Residence'),
                           color = "black")
# Lollipop head
lol2= lol2 + geom_point(size=2)
# theme:
```

```
lol2 = lol2 + theme_classic()
# titles and aligment later in matplotlib
# repositioning
lol2 = lol2 + scale_x_discrete(limits=rePOSITION_2)
#flipping
lol2 = lol2 + coord_flip()
# Vertical axis changes
lol2 = lol2 + theme(axis_title_y=element_blank(),
                    axis_text_y=element_blank(),
                    axis_ticks_major_y = element_blank(),
                    axis_line_y = element_blank())
# Horizontal axis changes
lol2 = lol2 + scale_y_continuous(breaks=CountToShow)
lol2 = lol2 + theme(axis_line_x = element_blank())
lol2 = lol2 + theme(panel_grid_major_x =
                    element_line(color = "silver",
                                 linetype = "dashed"))
# annotations: text near dot
lol2 = lol2 + geom_text(aes(label='Residence'),
                        ha = 'left',
                        nudge_y = 0.1,
                        size=4.5)
```

As before, *matplotlib* will be needed for the titles and source:

```
import matplotlib.pyplot as plt

fig = lol2.draw()
fig.text(x=0.1,y=-0.02,s=texts_2['SOURCE'])
plt.suptitle(texts_2['TITLE'], y=0.97, fontsize=14)
plt.title(texts_2['sTITLE'], fontsize=10)
```

4.4 Categorical III: Diversity and Inequality

Frequency tables for nominal variables do not normally use cumulative values, as the order of frequency table rows can be arbitrary. However, the fact that you can order by frequency instead of alphabetic order of the categories allows you to represent how diverse or unequal a distribution can be.

This time, I will focus on the distribution of crimes in Seattle. Since inequality means that a few take most of the whole, a plot can inform us if every crime matters, or which are the main crimes. I have prepared a dataset using the Seattle Open Data Portal[2]. Let me open the file and prepare the frequency table for the variable *cat*(which I organized from the column Crime.Subcategory):

```
> linkRepo='https://github.com/resourcesbookvisual/data/'
> linkCRI='raw/master/crime.csv'
> fullLink=paste0(linkRepo,linkCRI)
> crime=read.csv(fullLink,stringsAsFactors = F)
> # preparing frequency table
```

[2] https://data.seattle.gov/Public-Safety/Crime-Data/4fs7-3vj5

```
> library(questionr)
> #rename missing values
> crime$crimecat[is.na(crime$crimecat)]='UNcategorized'
> FTcri=freq(crime$crimecat, sort = "dec", total = F,
+               valid = F,digits = 3,cum = T)
> #result:
> FTcri
```

	n	%	%cum
THEFT	170946	34.210	34.210
CAR PROWL	142447	28.507	62.716
BURGLARY	76630	15.335	78.052
AGGRAVATED ASSAULT	21315	4.266	82.317
NARCOTIC	16864	3.375	85.692
ROBBERY	16832	3.368	89.061
TRESPASS	15919	3.186	92.246
DUI	12205	2.442	94.689
FAMILY OFFENSE-NONVIOLENT	6601	1.321	96.010
SEX OFFENSE-OTHER	6050	1.211	97.221
WEAPON	4751	0.951	98.171
PROSTITUTION	3555	0.711	98.883
RAPE	1859	0.372	99.255
LIQUOR LAW VIOLATION	1619	0.324	99.579
ARSON	1040	0.208	99.787
DISORDERLY CONDUCT	268	0.054	99.841
HOMICIDE	267	0.053	99.894
UNcategorized	262	0.052	99.946
PORNOGRAPHY	166	0.033	99.980
LOITERING	85	0.017	99.997
GAMBLE	17	0.003	100.000

The object FTcri was easily created with help from the package *questionr* (Barnier et al., 2018). I will send the row names as a data frame column:

```
> FTcri$Crimes=row.names(FTcri)
> row.names(FTcri)=NULL
```

From the frequency table you realize that the first ones from the top account for the most trouble in the city. It is important to recall that the **mode** is the value with the highest frequency; however, that does not illustrate the unequal distribution of counts. A good arithmetical strategy can be to compute the **Herfindahl-Hirschman** index (HH-index) (Woerheide, 1993):

```
> # sum of the squares of the percents:
> (HH=sum((FTcri$`%`/100)**2))
```

```
[1] 0.22801
```

When the HH-index is zero, this means we can expect an equal distribution or a very high diversity, but as soon as the index is above 0.25, you can expect an unequal distribution or less diversity. Then, from the value computed, you expect there to be clear signs of inequality, which confirms what we saw in the frequency table. I can also tell you that if you want to know *how many* categories seem to stand out from the rest, you could take the inverse of the HH-index:

```
> # Inverse Simpson or Laakso-Taagepera Index
> 1/HH
```

```
[1] 4.385772
```

The value obtained suggests that there are no more than four groups that are salient from the rest. This value is a measure of *salient presence* in the group, and is known as the Inverse Simpson Index (Simpson, 1949) and also as the Laakso-Taagepera Index of Effective Number of Parties (Laakso and Taagepera, 1979). Now I have this information, let me find a way to visually represent it.

Distribution with One Vertical Axis

I will make a barplot, but I know that I should highlight four bars. Let me prepare a palette with two colors, so that the top crimes are highlighted:

```
> # palette for highlighting the top crimes
> bigCrimes=FTcri$Crimes[1:4]
> TOPS = ifelse(FTcri$Crimes %in% bigCrimes, 'black', 'grey60')
```

I have the colors that will help differentiate the four top crimes from the rest; now, let's use this and the frequency table to prepare the visual:

1. The usual first step:

```
> # base
> info5=ggplot(FTcri,aes(x=Crimes,y=`%cum`)) + theme_classic()
```

2. I will next add a reference line. I can do this as long as I know what the valid values in %cum are. However, my decision to have the reference at **80** is based on the Pareto Principle (Clayton, 2018; Juran, 2019) which proposes that 80 percent of an event is caused by a minority (the 20 percent). Notice that I am doing this so the bars are drawn on top of the line.

```
> # horizontal reference line
> annot1= info5 + geom_hline(yintercept = 80, linetype='dashed')
```

3. Adding the bars. Notice I am making thin bars to avoid *The Moiré Effect* (Saveljev et al., 2018). This is the first time I will use my **TOPS** palette:

```
> # creating bars, applying palette to bar border
> cumBar1= annot1 + geom_bar(stat = 'identity',
+                            fill='white',
+                            colour=TOPS, #border
+                            width = 0.2) # thining
```

4. Now, I should force the order of the bars (otherwise bars will appear in the alphabetic order of crimes):

```
> # reordering bars
> cumBar1=cumBar1+ scale_x_discrete(limits=FTcri$Crimes)
```

5. Another change of defaults, this time for the vertical axis. The intention is to see the Pareto value and other relevant values:

```
> # showing some y axis tick values
> cumBar1=cumBar1 + scale_y_continuous(breaks = c(20,50,80,100))
```

6. The last step for creating a basic plot will be to make sure the tick labels for the top crimes are different from the rest:

```
> # applying palette to text
> cumBar1=cumBar1 + theme(axis.text.x=element_text(angle = 45,
+                                                  hjust = 1,
+                                                  colour=TOPS))
```

The code above is not complete, as there are titles and other elements missing or in need of modification; also, you need to get rid of elements that do not add much (ticks, for instance). I think it would be a good exercise for you to finish the plot, which you can do with the codes given so far. The resulting visual is shown in Figure 4.5:

The **Python** version is shown next. First, the opening of the data and the preparation of the frequency table:

```
import pandas as pd

#link to data
linkRepo='https://github.com/resourcesbookvisual/data/'
linkFile='raw/master/crime.csv'
fullLink=linkRepo+linkFile
crime=pd.read_csv(fullLink)

# Frequency table
FTcri = pd.value_counts(crime.cat,
                        ascending=False,
                        dropna=False).reset_index()
FTcri.columns = ['Crimes','Counts']
```

Then, I add the cumulative percent and rename the missing value. Notice that cumsum and sum are *Pandas* functions that are applied to each column.

```
# adding column
FTcri['CumPercent']=100*FTcri.Counts.cumsum()/FTcri.Counts.sum()
# renaming missing values
FTcri['Crimes'].fillna('UNCATEGORIZED', inplace=True)
```

Here, I prepare the palette. I first prepared a condition using the isin function from *Pandas*, and then used the function where from **numpy**:

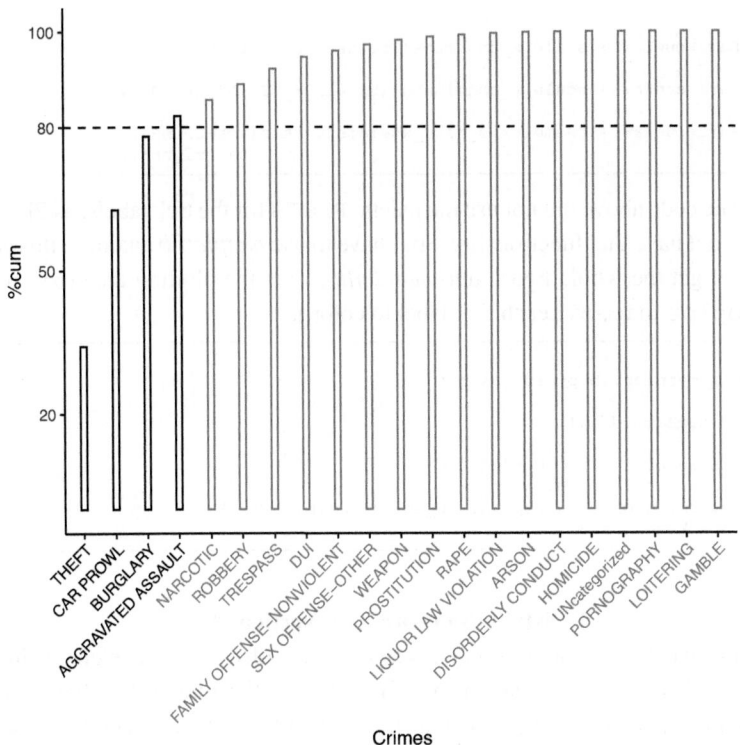

Figure 4.5 Cumulative bars for diversity

Using cumulative bars to show how few crimes are the biggest concern in Seattle. Data from Seattle Open Data Portal (City of Seattle, 2019).

```
import numpy as np

condition=FTcri.Crimes.isin(FTcri.Crimes[0:4])
TOPS =tuple(np.where(condition, 'black', 'silver'))
```

Then, I follow the same steps I took for creating Figure 4.5. The coding strategy is almost the same.

```
from plotnine import *

#1
info5=ggplot(FTcri,aes(x='Crimes',y='CumPercent')) + theme_classic()
#2
annot1=info5 + geom_hline(yintercept = 80, linetype='dashed')
#3
cumBar1=annot1 + geom_bar(stat = 'identity',
                          fill='white',
                          color=TOPS,
                          width = 0.2)
```

```
#4
cumBar1=cumBar1+ scale_x_discrete(limits=FTcri.Crimes)
#5
cumBar1=cumBar1+ scale_y_continuous(breaks = (20,50,80,100))
#6a
cumBar1=cumBar1+ theme(axis_text_x=element_text(rotation=45,
                                                 ha='right'))
```

The code above did not use the palette PLOTS for the tick labels, as Plotnine does not have that functionality. So, I have to use *matplotlib* again. In this case, after I get the whole figure into *matplotlib*, I get the plotting area (ax) using subplot to recover each tick label to color it.

```
# 6b
import matplotlib.pyplot as plt

fig = cumBar1.draw()

ax=plt.subplot() # the plot area
# coloring each label
for aTick, aColor in zip(ax.get_xticklabels(), TOPS):
    aTick.set_color(aColor)
```

Distribution with Two Vertical Axes

Using two vertical axis is not always a good idea, as each element in the plot will have two measurements. However, if the plot is familiar in your community, it is worth producing it. The *Pareto Chart* is a good choice for categorical data. It is a modified barplot that depicts the group of categories that represent the biggest concern for the organization (Wilkinson, 2006). The plot uses bars in decreasing order, and a line element to represent the cumulative percent.

Let me first prepare a *Pareto Chart* using R. It can be in fact a long process but using the library **ggQC** (Grey, 2018) it can be very easy:

```
> library(ggQC)
> info6=ggplot(FTcri, aes(x=Crimes, y=n)) + theme_classic()
> paret=info6 + stat_pareto()
```

I will not show the result from the code above, but I recommend you do this. When you do, you will realize there is still a lot of work to be done. Fortunately, the library *ggQC* is easily integrated with *ggplot*. Let me now offer you one version, not necessarily complete, for our case:

```
> #base
> info6=ggplot(FTcri, aes(x=Crimes, y=n)) + theme_classic()
> #horizontal reference line at   80%
> info6=info6 + geom_hline(yintercept = sum(FTcri$n)*0.80,
+                          linetype = "dashed",color='grey90')
> #vertical reference line at   4th bar
```

```
> info6=info6 + geom_vline(xintercept = 4,
+                          linetype = "dashed",color='grey90')
> #order of the bars
> info6=info6 + scale_x_discrete(limits=FTcri$Crimes)
> #angle for x ticks labels, to ease visibility
> info6=info6 + theme(axis.text.x =element_text(angle=45,hjust = 1))
> #add the Pareto, but shringk the dots, and recolor bar
> paret=info6 + stat_pareto(point.size = 0.5,bars.fill = "grey")
```

The previous code will produce a nice plot, but the default values of the secondary axis values are not the ones I want. So, I will change them with some extra manipulation. For that, I simply type `stat_pareto` in the **R** console to identify its default configuration in order to know how to change the name and the breaks of the secondary axis. Notice that the primary y-axis will produce, by default, labels with a scientific format if the values are big. Add this layer to accomplish the last changes:

```
> paret=paret +
+       scale_y_continuous(
+         sec.axis=sec_axis(trans = ~./(max(.)*0.95)*100,
+                           name="Cumulative %",
+                           breaks=c(20,50,80,100)),
+         labels=function(x) format(x,scientific=F))
```

The result of the `paret` object can be seen in Figure 4.6. There are elements missing, but we have the tools to finish it, by adding more layers using the *ggplot* functions. I also recommend altering the order of the layers in case you want to see what should or should not be moved.

Python can produce a visual similar to Figure 4.6 with the help of the *Pareto Chart* library, created by Lee (2013), and modified by Jesus (2019) (please install it before running the code). The basic functionality is limited, so I have to use *matplotlib* to add the reference lines. Notice that the vertical line value was very easy to produce, compared to the computation needed in *ggplot*.

```
from paretochart import pareto

#using pareto
ax=pareto(FTcri.Counts, FTcri.Crimes,
       line_args=('k'), #'k' is 'black'
       data_kw={'color': 'grey'})

#reference lines using matplotlib
plt.axvline(x=3,ls='--',c='silver',lw=1)
plt.axhline(y=80,ls='--',c='silver',lw=1)

#modifying tick labels
plt.setp(ax[1].get_xticklabels(), ha="right",rotation=45)
plt.show()
```

Notice in the code above that I saved the *Pareto Chart* in `ax` (a tuple with three elements), then I added layers to the plot using `plt`. Finally, the ticks of the horizontal are modified (`ax[1]`).

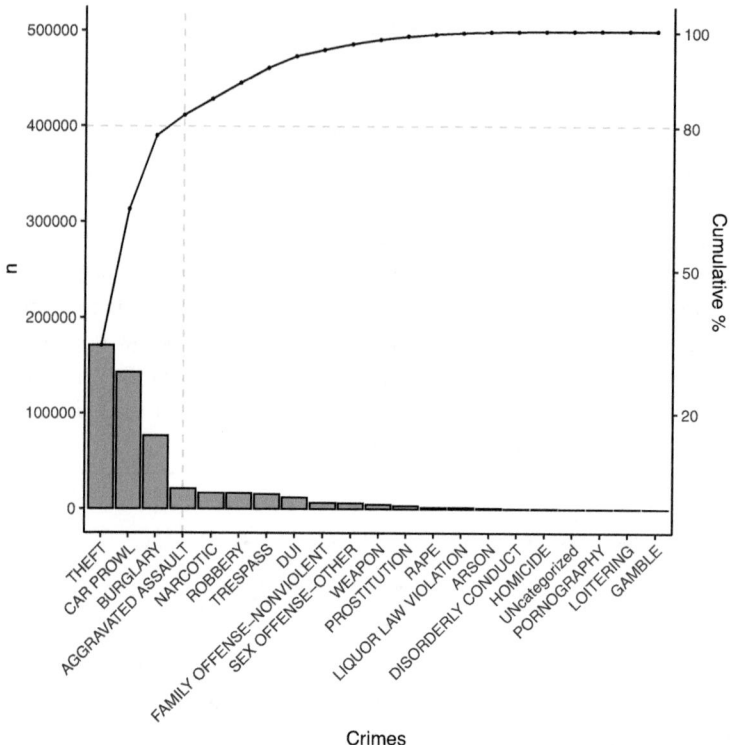

Figure 4.6 *Pareto Chart*

The intersection between the 80 percent value of the secondary axis, and the fourth bar is shown. The fourth bar was selected based on the Inverse Simpson Index (Simpson, 1949). Data from Seattle Open Data Portal (City of Seattle, 2019).

4.5 Categorical IV: Symmetry and Position

The previous examples used nominal data. In those cases, bars were reordered because they did not need to respect any sequence. In ordinal data, you could reorder, but since these data do have order, you should consider highlighting their own properties. For example, take a look at the categories present in the variable High.Grade from the data frame eduwa.

```
> table(eduwa$High.Grade,useNA = "ifany")

  1   10   11   12   13    2    3    4    5    6    7    8    9   KG   PK
  6    7    5  757    9   16   19   45  755  266   11  427   15    7   82
```

This represents the highest grade offered per school. However, ordinal data usually needs to be formatted, as most programs will have recognized it as text or nominal by default. This is the case with this variable. Let's make the change with the command `ordered`:

```
> #get levels
> levelsHG=names(table(eduwa$High.Grade))
> #reorder levels
> ordLabels=c(levelsHG[c(15,14)],
+    sort(as.numeric(levelsHG[c(1:13)])))
> #apply that to the column
> eduwa$High.Grade=ordered(eduwa$High.Grade,levels=ordLabels)
```

The process to format ordinal data requires a little more work in **Python** than in **R** (five steps instead of three)[3]:

```
from pandas.api.types import CategoricalDtype

# get the levels
levels=eduwa['High.Grade'].value_counts().index.sort_values()
#reorder levels
ordLabels=levels[-2:].tolist()[::-1]+sorted(map(int,levels[:-2]))
# turn previous result into a list of strings
ordLabels=list(map(str,ordLabels))
# use that list of levels to create ordinal format
HGtype= CategoricalDtype(categories=ordLabels,ordered=True)
# apply that format to the column
eduwa['High.Grade']= eduwa['High.Grade'].astype(HGtype)
```

Since I have an ordinal column, I should consider that I can highlight:

- Position. Order gives you position, then you can speak in terms of "greater than," "less than," and the like. So you can try computing quartiles (which include the median). When you explore positions, you may find **outliers** – unusual values that are very far from the rest. These are not values to be disregarded, but values whose presence you should try to understand.
- Symmetry. If you have a middle value, you can see how similar the distribution to left of the middle is to the distribution to the right.

A key statistic in ordinal data is the median, which can be easily identified in the frequency table using the cumulative percent (the category that accumulates half or less of the counts):

```
> library(questionr)
> FThg=freq(eduwa$High.Grade, total=F,valid=F,digits=3,cum=T)
> # some changes to FThg:
> FThg$MaxOffer=row.names(FThg)
> row.names(FThg)=NULL
> FThg=FThg[c(4,1:3)]
> names(FThg)[2:4]=c("Counts","Percent","CumPercent")
> FThg
```

---

[3] The third step in **Python** was done by default in **R** the second step, and the fourth step in **Python** is included in the last step in R.

```
    MaxOffer Counts Percent CumPercent
1        PK     82   3.379      3.379
2        KG      7   0.288      3.667
3         1      6   0.247      3.914
4         2     16   0.659      4.574
5         3     19   0.783      5.356
6         4     45   1.854      7.211
7         5    755  31.108     38.319
8         6    266  10.960     49.279
9         7     11   0.453     49.732
10        8    427  17.594     67.326
11        9     15   0.618     67.944
12       10      7   0.288     68.232
13       11      5   0.206     68.438
14       12    757  31.191     99.629
15       13      9   0.371    100.000
```

You can get the same table (without the percent column) using Python:

```
# Frequency table
FThg = pd.value_counts(eduwa['High.Grade'],
                       ascending=False,sort=False,
                       dropna=False).reset_index()
FThg.columns = ['MaxOffer','Counts']
# adding column
FThg['CumPercent']=100*FThg.Counts.cumsum()/FThg.Counts.sum()
```

From the frequency table, you know:

- The first quartile: 25 percent of the public Schools offer at most 5th grade.
- The median or secon quartile: 50 percent of the public Schools offer at most 8th grade.
- The third quartile: 75 percent of the public Schools offer at most 12th grade (25 percent of the schools offer at least 12th grade).

The median and the other positional values do not belong to the nominal data statistics realm, but all the statistics from nominal data can be used in ordinal ones. Let me get the median of this ordinal in **R** using function **Median** from the package **DescTools**[4] by Signorell et al. (2019):

```
> library(DescTools)
> medianHG=as.vector(Median(eduwa$High.Grade))
> # then
> medianHG
```

```
[1] "8"
```

You need to prepare a function in **R** to compute the other quartiles.[5] Since **Python** does not have a median function for ordinal data, let me give an example on how to prepare one to get all quartiles:

---

[4] The function **median** in **R** only works with numeric data.
[5] *DescTools* can not compute other positional values for ordinals.

```
# function for quartiles in ordinal data
def Quart_Pos(cumFT,q=1): # q can be 1,2 or 3.
    position=0
    for percent in cumFT:
        if percent ≤ 25*q: position +=1
        else: break
    return position # returns a position

# applying function
medianHG=FThg.MaxOffer[Quart_Pos(FThg.CumPercent,2)]
```

My **Python** function gives you back the position of the quartile requested (**2** gives me the median). So, I used that value to get the grade that occupies that position.

Having the median will allow me to explore the ordinal characteristics. Let me first make a barplot with the median highlighted:

```
> # color to highlight median
> colCondition=ifelse(ordLabels==medianHG,'black','grey')
> #
> # usual
> info7=ggplot(FThg, aes(MaxOffer,Counts)) + theme_classic()
> barFThg=info7 + geom_bar(stat='identity',
+                          fill=colCondition)
> barFThg=barFThg + scale_x_discrete(limits=ordLabels)
```

As usual, the **Python** version using *plotnine* is almost identical:

```
# color to highlight median
condition=[medianHG==test for test in ordLabels]
colCondition=tuple(np.where(condition, 'black', 'silver'))

# usual
info7=ggplot(FThg, aes('MaxOffer','Counts')) + theme_classic()
barFThg=info7 + geom_bar(stat='identity',fill=colCondition)
barFThg=barFThg + scale_x_discrete(limits=ordLabels)
```

Figure 4.7 renders the object barFThg. Can you find signs of symmetry in that plot?

You can clearly see the lack of symmetry: the distribution to the left of the median ('Grade 8') is not mirroring the distribution to the right. Also, from the frequency table FThg, we know the big grey bars are the first and third quartiles. However, you can not directly identify positional values in barplots without the support of frequency tables.

Your next option is the **boxplot** (Spear, 1969; Tukey, 1977). Boxplots have the advantage of not requiring a frequency table as input; however, they are not that common to understand if you are not familiar with quartiles. Also, **R** and **Python** require a numeric version of the variable. So, let me start by creating a numeric version of the ordinal column:

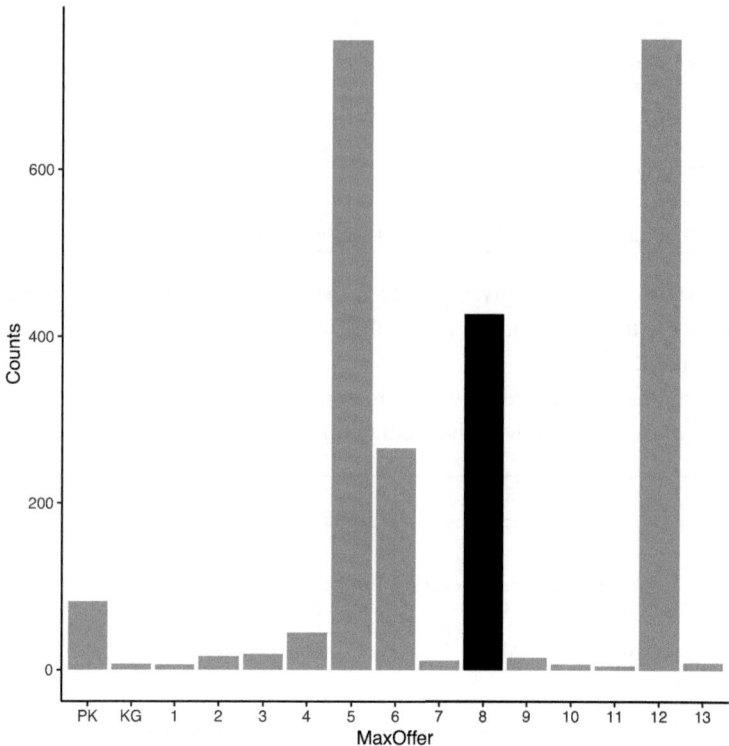

Figure 4.7 Ordinal barplot

The median is highlighted.

Data Source: The Common Core of Data from the US Department of Education, available at
`https://nces.ed.gov/ccd/`.

```
> # from ordinal to numeric
> eduwa$High.Grade.Num=as.numeric(eduwa$High.Grade)
```

You can now create a boxplot with this new variable. The result will be shown in Figure 4.8.

```
> info8=ggplot(eduwa,aes(x=0,y=High.Grade.Num)) + theme_classic()
> boxHG =info8 + geom_boxplot() + coord_flip()
> boxHG = boxHG + scale_y_continuous(labels=ordLabels,breaks=1:15)
```

This will be the **Python** version to get Figure 4.8:

```
# from ordinal to numeric
eduwa['High.Grade.Num']=eduwa['High.Grade'].cat.codes

info8=ggplot(eduwa,aes(x=0,y='High.Grade.Num')) + theme_classic()
```

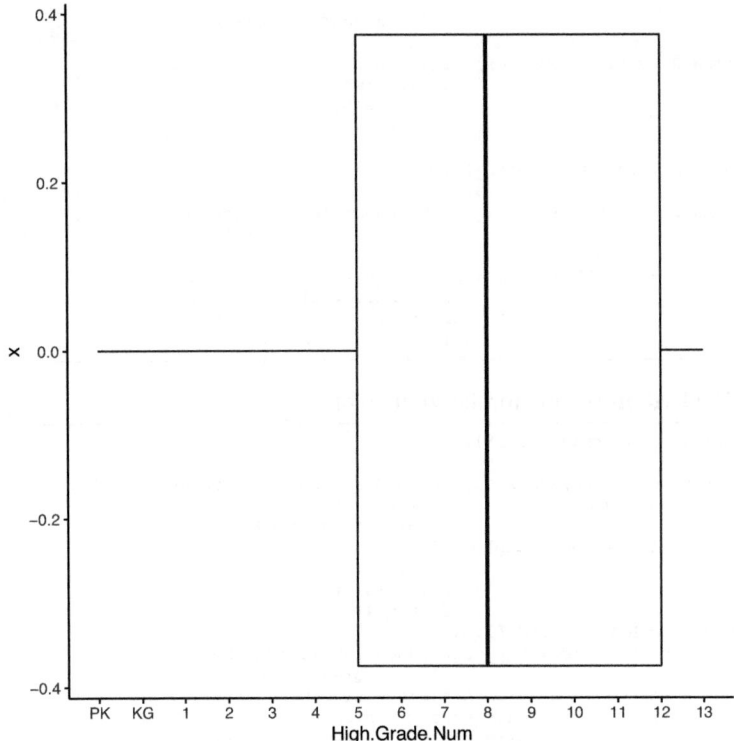

Figure 4.8 Boxplot

The median is highlighted.

Data Source: The Common Core of Data from the US Department of Education, available at https://nces.ed.gov/ccd/.

```
boxHG =info8+ geom_boxplot()
boxHG =boxHG + coord_flip()
boxHG = boxHG + scale_y_continuous(labels=ordLabels,
                                    breaks=list(range(0, 15)))
```

Boxplots can confirm that you have symmetry when the distance of each *whisker* to the *box* is the same, and when the thick line (the median) is in the middle of the box. Since you have a *left tail*, you can say this variable has *negative symmetry*.

Boxplots do not replace barplots. The boxplot is hiding the peaks you can see in bars. However, you can reveal that if you combine the boxplot with a **violin plot**:

```
> info8=ggplot(eduwa,aes(x=0,y=High.Grade.Num)) + theme_classic()
> # first the violin:
> viol =info8 + geom_violin(width=1.4, # play with this value
```

```
+                           fill="black", color=NA)
> #now the bxplot
> boxHG2 =vio1 + geom_boxplot(width=0.2,# play with this value
+                             fill='white',
+                             color='grey',
+                             fatten=4) #thicker median
> # flipping
> boxHG2 = boxHG2 + coord_flip()
> # right order of tick labels
> boxHG2 = boxHG2 + scale_y_continuous(labels=ordLabels,
+                             breaks=1:15)
> # erase unneeded elements.
> boxHG2 = boxHG2 + theme(axis.ticks = element_blank(),
+                         axis.text.y = element_blank(),
+                         axis.title.y = element_blank(),
+                         axis.line.y  = element_blank())
```

The **Python** version for the Violin plot:

```
theBreaks=list(range(0, 15))

info8=ggplot(eduwa,aes(x=0,y='High.Grade.Num')) + theme_classic()
vio1 =info8 + geom_violin(width=1.4,
                          fill="black", color=None)
boxHG2 = vio1 + geom_boxplot(width=0.2,
                             fill='white',
                             color='silver',
                             fatten=4)
boxHG2 = boxHG2 + coord_flip()
boxHG2 = boxHG2 + scale_y_continuous(labels=ordLabels,
                                     breaks=theBreaks)
boxHG2 = boxHG2 + theme(axis_ticks = element_blank(),
                        axis_text_y = element_blank(),
                        axis_title_y = element_blank(),
                        axis_line_y  = element_blank())
```

Then, the object boxHG2 is represented in Figure 4.9.

Figures 4.8 and 4.9 have a negative asymmetry, but there is no presence of outliers. If there were, the boxplot would identify them with dots. In future visuals, we may see some outliers. Those boxplots are also a good example of the difference between labels and limits of an axis. Previously, I could customize the axis just by indicating the values I wanted, but in all those cases we just dealt with numeric values. In this case, I needed to indicate the numeric values and the labels each tick will have. Also, pay attention to the data structure needed for each argument. In R, labels and breaks, use *vectors*; while in **Python**, both arguments need *lists*.

4.6 Numerical I: Dispersion

Bars or similar elements have allowed you to see the dispersion of a variable; however, I have not paid so much attention to this property in nominal or ordinal variables as generally they do not take that many values, while

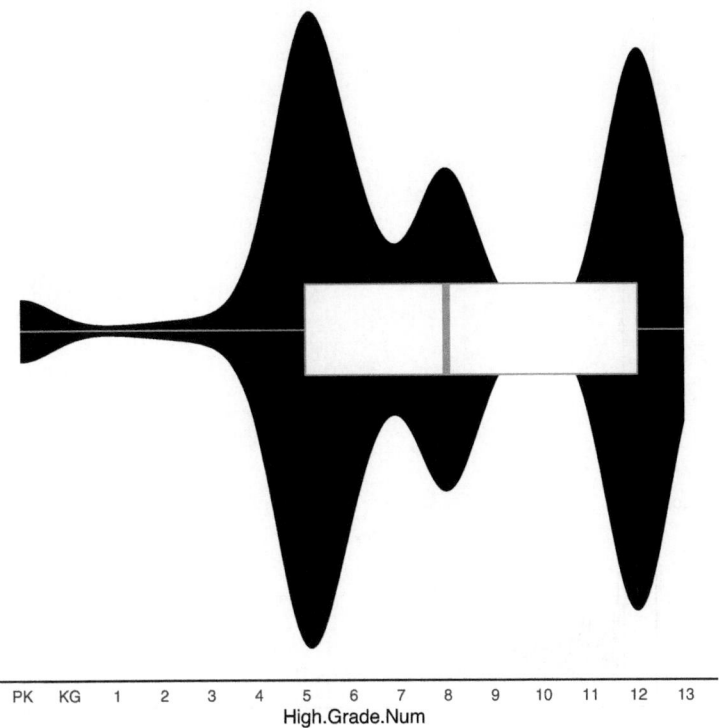

PK KG 1 2 3 4 5 6 7 8 9 10 11 12 13

High.Grade.Num

Figure 4.9 Box and Violin plot combined

Data Source: The Common Core of Data from the US Department of Education, available at
https://nces.ed.gov/ccd/.

numerical do. Let me use a barplot to show you the dispersion in the variable
Reduced.Lunch, which informs how many kids there are in each school that
have lunch for a reduced price, simply using a barplot:

```
> info9= ggplot(eduwa,aes(x = Reduced.Lunch)) + theme_classic()
> displ= info9 + geom_bar()
```

Figure 4.10 has 172 bars, as there are that many different values, a lot more
than what you find in categorical data. This prevents bars from being an option;
so we need to find an alternative. Keeping in mind that when your purpose is
to inform about dispersion, it is because you want to show that:

- most values are well represented by central values (median / mean).
  A boxplot can help, as its central box is showing the dispersion in the
  neighborhood of the median;

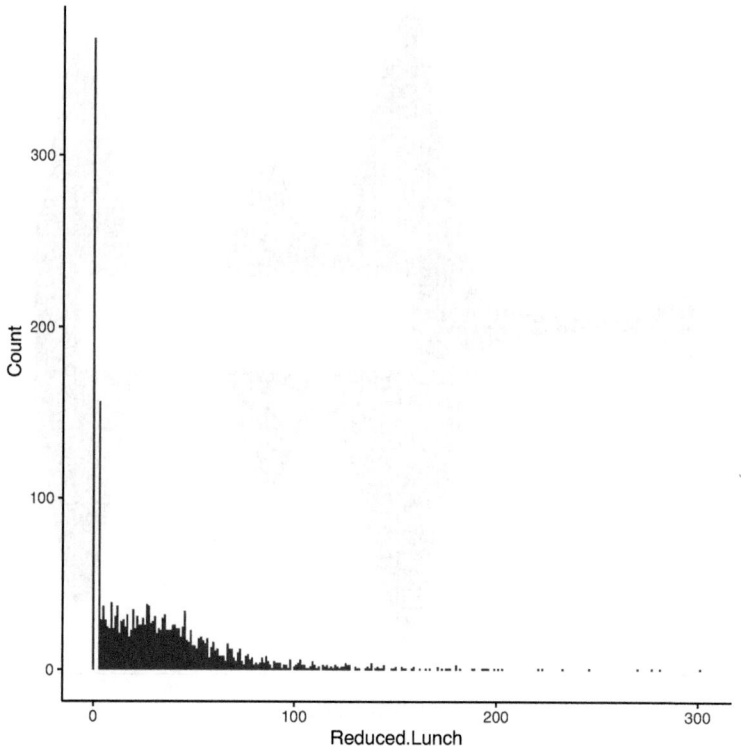

Figure 4.10 Dispersion using bars

Data Source: The Common Core of Data from the US Department of Education, available at
https://nces.ed.gov/ccd/.

- the dispersion pattern allows for outliers. A boxplot will automatically illustrate of that;
- the dispersion around the central values (median/mean).

You can see from what I have just mentioned that a first option can be a **boxplot**. However, before plotting, I recommend you get information on your data:

- Get the basic statistics:

```
> (statVals=summary(eduwa$Reduced.Lunch)) # just values

   Min. 1st Qu.  Median    Mean 3rd Qu.    Max.   NA's
   0.00    5.00   25.50   33.53   47.00  301.00    131

> # In R, you need to get the standard deviation (NOT in Python):
> statVals['std']=sd(eduwa$Reduced.Lunch,na.rm = T)
```

When readers know the median and the mean, most will believe these are representative values of the population. You need to show how representative these actually are by showing the dispersion of the data. Notice that the command `summary` produced a *table* structure, which produces "named" values (there is a name for each value); this is how I added the standard deviation to `statVals`, which is a measure of dispersion relative to the mean.

- Turn the basic statistics into values you can use later:

```
> (statVals=ceiling(statVals))

   Min. 1st Qu.  Median    Mean 3rd Qu.    Max.     std   NA's
      0       5      26      34      47     301      37    131
```

The function `ceiling` will round up the values. This is an optional step, which I may use for annotating.

- Thresholds to detect outliers:
  - Distance between quartiles (the measure of dispersion for the median):

    ```
    > IQR=statVals['3rd Qu.']-statVals['1st Qu.']
    ```

  - Compute the upper and lower thresholds to detect outliers:

    ```
    > statVals['upper']=1.5*IQR + statVals['3rd Qu.']
    > statVals['lower']=statVals['1st Qu.']-1.5*IQR
    ```

    Any value above or below will be considered an outlier.

- Prepare annotations for the plot:
  - Values for axis:

    ```
    > # no 'lower' this time
    > axisKeys=c('Min.','1st Qu.','Median','Mean',
    +            '3rd Qu.','upper','Max.')
    > myTicks=as.vector(statVals[axisKeys])
    ```

    The object `myTicks` is a vector, a structure needed for the axis in *ggplot*.
  - Compute the share of values considered as outliers:

    ```
    > # Share of values considered outliers:
    > theVariable=eduwa$Reduced.Lunch
    > theVariable = theVariable[!is.na(theVariable)]
    > countOutliersUp=sum(theVariable>statVals['upper'])
    > shareOut=ceiling(countOutliersUp/length(theVariable)*100)
    > # message using the value computed:
    > labelOutliers=paste0("Outliers:\n", shareOut,"% of data")
    ```

The **Python** code for the previous computations is shown next:

```
# get stats as DICT: count, mean,std,min,q1,q2,q3,max
statVals=eduwa['Reduced.Lunch'].describe().to_dict()

# Turn into DICT of integers (rounding up)
from math import ceil
```

```python
statVals={key: ceil(val) for key, val in statVals.items()}

# Thresholds to detect outliers:

## distance between quartiles
IQR=statVals['75%']-statVals['25%']
## Thresholds:
statVals['upper']=1.5*IQR + statVals['75%']
statVals['lower']=statVals['25%'] - 1.5*IQR

#prepare annotations:
axisKeys=['min','25%','50%','mean','75%','upper','max']
myTicks = {axKey: statVals[axKey] for axKey in axisKeys}

# Share of values considered outliers:
theVariable=eduwa['Reduced.Lunch']
theVariable = theVariable.dropna()
countOutliersUp=sum(theVariable>statVals['upper'])
shareOut=ceil(countOutliersUp/len(theVariable)*100)
# message using the value computed:
labelOutliers="Outliers:\n" + str(shareOut) + "% of data"
```

Next, let me produce an annotated boxplot in R:

```r
> # x=0, 0 is the position of line that goes accross the boxplot
> info10= ggplot(eduwa,aes(x=0,y=Reduced.Lunch)) + theme_classic()
> #
> # Changing defaults
> ## axis 'breaks'
> info10= info10 + scale_y_continuous(breaks=myTicks)
> #
> ## this is the x-axis limits, useful for annotation positions
> info10= info10 + xlim(c(-0.25,0.3)) + coord_flip()
> #
> # changing width of boxplot
> disp2= info10 + geom_boxplot(width=0.25,outlier.alpha = 0.2)
> #
> # ANNOTATING
> ## Standard deviation:
> ## this is a segment showing one standard deviation interval
> disp2=disp2 + annotate("pointrange",
+                     x=0.15, y=statVals['Mean'],
+                     ymin = (statVals['Mean']+5)-statVals['std'],
+                     ymax = (statVals['Mean']+5)+statVals['std'],
+                     colour = "gray80", size = 1)
> ## mean
> ### the line
> disp2=disp2 + geom_hline(yintercept = statVals['Mean'],
+                      linetype='dotted')
> #
> ### the text: notice I add '5', to move text
> disp2=disp2 + annotate(geom="text", fill='white',
+                     x=0.2, y=statVals['Mean']+5,
+                     label="Mean",angle=90,size=3)
> ## median
> ### the line
> disp2=disp2 + geom_hline(yintercept = statVals['Median'],
+                      linetype='dotted')
> #
> ### the text: notice I substract '5', to move text
> disp2=disp2 + annotate(geom="text",
+                     x=-0.2, y=statVals['Median']-5,
+                     label="Median",angle=90,size=3)
```

```
> ## outliers
> ### the line
> disp2=disp2 + geom_hline(yintercept = statVals['upper'],
+                          linetype='dashed',color='grey50')
> #
> ### the text
> disp2=disp2 + annotate(geom="label",
+                        x=0.1, y=statVals['Max.'],
+                        label=labelOutliers,size=5,hjust=1,
+                        color='grey50')
> # erasing
> disp2=disp2 + theme(axis.ticks.y = element_blank(),
+                     axis.line.y = element_blank(),
+                     axis.text.y = element_blank(),
+                     axis.title.y = element_blank())
```

The object `disp2` is shown in Figure 4.11. This plot includes statistical information which is appropriate in case your audience has some basic training. You are clearly showing that the mean and the median are not at the center of the distribution, and that the amount of outliers is probably worth considering.

You can see the **Python** version of Figure 4.11 below. Notice that I am using dictionaries in Python; I have done that before to use *keys* instead of indexes (numbers). I followed a similar approach in **R** with the table structure. This is optional, but I think it improves not only readability but it gets easier to remember:

```
info10= ggplot(eduwa,aes(x=0,y = 'Reduced.Lunch')) + theme_classic()
info10=info10 + scale_y_continuous(breaks =list(myTicks.values()))
info10=info10 +xlim(-0.25,0.3) +coord_flip()
disp2= info10 + geom_boxplot(width=0.25,outlier_alpha = 0.2)

# annotating
## standard deviation
disp2=disp2 + annotate("pointrange",
                       x=0.15, y=statVals['mean'],
                       ymin = (statVals['mean']+5)-statVals['std'],
                       ymax = (statVals['mean']+5)+statVals['std'],
                       colour = "silver", size = 1)
## mean
disp2=disp2 + geom_hline(yintercept = statVals['mean'],
                         linetype='dotted')
disp2= disp2 + annotate(geom="text",
                        x=0.2, y=statVals['mean']+5,
                        label="Mean",angle=90,size=10)
## median
disp2=disp2 + geom_hline(yintercept = statVals['50%'],
                         linetype='dotted')
disp2= disp2 + annotate(geom="text",
                        x=-0.2, y=statVals['50%']-5,
                        label="Median",angle=90,size=10)

## outliers
disp2=disp2 + geom_hline(yintercept = statVals['upper'],
                         linetype='dashed',color='silver')
disp2=disp2 + annotate(geom="label",
                       x=0.1,y=statVals['max'],
                       label=labelOutliers,size=12,ha='right',
                       color='silver')
```

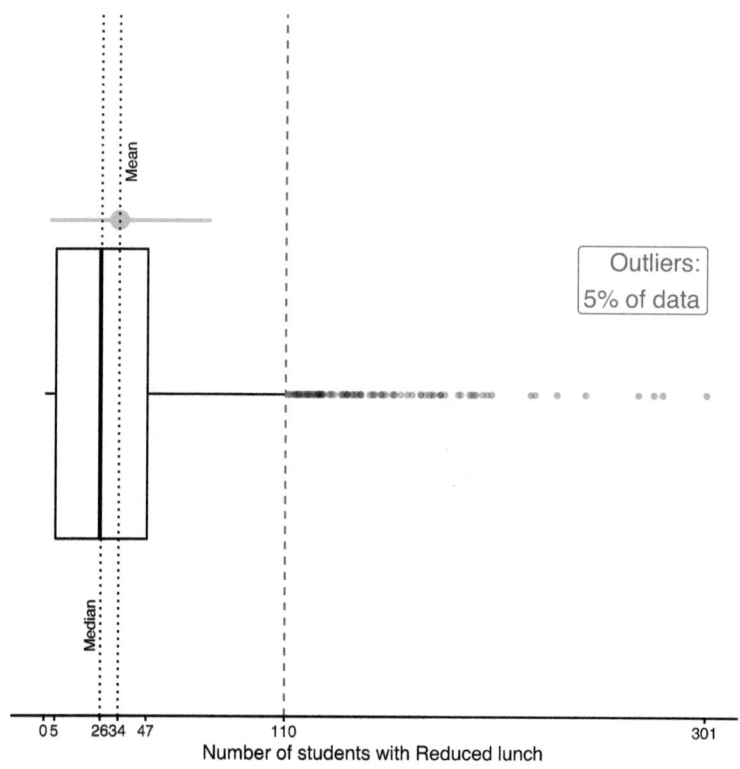

Figure 4.11 Dispersion using a boxplot

Data Source: The Common Core of Data from the US Department of Education, available at
`https://nces.ed.gov/ccd/`.

```
# erasing
disp2=disp2 + theme(axis_ticks_major_y = element_blank(),
                    axis_line_y = element_blank(),
                    axis_text_y = element_blank(),
                    axis_title_y = element_blank())
```

Keep in mind that the features we have been highlighting in the previous
subsections can all be applied to numeric data, but dispersion and shape
feature, coming next, are more natural to numeric data.

4.7 Numerical II: Shape

Shape and dispersion combined allow for a comprehensive analysis of numeric
data. Shape of data distribution can resemble several well-known statistical distributions. However, most of the time you will be interpreting data comparing

them to a distribution known as the *normal distribution*. A normal distribution is bell-shaped and symmetrical, and, in that situation, its mean and median are the same. However, even if symmetry is accomplished, you need to find out if it has an interesting relationship between its mean (M) and its standard deviation (STD):

- Approximately 68 percent of the data fall within 1 STD of the M.
- Approximately 95 percent of the data fall within 2 STDs of the M.
- Approximately 99.7 percent of the data fall within 3 STDs of the M.

When symmetry is satisfied, but the above conditions are not met, you explore the *kurtosis*: if the bell is too flat, the kurtosis becomes negative and you have a platycurtik shape; if the bell is thin, you have a leptokurtic shape. The normal distribution is mesokurtic.

Boxplots do not show shape very well; so, you should use the **histogram** for this feature. The histogram is very similar to a barplot, as the height of the bars also represents a count or a percent; however, the bars in a histogram are contiguous, and each bar width represents an interval of numbers, instead of a category.

Next, let me explore the shape of the variable on reduced lunch. I have to complete two basic steps:

a) Compute the input elements to create a frequency table of the data intervals:

1. Decide the starting value and the width of the interval. In our case it will be 10.

```
> theStart=statVals['Min.']
> width=10
```

2. Since the maximum value of the data may not be a multiple of the width selected, I will need to select the smallest multiple of 10 as the new maximum value.

```
> oldMax=statVals['Max.']
> newMax=ifelse(oldMax%%width<width,
+               oldMax+(width-oldMax%%width),oldMax)
```

3. With the previous information, I will produce all the interval breaks.

```
> TheBreaks=seq(theStart,newMax,width)
```

4. The object TheBreaks will be used in the histogram. You can cut the variable with TheBreaks to produce a frequency table, but I only need the maximum frequency:

```
> intervals=cut(eduwa$Reduced.Lunch,
+                  breaks=TheBreaks,include.lowest = T)
> topCount=max(table(intervals))
```

I need the `topCount` to determine the values on the vertical axis.

5. Compute the vertical axis values:

```
> widthY=50
> top_Y=ifelse(topCount%%widthY<widthY,
+                  topCount+widthY-topCount%%widthY,topCount)
> vertiVals=seq(0,top_Y,widthY)
```

The **Python** code that computes the same is shown next:

```
#1
theStart=statVals['min']
width=10
#2
oldMax=statVals['max']
reminderMax=oldMax%width
newMax= oldMax+(width-reminderMax) if reminderMax<width else oldMax
#3
TheBreaks=list(range(theStart,newMax+width,width))
#4
intervals=pd.cut(eduwa['Reduced.Lunch'],
               bins=TheBreaks,include_lowest=True)
topCount=intervals.value_counts().max()
#5
widthY=50
reminderY=topCount%widthY
top_Y=topCount+widthY-reminderY if reminderY<widthY else topCount
vertiVals=list(range(0,top_Y+widthY,widthY))
```

a) Compute the normal curve for the data[6]. This will let you know how far the actual shape is from the normal one. These are the steps:

1. Set the input parameters:

```
> N = sum(!is.na(eduwa$Reduced.Lunch)) # number of elements
> MEAN = as.vector(statVals['Mean'])
> STD = as.vector(statVals['std'])
```

2. Create the function, modifying output to resemble counts:

```
> NormalHist=function(x) dnorm(x,mean =MEAN,sd =STD)*N*width
```

The previous function looks like this in **Python**:

```
#1
N = statVals['count']
MEAN = statVals['mean']
STD = statVals['std']
#2
```

---

[6] The function for the normal curve requires the input of mean and the standard deviation.

```
def NormalHist(x,m=MEAN,s=STD,n=N,w=width):
    import scipy.stats as stats
    return stats.norm.pdf(x, m, s)*n*w
```

Then, I can create my histogram like this:

```
> info11= ggplot(eduwa, aes(x = Reduced.Lunch)) +
+          theme_classic() +
+          ylab("Number of students with Reduced lunch")
> # the histogram
> disp3= info11 + geom_histogram(binwidth = width,
+                                #start of first bar
+                                boundary=theStart,
+                                fill='white',color='grey60')
> # the normal curve
> disp3= disp3 + stat_function(fun = NormalHist,
+                 color = "black", size = 1,linetype='dashed')
> # the vertical axis values
> disp3= disp3 + scale_y_continuous(breaks = vertiVals)
```

The result can be seen in Figure 4.12.
The **Python** version for Figure 4.12 is:

```
info11= ggplot(eduwa, aes(x = 'Reduced.Lunch')) + theme_classic()
disp3= info11 + geom_histogram(binwidth = width,
                               boundary=theStart,
                               fill='white',color='silver')
disp3= disp3 + stat_function(fun = NormalHist,
                color = "black", size = 1,linetype='dashed')

disp3= disp3 + scale_y_continuous(breaks = vertiVals)
```

4.8 Numerical III: Numerical Inequality

Some people would like to know how much a particular share of schools are receiving a particular share of benefits. In situations like this, some people want to see a **Lorenz Curve** (Lorenz, 1905). This curve is always compared to a diagonal: the closer to the diagonal, the more equal the distribution of the variable. Most of the time, the curve is accompanied by the **Gini Index** (Gini, 1912, 1921).

Plotting a Lorenz curve and computing the Gini index can be done by learning particular formulas. You can save some time when producing a Lorenz curve by using the library *gglorenz* (Chen, 2018) in R, which combines perfectly with *ggplot*; and you can also get the Gini Index using the library *DescTools* (Signorell et al., 2019), previously introduced, which has a function **Gini**.

```
> library(gglorenz)
> #for titles
```

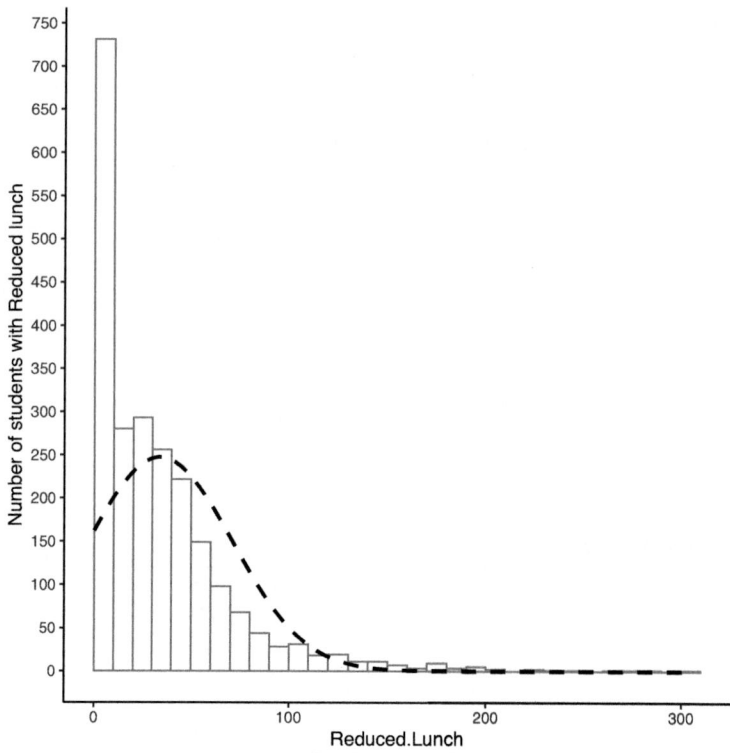

Figure 4.12 Shape using a histogram and normal curve

The normal curve has been created using the mean and standard deviation of the variable.

Data Source: The Common Core of Data from the US Department of Education, available at
https://nces.ed.gov/ccd/.

```
> HorizontalTitle="Percent of Schools by benefit received"
> VerticalTitle="Cummulative percent of benefit"
> plotTitle="How much receives\nthe 20% that receives most?"
> sourceText="Source: US Department of Education"
> # text for annotation
> ## computing
> gini=Gini(eduwa$Reduced.Lunch,na.rm = T)
> ## pasting message
> GINItext=paste("Gini:",round(gini,3))
> # plot Lorenz curve
> lorenz=info11 + stat_lorenz()
> #
> # diagonal
> lorenz= lorenz + geom_abline(linetype = "dashed")
> #
> # annotations
> ## vertical and horizontal lines
> lorenz= lorenz + geom_vline(xintercept = 0.8,
+                                     color='grey80',
```

```
+                          lty='dotted') +
+              geom_hline(yintercept = 0.5,
+                          color='grey80',
+                          lty='dotted')
> #
> # changing default axis tick values, positions and aspect
> lorenz= lorenz + scale_y_continuous(breaks = c(0,0.5,0.8),
+                                      position = 'right') + #position
+              scale_x_continuous(breaks = c(0,0.5,0.8)) +
+              coord_fixed() #aspect
> # annotating: adding Gini Index value
> lorenz= lorenz + annotate(geom="text",
+                          x=0.4, y=0.25,size=3,
+                          label=GINItext)
> # texts
> lorenz= lorenz +  labs(x = HorizontalTitle,
+                        y = VerticalTitle,
+                        title = plotTitle,
+                        caption = sourceText)
```

The object `lorenz` is represented in Figure 4.13.

You should have realized by now that for the categorical case I, represented inequality using *Pareto Charts* plus the Herfindahl-Hirschman Index, and for the numerical (or continuous case), I have used the Lorenz Curve and the Gini Index.

You can also prepare a **Python** version of Figure 4.13. However, this time I can not use *plotnine* (unless I want to implement it from scratch or adapt the code from `stat_lorenz()`). I recommend the use of the **ineqpy** library. Once you have installed it,[7] you need first to create a data frame where one column is the variable and another one is the counts of that variable (like a frequency table). However, our variable is not a frequency table, so I just create a column of *ones* instead:

```
import ineqpy as ineq

#new data frame (one column)
dfTest=pd.DataFrame(eduwa['Reduced.Lunch'].dropna())
## add a columns, where each value is number '1':
dfTest['count']=np.ones(dfTest.size)
```

The `dfTest` data frame will now be converted into a *survey* object:

```
# data frame to survey object
dfIneq = ineq.api.Survey(dfTest, weights='count')
```

The function from *ineqpy* can now be applied to the object **dfIneq** to create a **Python** version of Figure 4.13:

```
#for titles
txtLz={'HorizontalTitle':"Percent of Schools by benefit received",
       'VerticalTitle':"Cummulative percent of benefit",
```

---

[7] Use: pip install git+https://github.com/mmngreco/IneqPy.gittoinstallit.

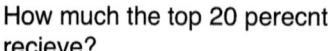

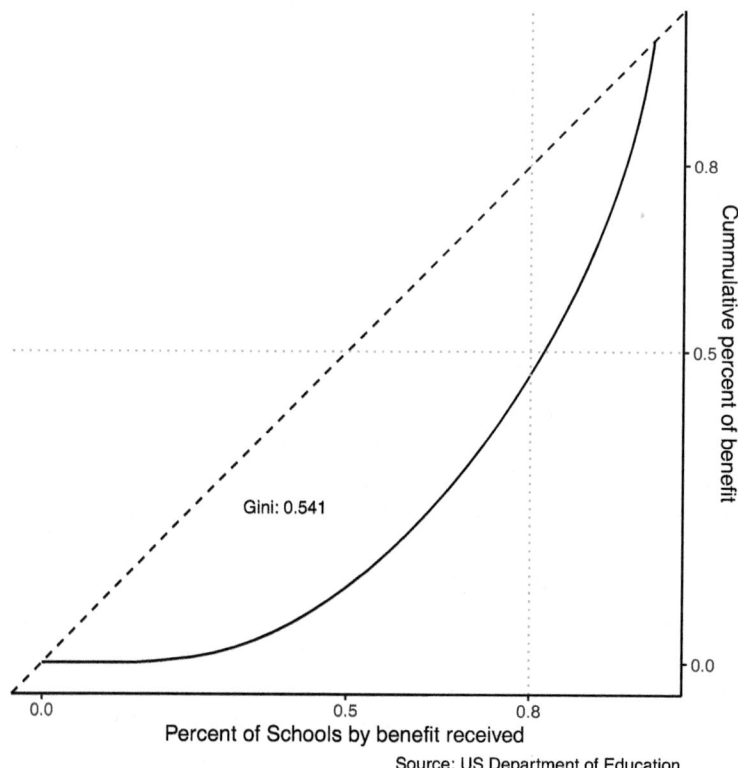

Source: US Department of Education

Figure 4.13 Lorenz curve for reduced lunch

You can see that the top 20% of schools that receive reduced lunches represent more then 50% of the whole system.

Data Source: The Common Core of Data from the US Department of Education, available at https://nces.ed.gov/ccd/.

```
        'plotTitle':"How much receives\nthe 20% that receives most?",
        'sourceText':"Source: US Department of Education"}

# text for annotation
## computing
gini=dfIneq.gini('Reduced.Lunch')
## pasting message (number to text before pasting)
GINItext='Gini:' + str(gini.round(3))

# plot diagonal (automatic) and Lorenz curve (in that order)
symbols=['k--',"k-"] # color (black) and line type (respect order).
ax1=dfIneq.lorenz('Reduced.Lunch').plot(legend=False,style=symbols)

# annotations
## vertical and horizontal lines (matplotlib)
```

```
plt.axvline(x=0.8,ls=':',c='silver',lw=1)
plt.axhline(y=0.5,ls=':',c='silver',lw=1)

# changing default axis tick values, positions and aspect
plt.yticks((0,0.5,0.8))
plt.xticks((0,0.5,0.8))
ax1.yaxis.set_label_position("right")
ax1.yaxis.set_ticks_position("right")
plt.axes().set_aspect('equal')

# annotating: adding Gini Index value
plt.text(0.4, 0.25,GINItext, fontsize=8)

# texts
plt.title(txtLz['plotTitle'])
plt.ylabel(txtLz['VerticalTitle'])
plt.xlabel(txtLz['HorizontalTitle'])
```

I hope these topics serve you well for plotting one variable. It is time now to pay attention to pairs of variables.

5

Insights from TWO Variables

We analyze two variables to find out if there might be some kind of relationship between them. This is a step needed in social and policy analysis to identify possible candidates of association or cause–effect relationships. As before, the nature of the data types allows for some particular analytical techniques; that is, the visual will depend on the data type of the two variables of under exploration.

I will continue to use the data on crime we saw in Chapter 4. Allow me to reload it again:

```
> # opening file
> linkRepo='https://github.com/resourcesbookvisual/data/'
> linkCRI='raw/master/crime.csv'
> fullLink=paste0(linkRepo,linkCRI)
> crime=read.csv(fullLink,stringsAsFactors = F)
```

Let me see what data types we have:

```
> str(crime,width = 60,strict.width='cut')
```

```
'data.frame':    499698 obs. of  17 variables:
 $ ReportNumber             : num  2.01e+13 2.01e+13 2.01..
 $ OccurredDate             : chr  "2013-07-09" "2013-07"..
 $ year                     : int  2013 2013 2013 2013 20..
 $ month                    : int  7 7 7 7 7 7 7 7 7 ...
 $ weekday                  : chr  "Tuesday" "Tuesday" ""..
 $ OccurredTime             : int  1930 1917 1900 1900 18..
 $ OccurredDayTime          : chr  "evening" "evening" ""..
 $ ReportedDate             : chr  "2013-07-10" "2013-07"..
 $ ReportedTime             : int  1722 2052 35 1258 1846..
 $ DaysToReport             : int  1 0 1 1 0 0 0 0 1 0 ...
 $ crimecat                 : chr  "NARCOTIC" "BURGLARY""..
 $ CrimeSubcategory         : chr  "NARCOTIC" "BURGLARY-"..
 $ PrimaryOffense.Description: chr  "NARC-FRAUD-PRESCRIPT"..
 $ Precinct                 : chr  "NORTH" "NORTH" "SOUT"..
 $ Sector                   : chr  "U" "L" "R" "U" ...
 $ Beat                     : chr  "U3" "L3" "R2" "U3" ...

 $ Neighborhood             : chr  "SANDPOINT" "LAKECITY"..
```

Based on what we have, let me present the type of plots you can use to reveal the possible relationships between two variables.

5.1 Cat–Cat Relationships

If you consider two categorical variables that are related, you need to first prepare a **contingency table** or **crosstab**.

```
> #contingency table of counts
> (PrecintDaytime=table(crime$Precinct,crime$OccurredDayTime))
```

```
           afternoon   day evening night
EAST           20774 15976   17380 19880
NORTH          48754 33744   39867 37942
SOUTH          22147 17322   16240 15497
SOUTHWEST      14221 10595   11169 11034

WEST           48931 30366   33766 30925
```

The contingency table shows the concurrent counts for every category. We can get the total and marginal counts using `addmargins`:

```
> #sum per rows and columns
> addmargins(PrecintDaytime)
```

```
           afternoon    day evening  night    Sum
EAST           20774  15976   17380  19880  74010
NORTH          48754  33744   39867  37942 160307
SOUTH          22147  17322   16240  15497  71206
SOUTHWEST      14221  10595   11169  11034  47019
WEST           48931  30366   33766  30925 143988
Sum           154827 108003  118422 115278 496530
```

Keep in mind that when a table tries to hypothesize a relationship, you should have the *independent* variable in the columns, and the *dependent* one in the rows; then, the percent should be calculated by column, to see how the levels of the dependent variable vary by each level of the independent one, and compare along rows:

```
> #marginal per column (column adds to 1)
> (PrecDayti_mgCol=prop.table(PrecintDaytime,
+                           margin = 2))
```

```
           afternoon        day    evening       night
EAST      0.13417556 0.14792182 0.14676327 0.17245268
NORTH     0.31489340 0.31243577 0.33665197 0.32913479
SOUTH     0.14304353 0.16038443 0.13713668 0.13443155
SOUTHWEST 0.09185090 0.09809913 0.09431525 0.09571644

WEST      0.31603661 0.28115886 0.28513283 0.26826454
```

Let me use the object `PrecDayti_mgCol` to prepare the input for *ggplot*:

```
> #making a data frame from contingency table
> PrecDaytiDF=as.data.frame(PrecintDaytime)
> names(PrecDaytiDF)=c("precinct","daytime","counts")
> #adding marginal columns percents:
> PrecDaytiDF$pctCol=as.data.frame(PrecDayti_mgCol)[,3]
> # we have:
> PrecDaytiDF # see result below
```

```
      precinct   daytime counts      pctCol
1         EAST afternoon  20774 0.13417556
2        NORTH afternoon  48754 0.31489340
3        SOUTH afternoon  22147 0.14304353
4    SOUTHWEST afternoon  14221 0.09185090
5         WEST afternoon  48931 0.31603661
6         EAST       day  15976 0.14792182
7        NORTH       day  33744 0.31243577
8        SOUTH       day  17322 0.16038443
9    SOUTHWEST       day  10595 0.09809913
10        WEST       day  30366 0.28115886
11        EAST   evening  17380 0.14676327
12       NORTH   evening  39867 0.33665197
13       SOUTH   evening  16240 0.13713668
14   SOUTHWEST   evening  11169 0.09431525
15        WEST   evening  33766 0.28513283
16        EAST     night  19880 0.17245268
17       NORTH     night  37942 0.32913479
18       SOUTH     night  15497 0.13443155
19   SOUTHWEST     night  11034 0.09571644
20        WEST     night  30925 0.26826454
```

Notice that the data types may need some formatting:

```
> summary(PrecDaytiDF)
```

```
     precinct        daytime       counts          pctCol
 EAST     :4   afternoon:5   Min.   :10595   Min.   :0.09185
 NORTH    :4   day      :5   1st Qu.:15856   1st Qu.:0.13437
 SOUTH    :4   evening  :5   Median :20327   Median :0.15415
 SOUTHWEST:4   night    :5   Mean   :24826   Mean   :0.20000
 WEST     :4                 3rd Qu.:33750   3rd Qu.:0.29196
                             Max.   :48931   Max.   :0.33665
```

The column `daytime` should be formatted as ordinal:

```
> # reformatting ordinal data
> RightOrder=c("day","afternoon","evening","night")
> PrecDaytiDF$daytime=ordered(PrecDaytiDF$daytime,
+                             levels=RightOrder)
```

5.1.1 Within-/Between-Group Differences

When we want to represent the counts we have in the contingency table, we can use the **grouped barplot** or **dodged barchart** :

```
> library(ggplot2)
> base1=ggplot(data=PrecDaytiDF,
+               aes(x=precinct,
+                  y=counts,
+                  fill=daytime)) + theme_classic()
> barDodge1= base1 +  scale_fill_brewer(palette = "Greys")
> barDodge1= barDodge1 + geom_bar(stat="identity",
+                          position="dodge", # DODGE
+                          color='grey') #border of bar
```

In this grouped barplot, the precinct serves as the grouping variable, so you can visualize the particular behavior of the daytime categories *within* each precinct. At the same time, you can analyze how a particular level of the daytime categories behaves *between* precincts. The default grouped bar chart is shown in Figure 5.1, using the *Greys* sequential color palette (Brewer, 2009).

If the default plot is not facilitating that within-/between-group exploration, you may need to make some changes. For instance, let me this time change the order of `precincts` in ascending order of the minimal count of `daytime`:

```
> minMargiPrecint=apply(PrecintDaytime,1,min)
> sortedMinPrecint=sort(minMargiPrecint)
> sortedMinPrecint
```

SOUTHWEST	SOUTH	EAST	WEST	NORTH
10595	15497	15976	30366	33744

I can use that precinct order to change the horizontal axis as we have done before:

```
> # improved values for horizontal axis
> newHorizontals=names(sortedMinPrecint)
> newHorizontals
```

```
[1] "SOUTHWEST" "SOUTH"    "EAST"     "WEST"     "NORTH"
```

However, this time, I will use the function `reorder`[1].

```
> base2=ggplot(data=PrecDaytiDF,
+               # using reorder
+               aes(x=reorder(precinct,counts,FUN = min),
+                  y=counts,
+                  fill=daytime)) + theme_classic()
> base2 = base2 + labs(x="precinct") # not needed in Python
> barDodge2= base2 +  scale_fill_brewer(palette = "Greys")
> barDodge2= barDodge2 + geom_bar(stat="identity",
+                          position="dodge", # DODGE
+                          color='grey')
```

---

[1] Notice that every time I use `reorder` in **R**, I need to change the axis title explicitly. I will not need to do that in **Python** as I will enter the order of the levels in the same way I did before (using the argument `limits` in the scale).

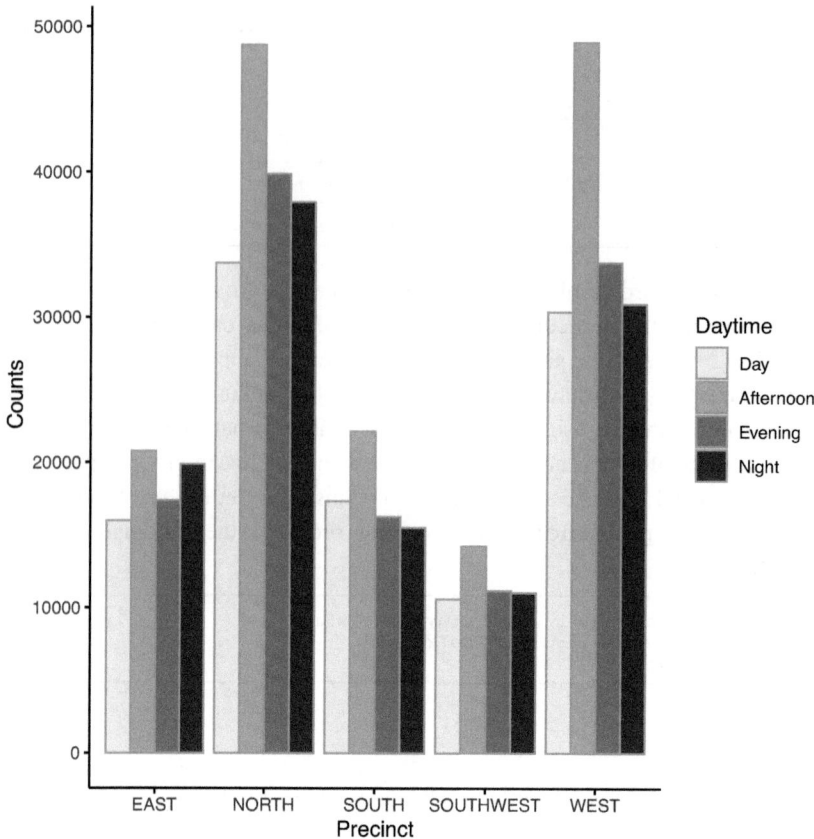

Figure 5.1 Grouped barplot (default)
Data from Seattle Open Data Portal (City of Seattle, 2019).

You can see the result in Figure 5.2.

If you wanted to add the counts on top of the bars, you could use this code:

```
> barDodge2= barDodge2 + geom_text(aes(label=counts),
+                              angle=0,
+                              vjust=0,
+                              hjust=0.5,
+                  position = position_dodge(width =0.9))
```

The code above used the command `position_dodge`. You need this command to distribute the labels along the bars. If you omit it, all the labels will appear one on over the other along in each group. You can alter the `width` parameter (currently 0.9) as needed.

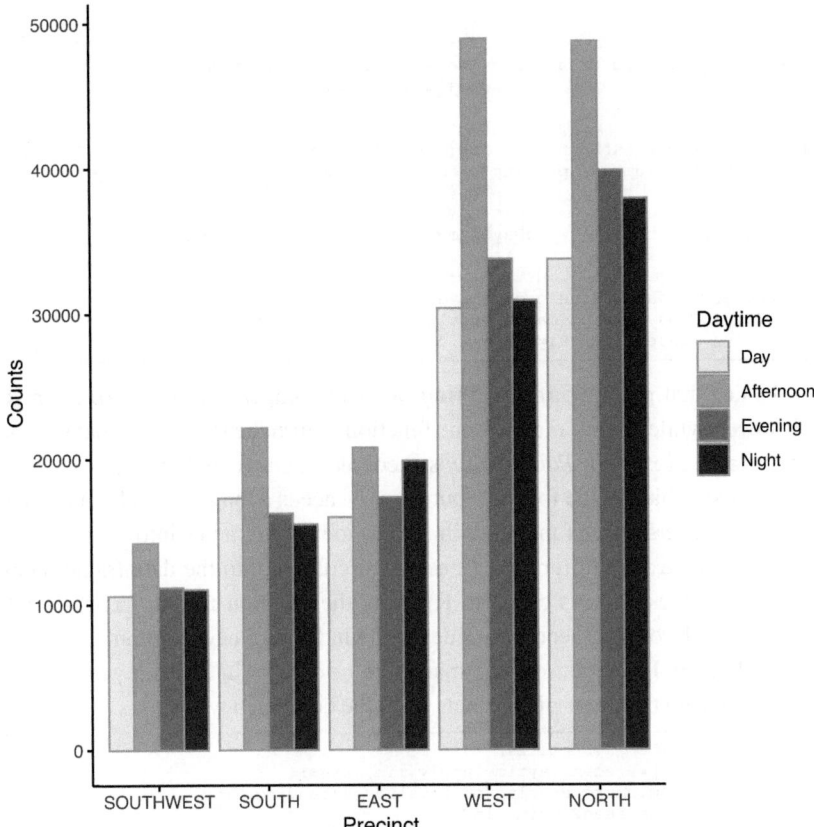

Figure 5.2 Grouped barplot (improved)
Groups have reorganized in an ascending fashion using command `reorder`. Data from Seattle Open Data Portal (City of Seattle, 2019).

Let me prepare my **Python** version. As always, I get the data:

```
import pandas as pd

#link to data
linkRepo='https://github.com/resourcesbookvisual/data/'
linkFile='raw/master/crime.csv'
fullLink=linkRepo+linkFile
crime=pd.read_csv(fullLink)
```

Once the data are available I can prepare the contingency table for *Pandas* and *plotnine*:

```
#contingency table of counts
PrecintDaytime=pd.crosstab(crime.Precinct,crime.OccurredDayTime)
```

```
#marginal per column (column adds to 1)
PrecDayti_mgCol=pd.crosstab(crime.Precinct,crime.OccurredDayTime,
                            normalize='columns')

#making a data frame from contingency table
PrecDaytiDF=PrecintDaytime.stack().reset_index()
PrecDaytiDF.columns=["precint","daytime","counts"]

#adding marginal columns percents:
PrecDaytiDF['pctCol']=PrecDayti_mgCol.stack().reset_index().iloc[:,2]

# reformatting ordinal data
RightOrder=["day","afternoon","evening","night"]
PrecDaytiDF.daytime=pd.Categorical(PrecDaytiDF.daytime,
          categories=RightOrder,ordered=True)
```

Notice that pd.crosstab brings a result comparable with table in **R**. However, while **R** only requires one function to turn the table into a data frame (as.data.frame), *Pandas* needs a couple: stack and reset_index. The crosstab has a wide format[2]; but *plotnine* needs a long (or stacked) format, see p. 19. The stack function will turn "wide" data frames into "long" ones. However, stack will turn the Precinct column into the data frame index (or "row names" as it is called in **R**); then, the function reset_index will number each row and send the values in the index as a new column.

In **Python**, I cannot use a command like reorder in **R** inside *plotnine*, so I need to keep the order of precincts from the contingency tab:

```
# improved values for horizontal axis
minMargiPrecint=PrecintDaytime.apply(min,axis=1)
sortedPrecint=minMargiPrecint.sort_values(ascending=True)
newPrecintAxis=sortedPrecint.index
```

Then, I can replicate Figure 5.2, including labels for each bar with this code:

```
from plotnine import *

base2= ggplot(PrecDaytiDF,
             aes(x='precint',y='counts',
                 fill='daytime')) + theme_classic()

barDodge2 = base2 +  geom_bar(stat="identity",
                              position="dodge",
                              color='grey')

barDodge2 += scale_fill_brewer(palette = "Greys")

barDodge2 += scale_x_discrete(limits=newPrecintAxis)

barDodge2 += geom_text(aes(label='counts'),angle=0,
                  va='bottom',ha='center',
                  position=position_dodge(width=0.9))
```

---

[2] see Section 2.3.1.

Notice that in the previous code, I started using the symbol **+=**, which simpifies the code a little. This cannot be used in **R**.

5.1.2 Whole-Part Differences

The **stacked barplot** is the most familiar option to highlight the difference that each category makes to another category. In this situation, we can use the same counts we had before. This time, let me draw the bars in a descending fashion.

```
> base3= ggplot(data=PrecDaytiDF,
+              aes(x=reorder(precinct,-counts,FUN=max), #- counts
+                  y=counts,
+                  fill=daytime)) + theme_classic()
> base3 = base3 + labs(x="precinct") # not needed in Python
> barStacked1 = base3 + scale_fill_brewer(palette = "Greys")
> barStacked1 = barStacked1 + geom_bar(stat = "identity",
+                               color='grey') # no position
>                                            # stack is default
```

Object *barStacked1* can be seen in Figure 5.3.

If you need to change the order of the colors in Figure 5.3, you need to do a couple of things:

- Create a copy of daytime, but with an inverse ordering

```
> # inversed copy
> PrecDaytiDF$daytime2 = factor(PrecDaytiDF$daytime,
+                        levels = rev(levels(PrecDaytiDF$daytime)))
```

- Use that new variable in the `fill` aesthetics:

```
> base3= ggplot(data=PrecDaytiDF,
+              aes(x=reorder(precinct,-counts,FUN=max),
+                  y=counts,
+                  fill=daytime2)) + theme_classic()
> base3 = base3 + labs(x="precinct") # not needed in Python
```

- Add `direction` in the color palette with the value **-1**. And no more changes.

```
> barStacked2 = base3 + scale_fill_brewer(palette = "Greys",
+                                  direction = -1)
> # no changes here:
> barStacked2 = barStacked2 + geom_bar(stat = "identity",
+                                color='grey')
```

The result can be seen in Figure 5.4.

If you want to annotate the bars, you have to do it within them. In that situation you need to use the `position_stack` parameter in the `geom_ text`:

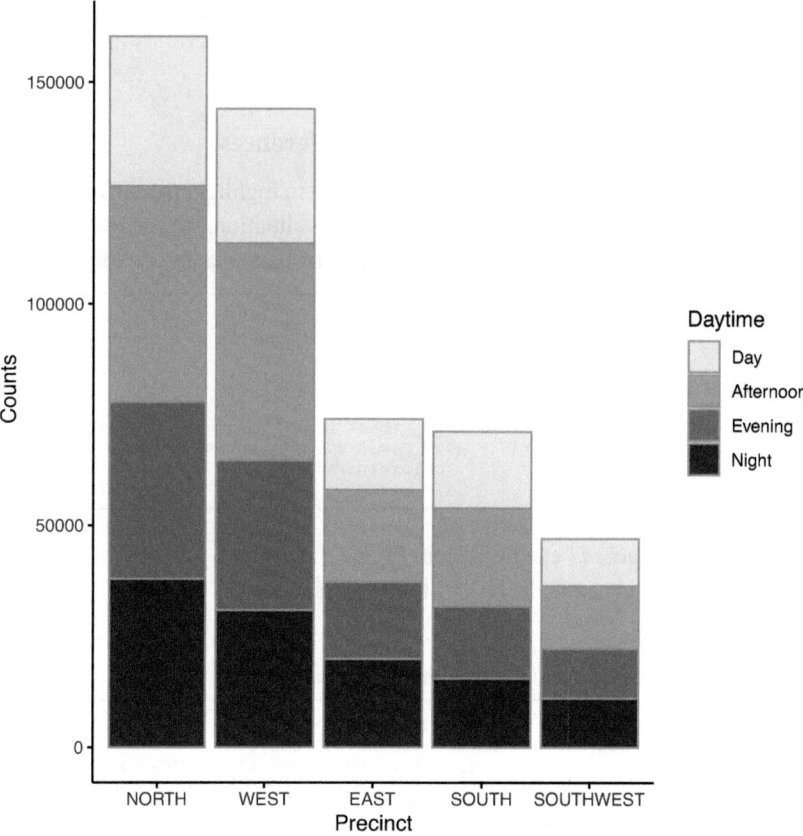

Figure 5.3 Stacked barplot
Groups have been reorganized in a descending fashion using command `reorder`. Data from
Seattle Open Data Portal (City of Seattle, 2019).

```
> barStacked2b= barStacked2 + geom_text(aes(label=counts),
+                                   size = 3,
+                                   color='black',
+                        position = position_stack(vjust = 0.5))
```

However, you might have a hard time reading some of the texts because of
the lack of contrast, as you can see in Figure 5.5.

A possible solution is to create a set of colors that deal with that:

```
> # ad-hoc set of colors
> adHoc=c('white','white','black','black')
```

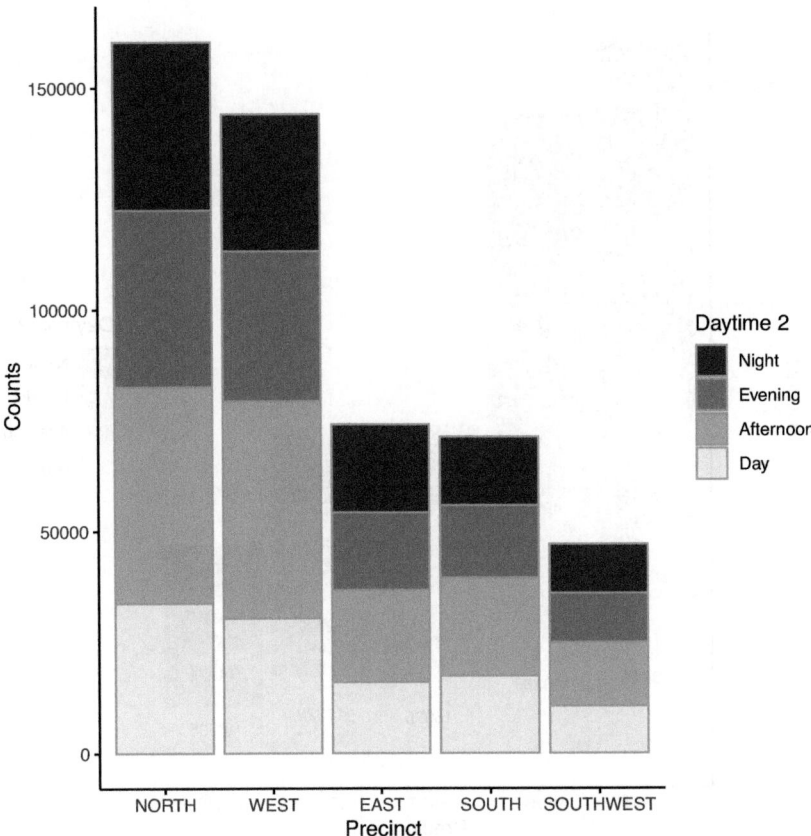

Figure 5.4 Stacked barplot recolored
Colors have been reorganized by changing the palette order and the order of the ordinal variable daytime. Data from Seattle Open Data Portal (City of Seattle, 2019).

Then, use those values for the label color:

```
> # annotating with color (default color will be assigned)
> barStacked2c= barStacked2 + geom_text(aes(label=counts,
+                                            color=daytime2),
+                                        size = 3,
+                                    position = position_stack(vjust = 0.5))
> # customized colors
> barStacked2c= barStacked2c + scale_colour_manual(values = adHoc)
> # use this to avoid text over legend symbols
> barStacked2c= barStacked2c + guides(color=FALSE)
```

Figure 5.6 shows you the result of the previous code.

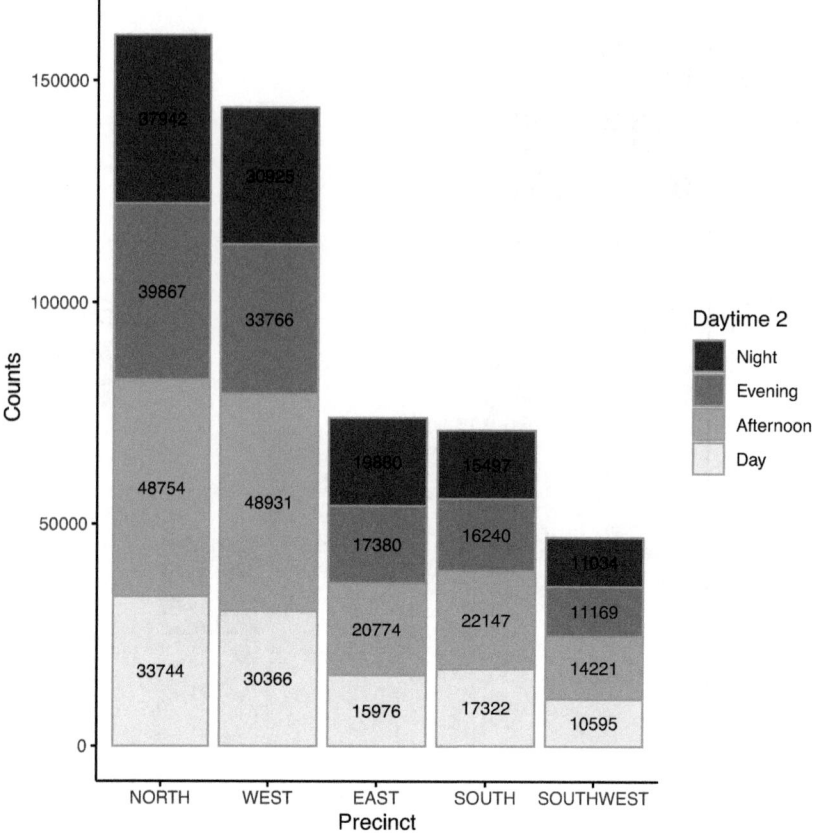

Figure 5.5 Stacked barplot annotated

Count annotations are difficult to see in some bars. Data from Seattle Open Data Portal (City of Seattle, 2019).

Notice the trick of coloring the text using aesthetics, to later assign color manually. This will have an annoying result: a letter a will appear over each legend symbol. I avoided that with the last line (color=FALSE).

You can follow similar steps to reproduce Figure 5.6 in Python:

- Change order of groups:

```
# improved values for horizontal axis
minMargiPrecint=PrecintDaytime.apply(min,axis=1)
sortedPrecint2=minMargiPrecint.sort_values(ascending=False)
newPrecintAxis2=sortedPrecint2.index
```

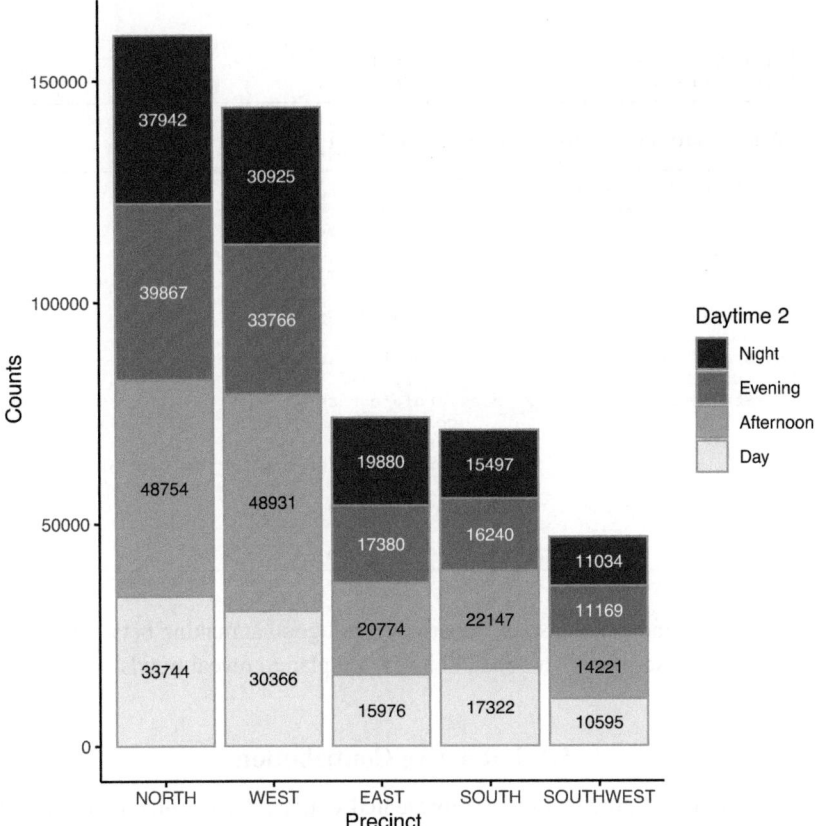

Figure 5.6 Stacked barplot with improved annotations

Count annotations are easier to see in comparison to Figure 5.5. Data from Seattle Open Data Portal (City of Seattle, 2019).

- Create copy of `daytime`:

```
# inversed copy
PrecDaytiDF['daytime2']=pd.Categorical(PrecDaytiDF.daytime,
                        categories=RightOrder[::-1],
                        ordered=True)
```

- Create a set of colors. Notice that I can not reverse the Brewer palette in *plotnine*, so I just call the amount of brewer colors I need from the *Greys* palette in `mizani`[3] (Kibirige, 2020a) to input them manually.

```
# ad-hoc set of colors
adHoc=['white','white','black','black']
```

---

[3] This library should be already among your libraries, as *plotnine* requires it.

```
# manual colors according to Brewer.
from mizani.palettes import brewer_pal
Greys4=brewer_pal(palette='Greys')(4)[::-1]
```

- Add this to the previous code to reproduce Figure 5.6:

```
base3= ggplot(PrecDaytiDF,
              aes(x='precint', y='counts',
                  fill='daytime2')) + theme_classic()
# order of horizontal
barStacked2c = base3 +scale_x_discrete(limits=newPrecintAxis2)
# manual Brewer palette
barStacked2c += scale_fill_manual(values=Greys4)
# usual
barStacked2c += geom_bar(stat="identity", color='grey')
# annotating with color (default color will be assigned)
barStacked2c += geom_text(aes(label='counts',
                              color='daytime2'),
                          size = 8,
                          position = position_stack(vjust = 0.5))
# customized colors
barStacked2c += scale_colour_manual(values = adHoc)
# use this to avoid text on top of legend symbols
barStacked2c += guides(color=False) # want to omit?
```

Keep in mind that the stacked barplot is not good at making between-group comparisons; so it is not a good choice if you plan to reveal trends.

5.1.3 Relative Contribution

The bars in the previous cases represented counts. As we mentioned at the begining of Section 5.1 we first prepared a contingency table and took it from there, so any of the previous plots could have changed what goes into a row or a column. In this subsection, however, we should have decided clearly what will be the row and the column variable, as we will use *marginal* shares. Take a look again at the marginals I am computing with totals per row and column:

```
> addmargins(PrecDayti_mgCol)
```

	afternoon	day	evening	night	Sum
EAST	0.13417556	0.14792182	0.14676327	0.17245268	0.60131333
NORTH	0.31489340	0.31243577	0.33665197	0.32913479	1.29311592
SOUTH	0.14304353	0.16038443	0.13713668	0.13443155	0.57499619
SOUTHWEST	0.09185090	0.09809913	0.09431525	0.09571644	0.37998172
WEST	0.31603661	0.28115886	0.28513283	0.26826454	1.15059284
Sum	1.00000000	1.00000000	1.00000000	1.00000000	4.00000000

That information is already in the `PrecDaytiDF` data frame which we have been using for the previous plots, and since the percentage stacked bar represents the relative contribution of a category to a level of the other, each of our bars must represent 100 percent. There will be several instructions that have changed, so let me guide you:

- The new base information will need different variables in the aesthetics:

```
> base4=ggplot(data=PrecDaytiDF,
+               aes(x=daytime, # changes in aes!
+                   y=pctCol,
+                   fill=precinct)) + theme_classic()
```

- Since the horizontal is daytime, the precinct bars will represent the contribution. Notice that precinct is a nominal variable, then we should look for a qualitative palette. I will choose Paired as my palette. This palette is the only safe palette for color-blindness (Brewer, 2009), and it is also safe for printing (not for photocopying) if you have four levels; so it is safe for our case.[4]

```
> barStPct1= base4 + scale_fill_brewer(type='qual', #not needed
+                                       palette = 'Paired')
```

Notice that if I write the palette name, I do not need to specify the type.

- By now, you should have realized that the vertical axis is not needed (it was not needed in other previous plots). Let me remind you how to get rid of it:

```
> barStPct1= barStPct1 + theme(axis.title.y = element_blank(),
+                              axis.text.y  = element_blank(),
+                              axis.line.y  = element_blank(),
+                              axis.ticks.y = element_blank())
```

- Finally, just set the position to fill in the geom_bar:

```
> barStPct1= barStPct1 + geom_bar(stat = "identity",
+                                 position="fill") # you need this
```

Figure 5.7 shows you the result of plotting the barStPct1 object.

Annotating the bars requires transforming the values, currently from 0 to 1, into percentages, and also adding the percent symbol. In this situation, *ggplot* needs the help of the library *scales* (Wickham et al., 2019b).

```
> library(scales) # for labelling
>                  #label in % with ONE decimal position
> barStPct2= barStPct1 + geom_text(aes(label=percent(pctCol,
+                                                     accuracy=0.1)),
+                 size = 4, fontface='bold',
+                 position = position_fill(vjust = 0.5))
```

---

[4] No qualitative Brewer palette is safe for colorblindness, neither photocopying nor printing if you have more than four levels.

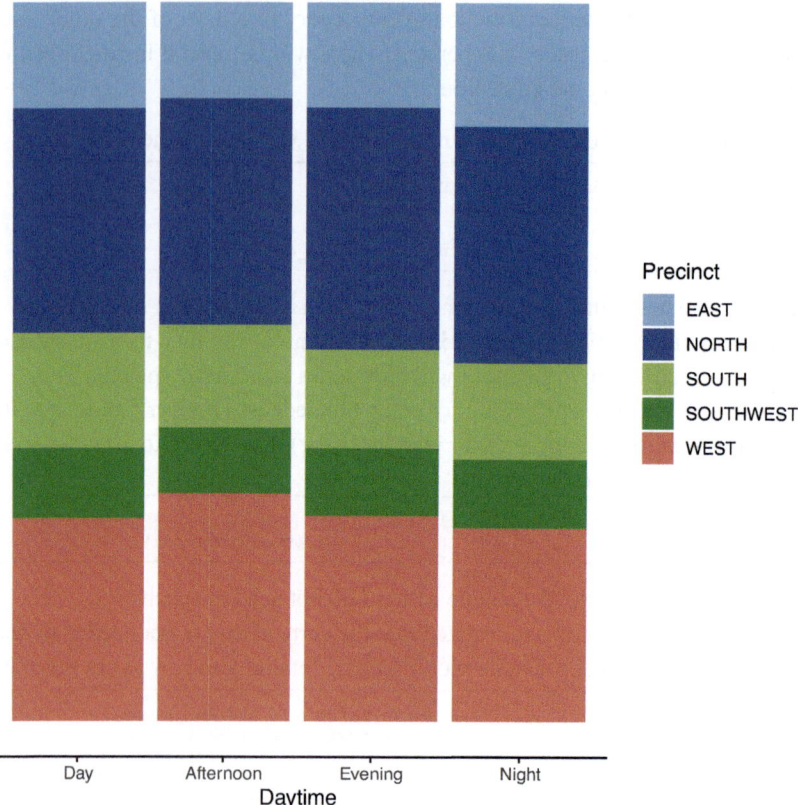

Figure 5.7 Percentage stacked bar chart
Data from Seattle Open Data Portal (City of Seattle, 2019).

Remember that you may clutter your plot with these annotations, so if you just need the audience to realize the qualitative contribution of each row level, it is better to omit them.

Let me plot object `barStPct2` in **Python**, which will include the elements from object `barStPct1`:

```
base4= ggplot(PrecDaytiDF,
              aes(x='daytime',y='pctCol',
                  fill='precint')) + theme_classic()

barStPct2 = base4 + scale_fill_brewer(type='Qualitative',
                                      palette = "Paired")

barStPct2 += theme(axis_title_y = element_blank(),
                   axis_text_y  = element_blank(),
                   axis_line_y  = element_blank(),
```

```
                 axis_ticks_major_y=element_blank())

barStPct2 += geom_bar(stat="identity",
                      position='fill')

barStPct2 += geom_text(aes(label='pctCol*100'),
                       format_string='{:.1f}%',
                       size = 8, fontweight='bold',
                       position = position_fill(vjust = 0.5))
```

5.1.4 Bigger Tables: Focusing on Highs/Lows

Categorical data do not usually have several levels, but there are circumstances when they do. The plots we have just seen may not suit more complex situations. Take a look at this contingency table:

```
> #contingency table of counts
> (CrimeDay=table(crime$crimecat,crime$OccurredDayTime))
```

	afternoon	day	evening	night
AGGRAVATED ASSAULT	5366	3564	4884	7501
ARSON	167	196	191	486
BURGLARY	22288	24139	14121	16082
CAR PROWL	38273	26740	42595	34839
DISORDERLY CONDUCT	81	41	67	79
DUI	939	706	2038	8522
FAMILY OFFENSE-NONVIOLENT	2516	1748	1217	1120
GAMBLE	4	4	7	2
HOMICIDE	46	41	49	131
LIQUOR LAW VIOLATION	491	112	410	606
LOITERING	31	20	25	9
NARCOTIC	6416	2415	3924	4109
PORNOGRAPHY	53	65	17	31
PROSTITUTION	675	115	1425	1340
RAPE	318	332	354	854
ROBBERY	4737	2584	4139	5372
SEX OFFENSE-OTHER	1759	1501	1014	1776
THEFT	64868	38687	38980	28410
TRESPASS	5184	4848	2598	3289
WEAPON	1445	735	947	1624

In situations like this, you can represent the contingency table with other elements but the possibility of finding a clear relationship gets more troublesome, so the next plots will mainly allow you to identify worst or best situations, or patterns.

Let me turn the table into a data frame before plotting:

```
> #marginal per column (column adds to 1)
> CrimeDay_mgCol=prop.table(CrimeDay,margin = 2)
> #making a data frame from contingency table
> CrimeDayDF=as.data.frame(CrimeDay)
> names(CrimeDayDF)=c("crime","daytime","counts")
> #adding marginal columns percents:
> CrimeDayDF$pctCol=as.data.frame(CrimeDay_mgCol)[,3]
```

```
> # reformatting ordinal data
> CrimeDayDF$daytime=factor(CrimeDayDF$daytime,
+                           levels = RightOrder,
+                           ordered=TRUE)
```

You need to do the same thing in **Python**:

```python
#contingency table of counts
CrimeDay=pd.crosstab(crime.crimecat,crime.OccurredDayTime)

#marginal per column (column adds to 1)
CrimeDay_mgCol=pd.crosstab(crime.crimecat,crime.OccurredDayTime,
                           normalize='columns')

#making a data frame from contingency table
CrimeDayDF=CrimeDay.stack().reset_index()
CrimeDayDF.columns=["crime","daytime","counts"]

#adding marginal columns percents:
CrimeDayDF['pctCol']=CrimeDay_mgCol.stack().reset_index().iloc[:,2]

# reformatting ordinal data
RightOrder=["day","afternoon","evening","night"]
CrimeDayDF.daytime=pd.Categorical(CrimeDayDF.daytime,
                                  categories=RightOrder,
                                  ordered=True)

# reformatting ordinal data
maxMargiCrime=CrimeDay.apply(max,axis=1)
sortedCrime=maxMargiCrime.sort_values(ascending=True)
newCrimeAxis=sortedCrime.index
```

Once I have the data frame, I can reproduce the percentages for this crosstab with a **dot plot** with a **theme_minimal**:

```
> # reorder table vertically by max count per daytime
> base5 = ggplot(CrimeDayDF,aes(x=daytime,
+                 y=reorder(crime, pctCol,FUN=max))) + theme_minimal()
> base5 = base5 + labs(y="crime") # not needed in Python
> # plot value as point, size by value of percent
> BTableDot = base5 + geom_point(aes(size = pctCol))
> # label points, label with 2 decimal positions (accuracy)
> # percent() need library "scale"
> BTableDot = BTableDot + geom_text(aes(label = percent(pctCol,
+                                        accuracy = 0.01)),
+                                    # push text to the right
+                                    nudge_x = 0.4,
+                                    size=3)
> # no need for legend
> BTableDot = BTableDot + theme(legend.position="none")
```

The object `BTableDot` is shown in Figure 5.8.

The **Python** code to get Figure 5.8 is:

```python
# reorder table vertically by max count per daytime
base5 = ggplot(CrimeDayDF,
               aes(x='daytime',
                   y='crime')) + theme_minimal()
```

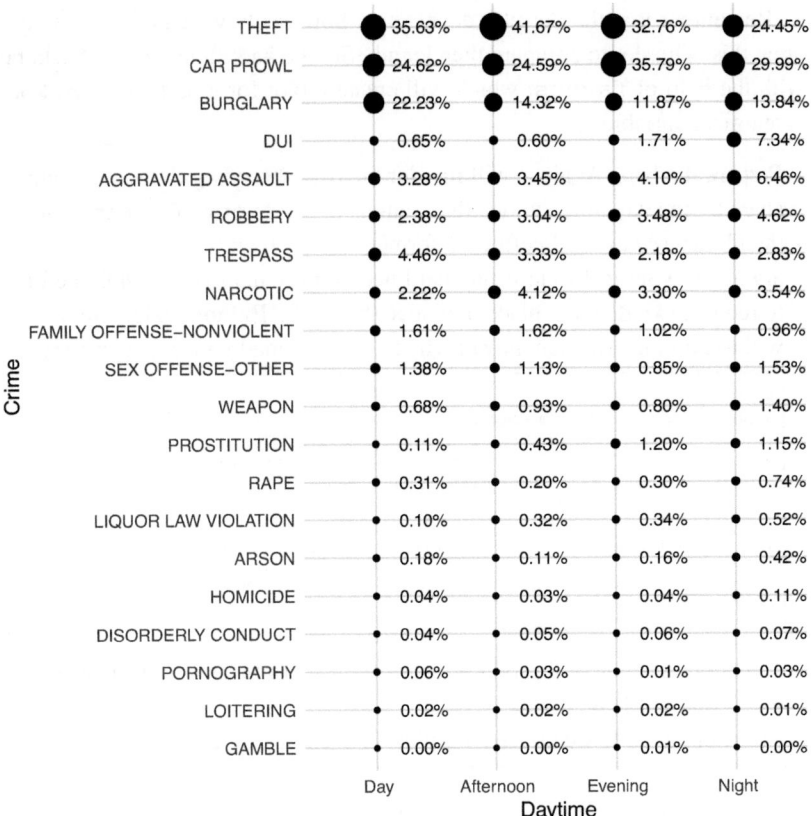

Figure 5.8 Dot plot for big crosstab
Data from Seattle Open Data Portal (City of Seattle, 2019).

```
base5 += scale_y_discrete(limits=newCrimeAxis)

# plot value as point, size by value of percent
BTableDot = base5 + geom_point(aes(size = 'counts'))

# label points, label with 2 decimal positions:
BTableDot += geom_text(aes(label = 'pctCol*100'),
                           format_string='{:.2f}%',
                           # push text to the right
                           nudge_x = 0.3,
                           size=8)
# no need for legend
BTableDot += theme(legend_position="none")
```

The plot looks nice, but unless the differences are notorious, you may see more noise than information, which distracts and delays decision-making.

Remember that the dot plot depends on how easily we can decode size or area; this is harder to compare than length. So, the bars should come back, but with the help of `facets`, which will create a plot for a particular level of a categorical variable:

- Prepare the bars. Again, I will reorder the bars according to the maximum share by the day time. Notice that I am using `percent_format`, from the library *scales* used before, to format the axis text; the `accuracy` argument is set to **1** to indicate that I need no decimals (I used **0.01** before to request two decimal places). Notice that in the **Python** code, *plotnine* will use a function from *mizani* which is also named `percent_format`.

```
> #crime ordered
> base6   = ggplot(CrimeDayDF,
+                        aes(x = reorder(crime,pctCol,FUN=max),
+                            y = pctCol) ) + theme_minimal()
> base6 = base6 + labs(x="crime") # not needed in Python
> #formatting text axis
> base6 = base6 +
+          scale_y_continuous(labels = percent_format(accuracy = 1))
> #basic bar
> BTableBar = base6 + geom_bar( stat = "identity" )
>
```

The previous code will produce a bar for each crime, as no information on `daytime` has been input.

- Partitioning. Now we create a barplot for each day time:

```
> #Facetting: one plot per 'daytime'
> BTableBar = BTableBar + facet_grid(.~daytime)
```

- Flipping. Now I flip the plot so that it resembles the original crosstab:

```
> #Flipping
> BTableBar= BTableBar + coord_flip()
```

You could make some changes to the text of the crimes:

```
> # altering axis text for crime
> BTableBar= BTableBar + theme(axis.text.y = element_text(size=8,
+                                                  angle = 45))
> # altering axis text for percent
> BTableBar= BTableBar + theme(axis.text.x = element_text(size=6,
+                                                  angle = 45))
>
```

Figure 5.9 shows how the `BTableBar` object is drawn.

Figure 5.9 allows you to clearly identify the worst crimes in the region, even if there is not a clear relationship at the variable level.

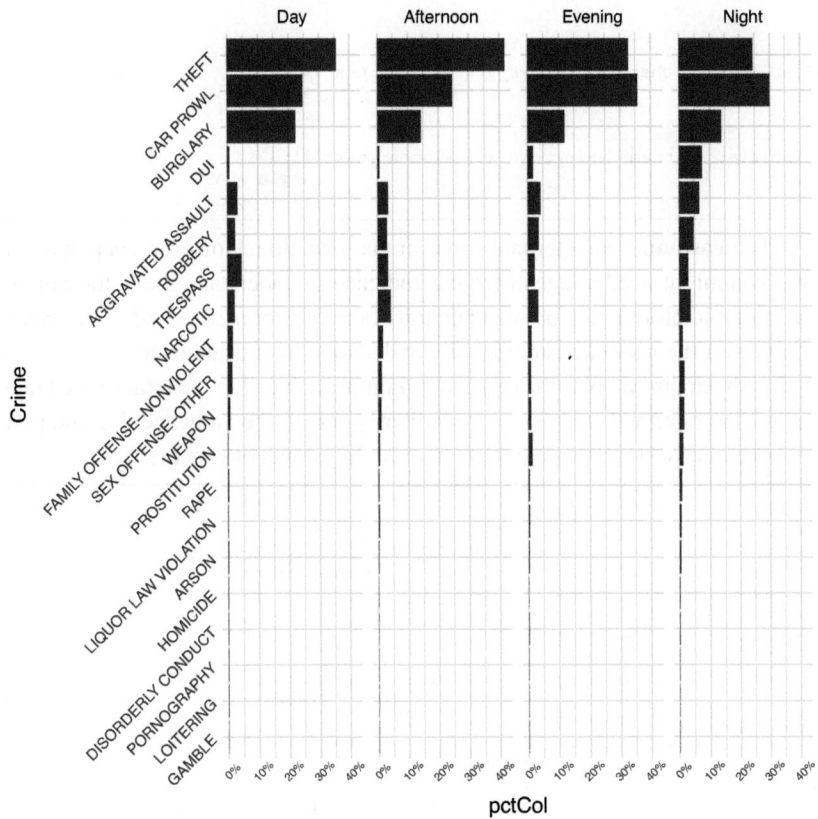

Figure 5.9 Barplot facetted and flipped
Data from Seattle Open Data Portal (City of Seattle, 2019).

The **Python** code to get Figure 5.9 is:

```python
from mizani.formatters import import percent_format

#crime ordered
base6   = ggplot(CrimeDayDF,
                   aes(x = 'crime',
                       y = 'pctCol') ) + theme_minimal()
#formatting text axis
base6 += scale_x_discrete(limits=newCrimeAxis)
base6 += scale_y_continuous(labels = percent_format())

#basic bar
BTableBar = base6 + geom_bar( stat = "identity" )

#Facetting
BTableBar += facet_grid('~ daytime')

#Flipping
BTableBar += coord_flip()
```

```
# altering axis text for crime
BTableBar += theme(axis_text_y = element_text(size=8,
                                              angle = 45,
                                              va='top'))
# altering axis text for percent
BTableBar += theme(axis_text_x = element_text(size=6,
                                              angle = 45,
                                              va='bottom'))
```

The **heatmap** is an alternative in a similar situation. However, keep in mind that you might need a legend for the audience to understand the color weight and to avoid plotting the numbers on top of the cells or *tiles*. Besides, you need to assess if the heatmap can be easily understood by the audience.

The heatmap can plot the relative weight of each cell to the total of the table or just the marginal, so make sure to clarify this to the audience. Let me plot this one relative to the whole table (reorder by counts of crimes):

```
> base7  = ggplot(CrimeDayDF,
+                 aes(x = daytime,
+                     y = reorder(crime, counts,FUN=max),
+                     fill = counts)) + theme_minimal()
> base7 = base7 + labs(y="crime") # not needed in Python
> # default heatmap
> heat1 = base7 +  geom_tile()
> # customizing color
> heat1 = heat1 +scale_fill_gradient(low = "gainsboro",
+                                    high = "black")
> # moving legend to the top
> heat1 = heat1 + theme(legend.title = element_blank(),
+                       legend.position="top")
> # making legend colorbar wider
> heat1 = heat1 + guides(fill=guide_colorbar(barwidth=10))
```

Figure 5.10 shows how `heat1` object is drawn.

This is the first time that I am representing a color weight relative to the whole table, in all the previous cases the weight for areas or length was computed per column. Our data frame `CrimeDayDF` does not have the relative share to the whole table, only per column,[5] so I just used the counts.

The **Python** code to get Figure 6.2 is given next:

```
base7 = ggplot(CrimeDayDF,
               aes(x = 'daytime',y = 'crime',
                   fill = 'counts')) + theme_minimal()
base7 += scale_y_discrete(limits=newCrimeAxis)

# default heatplot
heat1 = base7 + geom_tile()
# customizing color
heat1 += scale_fill_gradient(low = "gainsboro",
                             high = "black")
# moving legend to the top
```

---

[5] You can easily add that column to `CrimeDayDF`; you just need to request `prop.table` without using the `margin` argument.

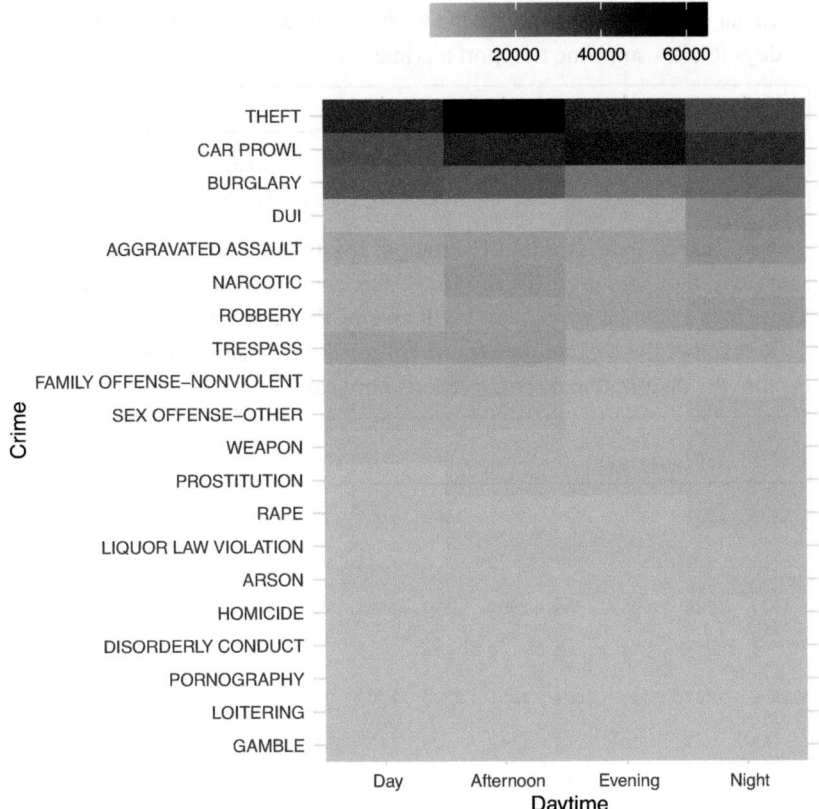

Figure 5.10 Heatmap – tiles weighted relative to total

The darker the greater the count of crimes for the whole table. Data from Seattle Open Data Portal (City of Seattle, 2019).

```
heat1 += theme(legend_title = element_blank(),
               legend_position="top")
# making legend colorbar wider
heat1 += guides(fill=guide_colorbar(barheight=200))
```

5.2 Cat–Num Relationship

In this section, I am interested in how a categorical variable can help us better understand the behavior of a numeric variable. Given the data we will be using, the curiosity and experience of the analyst is critical in mining the data to reveal some insight, as numerical data have longer value ranges than categorical data.

In our current `crime` data frame we had a variable that informs the amount of days it takes someone to report a crime:

```
> summary(crime$DaysToReport)
```

Min.	1st Qu.	Median	Mean	3rd Qu.	Max.	NA's
0.00	0.00	0.00	7.65	1.00	36525.00	2

You can see there is a lot of variation: from crimes that were reported the same day they occurred (**0**) to crimes that took around 100 years (**36525**). These data might be wrong, but I will assume they are not.

Remember the `crime` data frame collected information per year, so let me explore the distribution of crime reports per year:

```
> # counting crimes per year
> table(crime$year)
```

```
 1908  1964  1973  1974  1975  1976  1977  1978  1979  1980  1981  1985
 1986
    1     1     1     1     2     2     1     1     2     2     2
 2     1
 1987  1988  1989  1990  1991  1993  1994  1995  1996  1997  1998  1999
 2000
    1     1     1     2     2     5     2     6     4     5    20
 8    40
 2001  2002  2003  2004  2005  2006  2007  2008  2009  2010  2011  2012
 2013
   53    17    28    41    49    99   627 42792 45055 43350 41296 41005
 45548
 2014  2015  2016  2017  2018
49315 47687 49202 50302 43114
```

Let me keep the crimes since 2008, as the counts in that year are of the same magnitude as the remaining years. I am not saying you should do this in other cases, but the other years may be still in the process of being digitalized.[6]

```
> # keeping years since 2008
> crime2=crime[crime$year≥2008,]
```

Let me get rid of missing rows in the numeric variable, and rename the missing crime categories this way:

```
> # making data without missing values
> crime2=crime2[complete.cases(crime2$DaysToReport),]
> crime2$crimecat[is.na(crime2$crimecat)]='UNcategorized'
```

[6] The portal does state that the data are available from 2008 https://data.seattle.gov/Public-Safety/SPD-Crime-Data-2008-Present/tazs-3rd5.

The **Python** code for this pre-processing stage is shown next:

```python
# counting crimes per year
crime.year.value_counts()

# keeping years since 2008
crime2=crime[crime.year>=2008].copy()

# making data without missing values
crime2.dropna(subset=['DaysToReport'],inplace=True)
crime2.fillna(value={'crimecat': 'UNcategorized'},inplace=True)

# sorting crimes for plotting
maxD=crime2.groupby('crimecat').describe()['DaysToReport'][['max']]
maxDSort=maxD.sort_values(by=['max'],ascending=True).index
```

Now, let me show you how to explore the time it takes to report a crime by crime category:

```
> base8 = ggplot(data=crime2,
+               aes(x=reorder(crimecat,DaysToReport,FUN=max),
+                   y=DaysToReport))  + theme_minimal()
> base8= base8 + labs(x="crime")
> boxCrime=base8 + geom_boxplot() + coord_flip()
```

Figure 5.11 presents `boxCrime` object using boxplots. As you can see, I have used a boxplot to display the distribution of `DaysToReport` for every category:

As shown in Figure 5.11, most crimes take a few days to report, but the presence of outliers makes it difficult to find some other pattern. The code to reproduce Figure 5.11 in **Python** is the following:

```python
base8=ggplot(crime2,
             aes(x='crimecat',
                 y='DaysToReport')) + theme_minimal()
base8 += labs(x="crime")
base8 += scale_x_discrete(limits=maxDSort)
boxCrime=base8 + geom_boxplot() + coord_flip()
```

Discovering some pattern in the variability requires that we focus on a subset of the data. In situations like this, I recommend you compute the second and third quartile to decide what to keep:

```
> # computing quartiles 2 and 3
> q23=function(x){quantile(x,probs = c(0.5,0.75))}
> aggregate(data=crime2,DaysToReport~crimecat,q23)
```

	crimecat	DaysToReport.50%	DaysToReport.75%
1	AGGRAVATED ASSAULT	0	0
2	ARSON	0	0
3	BURGLARY	0	1
4	CAR PROWL	1	1
5	DISORDERLY CONDUCT	0	0
6	DUI	0	0
7	FAMILY OFFENSE-NONVIOLENT	0	0

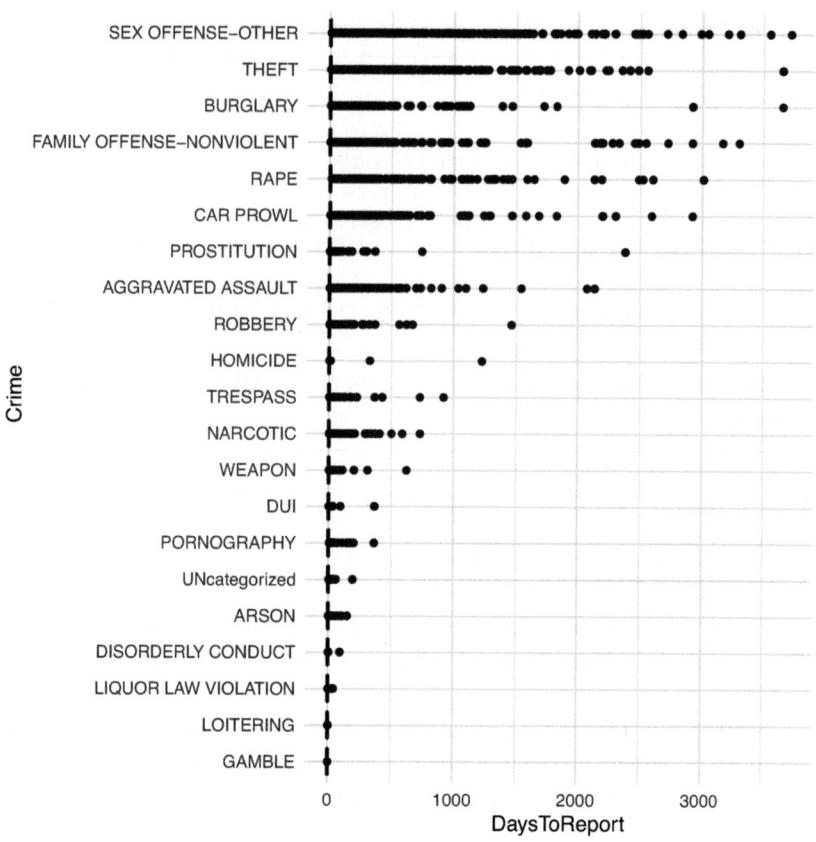

Figure 5.11 Boxplots per category

Categories have been reordered. Data from Seattle Open Data Portal (City of Seattle, 2019).

8	GAMBLE	0	0
9	HOMICIDE	0	0
10	LIQUOR LAW VIOLATION	0	0
11	LOITERING	0	0
12	NARCOTIC	0	0
13	PORNOGRAPHY	0	2
14	PROSTITUTION	0	0
15	RAPE	1	5
16	ROBBERY	0	0
17	SEX OFFENSE-OTHER	0	2
18	THEFT	0	1
19	TRESPASS	0	0
20	UNcategorized	0	1
21	WEAPON	0	0

The code in **Python** for this operation is:

```
q23=['50%','75%'] # list of quartiles
crime2.groupby('crimecat').describe()['DaysToReport'][q23]
```

These confirms that 75 percent of the crimes took less than a week (five days in worst case) to be reported. Let me keep the cases that took a year or longer to report for my next plot:

```
> #subsetting
> crimeYear=crime2[crime2$DaysToReport≥365,]
> #creating new variable
> crimeYear$YearsToReport=crimeYear$DaysToReport/365
```

Now, let's try a similar plot, this time ordering the crimes by the third quartile of `YearsToReport` (notice I am using the extra argument `probs` in `FUN` for the function `quantile`):

```
> base9=ggplot(data=crimeYear,
+             aes(x=reorder(crimecat,YearsToReport,
+                           FUN=quantile,probs=0.75),
+                 y=YearsToReport)) + theme_minimal()
> base9= base9 + labs(x="crime")
> boxCrimeY=base9 + geom_boxplot() + coord_flip()
```

Object `boxCrimeY` can be seen in Figure 5.12.

Remember that *plotnine* does not have the exact functionality of `reorder` from **R**'s *ggplot*; so, you need to get the crime names ordered by the third quartile or Q75 (75th quantile) first:

```
#subsetting
crimeYear=crime2[crime2.DaysToReport>365].copy()

#creating new variable
crimeYear['YearsToReport']=crimeYear.DaysToReport/365

# ordering the crimes by the q75 of YearsToReport
## subset with variables needed
subCrimeYear=crimeYear[['crimecat','YearsToReport']]
## grouping the subset by Q75
Q75=subCrimeYear.groupby('crimecat').quantile(q=0.75)
## sorting the grouping by Q75 of 'YearsToReport'
Q75Sort=Q75.sort_values(by=['YearsToReport'],ascending=True)
## just getting the names in order
sortedCrimesbyQ75=Q75Sort.index
```

The object `sortedCrimesbyQ75` in **Python** is just the names of the crimes, not a data frame. I can use those names to reproduce Figure 5.12:

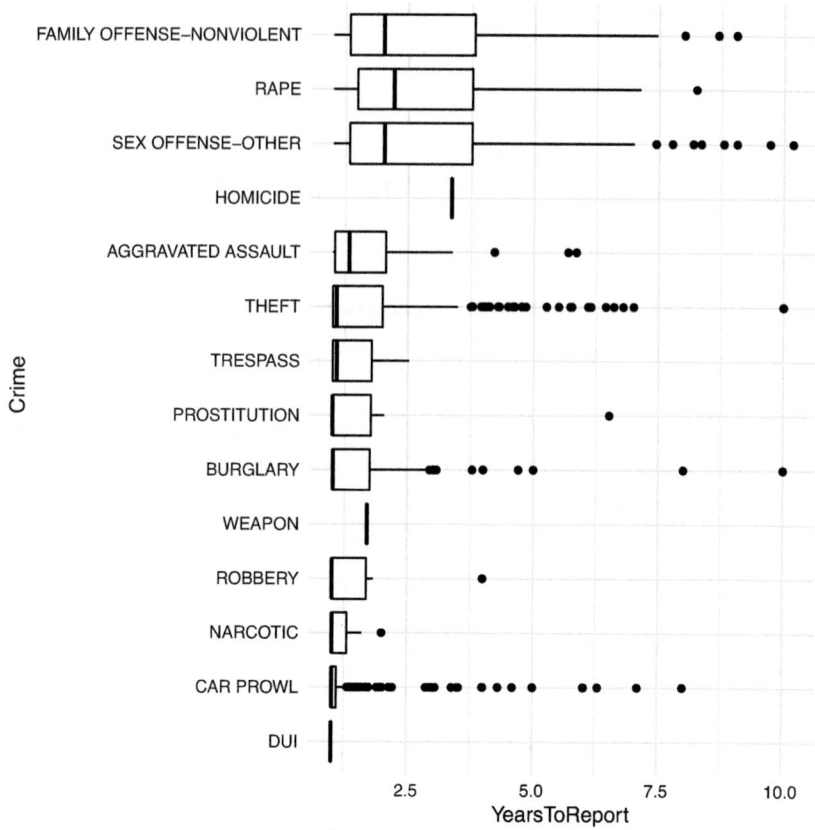

Figure 5.12 Boxplots per category (II) for crimes that took a year or longer to report

Categories have been reordered. Data from Seattle Open Data Portal (City of Seattle, 2019).

```
base9=ggplot(crimeYear,
             aes(x='crimecat',
                 y='YearsToReport')) + theme_minimal()
base9 += labs(x="crime")
#manually sorting
base9 += scale_x_discrete(limits=sortedCrimesbyQ75)
boxCrimeY = base9 + geom_boxplot() + coord_flip()
```

Figure 5.12 still has several crimes with outliers but you can see a better ordering of crimes and prepare an explanation for the crimes that take longer to report. Pay attention to the top three types of crime whose third quartiles are the highest: the crimes that take longer to report since 2008 are related to family and sex offenses (notice the horizontal dimension is showing counts in years).

The problem with Figure 5.12 is that boxplots are not a very common visual for non-academic audiences. Let me plot the third quartiles only, following the next steps:

- Prepare a function. Functions that require *one* argument to compute an statistic can be used immediately with *ggplot*, but in this case the quantile function requires two. I did not need it above, because the reorder function allows adding another argument. So, let me create my **q3** function:

```
> # ad-hoc q3
> q3=function(x){quantile(x,probs = 0.75)}
> theQ3='75%'## Labels for 'color'
```

- **Group** all the third quantiles and draw a line connecting them. Notice the color in aes is a label – it is a constant value, as the color will not change for every crime:

```
> # line of q3 grouped using last base9
> q3Y = base9 + stat_summary(aes(group=T, color=theQ3),
+                            fun=q3,
+                            geom="line",
+                            size=4)
```

- Flip the coordinates (optional):

```
> #flipping
> q3Y = q3Y + coord_flip()
```

The object q3Y is drawn in Figure 5.13. Notice this plot gives you a default color, as the color in aes was just a label.

The code in **Python** to reproduce Figure 5.13:

```
# ad-hoc q3
import numpy as np

q3=lambda x:np.quantile(x,0.75)
theQ3='75%'## Labels for 'color'

# line of q3 grouped using last base9
q3Y = base9 + stat_summary(aes(group=True,color='theQ3'),
                           fun_y=q3,
                           geom='line',
                           size=5)
# flipping
q3Y = q3Y + coord_flip()
```

Let me show you how to add the minima and maxima values to the plot, by following the same strategy:

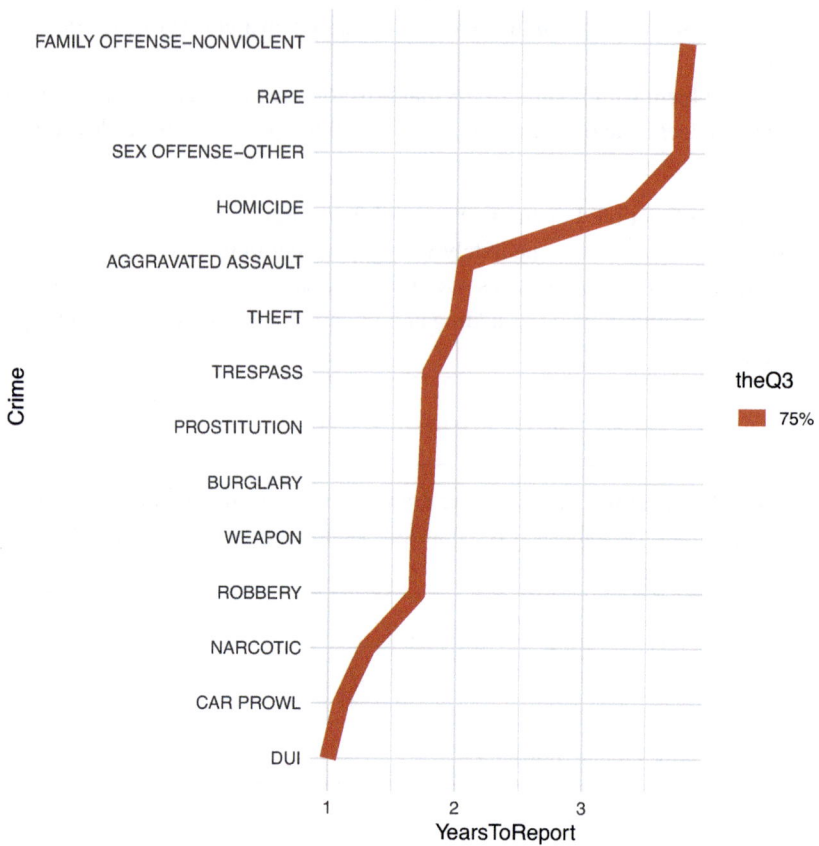

Figure 5.13 Line plot for grouped values

The line shows the third quartile of the time it takes to report a crime, separated by crime.
Data from Seattle Open Data Portal (City of Seattle, 2019).

```
> # More labels for 'color'
> theMin='Minima'
> theMax='Maxima'
> #adding minima (group of minima):
> mq3Y =q3Y + stat_summary(aes(group=T, color=theMin),
+                          fun=min,
+                          geom="point",
+                          size=3)
> #
> #adding maxima (group of maxima):
> Mmq3Y=mq3Y + stat_summary(aes(group=T, color=theMax),
+                           fun=max,
+                           geom="point",
+                           size=1)
```

If I plot the Mmq3Y object, I will get default colors. If I want my own colors, I should do this:

```
> #customizing legend and colors
> orderStats=c("Minima","75%","Maxima")
> cols_orderStats=c("grey80","grey50","black")
> Mmq3Yfin= Mmq3Y + scale_colour_manual(name='Stats',
+                                         limits = orderStats,
+                                         values = cols_orderStats)
```

The object Mmq3Yfin is shown in Figure 5.14. Notice that combining the grey scale I made every *geom* visible.

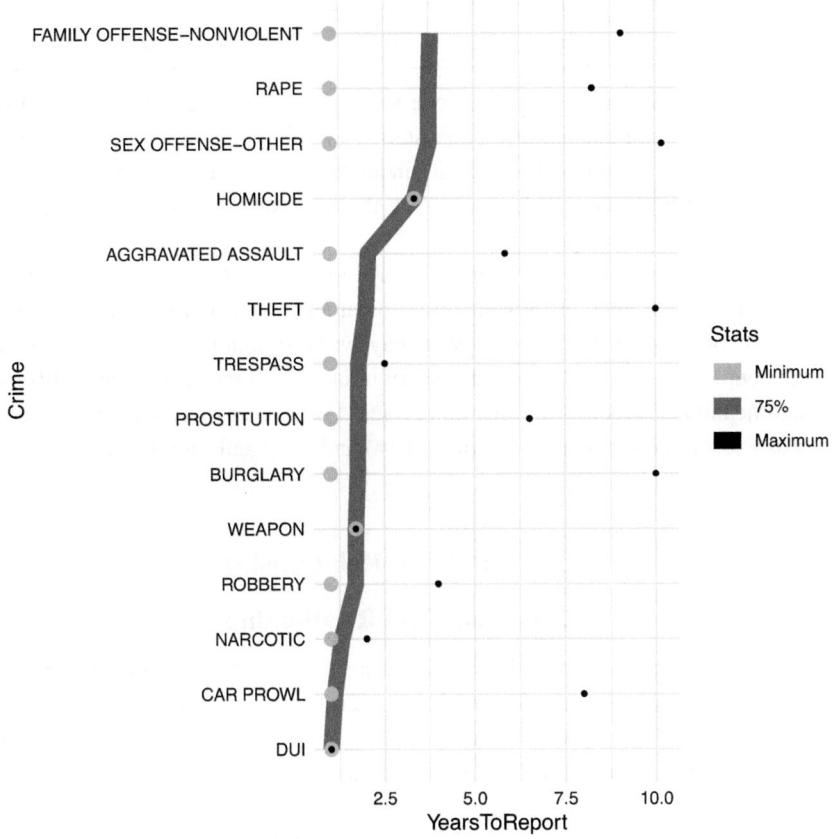

Figure 5.14 Line plot for grouped values
The line shows the third quartile of the time it takes to report a crime, separated by crime.
Data from Seattle Open Data Portal (City of Seattle, 2019).

The **Python** version for the object `Mmq3Yfin`:

```
#Labels for colors
theMin='Minima'
theMax='Maxima'

mq3Y = q3Y  + stat_summary(aes(group=True,color='theMin'),
                           fun_y=np.min,
                           geom='point',
                           size=4)
Mmq3Y = mq3Y + stat_summary(aes(group=True,color='theMax'),
                            fun_y=np.max,
                            geom='point',
                            size=1)

#customizing legend and colors
orderStats=["Minima","75%","Maxima"]
cols_orderStats=['silver','grey','black']
Mmq3Yfin= Mmq3Y + scale_color_manual(name='Stats',
                                     limits = orderStats,
                                     values = cols_orderStats)
```

You are welcome to alter the code to produce the object `Mmq3Yfin`, for instance, you can change any other statistical value you believe summarizes the numerical variable. Most people understand the `mean`, but in a situation where there is too much skewness, like the ones shown in Figures 5.12 and 5.14, you may prefer quartiles.

Also, the cat–num relationships are used to reveal if the summary statistics differ from one another. Several tests, parametric and non-parametric, exist to test for those differences, so you may want to annotate those plots with the coefficient that confirms if the distribution of a numerical variable differs significantly between or among categories. For further information on these tests I recommend you review Pons (2014) and Alvo and Yu (2018).

5.3 Num–Num Relationship

5.3.1 Num–Date Relationship

Time belongs to the interval scale (Stevens, 1946). The *zero* does not mean absence of time, the multiplicative interpretations do not make sense (16:00 is not twice 08:00), and the difference between two pairs of values is comparable (the time differences between 18:00 and 15:00, and 11:00 and 8:00, are the same).

I have a column with dates in the *crime2* data frame:

```
> str(crime2$OccurredDate)
```

```
 chr [1:498666] "2013-07-09" "2013-07-09" "2013-07-09" "2013-07-09" ...
```

Let me create a frequency table with that column, so I can see how many crime events have happened per day:

```
> # frequency of events
> allCrimes=as.data.frame(table(crime2$OccurredDate))
> names(allCrimes)=c('dates','count')
> head(allCrimes)
```

```
      dates count
1 2008-01-01   178
2 2008-01-02   103
3 2008-01-03   116
4 2008-01-04   114
5 2008-01-05   104
6 2008-01-06    95
```

The next code **should not be run**.

```
> baset=ggplot(allCrimes, aes(x=dates, y=count)) + theme_classic()
> # line of time by count:
> tsl=baset + geom_line(alpha=0.25)
> # result:
> tsl
```

There is nothing wrong with the code itself, the problem is the data frame format:

```
> str(allCrimes,width = 65,strict.width='cut')
```

```
'data.frame':   3963 obs. of  2 variables:
 $ dates: Factor w/ 3963 levels "2008-01-01","2008-01-02",..: 1..
 $ count: int  178 103 116 114 104 95 105 114 131 100 ...
```

The column date is currently in text format, so we need to convert it into **Date** format. For that, you first need to know the symbols used for formatting dates:

- For a date number (0–31): **%d**.
- For weekday:

  – For abbreviated weekday (Mon, Tue, etc): **%a**.
  – For non-abbreviated weekday (Monday, Tuesday, etc): **%A**.

- For month:

  – For month number (00–12): **%m**.
  – For abbreviated month (Jan., Feb., etc): **%b**.
  – For non-abbreviated month: **%B**.

- For year:

  - For a 2-digit year: **%y**.
  - For a 4-digit year: **%Y**.

Also, you may need to use some symbol, like *dash* or *slash*, to concatenate date elements.

Then, you can convert the column **allCrimes$date** into a date format like this:

```
> #formatting date (respect the format found in text):
> allCrimes$dates=as.Date(allCrimes$dates,format="%Y-%m-%d")
```

Once it is in the right format, you can request a statistic:

```
> median(allCrimes$dates)
```

```
[1] "2013-06-04"
```

The code in **Python** to accomplish the same follows:

```
allCrimes = pd.value_counts(crime2.OccurredDate).reset_index()
allCrimes.columns=['dates','counts']
allCrimes['dates']=pd.to_datetime(allCrimes.dates,
                                  format="%Y-%m-%d")
```

Now, this code will work:

```
> baset = ggplot(allCrimes,
+                aes(x=dates, # already a DATE
+                    y=count)) + theme_classic()
> # lines highly transparent:
> tsl=baset + geom_line(alpha=0.2)
```

The object `tsl` is plotted in Figure 5.15.

The **Python** code is almost the same (with the variable names in quotations):

```
baset= ggplot(allCrimes,
              aes(x='dates', # already a DATE
                  y='counts')) + theme_classic()
tsl = baset + geom_line(alpha=0.2)
```

Time data are generally plotted with lines to show continuity, but the use of dots can be a good alternative to show the date-to-date behavior:[7]

```
> # Using previous dots with some transparency (same 'baset')
> tsp=baset + geom_point(alpha=0.2, #transparency
+                        shape=4)
```

---

[7] Remember that I presented the **R** symbols for dots in Figure 3.8 (For **Python** you should visit `https://matplotlib.org/3.1.1/api/markers_api.html`).

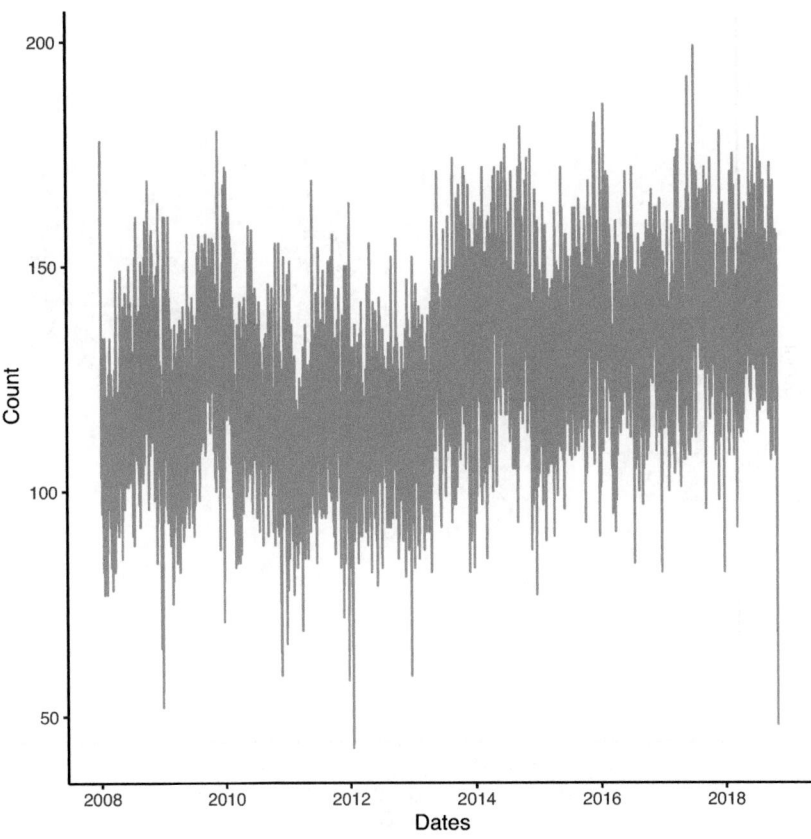

Figure 5.15 Basic time series
The horizontal dimension should be of *date* data type for *ggplot* to understand this is a time series. The frequency is the count of crime events on a particular day since 2008. Data from Seattle Open Data Portal (City of Seattle, 2019).

Now, I can use a line to show some pattern in time. Let me use a local regression line, also known as **loess** (Fox and Weisberg, 2019), for that purpose:

```
> tsp=tsp +geom_smooth(fill='grey70', #color around line
+                      method = 'loess', # to compute line
+                      color='black') #color of line
```

The date format on the horizontal axis can be customized in two ways. First, you can customize the text of the date shown (date_labels) and where you need the ticks (date_breaks). So, you may need to add some elements to the object tsp:

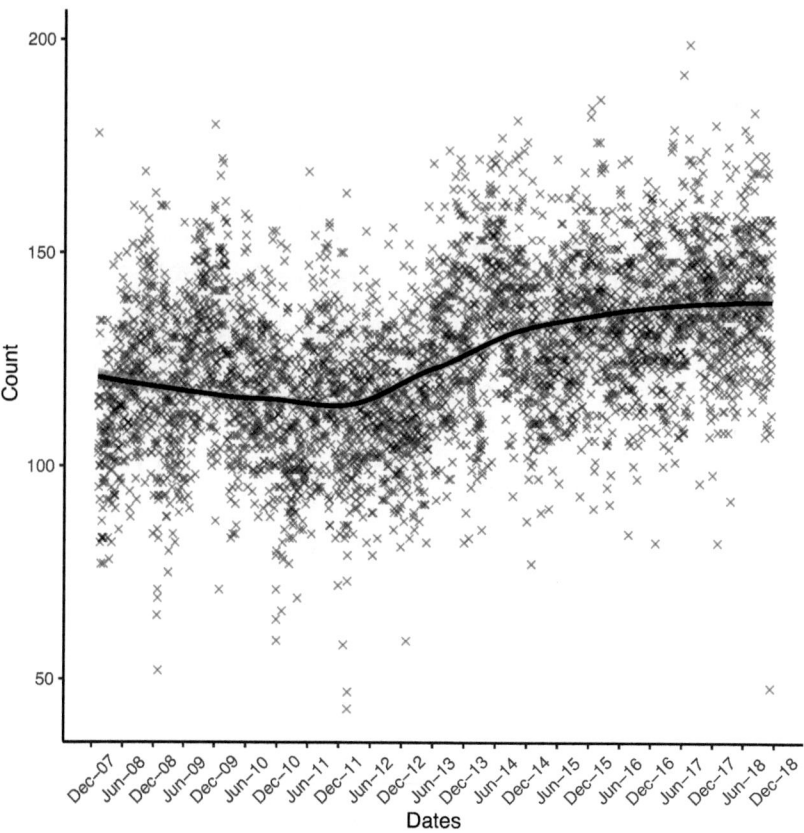

Figure 5.16 Time series using dots and lines

The dots represent the count of crime events per day since 2008; the line summarizes the long run pattern using a local regression approach. Data from Seattle Open Data Portal (City of Seattle, 2019).

```
> #add format to axis:
> tsp= tsp+scale_x_date(date_labels = "%b-%y", #how
+                       date_breaks = "6 months") #where
> #set up text values on each tick:
> tsp= tsp + theme(axis.text.x = element_text(angle=45,
+                                             vjust=0.5))
```

The object `tsp` is plotted in Figure 5.16.

Let me share the **Python** code to produce a result similar to Figure 5.16.[8] Notice that the text alignment using `vjust` in `element_text`, was not needed in **Python**.

---

[8] You may need to install *scikit-misc* (Kibirige, 2020b) for **loess** to work. Please follow instructions from `https://github.com/has2k1/scikit-misc`.

```
# dots with some transparency (same 'baset')
tsp= baset + geom_point(alpha=0.2,
                             shape='+')
#line for pattern
tsp += geom_smooth(fill='silver',
                     method='loess',
                     color='black')
#add format to axis:
tsp += scale_x_datetime(date_labels='%b-%Y',
                         date_breaks='6 months')
#set up text values on each tick:
tsp += theme(axis_text_x = element_text(angle=45))
```

We have used the dates as we found them. However, aggregating data may prove a useful option you can explore. Let me aggregate my daily data into week averages:

```
> library(lubridate)
> library(magrittr)
> library(dplyr)
> weekCrimes=allCrimes %>%
+           group_by(weekly=ceiling_date(dates, "week")) %>%
+             summarize(averages=mean(count)) %>% #create variable
+               as.data.frame()
```

The previous code produced an aggregated data frame where you have the last day of the week as the label for the average of that week using the `ceiling_date` function from the *lubridate* package (Grolemund and Wickham, 2011). This is the first time I have used the *pipe* operator (%>%); which requires the package *magrittr* (Bach and Wickham, 2014b). I used the pipes to concatenate a series of actions; in this case, `group_by`, and `summarize` (which creates a variable named `averages`), both functions from the package *dplyr*(Wickham et al., 2020a). Each operation concatenated with a pipe receives the output of the previous action.

Notice that the product of this aggregation kept the date format:

```
> str(weekCrimes)
```

```
'data.frame':    567 obs. of  2 variables:
 $ weekly  : Date, format: "2008-01-06" "2008-01-13" ...
 $ averages: num  123 113.6 104 106.9 92.1 ...
```

Notice that using the function `ceiling_date` you kept the date format.[9] This function will take the first day available in the data for the first week; so, in this case, the mean could be computed for less than 7 days.

Let me produce the same aggregation using **Python**. *Pandas* has the function `resample`, which simplifies the previous **R** code. The function `mean` was then applied.

---

[9] You can get the week average per year with other classic functions, like *tapply*, but you will need to reformat the date column

```
myArguments={'rule':'W', 'on':'dates', 'closed':'left'}
#using myArguments in resample with **
weekCrimes=allCrimes.resample(**myArguments).mean()
```

Notice that I have used a nice **Python** feature to input the arguments using a dictionary. You simply prepare the arguments using the names (keys) and values the function requires; notice that the keys have to be written as text (inside quotations). The function `resample`, or any other function, simply uses the dict by prefixing `**`.

Then, let me prepare a code similar to the one that produced Figure 5.16 with the `weekCrimes` data frame:

```
> basetW = ggplot(weekCrimes,
+                     aes(x=weekly, # formatted as DATE
+                         y=averages)) + theme_classic()
> tspW=basetW + geom_point(alpha=0.2, #transparency
+                         shape=4)
> tspW=tspW +geom_smooth(fill='grey70', #color around line
+                         method = 'loess', # to compute line
+                         color='black') #color of line
> #add format to axis:
> tspW=tspW+scale_x_date(date_labels = "%b-%y", #how
+                         date_breaks = "6 months") #where
> #set up text values on each tick:
> tspW=tspW + theme(axis.text.x = element_text(angle=45,
+                                               vjust=0.5))
>
```

The object `tspW` is represented in Figure 5.17. Notice that I needed to adjust the vertical alignment of the tick labels (not needed in Python).

Let me show you the code in **Python**. Notice that the previous use of `resample` sent the dates column as the *index* of the *Pandas* data frame (the row names in **R**); so I have to specify that in the aesthetics.

```
basetW = ggplot(weekCrimes,
                aes(x='weekCrimes.index', #for index
                    y='counts')) + theme_classic()

tspW= basetW + geom_point(alpha=0.2,
                        shape='+')

tspW += geom_smooth(fill='silver',
                    method='loess',
                    color='black')

tspW += scale_x_datetime(date_labels='%b-%Y',
                        date_breaks='6 months')

tspW += theme(axis_text_x = element_text(angle=45))
```

The previous plots have allowed you to become familiar with basic time series plotting; however, we have counted all the crime types in the previous plots. Remember that there are several crimes in the `crime2` data frame.

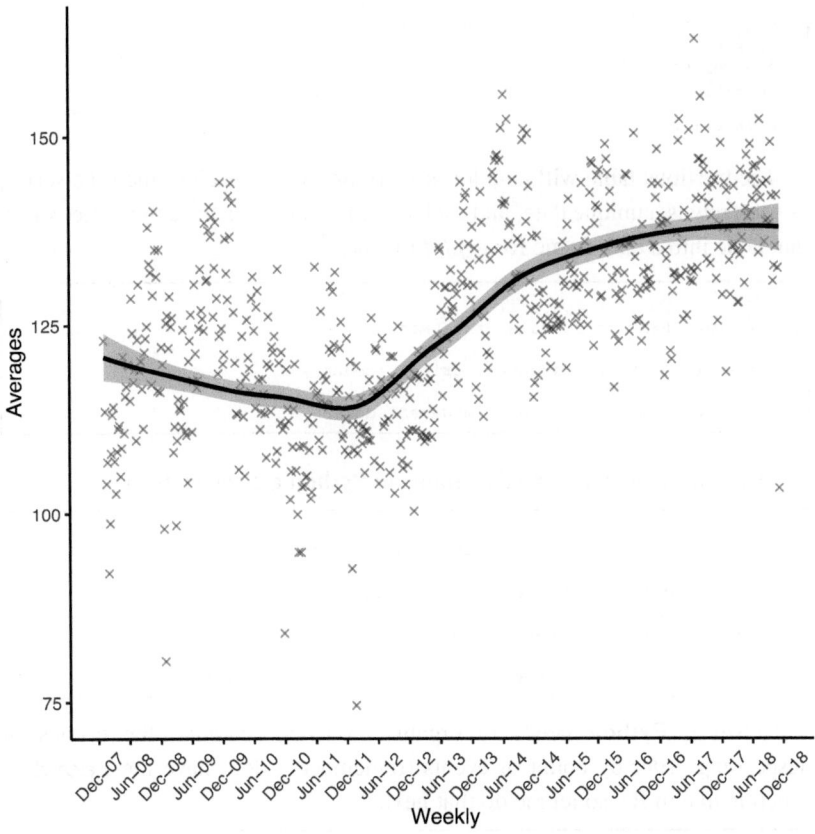

Figure 5.17 Aggregated time series using dots and lines

The dots represent the average of crime events per week since 2008; the line summarizes the long-run pattern using a local regression approach. Data from Seattle Open Data Portal (City of Seattle, 2019).

Let me make a contingency table between `OccurredDate` and `crimecat` to see time series of counts per crime:

```
> # making table
> crimeDate=table(crime2$OccurredDate,crime2$crimecat)
> # seeing first ten counts of four crimes:
> crimeDate[1:10,1:4]
```

```
           AGGRAVATED ASSAULT ARSON BURGLARY CAR PROWL
2008-01-01                 13     0       18        25
2008-01-02                  1     0       15        32
2008-01-03                  2     0       27        33
2008-01-04                  2     1       27        33
2008-01-05                  5     0       17        22
```

2008-01-06	6	0	12	25
2008-01-07	3	0	17	26
2008-01-08	4	0	24	28
2008-01-09	3	0	24	40
2008-01-10	3	0	6	25

The previous table will be a lot of help for plotting each crime time series, as each row is a unique date, and each column represents the counts. Let's turn that table into a data frame for *ggplot* to work:

```
> #table of dates to data frame
> crimeDateDF=as.data.frame(crimeDate)
> #renaming columns
> names(crimeDateDF)=c("date",'crime','count')
> # formatting date column as Date type
> crimeDateDF$date=as.Date(crimeDateDF$date)
```

The steps to get the same data frame in **Python** are shown below:

```
# making table
crimeDate=pd.crosstab(crime2.OccurredDate,crime2.crimecat)
#table of dates to data frame
crimeDateDF=crimeDate.stack().reset_index()
#renaming columns
crimeDateDF.columns=['date','crime','count']
# formatting date column as Date type
crimeDateDF['date']=crimeDateDF['date'].astype('datetime64')
```

However, **Python** needs to organize, outside *plotnine*, the crimes in descending order by count of events (remember it does have the `reorder` function like in **R**), so let me do that next:

```
# sum by crimes, resulting in data frame:
ordCrime=crimeDateDF.groupby('crime').sum().reset_index()
# sum by crimes, resulting in data frame:
ordCrimeSort=ordCrime.sort_values(by=['count'],
                                  ascending=False)
#saving only names of crimes
descendCrimes=ordCrimeSort.crime.values
#setting the variable as an ordinal
crimeDateDF['crime']=pd.Categorical(crimeDateDF.crime,
                                    ordered=True,
                                    categories=descendCrimes)
```

Let's pay attention to these two crimes and make a subset:

```
> selection=c("AGGRAVATED ASSAULT", 'WEAPON')
> crimeDateDF_sub=crimeDateDF[crimeDateDF$crime %in% selection,]
```

Let me do the subsetting in **Python**, but we will need some extra steps. Since we reformatted the *crime* variable as an ordinal category in the `crimeDateDF` *Pandas* data frame, we need to get rid of the **unused** categories:

```
selection=["AGGRAVATED ASSAULT", 'WEAPON']
crimeDateDF_sub=crimeDateDF[crimeDateDF.crime.isin(selection)]

#extra step, get rid of values NOT used
crimeDateDF_sub.crime.cat.remove_unused_categories(inplace=True)
```

You may have needed to do that in **R** if *ggplot* could not use the `reorder` function. The **R** data frame has crimes as *text* or character type, so you do not need to do anything to make the unused categories disappear (see also Figure 6.1). However, **R** has its function `droplevels` to serve that purpose.

Let me set two date points to zoom into some date range when I plot my series:

```
> mini = as.Date("2014/1/1")
> maxi = as.Date("2018/12/31")
```

After the previous steps, let me share the code to see the behavior of both crimes during this particular range of time:

```
> basetSub = ggplot(crimeDateDF_sub,
+                    aes(x=date,y=count)) + theme_minimal()
> # all points for both crimes
> tspSub = basetSub + geom_point(alpha=0.3,
+                                shape=4,
+                                color='grey70')
> # loess lines for each crime
> tspSub = tspSub + geom_smooth(aes(color=crime),
+                               fill='white',size=2,
+                               method='loess',alpha=1)
> # color for each loess line
> tspSub = tspSub + scale_color_manual(values = c("grey", "black"))
> # format for dates on the horizontal
> tspSub = tspSub + scale_x_date(date_labels = "%b/%Y",
+                                date_breaks='2 months',
+                                limits = c(mini,maxi),
+                                expand=c(0,0)) # to look better!
> # Changing legend defaults and horizontal text default
> tspSub=tspSub+ theme(legend.title = element_blank(),
+                      legend.position="top",
+                      axis.text.x = element_text(angle=90,
+                                                 vjust=1,
+                                                 size=6))
```

Notice that I have included the argument `expand` in `scale_x_date`. Using those values avoids extra space before and after the date limits. I have used the same in **Python**. You can observe the parallel behavior of the crimes in object `tspSub`, represented in Figure 5.18.

The **Python** code to replicate Figure 5.18 follows below. Notice the code used to set the text values as date format using `Timestamp` from *Pandas*.

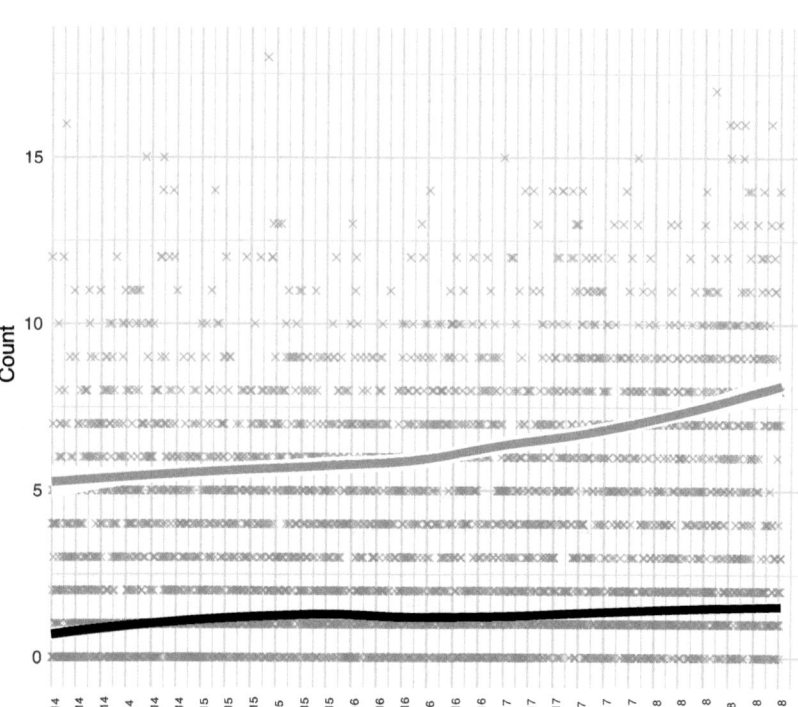

Figure 5.18 Multiple time series

The dots represent the daily count of both crime events, and the loess lines represent the
pattern of the crimes selected. Data from Seattle Open Data Portal (City of Seattle, 2019).

```
mini = pd.Timestamp("2014/1/1") #51
maxi = pd.Timestamp("2018/12/31")

basetSub=ggplot(crimeDateDF_sub,
                aes(x='date',y='count')) + theme_minimal()

tspSub  = basetSub + geom_point(alpha=0.3,
                                shape='x',
                                color='silver')

tspSub += geom_smooth(aes(color='crime'),
                      fill='white',size=2,
                      method='loess',alpha=1)

tspSub += scale_color_manual(values = ["grey", "black"])
```

```
tspSub += scale_x_datetime(date_labels='%b/%y',
                           date_breaks='2 months',
                           limits = [mini,maxi],
                           expand=[0,0])

tspSub += theme(legend_title = element_blank(),
                legend_position="top",
                axis_text_x = element_text(angle=90,
                                           va='top',
                                           size=6))
```

You should not go for areas as your first option for comparison purposes; however, you may try them and see if some pattern appears. Let me use a set of density plots, also known as *ridge plots*:

```
> baseTR = ggplot(allCrimes,
+                 aes(x = count)) + theme_void()
> tsDens = baseTR + geom_density(fill='grey', color=NA)
> tsRidge= tsDens + facet_grid(year(dates)~.) #lubridate
> tsRidge= tsRidge + theme(axis.text.x   = element_text())
```

The object `tsRidge` is plot in Figure 5.19.

The **R** version extracted the years directly in the `facet_grid` command using the function `year` from *lubridate*. The **Python** version is almost identical, but the year will be recovered as an attribute using `dt.year`:

```
baseTR  = ggplot(allCrimes,
                 aes(x = 'counts')) + theme_void()
tsDens  = baseTR + geom_density(fill='grey')
tsRidge = tsDens + facet_grid("allCrimes.dates.dt.year~")
tsRidge += theme(axis_text_x   = element_text())
```

In this case, this plot can complement the previous ones. Also, think how you can adapt Figure 5.14 to represent this time series data.

5.3.2 Correlation

The study of bivariate relationships among numerical variables is known as correlation analysis. The data we have been using has few numerical columns, but I will produce two by aggregating the original data since 2015 by neighborhood.

Let me first prepare my subset of data:

```
> #subsetting the data:
> crime2015=crime[crime$year≥2015,]
> # keeping non missing
> crime2015=crime2015[complete.cases(crime2015),]
```

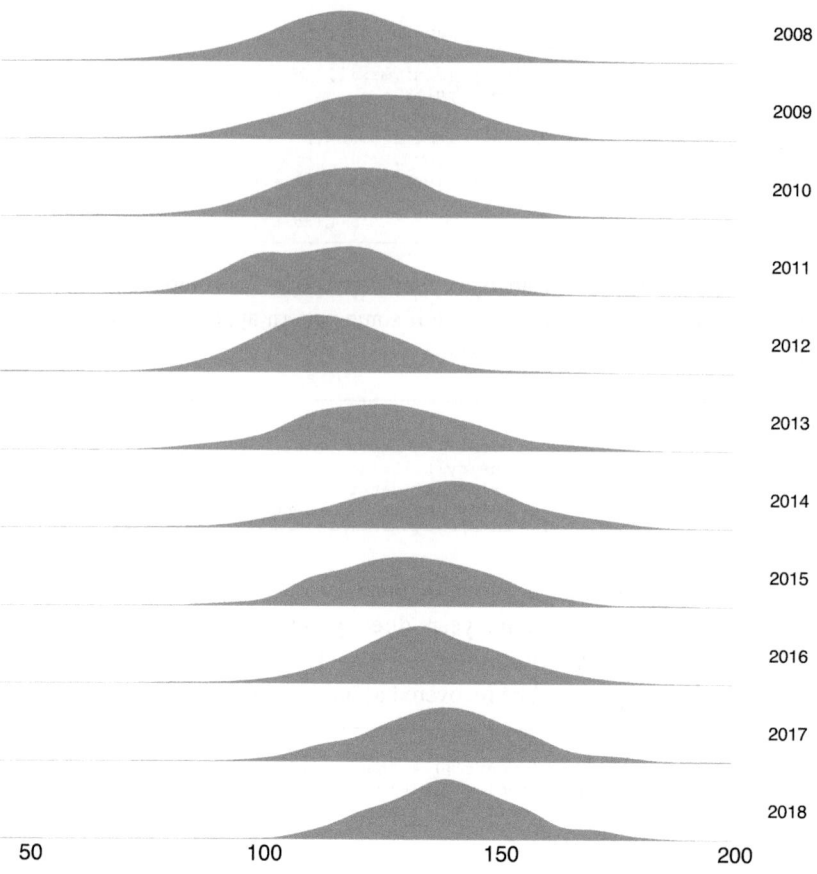

Figure 5.19 Time data as a ridge

Each year is a density plot. Data from Seattle Open Data Portal (City of Seattle, 2019).

You can do the same in **Python** like this:

```
baseTR  = ggplot(allCrimes,
                aes(x = 'counts')) + theme_void()
tsDens  = baseTR + geom_density(fill='grey')
tsRidge = tsDens + facet_grid("allCrimes.dates.dt.year~")
tsRidge += theme(axis_text_x   = element_text())
```

Now, I want a data frame, num_num, where every row is a neighborhood. This will have two columns, the first one will have the mean of the time it takes to report a crime; and the second will have the share of total crimes.

Let me create this first:

```
> num_num= crime2015%>%
+           group_by(Neighborhood) %>%
+             summarise(meanDaysToReport=mean(DaysToReport),
+                       CrimeShare=length(Neighborhood))
> head(num_num)
```

```
# A tibble: 6 x 3
  Neighborhood     meanDaysToReport CrimeShare
  <chr>                       <dbl>      <int>
1 ALASKA JUNCTION              3.62       2901
2 ALKI                        3.92        838
3 BALLARD NORTH               4.25       4177
4 BALLARD SOUTH               3.84       6274
5 BELLTOWN                    2.50       5283
6 BITTERLAKE                  4.38       3504
```

As you see, the second column represents the count, not the share. Let me get it:

```
> num_num=num_num%>%
+           mutate(CrimeShare=100*CrimeShare/sum(CrimeShare))
> #you get
> head(num_num)
```

```
# A tibble: 6 x 3
  Neighborhood     meanDaysToReport CrimeShare
  <chr>                       <dbl>      <dbl>
1 ALASKA JUNCTION              3.62       1.53
2 ALKI                        3.92       0.443
3 BALLARD NORTH               4.25       2.21
4 BALLARD SOUTH               3.84       3.32
5 BELLTOWN                    2.50       2.79
6 BITTERLAKE                  4.38       1.85
```

The steps to get the num_num data frame in **Python** follows:

```python
# operation to perform in each column:
operations={'DaysToReport': 'mean','Neighborhood': 'count'}
# grouping and applying operation
num_num=crime2015.groupby('Neighborhood').agg(operations)
# computing the total crimes
sumOfCrimes=num_num.Neighborhood.sum()
# overwriting column
num_num['Neighborhood']=100*num_num.Neighborhood/sumOfCrimes
# renaming data frame
num_num.columns=['meanDaysToReport','CrimeShare']
# Neighborhood is the index (row names),
# moving it to a column
num_num.reset_index(inplace=True)
```

Having two numeric columns, you can produce a scatter plot (see Figure 5.20):

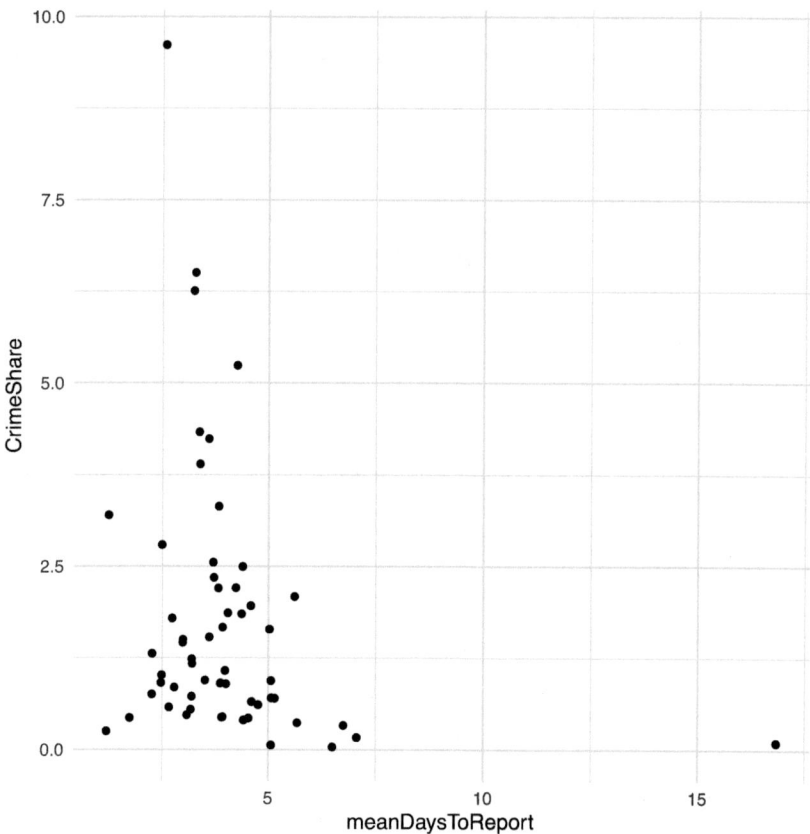

Figure 5.20 Basic scatter plot
The values of each variable serves to determine the position of each point; points represent a neighborhood. Data from Seattle Open Data Portal (City of Seattle, 2019).

```
> baseNN = ggplot(num_num,
+                 aes(x=meanDaysToReport,
+                     y=CrimeShare)) + theme_minimal()
> scat1 = baseNN +  geom_point(color='black')
```

Once you have a scatter plot, the usual next step is to highlight the level of correlation between the variables. This requires the computation of a correlation coefficient and its significance.

```
> # coefficient
> corVal=cor.test(num_num$meanDaysToReport,
+                 num_num$CrimeShare,method = 'spearman')$estimate
```

```
> # significance
> pVal=cor.test(num_num$meanDaysToReport,
+              num_num$CrimeShare,method = 'spearman')$p.value
> # rounding
> corVal=round(corVal,2); pVal=round(pVal,2);
> # building message
> TextCor=paste0('Spearman:\n',corVal,'\n(p.value:',pVal,')')
```

The **Python** code to the object `TextCor` follows:

```
import scipy.stats  as stats

corVal,pVal=stats.spearmanr(num_num.meanDaysToReport,
                            num_num.CrimeShare)

corVal=str(round(corVal,2))
pVal=str(round(pVal,2))
TextCor='Spearman:\n' + corVal +'\n(p.value:'+ pVal +')'
```

You can then produce an annotated scatter plot this way:

```
> scat2=scat1 + geom_smooth(method = lm,
+                           se=FALSE,
+                           color='grey60')
> scat2=scat2 + annotate(label=TextCor,
+                        geom = 'text',
+                        x=10,y=5)
```

The object `scat2` is plotted in Figure 5.21.

Scatter plots are easy to understand for people with a basic statistical background; for that reason, be careful with the annotations I included in Figure 5.21. That plot could be good for teaching purposes, but not for a short presentation to an audience that may not understand what *p.values* or correlation coefficients are.

You can use **Python** to replicate Figure 5.21 this way:

```
baseNN = ggplot(num_num,
                aes(x='meanDaysToReport',
                    y='CrimeShare')) + theme_minimal()
scat1  = baseNN +  geom_point(color='black')
#
scat2  = scat1 + geom_smooth(method = 'lm',
                             se=False,
                             color='silver')
scat2 += annotate(label=TextCor,
                  geom = 'text',
                  x=10,y=5)
```

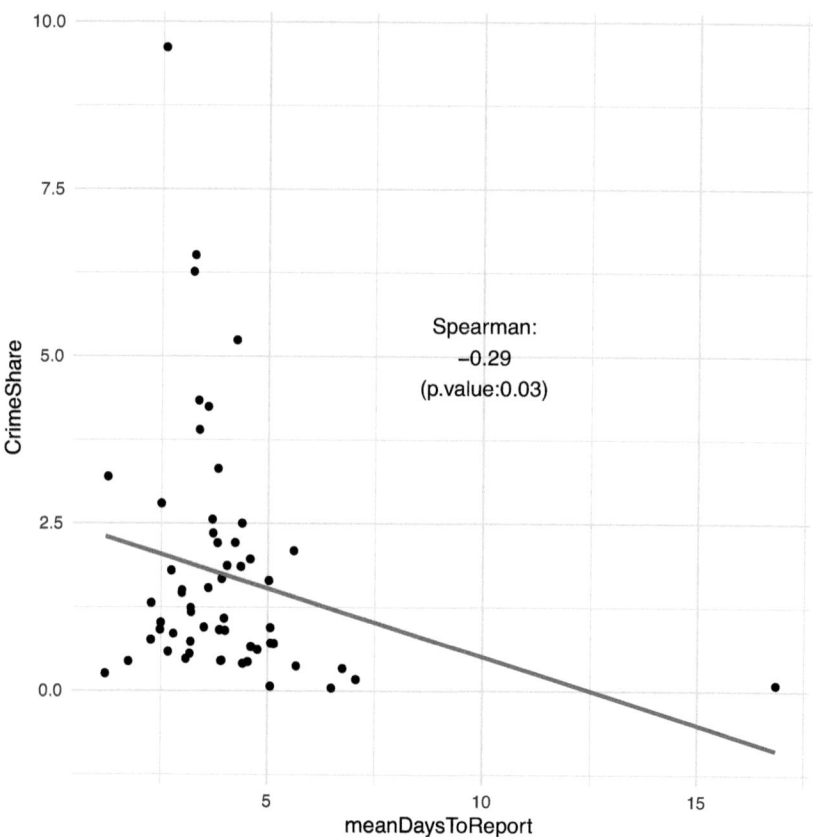

Figure 5.21 Scatter plot with correlation coefficient

The line has been computed using a lineal regression, and the text represents the Spearman's
rho. Data from Seattle Open Data Portal (City of Seattle, 2019).

5.3.3 Focusing

Beyond showing the weak negative correlation between these variables, you
can show some important information. In this case, as I have identified outlying
values, I could try computing which they are using a linear regression:

```
> #regression
> relationship=lm(CrimeShare~meanDaysToReport,data = num_num)
> #save cook distance in data frame
> num_num$cook=cooks.distance(relationship)
> #compute threshold
> threshold=4/nrow(num_num)
```

I have computed the *Cook* distance (Cook, 1979) and saved it as another column in my data frame. I will use that value to create a condition:

```
> # 'cond' will be the names of the neighborhood is 'cook'
> # is above the 'threshold'
> cond=ifelse(num_num$cook>threshold,
+             num_num$Neighborhood, "")
```

The **Python** code for both previous steps is shown next:

```
#library needed
from statsmodels.formula.api import ols

#regression
relationship = ols('CrimeShare~meanDaysToReport',num_num).fit()
#influential values
influences = relationship.get_influence()
#saving Cook distance
num_num['cook'], pval = influences.cooks_distance
#computing thresold
threshold=4/len(num_num)
# condition
condition=np.where(num_num['cook'] > threshold,
                   num_num['Neighborhood'],"")
```

Notice that in this case, I have called the *statsmodel* library (Seabold and Perktold, 2010), whose function `get_influence` will return some influential measures. I just saved the Cook distance. Notice you will get two values from `cooks_distance`; I have just saved the first one as a new column (I got rid of the *p-values*)

And then, with help of the library *ggrepel* (Slowikowski et al., 2020). I can make this code:

```
> library(ggrepel)
> scat3 = scat1 + geom_text_repel(aes(label=cond),
+                                 color='grey50')
```

Plotnine does not have a native solution like *ggrepel*; however, if you have at least *plotnine* version**6**, you can mimic the repelling text in Figure 5.22 by installing *adjustText* (Flyamer, 2019) and preparing a dictionary like this:

```
# needs installation: pip install adjustText
from adjustText import adjust_text

## parameters as a dictionary
# 'expand_objects'expand the bounding box of
# texts when repelling them from other object
# 'arrowstyle' can also be '->' or '←'
adjustParams= {'expand_points': (0,0),
               'arrowprops': {'arrowstyle': '-',
                              'color': 'silver'}}
```

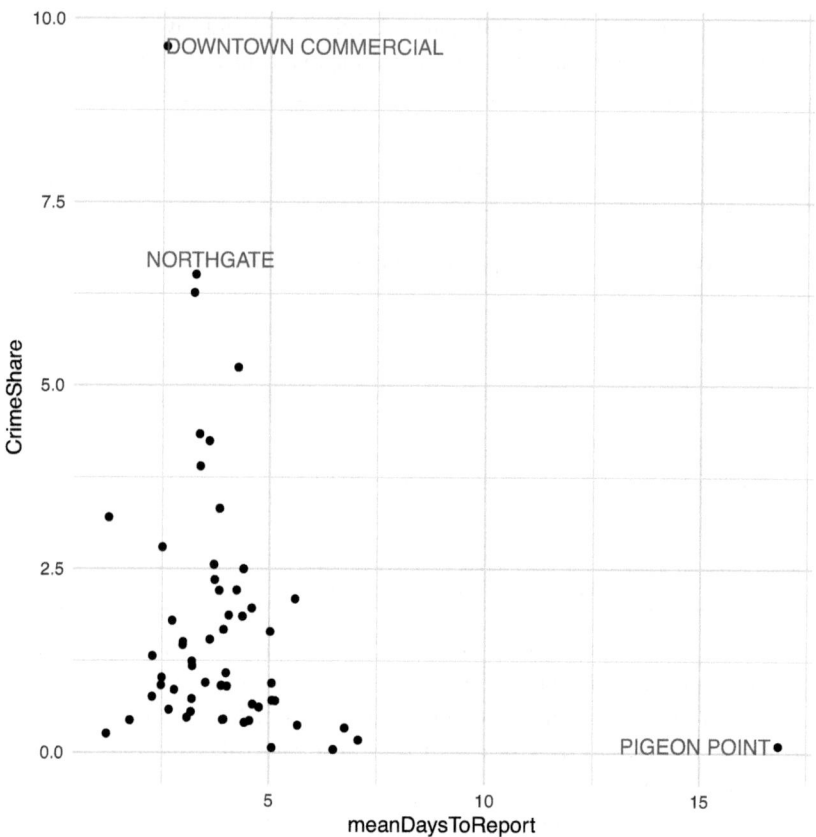

Figure 5.22 Scatter plot with annotated outliers

Outliers have been computed using the *cook distance* from a linear regression model. Data from Seattle Open Data Portal (City of Seattle, 2019).

You can get a similar result to Figure 5.22 using the following code:

```
scat3 = scat1 + geom_text(aes(label=condition),
                          adjust_text=adjustParams) #repel!
```

5.3.4 Concentration

The symbols in the scatter plot are usually plotted on top of each other; so while outliers are easy to identify, areas where several symbols are overplotted may hide some information. One smart way to solve this is abandoning the use of dots and trying alternative ways. Let me first compute the most common values in our bivariate relationship for annotating my final visual:

```
> # library(dplyr) for function "between"
> xVals=num_num$meanDaysToReport
> yVals=num_num$CrimeShare
> tVals=num_num$Neighborhood
> num_num$CondText=ifelse(between(xVals,3, 5) &
+                         between(yVals,1, 3),
+                         tVals,"")
```

I have created the variable `CondText`, which will have a neighborhood names only if the other numerical variables are within a data range. The function `between` from *dplyr* (Wickham et al., 2020a) came in handy for that. Let me show you how to achieve the same with Python:

```
xVals=num_num.meanDaysToReport
yVals=num_num.CrimeShare
tVals=num_num.ConText


num_num['CondText']=np.where(xVals.between(3, 5) &
                             yVals.between(1, 3),
                             tVals,None)
```

Now that I have created a new variable, I need to reload the data frame:

```
> baseNN_Re = ggplot(num_num,
+                 aes(x=meanDaysToReport,
+                     y=CrimeShare)) + theme_minimal()
```

This will create an *hexabin plot*, which consists of hexagons whose width values represent the interval width in each axis, and whose color intensity will represent the count of cases in each hexagon; in this case, darker the more cases there are (you can represent the opposite by changing `direction` to -1).

```
> scatHex = baseNN_Re +  geom_hex(binwidth = 1)
> scatHex = scatHex + scale_fill_distiller(palette ="Greys",
+                                           direction=1)
```

The object `scatHex` will show you in Figure 5.23 where the cases are concentrated.

You can annotate the Figure 5.23. However, if your purposes is to label the cities in the darkest hexagons, consider this:

- Text will be cluttered, so you will need to zoom into the darkest area.
- Zooming in will make areas disappear (outliers will not be seen).
- You may need to highlight the text, because you will get closer to darkest areas which might hide some hexagons.

Let me illustrate those considerations:

```
> #Zooming in:
> scatHexAn = scatHex + ylim(c(1,4)) + xlim(c(1.5,7))
```

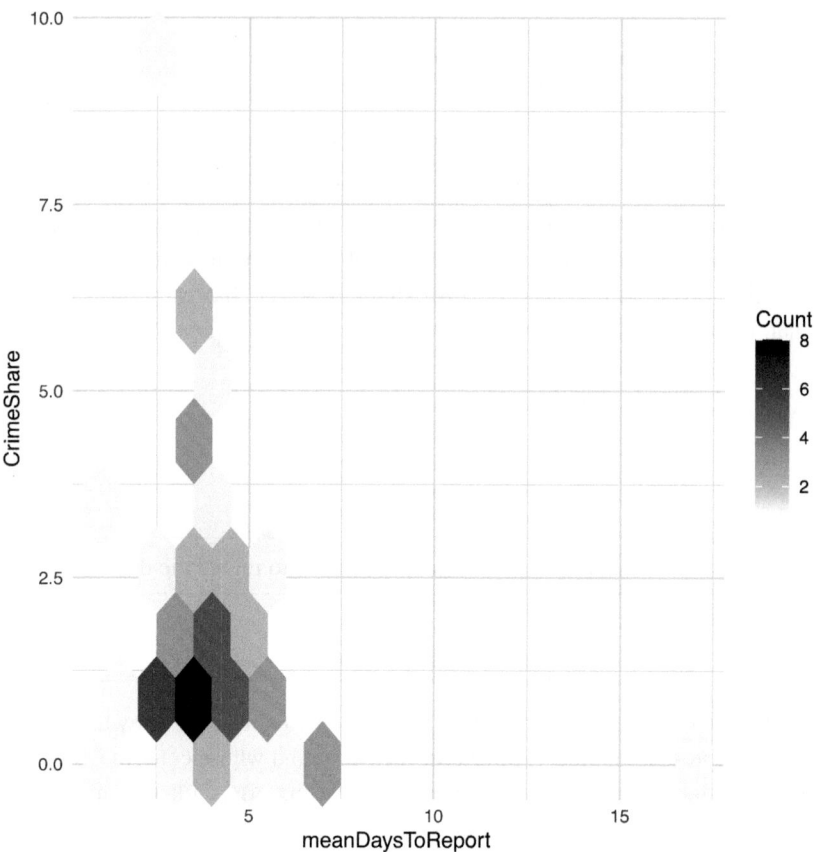

Figure 5.23 Basic Hexabin plot

This shows you the values where neighborhoods are concentrated. Data from Seattle Open Data Portal (City of Seattle, 2019).

```
>  #Annotating:
>  scatHexAn = scatHexAn + geom_label_repel(aes(label=CondText),
+                                           size=2.5,
+                                           color='grey50')
```

Figure 5.24 represents object scatHexAn.

Hexabin plots can be done in **Python**, but at the beginning of year 2020 it was not implemented in *plotnine*. Alternatives such as *seaborn*, or *Pandas* itself, facilitate making easy and fast hexabin plots, but lack some customization details. So, my best alternative is to use *matplotlib* and build it from scratch. Let me build this plot in several steps, until I reach Figure 5.24.

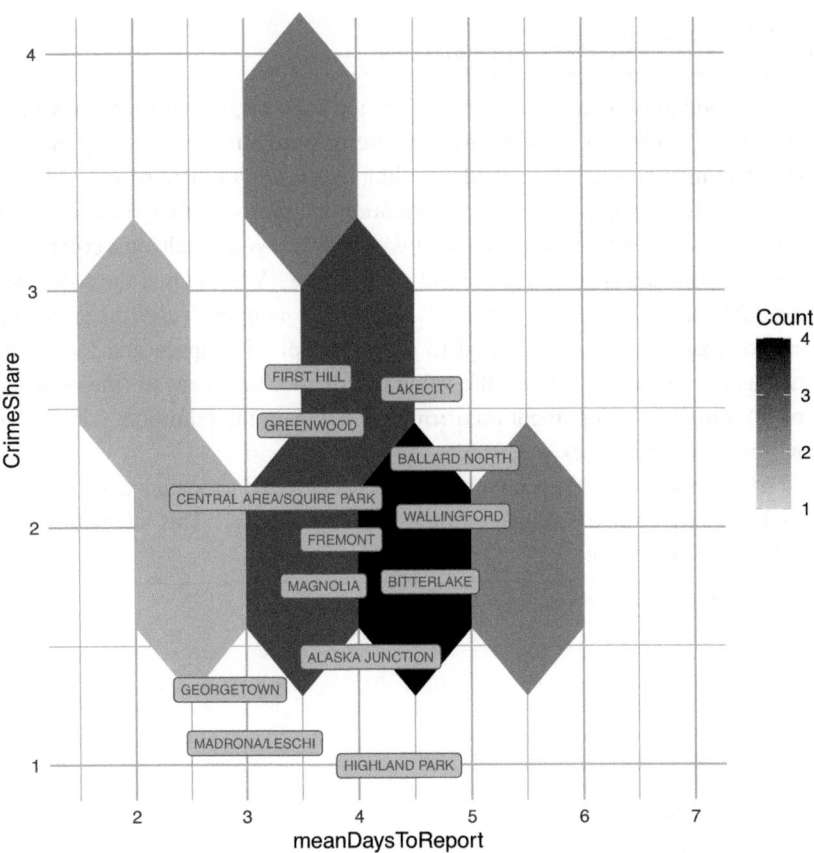

Figure 5.24 Annotated Hexbin plot

This plot shows you the locations where neighborhoods are concentrated. The plot has been zoomed-into to make labels visible. Data from Seattle Open Data Portal (City of Seattle, 2019).

The output of this **Python** code will closely resemble Figure 5.23:

```python
import matplotlib.pyplot as plt

# size of plot
plt.figure(figsize=(10,6))

# plot hexabin
plt.hexbin(xVals,
           yVals,
           cmap=plt.cm.Greys, #colormap
           gridsize=10,
           mincnt=1) # at least

# color bar that represents counts
```

```
TheLegend = plt.colorbar()
TheLegend.ax.set_title('Legend\nTitle')
```

The previous code shows how every step uses **plt**, which represents most of the *matplotlib* functionality. Most is pretty straightforward: setting the size (the plot may be small by default), calling the *hexabin* function, and adding a color bar for legend. However, pay attention to color selection. The argument cmap is calling a color map from *matplotlib*. When you decide on a color map, get the name and append it at the end of plt.cm. You can find the color bars available on *matplotlib*'s webpage.[10] Notice that *matplotlib* uses the argument gridsize, which will be used to divide the plotting space and locate the hexagons, so that the greater the value the smaller the hexagon (the opposite of **R**). Finally, the argument mincounts tells you the minimum counts that will make a hexagon exist.

The previous code will not control the background appearance, as we used to do it with theme_classic or theme_minimal. This adaptation will help you achieve that:

```
import matplotlib.pyplot as plt

plt.figure(figsize=(10,6))
# theme
plt.grid(color='silver') #lines color
plt.gca().set_facecolor("white") #background
#

plt.hexbin(xVals,
           yVals,
           cmap=plt.cm.Greys,
           gridsize=10,
           mincnt=1)
TheLegend = plt.colorbar()
TheLegend.ax.set_title('Legend\nTitle')
```

The last code gives me a good opportunity to share the difference between a *figure* and an *axis*. While a *figure* is the whole of what you see, including the space for the legend, the *axes* is the plotting area. Some properties have similar names in both, but that will create a different behavior. Obviously, figures have properties that axes do not, and vice versa. The function **gca**() recovers the current *axes* and makes changes there, so the function **set_facecolor** is an operation on *axes*, not on *figures*: this will change the background or the patches behind the grid. Also, notice that my color bar is an *axes* element too, so I give that axes a title.

The previous code can be adapted to perform the zooming in and the annotation. We need a couple of pieces. First, the zooming in:

[10] https://matplotlib.org/examples/color/colormaps_reference.html

```
#ZOOMING IN
plt.axis([1.5, 7, 1, 3])
```

That step was easy. The first two values of the list [1.5, 7, 1, 3] are the minimum and maximum of the horizontal, and the last two are the minimum and maximum of the vertical.

A harder piece of code is the annotation section. The annotations will use *labels* as we did in **R**. Labels have bounding boxes, This code will set up the bounding boxes:

```
## settings of the label bounding box
for_bbox = {'boxstyle':"round",
            'fc':"white"}
```

Then, I need to prepare the labels, which requires two steps. The first one is the creation of the labels. I will use the `text` function, a function that needs as input **each** coordinate of the text. So I need a **loop**:

```
## labels with bounding box
labels=[] #empty list of labels
for i in num_num.index:
    #creating each label
    labels.append(plt.text(xVals[i],yVals[i],
                           num_num.CondText[i],
                           color='gray',
                           fontsize=10,
                           bbox=for_bbox))
```

The loop visits each index, and uses that index, represented as `i` to retrieve the values for the coordinates (the numeric values) and the texts. Notice I am using the argument `bbox` explicitly. At this point, I need to repel the labels, so I will use again the `adjust_text` function:

```
## repelling text
adjust_text(labels,expand_text=(1.5, 1.5))
```

The only thing missing will the caption and titles. We have done that before in Subsection 3.3. The only thing you need to adapt in situations like the current one is the **x** coordinate of the caption:

```
## titles
plt.suptitle('The TITLE with matplotlib', y=1, fontsize=18)
plt.title('The SUBTITLE with matplotlib', y=1, fontsize=12)
plt.text(x=1.5,y=0.5,s="The Caption with matplotlib")
plt.xlabel('x-label with matplotlib')
plt.ylabel('y-label with matplotlib')
```

This final code integrates the previous pieces to produce the hexabin plot:

```
plt.figure(figsize=(10,6))
plt.grid(color='silver')
plt.gca().set_facecolor("white")
#
#ZOOMING IN
```

```
plt.axis([1.5, 7, 1, 3])
#
plt.hexbin(xVals,
           yVals,
           cmap=plt.cm.Greys,
           gridsize=10,
           mincnt=1)
#
#
# ANNOTATING
## settings of the label bounding box
for_bbox = {'boxstyle':"round",
            'fc':"white"}
## labels with bounding box
labels=[] #empty list of labels
for i in num_num.index:
    #creating each label
    labels.append(plt.text(xVals[i],yVals[i],
                           num_num.CondText[i],
                           color='gray',
                           fontsize=10,
                           bbox=for_bbox))
## repelling text
adjust_text(labels,expand_text=(1.5, 1.5))
#
#
TheLegend = plt.colorbar()
TheLegend.ax.set_title('Legend\nTitle')

## titles
plt.suptitle('The TITLE with matplotlib', y=1, fontsize=18)
plt.title('The SUBTITLE with matplotlib', y=1, fontsize=12)
plt.text(x=1.5,y=0.5,s="The Caption with matplotlib")
plt.xlabel('x-label with matplotlib')
plt.ylabel('y-label with matplotlib')
```

Another option for representing concentration is the *density plot*. The process is very similar to create object scatHexAn, you just replace function geom_hex with stat_density_2d using the parameters given, which will compute the density and represent it as a *raster* without *contours*.

```
> #limits
> scatDenAn = baseNN_Re + ylim(c(1,4)) + xlim(c(1.5,7))
> #palette
> scatDenAn= scatDenAn + scale_fill_distiller(palette="Greys",
+                                             direction=1)
> #2d density
> scatDenAn = scatDenAn +  stat_density_2d(aes(fill = ..density..),
+                                          geom = "raster",
+                                          contour = FALSE)
> #repelling text
> scatDenAn = scatDenAn + geom_label_repel(aes(label=CondText),
+                                          size=2,
+                                          color='grey50')
> #no legend
> scatDenAn = scatDenAn +  theme(legend.position='none')
```

Notice that I am not requesting a legend as it will not inform the counts, but the share of points. You can keep it by not using the last line.

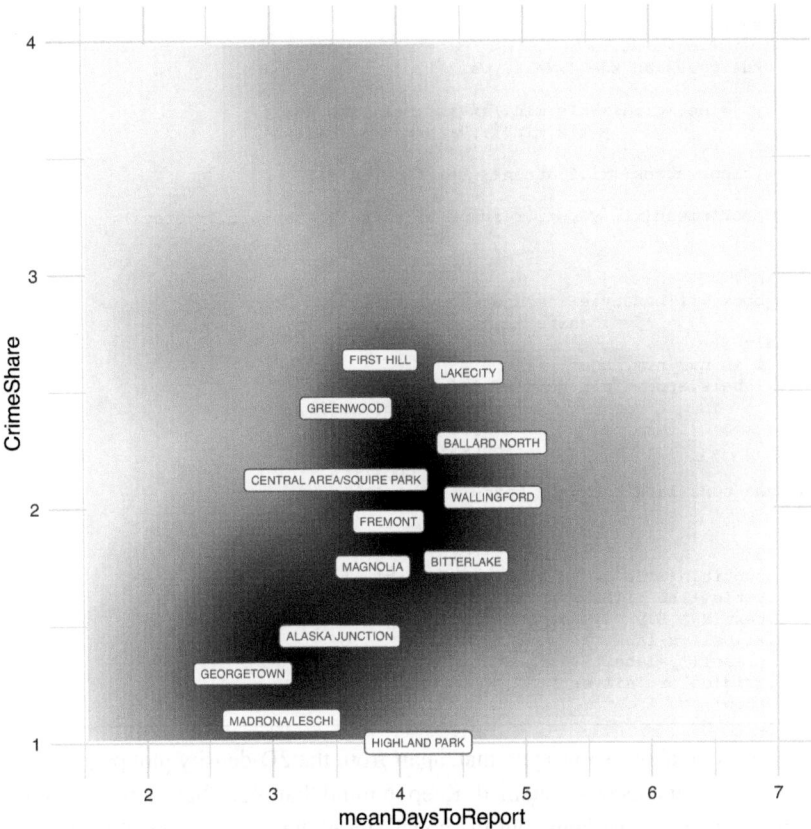

Figure 5.25 Annotated 2D-density plot

This plot lets you know the locations where neighborhoods are concentrated. The plot has been zoomed-into to make labels visible. Data from Seattle Open Data Portal (City of Seattle, 2019).

Let me replicate Figure 5.25 using **Python** and *matplotlib* again:

```
# libraries
import matplotlib.pyplot as plt
import numpy as np
from scipy.stats import kde

#LIMITS, THEME and ZOMING
plt.figure(figsize=(10,6))
plt.grid(color=None)
plt.gca().set_facecolor("white")
plt.axis([1.5, 7, 1, 3])
#
#
# MAKING THE DENSITY PLOT
## dividing plotting area
```

```
nbins=300
## computing densities
k = kde.gaussian_kde([xVals,yVals])
## preparing grid
xi, yi = np.mgrid[xVals.min():xVals.max():nbins*1j,
                  yVals.min():yVals.max():nbins*1j]
## preparing weights
zi = k(np.vstack([xi.flatten(), yi.flatten()]))
## preparing color palette
plt.pcolormesh(xi, yi, zi.reshape(xi.shape), cmap=plt.cm.Greys)
#
#
# ANNOTATING
for_bbox = {'boxstyle':"round",
            'fc':"white"}
labels=[]
for i in num_num.index:
    labels.append(plt.text(xVals[i],yVals[i],
                           num_num.CondText[i],
                           color='gray',
                           fontsize=10,
                           bbox=for_bbox))
adjust_text(labels,expand_text=(1.5, 1.5))
#
#
#TITLES
plt.suptitle('The TITLE with matplotlib', fontsize=18)
plt.title('The TITLE with matplotlib', fontsize=12)
plt.text(x=1.5,y=0.75,s="The Caption with matplotlib")
plt.xlabel('x-label')
plt.ylabel('y-label')
plt.grid(color='silver')
plt.show()
```

The code above shows you that, apart from the 2D-density plot preparation, the other elements were retained. Keep in mind that plots that show concentration have several variants, but the codes shared here can be easily adapted in case you require other alternatives.

6

Insights from THREE or More Variables

We all face multiple variables during the decision making process. We are also confident that the more information we have, the better the decision will be; so, we all crave for more rows and columns of data. If you have the good fortune of having "enough" and the "right" data, you need to decide whether you are going to use the data as they are, or you need to reduce their dimensionality.

If you plan to use the data as they are, you will face further challenges in trying to unravel the complexity. And, if you avoid using 3-D images, you will be making several univariate and bivariate plots. Of course, you can make use of different elements, as I will show later, but you need to be extremely careful in what you are trying to communicate.

On the other hand, if you believe that some reduction in dimensionality is necessary, you will produce better visuals. In that situation you will only need univariate and bivariate plots, and maybe some of the ones I will present in this chapter.

Whatever decision you make on this matter, you might need more than one plot to make your case.

6.1 Partitioning with Facets

Let me use the data frame on crimes that we were using at the chapter on bivariate plots. Remember that we subset the data frame `crimeDateDF` into the data frame `crimeDateDF_sub`, and with that data frame I prepared Figure 5.18.

Let me use the original data frame `crimeDateDF` to plot a time series per crime, using points and line patterns, in a descending order based on crime counts:

```
> library(ggplot2)
> #base
> basetF = ggplot(crimeDateDF,
+                 aes(x=date,
+                     y=count)) + theme_classic()
> #points
> tspF = basetF + geom_point(alpha=0.1,shape=4)
> tspF = tspF + geom_smooth(fill='grey90',
+                           method = 'loess',
+                           color='white')
> # format for horizontal text
>
> tspF = tspF + scale_x_date(date_labels = "%Y",
+                            date_breaks='2 years')
> tspF = tspF + theme(axis.text.x  = element_text(angle=90,
+                                                 size=7),
+                     axis.text.y  = element_text(size=7),
+                     strip.text = element_text(size = 8))
> # facetting
> tspF1 = tspF + facet_wrap(.~reorder(crime,-count),
+                           ncol=4,
+                           scales = "free_y")
>
```

We have used facets before for Figure 5.9 and Figure 5.19, in those cases we make use of **facet_grid**, but this time I am using **facet_wrap**. They do not work in exactly the same way:

- The ~ can connect two or more variables, which are categorical. So you can get particular plots, each representing a combination of those variables.
- If you request a *wrap* you will get a subplot for every existent combination of those categorical variables, but if you request a *grid* you will get a subplot for every possible combination, even non-existent ones in the data. Then, a *grid* might produce more subplots, but some might be empty.
- You can use only one variable in a *grid*, but you will get all the subplots in one column (using . ~) as in Figure 5.19; or in one row as in Figure 5.9 (using ~ .).[1]
- You can use only one variable in a *wrap* by using . ~ and *ggplot* will organize the result in several columns. In the code above, I am controlling the amount of columns.[2]
- In the code above, I have used scales with "free_y". That will give you subplots each with their own y-axis value range (you can also use "free_x" for the same purpose on the horizontal). If you omit that argument, the subplots will share the same range values.

The faceted object tspF1 is represented in Figure 6.1.

---

[1] You will notice in a while that *plotnine* in **Python** does not use the dot in either case.
[2] You will notice that *plotnine* in **Python** does not require any symbol before the variable name.

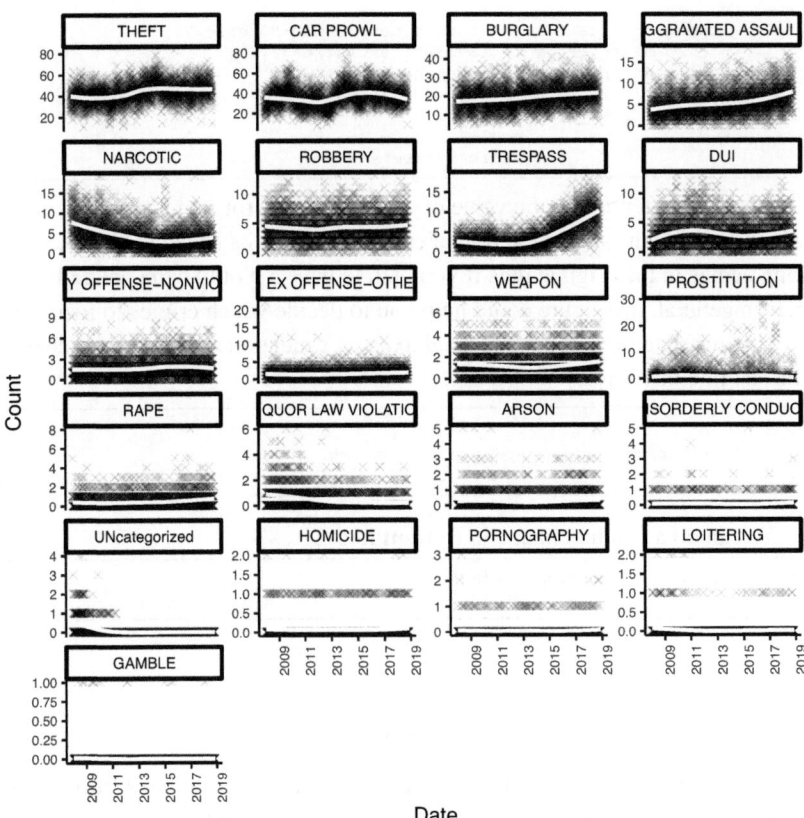

Figure 6.1 Faceted plot with independent axes

The vertical axes is free, so each plot has its own range of values on y. Each plot represents a particular crime. Data from Seattle Open Data Portal (City of Seattle, 2019).

The code in **Python** which outputs Figure 6.1 follows. Remember that we turned the variable crime into an ordinal. Notice that the code for formatting the dates axis is very similar; and in both languages you can even write '1 years' or '1 year' at date_breaks.

```
basetF = ggplot(crimeDateDF, aes(x='date',
                                 y='count')) +theme_classic()
basetF+= geom_point(alpha=0.1,shape='+')

tspF= basetF + geom_smooth(fill='silver',
                           method='loess',
                           alpha=1,
                           color='white')

tspF += scale_x_datetime(date_labels='%Y',
                         date_breaks='2 years')
```

```
tspF += theme(axis_text_x  = element_text(angle=90,size=7),
              axis_text_y  = element_text(size=7),
              strip_text = element_text(size = 6))

tspF1 = tspF + facet_wrap('crime',
                          ncol=4,
                          scales="free_y")
```

Also, pay attention to the value of `strip_text` (or `strip.text` in R), which controls the size of the title of each facet. You may need to change some long names in the original data if you plan to have a plot like the one in Figure 6.1. In general, that figure could help you to decide which crimes to focus on.

If you wanted a common vertical axis, as I mentioned before, just change the last line this way:

```
> # facetting
> tspF2 = tspF + facet_wrap(.~reorder(crime,-count),
+                            ncol=4)
```

Yo can do a similar change in **Python** like this:

```
tspF2 = tspF + facet_wrap('crime',
                          ncol=4)
```

6.2 Color Intensity

I have avoided the use of color as much as possible, but in this section I will make use of it. My main purpose is to play with color intensity or saturation. The choice to take advantage of color intensity is the *heatmap*.

Let me use a different data set this time. I will pay attention to the Safe Cities Index from the Economist (The Economist Intelligence Unit, 2017). I will call the data this way:

```
> linkRepo='https://github.com/resourcesbookvisual/data'
> linkCRI='/raw/master/safeCitiesIndexAll.csv'
> fullLink=paste0(linkRepo,linkCRI)
> safe=read.csv(fullLink,stringsAsFactors = FALSE)
```

Take a look at the variable names:

```
> names(safe)

 [1] "city"                          "D_In_PrivacyPolicy"
 [3] "D_In_AwarenessDigitalThreats"  "D_In_PubPrivPartnerships"
 [5] "D_In_TechnologyEmployed"       "D_In_CyberSecurity"
 [7] "D_Out_IdentityTheft"           "D_Out_CompInfected"
 [9] "D_Out_InternetAccess"          "H_In_EnvironmentPolicies"
[11] "H_In_AccessHealthcare"         "H_In_Beds_1000"
[13] "H_In_Doctors_1000"             "H_In_AccessFood"
```

```
[15]  "H_In_QualityHealthServ"        "H_Out_AirQuality"
[17]  "H_Out_WaterQuality"            "H_Out_LifeExpectY"
[19]  "H_Out_InfMortality"            "H_Out_CancerMortality"
[21]  "H_Out_AttacksBioChemRad"       "I_In_EnforceTransportSafety"
[23]  "I_In_PedestrianFriendliness"   "I_In_QualityRoad"
[25]  "I_In_QualityElectricity"       "I_In_DisasterManagement"
[27]  "I_Out_DeathsDisaster"          "I_Out_VehicularAccidents"
[29]  "I_Out_PedestrianDeath"         "I_Out_LiveSlums"
[31]  "I_Out_AttacksInfrastructure"   "P_In_PoliceEngage"
[33]  "P_In_CommunityPatrol"          "P_In_StreetCrimeData"
[35]  "P_In_TechForCrime"             "P_In_PrivateSecurity"
[37]  "P_In_GunRegulation"            "P_In_PoliticalStability"
[39]  "P_Out_PettyCrime"              "P_Out_ViolentCrime"
[41]  "P_Out_OrganisedCrime"          "P_Out_Corruption"
[43]  "P_Out_DrugUse"                 "P_Out_TerroristAttacks"
[45]  "P_Out_SeverityTerrorist"       "P_Out_GenderSafety"
[47]  "P_Out_PerceptionSafety"        "P_Out_ThreaTerrorism"

[49]  "P_Out_ThreatMilitaryConf"      "P_Out_ThreatCivUnrest"
```

These several variables are telling us information about the safety levels of some cities in the world, and are related to **D_**igital, **H_**ealth, **I_**nfrastructure, and **P_**ersonal_dimensions. For each of these dimensions, there are measures of actions taken (**In**), and results (**Out**). We have 49 variables. A great restriction for this many variables is that they share the same range of values (you will need to re scale the data in case it was not so); so, we are good as each variable ranges, at least theoretically, from zero to one hundred (0–100).

Let me use the heatmap to show you the whole data set, but first verify the *shape* of the data frame:

```
> #just four columns out of fifty
> head(safe[,c(1:4)])

        city D_In_PrivacyPolicy D_In_AwarenessDigitalThreats
1 Abu Dhabi                 50                          66.7
2 Amsterdam                100                         100.0
3    Athens                 75                         100.0
4   Bangkok                 25                          66.7
5 Barcelona                100                         100.0
6   Beijing                 75                          66.7
  D_In_PubPrivPartnerships
1                       50
2                       50
3                        0
4                        0
5                       50
6                        0
```

The current data frame is in *wide* format, but *ggplot* needs a long format; so let me reshape:

```
> library(reshape)
> safeAllLong=melt(safe, # all the data
+                  id.vars = 'city') #identifier
> head(safeAllLong)
```

```
      city            variable value
1 Abu Dhabi D_In_PrivacyPolicy    50
2 Amsterdam D_In_PrivacyPolicy   100
3     Athens D_In_PrivacyPolicy    75
4    Bangkok D_In_PrivacyPolicy    25
5 Barcelona D_In_PrivacyPolicy   100
6    Beijing D_In_PrivacyPolicy    75
```

The function melt from the *reshape* library (Wickham, 2018) helped us reshape the file. Notice that I only needed to tell what variables are the identifiers (in this case only "city"). Pay attention to the fact that the melting in **R** returned the variable, now in long format, as a categorical type:

```
> str(safeAllLong,width = 65,strict.width='cut')
```

```
'data.frame':   2940 obs. of  3 variables:
 $ city    : chr  "Abu Dhabi" "Amsterdam" "Athens" "Bangkok" ...
 $ variable: Factor w/ 49 levels "D_In_PrivacyPolicy",..: 1 1 1..
 $ value   : num  50 100 75 25 100 75 50 100 75 50 ...
```

Python can reshape in a very similar way but the resulting variable will not be categorical. Here is the code using melt from *Pandas*:

```
safeAllLong=pd.melt(safe, id_vars=['city'])
```

Let me keep just the variables that measure INPUT indexes. Fortunately, there is a pattern in the variable names, so you can apply some basic *regular expression* recovery technique:

```
> # "grep" will find coincidences and return positions
> positionsIN=grep("_In_", safeAllLong$variable)
> # using those positions to subset
> safeIN=safeAllLong[positionsIN,]
```

The use of grep avoided you having to look for the positions of these columns. You can do it manually in data frames with few columns, as we have done before, but with fifty columns I recommend you use regular expressions. You can achieve the same using the function str.contains from *Pandas* functions:

```
positionsIN=safeAllLong.variable.str.contains('_In_')
safeIN=safeAllLong[positionsIN]
```

The data frame safeIN is almost ready, the problem is that it still has unused categories in **R**:

```
> # the same amount of variables
> length(levels(safeIN$variable))
```

Since we had forty-nine variables in the data frame, the column `variable`, now a categorical, will have the same amount of levels, even though we have filtered half of them. You have two options:

```
> safeIN$variable=droplevels(safeIN$variable)
> # or
> safeIN$variable=as.character(safeIN$variable)
```

Notice that you do not need to apply both of the previous commands simultaneously. The first one will get rid of the unused levels but it will remain a category. The second one can work without the first one, and the variable will not be a category anymore. The purpose of the previous code was the introduction of the `droplevels` command . In **Python**, I do not need to do anything in this case (remember it did not create a category after melting).

Let me go ahead and prepare a heatmap with the next code. The result will be shown in Figure 6.2.

```
> library(ggplot2)
> base = ggplot(data = safeIN, aes(x = variable,
+                                  y = city))
> heat1 = base +  geom_tile(aes(fill = value))
```

The basic commands used to produce the object `heat1` may not be enough, as this kind of visual requires much more work to get a good result. Let me suggest some extra adjustments:

- Reorder columns and rows so that better and worse situations are easier to see. I am going to reorder the rows and columns without using the `reorder` function.

  - Here, I get the indexes (`variable`) sorted by median:

    ```
    > library(magrittr)
    > library(dplyr)
    > #median per index (variable)
    > medVar=safeIN %>%
    +     group_by(variable) %>%
    +         summarize(the50=median(value))
    > # varSorted has the indexes sorted
    > varSorted=medVar%>%
    +         arrange(the50)%>%as.data.frame()%>%
    +         .$variable%>%as.character()
    ```

  - Here, I get the cities (`city`) sorted by median:

    ```
    > #median per city
    > medCity=safeIN %>%
    +     group_by(city) %>%
    +         summarize(the50=median(value))
    > # citySorted has the cities sorted
    > citySorted=medCity%>%
    +         arrange(the50)%>%as.data.frame()%>%
    +         .$city%>%as.character()
    ```

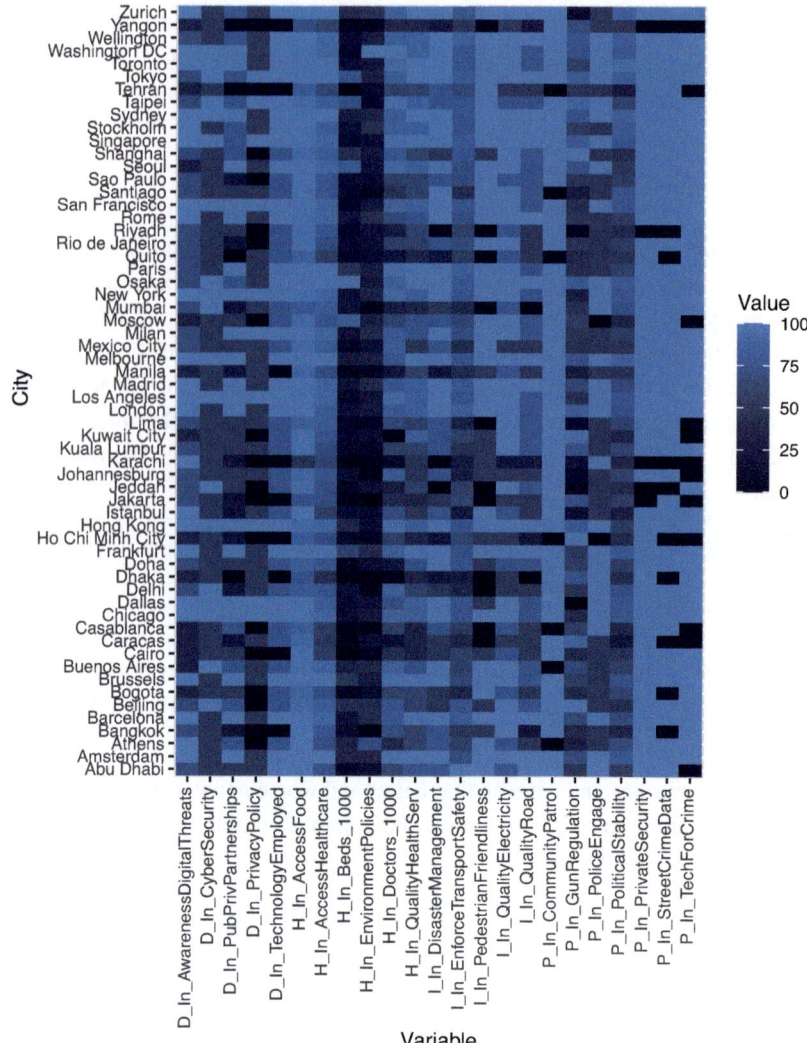

Figure 6.2 Basic heatmap

The legend indicates that the darker the lower the index in a particular city. Data from City Safety Index (The Economist Intelligence Unit, 2017).

— Reordering the labels in **Python** can be done this way:

```
medVar=safeIN.groupby('variable').describe()['value'][['50%']]
varSorted=medVar.sort_values(by=['50%'],ascending=True).index

medCity=safeIN.groupby('city').describe()['value'][['50%']]
citySorted=medCity.sort_values(by=['50%'],ascending=True).index
```

- Change the color palette to identify central values. In this case, you will need to use the `scale_fill_gradient2` command.
- Make sure texts on the axes are readable. If it is important, you should highlight a particular case.

  - Remember that the current labels of `varSorted` have this text in each one `_In_`, I am going to keep just the text after that string:

```
> library(stringr)
> #splitting each text, keeping second part (right)
> varLabel=str_split(varSorted,pattern = 'In_',simplify = T)[,2]
```

  - If you are interested in highlighting one of the cities, you can prepare an ad hoc set of colors:[3]

```
> colorCity=ifelse(citySorted=='Lima','red','black')
```

  - The previous two steps can be done in **Python** this way:

```
#new labels for ticks
varLabel=[v[1] for v in varSorted.str.split('In_')]

# color for one city
colorCity=['r' if text=='Lima' else 'k' for text in citySorted]
```

Let me build the changes on top of object `heat1`:

```
> #reordering
> heat2 = heat1+ scale_x_discrete(limits=varSorted,labels=varLabel)
> heat2 = heat2+ scale_y_discrete(limits=citySorted)
> #change palette to highlight top, bottom and average
> heat2 = heat2+ scale_fill_gradient2(midpoint = 50,
+                                      mid= 'white',
+                                      low = 'red',
+                                      high = 'darkgreen')
> # Readable text
> heat2 = heat2 + labs(x="",y="")
> heat2 = heat2 + theme(axis.text.x = element_text(angle = 90,
+                                      hjust = 1))
> # Highlighting one city (possible warning or error)
> heat2 = heat2 + theme(axis.text.y=element_text(colour=colorCity,
+                                      size=6))
```

Figure 6.3 is a good improvement from Figure 6.2.

You can reproduce Figure 6.3 using this code in **Python**:

```
#raw heatplot
base    = ggplot(safeIN, aes(x = 'variable',
                             y ='city'))
heat1   = base + geom_tile(aes(fill = 'value'))

#reordering
heat2   = heat1 + scale_x_discrete(limits=varSorted,
```

[3] You may get a warning in **R** when you use the vector `colorCity`, if the plot crashes some time in the future verify if avoiding this helps.

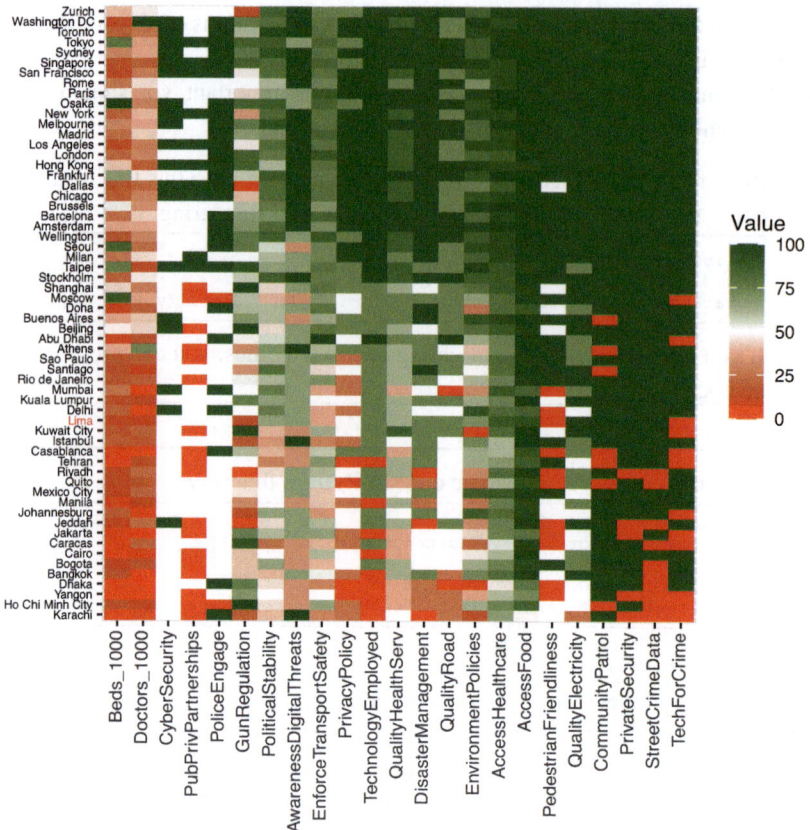

Figure 6.3 Improved heatmap
The palette helps identify different sectors (top, bottom, average). Rows and columns have
been ordered; and names of variables (horizontal labels) have been shrunk. Data from City
Safety Index (The Economist Intelligence Unit, 2017).

```
                                labels=varLabel)
heat2 += scale_y_discrete(limits=citySorted)

#change palette to highlight top, bottom and average
heat2 += scale_fill_gradient2(midpoint = 50,
                              mid= 'white',
                              low = 'red',
                              high = 'darkgreen')
# Readable text
heat2 += labs(x="",y="")
heat2 += theme(axis_text_x = element_text(angle = 90,
                                          va = 'top',
                                          size = 6),
               axis_text_y = element_text(size = 6))
```

The previous code is not highlighting the city name, *plotnine* needs these last lines using matplotlib to accomplish that:

```python
# Highlighting one city
import matplotlib.pyplot as plt

heat2FIG = heat2.draw() # plotnine to matplotlib
ax = heat2FIG.axes[0]    # the plotting area
labels = ax.get_yticklabels() #the city labels
# for every current city label:
for l, c in zip(labels, colorCity):
    l.set_color(c) # change color
```

You should by now realize that the heatmap is trying to use a two dimensional element to display multivariate patterns; so, we started from that basic idea and did our best to make patterns appear and highlight a situation of interest.

6.3 Simultaneity

I will use lines to see the whole behavior of the cases, expecting to find some patterns. The selected visual is the *parallel lines plot*. We used lines in time series data, but this time we do not have time on the horizontal axis but every column; and in the vertical axis the possible values of every column; so the same restriction we had for the heatmap remains here: the range of values for all the variables needs be the same.

Let me do some simple computations to reduce the number of variables (columns for the horizontal). I am going to compute an average (mean) of every city by type (Input/Output) and dimension (Digital, Health, Infrastructure, Personal):

```r
> safe$meanDIN=rowMeans(safe[,c(grep("D_In", names(safe) ))])
> safe$meanDOUT=rowMeans(safe[,c(grep("D_Out", names(safe) ))])
> safe$meanHIN=rowMeans(safe[,c(grep("H_In", names(safe) ))])
> safe$meanHOUT=rowMeans(safe[,c(grep("H_Out", names(safe) ))])
> safe$meanIIN=rowMeans(safe[,c(grep("I_In", names(safe) ))])
> safe$meanIOUT=rowMeans(safe[,c(grep("I_Out", names(safe) ))])
> safe$meanPIN=rowMeans(safe[,c(grep("P_In", names(safe) ))])
> safe$meanPOUT=rowMeans(safe[,c(grep("P_Out", names(safe) ))])
```

You can get the row means in **Python** using this code:

```python
safe['meanDIN']=safe.filter(regex='D_In').mean(axis=1)
safe['meanDOUT']=safe.filter(regex='D_Out').mean(axis=1)

safe['meanHIN']=safe.filter(regex='H_In').mean(axis=1)
safe['meanHOUT']=safe.filter(regex='H_Out').mean(axis=1)

safe['meanIIN']=safe.filter(regex='I_In').mean(axis=1)
```

```
safe['meanIOUT']=safe.filter(regex='I_Out').mean(axis=1)

safe['meanPIN']=safe.filter(regex='P_In').mean(axis=1)
safe['meanPOUT']=safe.filter(regex='P_Out').mean(axis=1)
```

We have increased the number of variables in the *safe* data frame. Let me just keep the columns with the averages of each of the "input" dimensions:

```
> safeINS=safe[,c(grep("IN$|^city", names(safe)))] # ends with
> NewNames=c("city",'DIGITAL','HEALTH','INFRA','PERSON')
> names(safeINS)=NewNames
```

Similarly, in **Python**:

```
safeINS=safe.filter(regex='IN$|^city')
safeINS.columns=["city",'DIGITAL','HEALTH','INFRA','PERSON']
```

As before, I would like to identify some cities from the rest. In this case, let me prepare another column for the `safeINS`; there, I will identify cities whose overall average is higher than 90 (100 is the most they can get):

```
> InValues=c('DIGITAL','HEALTH','INFRA','PERSON')
> safeINS$top=apply(safeINS[,InValues],1,mean)>90
```

The data frame is in wide format, so let me reshape it into a long one:

```
> safeINLongTop = melt(safeINS, id.vars = c('city','top'))
```

The last two steps can be achieved in **Python** like this:

```
InValues=['DIGITAL','HEALTH','INFRA','PERSON']
safeINS['top']=safeINS.loc[:,InValues].mean(axis=1)>90

# To long version
safeINLongTop = pd.melt(safeINS, id_vars = ['city','top'])
```

We can prepare the plot from here:

```
> library(ggrepel)
> #conditions
> conditionColor=ifelse(safeINLongTop$top,'black','grey90')
> conditionLabel=ifelse(safeINLongTop$top,safeINLongTop$city,"")
> # base
> basep1 = ggplot(safeINLongTop, aes(x = variable,
+                                     y = value,
+                                     group = city))
> basep1 = basep1 + theme_classic()
> # parallels using PATH
> paral1 = basep1 + geom_path(color=conditionColor)
> # annotating
> paral1 = paral1 + geom_text_repel(aes(label=conditionLabel),
+                                   size=4)
```

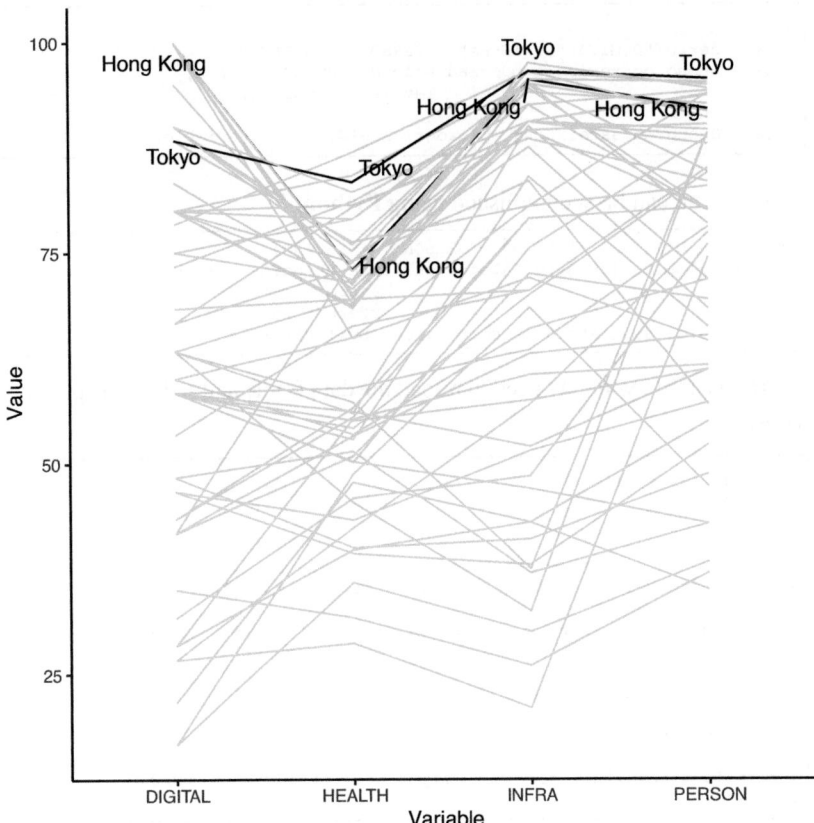

Figure 6.4 Parallel plot
Data from City Safety Index (The Economist Intelligence Unit, 2017).

Figure 6.4 can be easiliy replicated using **Python** like this:

```
import numpy as np

conditionColor=np.where(safeINLongTop['top'],
                  'black',"silver")
conditionLabel=np.where(safeINLongTop['top'],
                  safeINLongTop['city'],"")
basep1 = ggplot(safeINLongTop, aes(x = 'variable',
                                    y = 'value',
                                    group = 'city'))
basep1 += theme_classic()
parall  = basep1 +  geom_path(color=conditionColor)
parall+= geom_text(aes(label=conditionLabel))
```

Since the horizontal is not a date axis, and the column names do not represent a particular order, we can reorder those positions to make some patterns clearer. Let me do that next:

```
> #reordering
> newOrder=c("DIGITAL", "INFRA", "PERSON", "HEALTH")
> safeINLongTop$variable=ordered(safeINLongTop$variable,
+                                      levels = newOrder)
> #sorting the long data frame
> safeINLongTop=safeINLongTop[order(safeINLongTop$variable),]
```

The same can be accomplished using **Python**:

```
NewOrder=["DIGITAL", "INFRA", "PERSON", "HEALTH"]
safeINLongTop.variable=pd.Categorical(safeINLongTop.variable,
                                 categories=NewOrder,
                                 ordered=True)
safeINLongTop=safeINLongTop.sort_values(by=['variable'])
```

At this point, you may need to reload the data frame and redo some previous steps:

```
> library(ggrepel)
> #reloading
>
> # conditions:
> conditionColor=ifelse(safeINLongTop$top,'black','grey90')
> conditionLabel=ifelse(safeINLongTop$top,safeINLongTop$city,"")
> #base
> baseplb = ggplot(safeINLongTop, aes(x = variable,y = value,
+                                      group = city))
> #theme
> baseplb = baseplb + theme_classic()
> #lines
> parallb = baseplb +  geom_path(color=conditionColor)
> #text
> parallb = parallb + geom_text_repel(aes(label=conditionLabel),
+                                      size=4)
```

The object `parallb` has a different order of columns; you can see that in Figure 6.5.

You can replicate this plot in **Python** (after the `safeINLongTop` is reordered and sorted):

```
# reloading data frame

conditionColor=np.where(safeINLongTop['top'],
                    'black',"silver")
conditionLabel=np.where(safeINLongTop['top'],
                    safeINLongTop['city'],"")
baseplb = ggplot(safeINLongTop, aes(x = 'variable',
                              y = 'value',
                              group = 'city'))
baseplb += theme_classic()
parallb  = baseplb +  geom_path(color=conditionColor)
parallb += geom_text(aes(label=conditionLabel))
```

You can plot some cases, as I will do in Figure 6.6, using this code:

```
> basep2 = ggplot(safeINLongTop[safeINLongTop$top,],
+            aes(x = variable,
+                y = value, group = city)) + theme_classic()
```

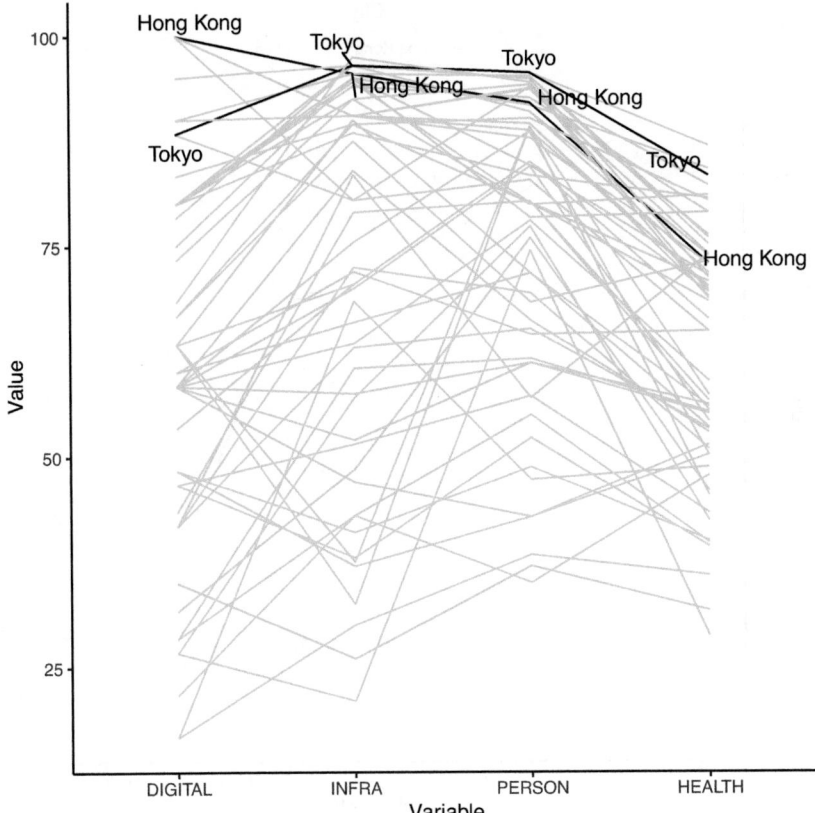

Figure 6.5 Parallel plot for selected cases

Data from City Safety Index (The Economist Intelligence Unit, 2017).

```
> paral2 = basep2 +  geom_path(aes(color=city))
> paral2 = paral2 + theme(legend.position="top",
+                           legend.title.align=0.5)
> paral2 = paral2 +  guides(color=guide_legend(nrow = 1,
+                                   title.position = "top"))
>
```

The **Python** version of Figure 6.6 follows next:

```
basep2 = ggplot(safeINLongTop[safeINLongTop.top],
                aes(x = 'variable',
                    y = 'value',
                    group = 'city')) + theme_classic()

paral2 = basep2 +  geom_path(aes(color='city'))

paral2 += theme(legend_position="top",
                legend_title_align="center")
```

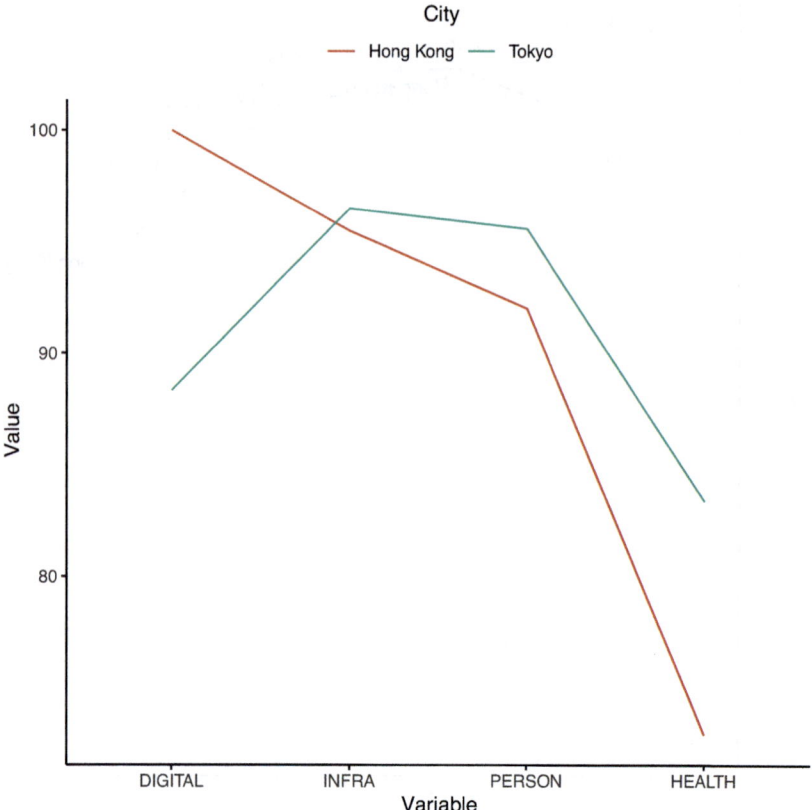

Figure 6.6 Parallel plot for selected cases

Data from City Safety Index (The Economist Intelligence Unit, 2017).

6.4 Area

The previous plot put the variables (columns) in the horizontal axis and you saw the level reached by each case (rows). We could use areas to represent the same. This strategy is called the *radial plot*. Imagine you are wrapping the horizontal and the values will form some polygon. Let me subset safeINS into safeRadarINS with some cities and without the top variable previously created:

```
> cities=c('Abu Dhabi', 'Lima' , 'Zurich','London')
> #safeRadar
> safeRadarINS=safeINS[safeINS$city %in% cities,]
> safeRadarINS$top=NULL
> row.names(safeRadarINS)=NULL
```

Let me do the same in **Python**. Notice that in **Python** I will set the index values with the city names:

```
cities=['Abu Dhabi', 'Lima' , 'Zurich','London']
# a copy (avoids changes to original)
safeRadarINS=safeINS.copy()
#index will be the city instead of usual numbers
safeRadarINS.index=safeRadarINS.city
#no need for column city, it is the index,
#and the column 'top' is deleted
safeRadarINS.drop(columns=['city','top'],inplace=True)
#choosing by index value with 'loc' (not 'iloc')
safeRadarINS=safeRadarINS.loc[cities,:]
```

As usual, *ggplot* in **R** needs the data in long format (Python will not need that as I will propose a different strategy):

```
> safeRadarINS_long=melt(safeRadarINS,id.vars = 'city')
```

Now the radar plot:

- Prepare the base layer:

```
> base   = ggplot(safeRadarINS_long,
+                 aes(x = variable,
+                     y = value,
+                     group = city))
> base   = base + theme_minimal()
```

- Draw a polygon using polar coordinates, so each value in the variable or index is a vertex or corner of the polygon:

```
> radar = base + geom_polygon(fill = 'gray90',
+                             size=2,
+                             col='black')
> radar = radar + coord_polar()
```

- By default, the radar plots may not use the whole range of possible values, in this case from 0 to 100, so you may want to make sure the whole range is shown:

```
> radar = radar +   scale_y_continuous(limits = c(0,100))
```

- You can customize some elements:

```
> # for the grid and text:
> GridChanges=element_line(size = 0.8,
+                          colour = "grey80")
> TextChanges= element_text(size=10,
+                           color = 'black')
> ### more customization
> radar = radar + theme(panel.grid.major = GridChanges,
+                       axis.text.x =TextChanges)
```

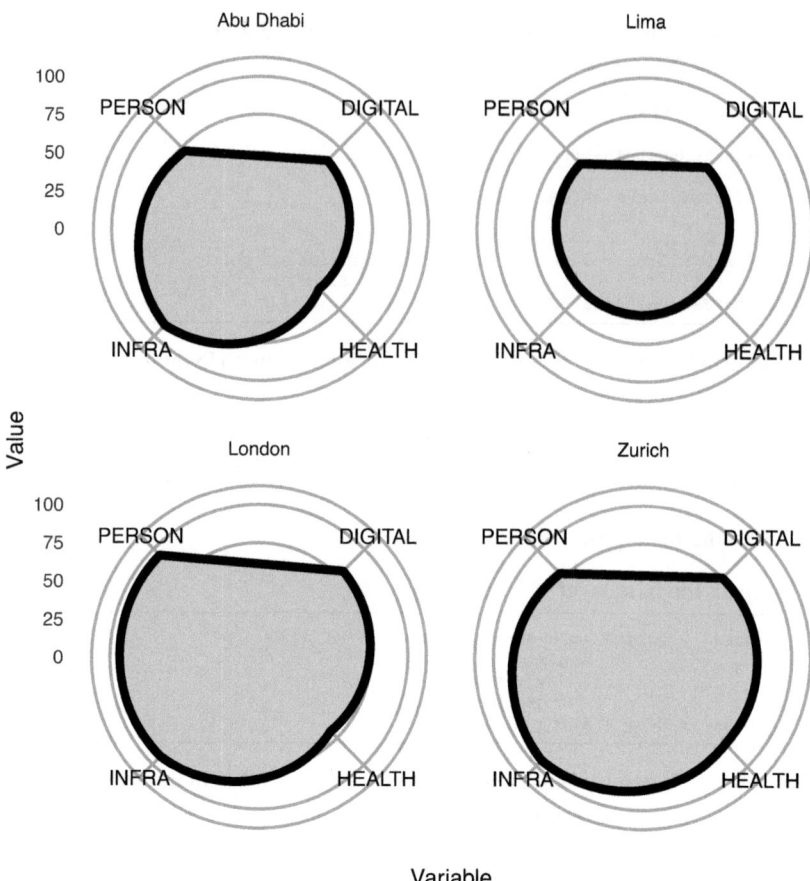

Figure 6.7 Area and Radar plot faceted
Data from City Safety Index (The Economist Intelligence Unit, 2017).

- Finally, you should use facets to plot a radar per city. If you do not use facets, each area will be plotted on top of the other. Use `facet_wrap` to control the amount of columns:

```
> radar = radar + facet_wrap(~city, # one plot per city
+                             ncol = 2)
```

The object `radar` can be seen in Figure 6.7.

Producing a similar plot using *plotnine* is not possible as it lacks `coord_polar` (as of January 2020). So, I decided to offer you a solution in *plotly* (Plotly Technologies Inc., 2015). *Plotly* allows different types of charts to be created but it has a different approach that does not follow the grammar of graphics (it is very declarative, as you will soon see).

Plotly does not require a long format data set, so I can use the current `safeRadarINS` data frame in **Python**. Let me first choose Abu Dhabi, the city in the first row of the data frame `safeRadarINS` (index 0). Remember that the cities are not a column, but the row name or index:

```
# city Name - index.values[0]= ABU DHABI
currentName=safeRadarINS.index.values[0]
# variableNames
VarNames=safeRadarINS.columns
```

The object `currentName` is simply a string; and the object `VarNames` has a list with all the variable names. Then, you need to use *plotly*, if it is installed, this way:

```
# calling plotly
import plotly.graph_objects as go
from plotly.offline import plot
```

In *ggplot*, we have been creating a *base* layer first, and then adding more layers on top. In *plotly*, we create the **figure**, and then add *traces*; you should understand a trace as a collection of data that defines a visual object. It is actually an element that will be part of the **figure**:

```
fig = go.Figure() # "fig" created, then add info:
fig.add_trace(go.Scatterpolar(
                      #data for each variable
                      r=safeRadarINS.loc[currentName],
                      #variable names
                      theta=VarNames))

fig.update_traces(fill='toself')#radar ends in the beginning
fig.update_layout(title = currentName)
```

The code above also used two "updating" functions: `update_traces` and `update_layout`. As the name implies, the former acts at the trace level and the latter at the **figure** level.

Finally, You need a little piece of code to see the final result. Below I am showing two lines; you need to use only one according to what environment you are using:

```
##for Jupyter-like notebooks
fig.show()

##for Spyder-like environments
plot(fig, auto_open=True)
```

The *plotly* result is represented in Figure 6.8.

From Figure 6.8 you can guess that if you need facets, you need to make a figure as a *grid*, and add a *trace* in each location. Let me guide you.

Abu Dhabi

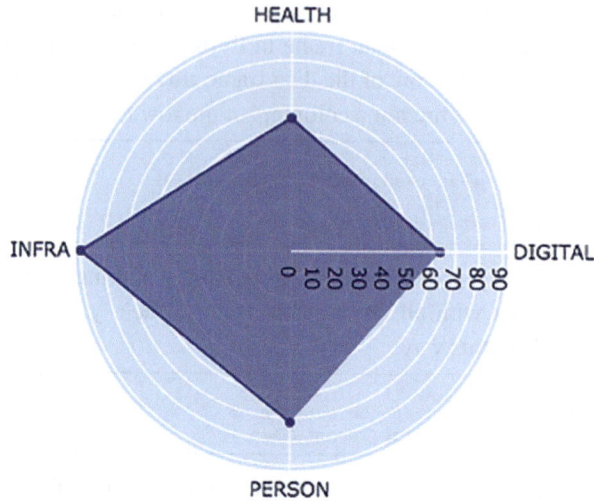

Figure 6.8 Plotly Radar plot
Data from City Safety Index (The Economist Intelligence Unit, 2017).

The first step is to import some libraries:

```
import plotly.graph_objects as go
from plotly.subplots import make_subplots
```

I used the first line before, so you may not need to call it again. The second line is important to create the grid:

```
fig = make_subplots(rows=2,
                    cols=2,
                    specs=[[{'type': 'polar'}]*2]*2)
```

This is a grid with two columns and two rows, and `specs` is setting each as a *polar* element. Now, add the subplots:

```
# the four subplots (traces)
currentName0=safeRadarINS.index.values[0]
fig.add_trace(go.Scatterpolar(
        name = currentName0,
        r = safeRadarINS.loc[currentName0],
        theta = VarNames),
        1, 1) # location of plot (row,column)

currentName1=safeRadarINS.index.values[1]
fig.add_trace(go.Scatterpolar(
        name = currentName1,
        r = safeRadarINS.loc[currentName1],
        theta = VarNames),
```

```
        1, 2) # location of plot
currentName2=safeRadarINS.index.values[2]
fig.add_trace(go.Scatterpolar(
        name = currentName2,
        r = safeRadarINS.loc[currentName2],
        theta = VarNames),
        2, 1) # location of plot

currentName3=safeRadarINS.index.values[3]
fig.add_trace(go.Scatterpolar(
        name = currentName3,
        r = safeRadarINS.loc[currentName3],
        theta = VarNames),
        2, 2) # location of plot

fig.update_traces(fill='toself')
```

The last big piece of code has created a figure with four subplots. However, if you finish there, each radar plot may not use the 0 to 100 range of values (you can try to see if this is the case). So, I need to add some more customization:

```
layoutTrace={'radialaxis' : {'range': [0, 100]}}
fig.update_layout(polar1 = layoutTrace,
                  polar2 = layoutTrace,
                  polar3 = layoutTrace,
                  polar4 = layoutTrace,
                  showlegend=False)
```

Notice that each subplot can be identified (`polar1`, `polar2`, etc.); now, I need to force each one to show the same range. Notice the layout is entered as a *dictionary*. If you want to plot, just use one of the two alternatives shown before (for Jupyter- or Spyder-like environments).

After seeing this process of creating a *plotly* visual, and if you like programming, you might be tempted to use a *loop* to produce the same result as above. I leave the code for you to have fun with (if you do not like programming just ignore it):

```
# libraries needed
from plotly.subplots import make_subplots
import plotly.graph_objects as go
from plotly.offline import plot

# variableNames
VarNames=safeRadarINS.columns
# cityNames
CaseNames=safeRadarINS.index.values

# making up my theme_minimal
layoutTrace={'radialaxis':{'visible':True,
                           'linecolor': 'black',
                           'gridcolor': 'silver',
                           'range' :[0, 100]},
             'angularaxis': {'gridcolor': 'silver',
                             'linecolor':'black'},
             'bgcolor': 'white'} #background
```

```
#number of rows and columns
nR=2;nC=2


# producing figure as collection of subplots
fig = make_subplots(rows=nR, cols=nC, #dimensions
                    specs=[[{'type': 'polar'}]*nC]*nR,
                    subplot_titles=CaseNames) #city name on top

# altering shape from linear list
# to list of two lists, each with two elements
CaseNames.shape = (nR,nC)

# each polar element requires a number
NumForPolar=1 # initial number for subplot name

for row in range(1,nR+1):
#do this for each row
    for column in range(1,nC+1):
    #do this for each column (create  subplotplot)
        # get city name
        currentName=CaseNames[row-1,column-1]
        # create a name for the polar
        # this will be: 'polar1','polar2', etc
        polar_name='polar'+str(NumForPolar)
        # creating one subplot
        figINFO=go.Scatterpolar(
                # basic details for Scatterpolar
                r=safeRadarINS.loc[currentName],
                theta=VarNames,
                name=currentName,
                subplot=polar_name) #polar1,polar2, etc
```

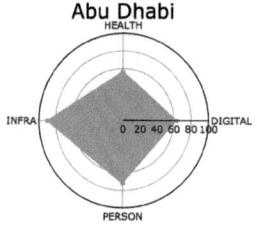
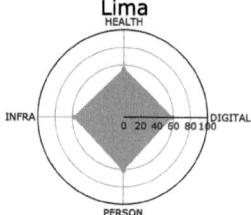
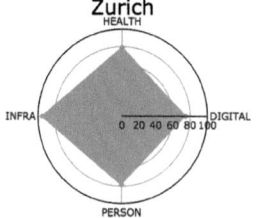
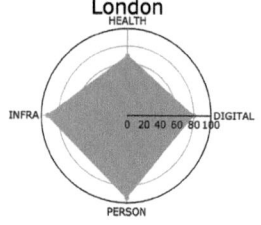

Figure 6.9 Plotly Radar plot in a grid

Data from City Safety Index (The Economist Intelligence Unit, 2017).

```
        #adding a trace with previous info
        fig.add_trace(figINFO,
                      row, column)# location of subplot

        fig.update_layout({polar_name:layoutTrace,
                        'showlegend':False})
        NumForPolar+=1 # number for next polarName


fig.update_traces(fillcolor = 'silver',
                  line_color = 'silver',
                  fill='toself')

fig.update_annotations({'font':{'size':25,
                                'color':'black'},
                        "xanchor": "center",
                        "yanchor": "bottom",
                        "yref": "paper",
                        "borderpad":12})

# choose one:
## jupyter
fig.show()
## spyder
plot(fig, auto_open=True)
```

The final result of this last code, shown in Figure 6.9, will be the closest you get to Figure 6.7 created in **R**.

PART THREE

Beyond Tabular Data

7

Geospatial Data

7.1 Data Suitable for Maps

Any data frame that gives you some spatial information is suitable for being represented in a map. These are some options:

- An address or a pair of coordinates: school address, airport address, home address, etc.
- An administrative unit: county, district, region, country, etc.
- A segment: roads, streets, routes, etc.

Addresses or coordinates (latitude-longitude) are generally represented using points; administrative units are generally represented using polygons;[1] segments are generally represented using lines. Points, polygons and lines are generally stored in *shapefiles*.

Let me show you some data I have collected on contributions to candidates and political committees in Washington State. These data are available at the WA State portal for open data.[2] Let's use this code to open the data in **R**:

```
> link1='https://github.com/resourcesbookvisual/data/'
> link2='raw/master/contriWA.RDS'
> LINK=paste0(link1,link2)
> #getting the data TABLE from the file in the cloud:
> contriWA=readRDS(file=url(LINK))
```

You can open it in **Python** like this (notice this is a CSV file):

```
import pandas as pd

link1='https://github.com/resourcesbookvisual/data/'
link2='raw/master/contriWA.csv'
contriWA=pd.read_csv(link1+link2)
```

---

[1] Points can also be used but this may not be an address but a representative coordinate, such as a 'centroid'.
[2] https://data.wa.gov/Politics/Contributions-to-Candidates-and-Political-Committe/kv7h-kjye

193

The data frame looks like this:

```
         id contributor_state contributor_zip amount election_year
1 6229365.rcpt               WA           98501 106.00          2019
2 6229366.rcpt               WA           98501 110.00          2019
3 6229367.rcpt               WA           98501  69.99          2019
4 6229368.rcpt               WA           98501  40.98          2019
5 6229369.rcpt               WA           98103 100.00          2019
6 6229371.rcpt               WA           98107  20.00          2019
      party cash_or_in_kind     contributor_location      Lat       Lon
1 NON PARTISAN      In kind (47.02872, -122.87765) 47.02872 -122.8777
2 NON PARTISAN      In kind (47.01362, -122.87553) 47.01362 -122.8755
3 NON PARTISAN      In kind (47.01362, -122.87553) 47.01362 -122.8755
4 NON PARTISAN      In kind (47.01362, -122.87553) 47.01362 -122.8755
5 NON PARTISAN         Cash (47.67672, -122.35165) 47.67672 -122.3517
6 NON PARTISAN         Cash (47.66897, -122.40436) 47.66897 -122.4044
```

These data look promising for using maps. First, it has information at the administrative level: the zip code (the state could be used, but not in this case, as it only has information from WA). Second, the location of the contributor, represented by the last three columns. Notice that each row is a contribution from somebody. Someone may have contributed several times, but in this data frame we do not have a way to identify a person; however, this is a simplified version, as the original data available at the open data portal does have the information of the contributor. Let's see the data types:

```
> str(contriWA,width = 60, strict.width = 'cut')
```

```
'data.frame':   3096599 obs. of  10 variables:
 $ id                  : chr  "6229365.rcpt" "6229366.rcp"..
 $ contributor_state   : chr  "WA" "WA" "WA" "WA" ...
 $ contributor_zip     : chr  "98501" "98501" "98501" "98"..
 $ amount              : num  106 110 70 41 100 ...
 $ election_year       : int  2019 2019 2019 2019 2019 201..
 $ party               : Factor w/ 9 levels "","CONSTITUT"..
 $ cash_or_in_kind     : Factor w/ 2 levels "Cash","In ki"..
 $ contributor_location: chr  "(47.02872, -122.87765)" "("..
 $ Lat                 : num  47 47 47 47 47.7 ...
 $ Lon                 : num  -123 -123 -123 -123 -122 ...
```

The data types seem right: the location, the contribution and the year have been read as numbers, and the zip codes have been read as strings. The other variables are in the right format, too. However, this data frame is not a map.

7.2 Map Files

Maps are available in different formats. But, you might have heard of the *shapefile* (Environmental Systems Research Institute, 1998). The shapefile

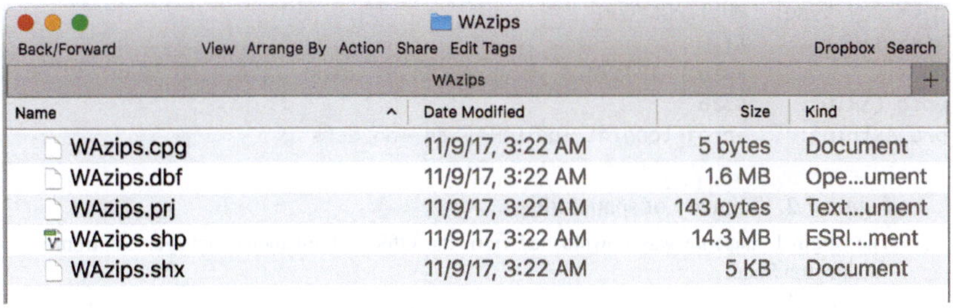

Figure 7.1 Contents of shapefile folder
The file was downloaded from the Office of Financial Management from Washington State.

has something that may sound confusing for the basic user: it is actually a collection or system of files. So, when you download or someone shares a shapefile with you, you actually need to get all those files. As the name implies, you get shapes from this file collection representing either lines, points or polygons.

For the data we have, we need a map where each element (shape) represents a zip code. So, I searched on Google for *Washington zipcode shapefile* and found one available.[3] I downloaded the file and the folder looks like Figure 7.1.

R can not read shapefile from an online repository as *GitHub*, which we have been using along this book, so the alternative is to read it from a folder on your computer:

```
> folderMap="WAzips"
> fileMap="WAzips.shp"
> locationMap=file.path(folderMap,fileMap)
```

The file in your computer can be read using the *sf* library (Pebesma, 2018). Once it is installed in **R**, you can simply call the file like this:

```
> library(sf)
> wazipMap=st_read(locationMap)
```

The function `st_read` creates a data frame with special a column: *geometry*, never get rid of it. That function will also send some information (see Figure 7.2). The *geometry type* informs your map and is made of polygons; the *dimension* confirms it is bidimensional; the *bbox* informs the corners of the rectangle in which the map is represented. The last two ones (*EPSG* and *proj4string*) inform the default coordinate system and projection of the map you have. Remember the world is not flat, so any bidimensional map

---

[3] www.ofm.wa.gov/washington-data-research/population-demographics/
gis-data/census-geographic-files

```
geometry type:   MULTIPOLYGON
dimension:       XY
bbox:            xmin: -124.7428 ymin: 45.54354 xmax: -116.9156 ymax: 49.0025
epsg (SRID):     4326
proj4string:     +proj=longlat +datum=WGS84 +no_defs
```

Figure 7.2 Summary of spatial file

The original shapefile was downloaded from the Office of Financial Management from
Washington State.

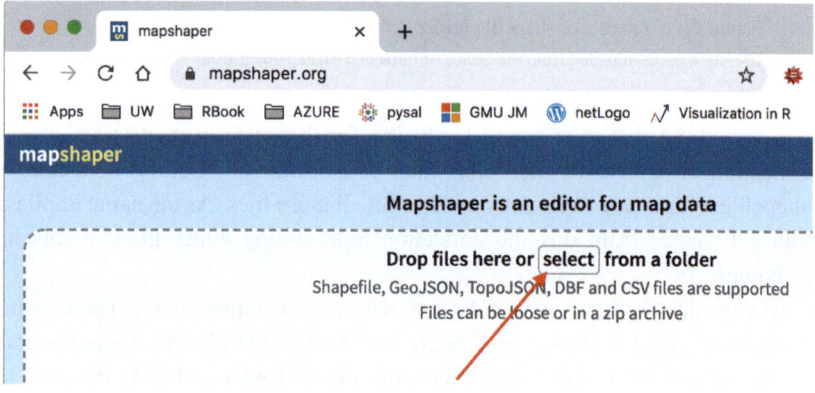

Figure 7.3 From SHP to *geojson* (1)

This steps requires you visit the website of **mapshaper** at `https://mapshaper.org/`.
The original shapefile was downloaded from the Office of Financial Management from
Washington State.

is a distorted representation of reality. Of course, there are several projection
possibilities. I will use the default to avoid dealing further with this matter.

I will read my map file from *GitHub*. A possible direction will be to
transform the original shapefile into another format: **geojson** (Butler et al.,
2016). Let me follow these steps:

1. Go to the website of *mapshaper*.[4] As I show in Figure 7.3, click on **select**.
2. When prompted, as shown in Figure 7.4, go to the folder with the shapefile
   and select all of them.
3. You can click **import** (see Figure 7.5) after you see *mapshaper* has
   selected the files needed. It may select less files than the ones you have in
   the folder.
4. After the last step, you will see the map of Seattle, where each polygon
   represents a zip code area. You will see the option to *simplify* the map,

---

[4] `https://mapshaper.org/`

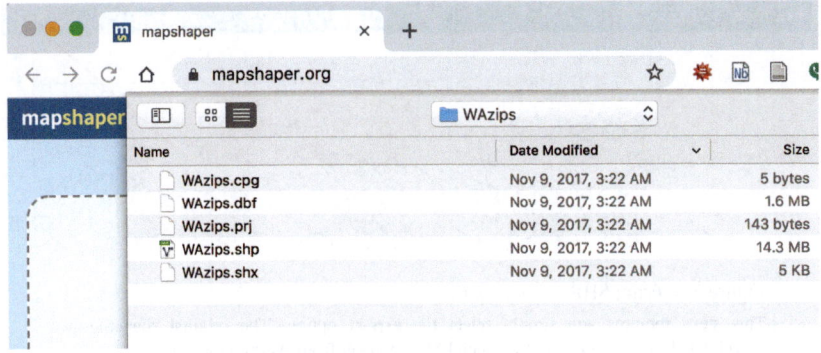

Figure 7.4 From SHP to *geojson* (2)

This steps requires you select all the files in the folder of the shapefile to be upooloaded to **mapshaper**. The original shapefile was downloaded from the Office of Financial Management from Washington State.

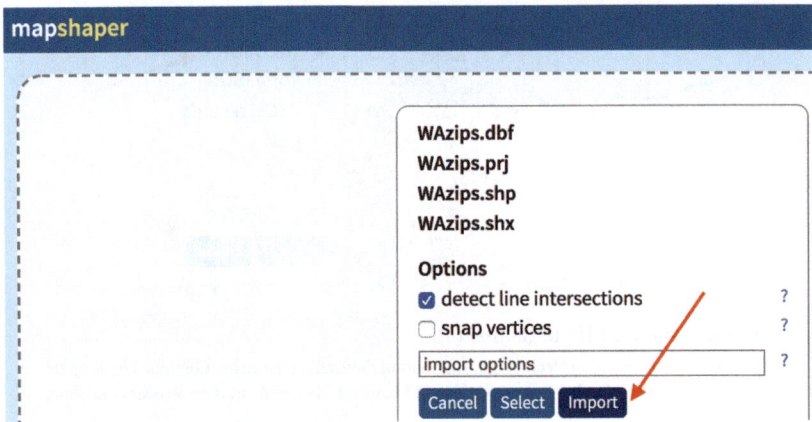

Figure 7.5 From SHP to *geojson* (3)

In this step, you simply import the files that mapshaper requires. The original shapefile was downloaded from the Office of Financial Management from Washington State.

which means you can optimize the current representation and get a map with a smaller size in terms of space occupied in bytes. If you want, you can simply leave the map as it is. When you are done, just click on **export** (see Figure 7.6).

5. At the export menu, select **geojson**, and then **Export**, as shown in Figure 7.7.

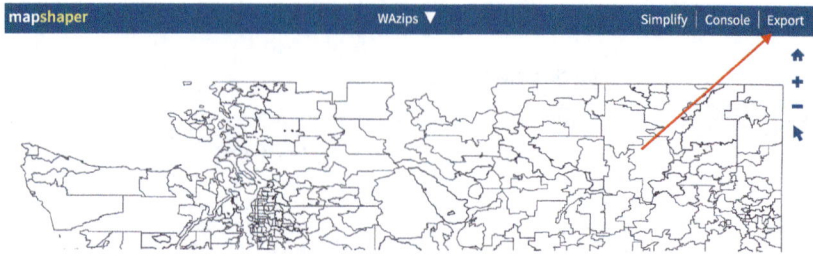

Figure 7.6 From SHP to *geojson* (4)

This steps requires you simply select the **export** option. The original shapefile was downloaded from the Office of Financial Management from Washington State.

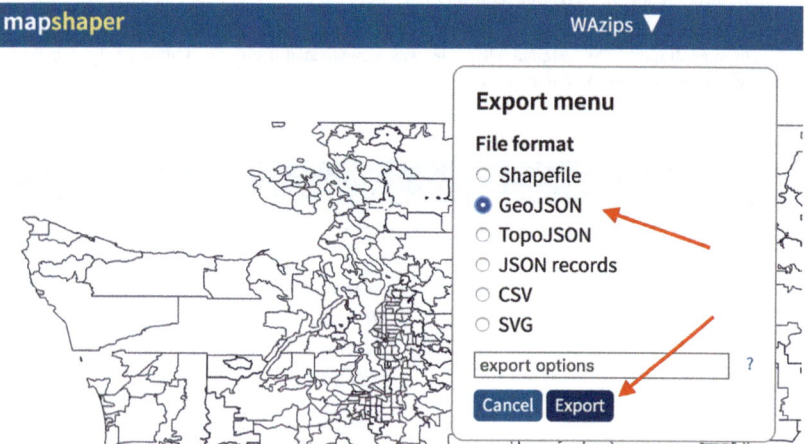

Figure 7.7 From SHP to *geojson* (5)

This steps requires you select the *geojson* option then select the **export** option. The original shapefile was downloaded from the Office of Financial Management from Washington State.

6. *Mapshaper* will ask you to save the file in **geojson** format in your computer. Save it anywhere, and then upload that file to *GitHub*. When it is in *GitHub*, click on the file name so that you see something similar to Figure 7.8. Once you are in that webpage, go to the download button and get the link by right-clicking on it.

By now you have copied a link to the *geojson* file. Let me save the link in an object in my code:

```
> myGit="https://github.com/resourcesbookvisual/data/"
> myGeo="raw/master/WAzipsGeo.json"
> mapLink=paste0(myGit,myGeo)
```

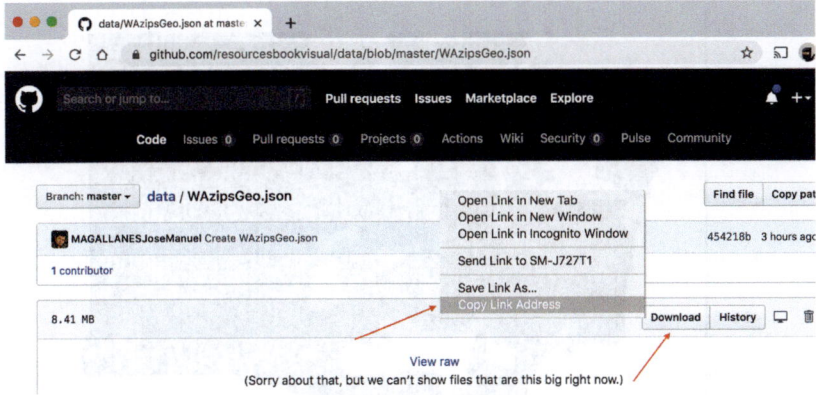

Figure 7.8 From SHP to *geojson* (6)

This step requires that you get the link of the *Geojson* file to be used in your code (R or Python). The original shapefile was downloaded from the Office of Financial Management from Washington State.

Once the link is in **R**, I can use the same functions from the *sf* package with the link to the *geojson* file in *GitHub*:

```
> library(sf)
> wazipMap=read_sf(mapLink)
```

Notice I used read_sf which is a popular alias to st_read in the sf package. I will keep using *ggplot* here, as it can work very well with the *sf* geojson object we have:

```
> library(ggplot2)
> base= ggplot(data=wazipMap) + theme_classic()
> basemap= base + geom_sf(fill='black', #color of polygon
+                         color=NA) #color of border
```

The object `basemap` is storing the visual map, which can be seen in Figure 7.9:

Python can recover the *geojson* file using *GeoPandas*, a library that has geospatial functions and which brings spatial data frames that can be accessed and manipulated like any *Pandas* data frame (Jordahl et al., 2020). This is how you load the file:

```
import geopandas as gpd

myGit="https://github.com/resourcesbookvisual/data/"
myGeo="raw/master/WAzipsGeo.json"
mapLink=myGit + myGeo

wazipMap = gpd.read_file(mapLink)
```

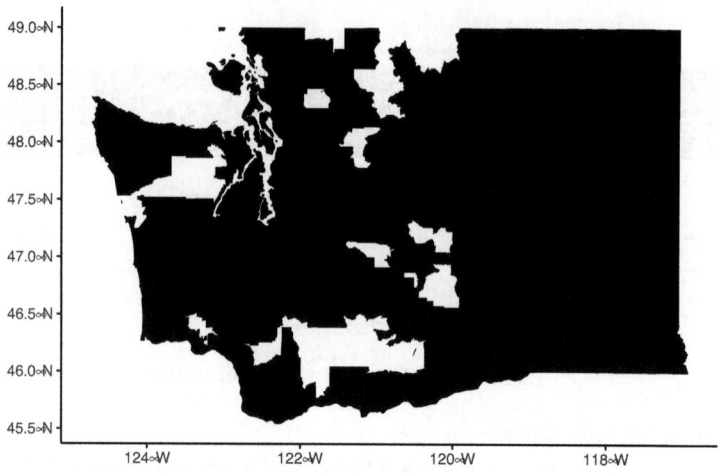

Figure 7.9 Simple map from *geojson* file
The geojson file was produced on the website of *mapshapper*.

Once you have a geodata frame, you can use the `plot` function in *geopandas* easily:

```
wazipMap.plot()
```

I recommend you also install *GeoPlot* (Bilogur et al., 2019), which may give some extra function for plotting *geopandas* dataframes:

```
import geoplot as gplt
gplt.polyplot(wazipMap)
```

7.3 Combining Maps and Data

Maps may come with data, in fact the object `wazipMap` has several columns (102). However, for combining maps and data, I have identified the column with the zip code: `ZCTA5CE10`,[5] let's see:

```
> str(wazipMap$ZCTA5CE10)
```

```
chr [1:598] "98001" "98002" "98003" "98004" "98005" "98006" "98007" ...
```

You can see that in **Python** too:

```
wazipMap.ZCTA5CE10.describe()
```

---

[5] ZCTA5CE10 stands form *2010 Census 5-Digit ZIP Code Tabulation Area*

However, while the map may not bring relevant columns for you, you can have a data frame (maybe a spreadsheet) with columns you wish to represent on a map. Then, recall you have information about contributions per zip code, and location of the contributor in Washington State (longitude and latitude). As a zip code is an administrative unit, you should work to put information about contributions in each polygon of `wazipMap`. The other alternative, the location coordinates of the contributor can not be merged into the `wazipMap` object, but can be an additional layer.

7.3.1 Merging

Merging data into maps is not different from common merging. As long as the map and the other data frame have a common column, the merging is possible. However, there is still some thinking. In our case, the data in `contriWA` has more than 3 million rows, and the map offers 598 polygons. In this situation, you need to aggregate the `contriWA` data by zip code. As `contriWA` has varied information, I need to do some filtering before aggregation, and then proceed to merge:

1. Filtering: Let's keep just the contributions in cash, directed to democrats or republicans, for the year 2012:

```
> library(dplyr)
> contriWAsub=contriWA %>%
+              filter(cash_or_in_kind=="Cash" &
+                     party%in%c("DEMOCRAT","REPUBLICAN") &
+                     election_year==2012)
```

The object `contriWAsub` can be obtained in **Python** using the `query` function. I have chained two queries to improve readability:

```
#conditions
condition1='election_year==2012 and cash_or_in_kind=="Cash"'
condition2='party.isin(["DEMOCRAT","REPUBLICAN"])'

#chained queries
contriWASub=contriWA.query(condition1).query(condition2)
```

Once you have the filtered data, you should explore what you have got:

- The count of contributions given:[6]

```
> nrow(contriWAsub)
```

```
[1] 230717
```

---

[6] This dataset does not have information on the contributor, but the original one does.

- The summary of numerical variables `contriWAsub`:

```
> # Distribution of contributions:
> summary(contriWAsub$amount)
```

Min.	1st Qu.	Median	Mean	3rd Qu.	Max.
0.0	36.0	75.0	208.2	200.0	1500000.0

- The frequencies in categorical data:

```
> # Destination of contributions:
> as.data.frame(table(contriWAsub$party))
```

	Var1	Freq
1		0
2	CONSTITUTION PARTY	0
3	DEMOCRAT	118356
4	INDEPENDENT	0
5	LIBERTARIAN	0
6	NON PARTISAN	0
7	NONE	0
8	OTHER	0
9	REPUBLICAN	112361

- The count of zip codes:

```
> # Destination of contributions:
> length(unique(contriWAsub$contributor_zip))
```

```
[1] 785
```

You have more zip codes than the map. You can verify the distribution on the zip codes in the data frame:

```
> summary(unique(as.numeric(contriWAsub$contributor_zip)))
```

| Min. | 1st Qu. | Median | Mean | 3rd Qu. | Max. |
| 98001 | 98251 | 98528 | 98585 | 98933 | 99403 |

Then, you can compare the previous values to the distribution on the zip codes in the map:

```
> summary(unique(as.numeric(wazipMap$ZCTA5CE10)))
```

| Min. | 1st Qu. | Median | Mean | 3rd Qu. | Max. |
| 98001 | 98281 | 98576 | 98620 | 98952 | 99403 |

Both data have the same minimum and maximum values, so whatever is not matching is between those values. It is possible that new zip codes were created after 2010, but I will not deal with that.

Once you have explored the data, you should decide if your audience will need to see a map or not. You can make several plots with the data you have; but if you prepare a map, it is because your audience has familiarity with the geography represented. That is, if your audience is in Brazil (or even from Atlanta), the map of Washington State may not be important; but if the audience is from King County, that map may be well received. If you are still planing to merge this data into the map, the next step will be to aggregate the information on contributions per zip area.

2. Aggregating. You have several rows (230,717) that could give a value to each of the polygons in the map (598). So, you need to create a "summary" at the zip level. The summary is a function of your choice (mean, max, min, etc), let me use sum to get the amount of money given to each party per zip, and the total amount per zip as well:

```
> contrisum=contriWAsub %>%
+            group_by(contributor_zip) %>%
+            summarise(REPUBLICAN=sum(amount[party=="REPUBLICAN"]),
+                      DEMOCRAT=sum(amount)-REPUBLICAN,
+                      total=sum(amount)) %>%
+            as.data.frame()
> # you get:
> head(contrisum)
```

```
  contributor_zip REPUBLICAN DEMOCRAT      total
1           98001   67723.12  44654.0  112377.12
2           98002   30372.22  19843.0   50215.22
3           98003  180465.00 242428.0  422892.95
4           98004  782610.28 291740.8 1074351.09
5           98005 2451978.61 147940.0 2599918.61
6           98006  326822.49 174507.0  501329.51
```

You can compute the object contrisum in **Python** like this:

```
contrisum=contriWASub.groupby(['contributor_zip','party'])
contrisum=contrisum.agg({'amount':'sum'}).reset_index().fillna(0)
contrisum=contrisum.pivot(index='contributor_zip',
                          columns='party',
                          values='amount').reset_index().fillna(0)
contrisum['total']=contrisum.DEMOCRAT + contrisum.REPUBLICAN
```

Even though you know by now that you do not have some zip codes, you are ready to merge the object contrisum into the map wazipMap, just keep in mind a couple of things:

- You could keep the columns you need from wazipMap, getting rid of what you do not need (this is optional):

```
> # keeping zip (column 2) and last column (the 'geometry')
>
> wazipMap=wazipMap[,c('ZCTA5CE10','geometry')]
```

- The map must go to the "left" (first object) during the merge (this is not optional):

```
> allZip=merge(wazipMap,contrisum,
+               by.x='ZCTA5CE10', by.y='contributor_zip',
+               all.x=TRUE)
```

You can get the map `allZip` in **Python** like this:

```
wazipMap=wazipMap.loc[:,['ZCTA5CE10','geometry']]
# contributor_zip as text (it was a number)
contrisum.contributor_zip=contrisum.contributor_zip.astype(str)
allZip=wazipMap.merge(contrisum,
                      left_on='ZCTA5CE10',
                      right_on='contributor_zip',
                      how='left')
```

The object `allZip` is a new map with the three extra columns on the
counts of people contributing to the campaign. As we included the option
`all.x=TRUE` in **R** or `how='left'` in **Python**, this merged map will have
the same amount of polygons as the original map. Keep in mind that choosing
that kind of merge can cause the new columns merged into the map to have
missing values.

```
> #same amount of rows?
> nrow(allZip)==nrow(wazipMap)
```

```
[1] TRUE
```

Now that we have a map merged with information from another data frame,
I can use the new object `allZip` as a normal data frame; for instance, let me
create a simple variable:

```
> #creating the dissolving column
> allZip$winnerREP=allZip$REPUBLICAN >allZip$DEMOCRAT
```

Keep in mind that the new variable might have some missing values, as
there might not have been some coincidences during merging:

```
> summary(allZip$winnerREP)
```

```
   Mode    FALSE    TRUE    NA's
logical    198     385      15
```

The missing values occurred when at least one NA was present in the values.
Pandas, in **Python**, does not give missing values when the missing values are
compared, so my code to create this variable is more verbose:

```
comparison=allZip.REPUBLICAN>allZip.DEMOCRAT
condition=allZip.loc[:,["REPUBLICAN","DEMOCRAT"]].any(axis=1)
allZip['winnerREP']=condition1
allZip['winnerREP']=np.where(condition,
                             comparison,
                             None)
```

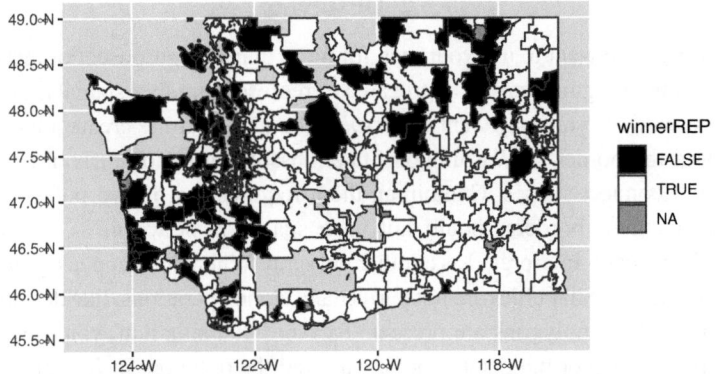

Figure 7.10 Plotting merged map

Notice the presence of missing values and its customization. The original shapefile was
downloaded from the Office of Financial Management from Washington State; and the data
on contributions was obtained from Washington State portal for open data.

In **Python**, I made sure to put a missing value if missing values were
compared; the function any(), used in the second condition, help me do that.
Now, I am ready to see if my merged map can plot the info that came from the
external data frame. Let me prepare the code:

```
> mergedMap = ggplot(data=allZip) +
+           geom_sf(aes(fill=winnerREP)) +
+           scale_fill_manual(values = c('black','white'),
+                             na.value = "grey")
```

You can see the object mergedMap in Figure 7.10. Notice that the color for
the polygons use fill instead of color (color can be used for the border
of the polygon). Also, as I wanted to use the variable winnerREP to color the
polygons, I put the fill argument inside the aes().

Let me use basic *geopandas* plotting capabilities to produce a map similar
to Figure 7.10. Notice that I used a particular palette (colormap) to resemble
that figure (gist_gray).

```
allZip.plot(column='winnerREP', #column to color
            categorical=True,
            edgecolor='black',
            legend=True,
            missing_kwds={'color': 'lightgrey'},
            cmap='gist_gray') # palette for column chosen
```

Notice that the legend for categorical data using **Python** was located on top
of the plot. I will show you how to improve that in subsection 7.5.2.

7.3.2 Dissolving

Sometimes you want to use your map for more than one purpose. For instance, these many polygons may be aggregated to represent another spatial aspect. In those situations, you may want to *dissolve* the map. Let me create a basemap just with the border of Washington State. Dissolving is not a trivial process, as it will connect shapes. Combining them requires that if two polygons are neighbors, their borders should not have spaces in-between, as any space might be visually interpreted as another polygon. When this happens, you have *sliver polygons*. Shapefiles are not perfect and some operations, like dissolving, can fail if sliver polygons are present. To avoid that situation, you can either simplify the map or build some buffers around the polygon. In **R**, simplifying is fairly easy using *rmapshaper* (Teucher et al., 2020):

```
> library(rmapshaper)
> waBetter=ms_simplify(wazipMap)
```

The object `waBetter` is just a cleaner version of `wazipMap` after using the function `ms_simplify`; it is now time to dissolve using `ms_dissolve`, another function from *rmapshaper*:

```
> waBorder ← ms_dissolve(waBetter)
```

The object `waBorder` can be plotted as before:

```
> borderMap=ggplot(waBorder) +
+          theme_classic() +
+            geom_sf(fill='white',
+                      color='black') # border color
```

You can see the result in Figure 7.11.

Let me get rid of possible sliver polygons by using the alternative strategy mentioned, that is, creating buffers in Python:

```
## a. make copy
waBorder=wazipMap.copy()
## b. Correct map with buffer (may not be needed)
waBorder['geometry'] = waBorder.buffer(0.01)
## c. create a constant column by which to dissolve
waBorder['dummy']=1
## d. dissolving
waBorder= waBorder.dissolve(by='dummy')
## e. plot the dissolved map
waBorder.plot(color='white',edgecolor='black')
```

In **Python**, I also needed to create a new column (a *dummy*) (the function requires one) to be used when dissolving. This process does not need to dissolve all the polygons into one. Notice that **R** dissolves all polygons by

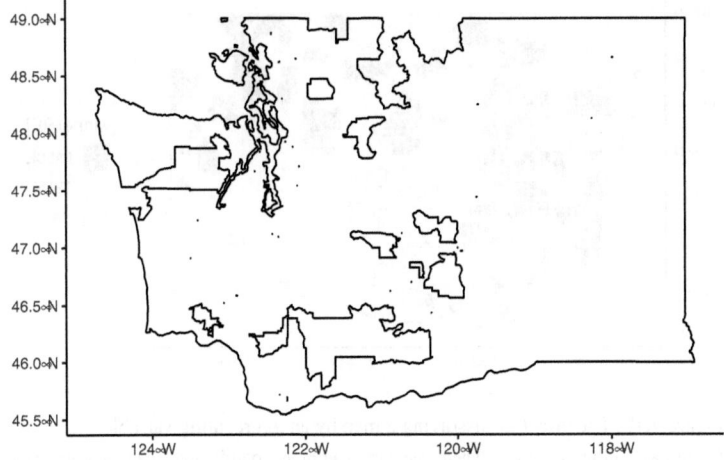

Figure 7.11 The effect of dissolving a map by a constant value

In this case all the internal borders between polygons dissappeared. The original shapefile was downloaded from the Office of Financial Management from Washington State; and the data on contributions were obtained from Washington State portal for open data.

default if no field is present in the function. However, if the "dissolving column" or field had more values, the result would be different. Let me show you that by using my `allZip` map and its `winnerREP` column:

```
> #optimizing
> allZipBetter=ms_simplify(allZip)
> #dissolving
> allZipREP=ms_dissolve(allZipBetter,field = "winnerREP")
> #plotting the dissolved map
> dividedZip= ggplot(data = allZipREP) + theme_classic() +
+               geom_sf(aes(fill=winnerREP))  +
+               scale_fill_manual(values = c('black','white'),
+                               na.value = "grey")
```

As you can see in Figure 7.12, you turn the whole set of polygons into a binary map (notice I show you a way to inform the polygons with missing data).

At this point, remember that simplifying or buffering is not strictly needed, but if your code fails without it, try including those processes. In this case, I needed to make the `allZipREP` object and produce Figure 7.12, whose similar version in **Python** can be achieved like this:

```
## a. make copy
allZipBetter=allZip.copy()
## a.1 saving missing values
```

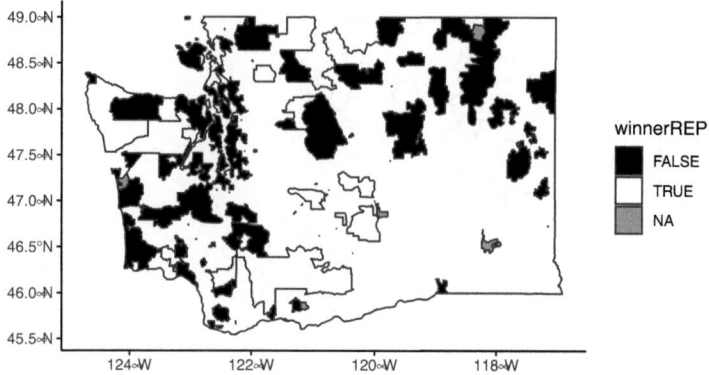

Figure 7.12 The effect of dissolving a map by an aggregating variable

In this case, all the zip codes where one party had more contributions than the other were dissolved. The original shapefile was downloaded from the Office of Financial Management from Washington State; and the data on contributions were obtained from Washington State portal for open data.

```
NAs = allZipBetter[allZipBetter.winnerREP.isna()]
## b. Correct map with buffer (may not be needed)
allZipBetter['geometry'] = allZipBetter.buffer(0.01)
## c. dissolving
allZipREP= allZipBetter.dissolve(by='winnerREP',as_index=False)
## d. plotting the dissolved map
allZipREP.append(NAs).plot(column='winnerREP', #column to color
                edgecolor='black',
                categorical=True,legend=True,
                missing_kwds={'color': 'grey'},
                cmap='gist_gray')
```

Notice that *geopandas* did not create missing values after dissolving. So, I had to save the missing values in the object NAs and append it to allZipREP before plotting it. It is a functionality not yet present in *geopandas*. However, it is important to think that if you want to have more control over your work, you should use maps with complete data, and take advantage of the *layering* capacities of **R** and **Python** (and every software for maps), which comes next.

7.3.3 Layering

When you have several maps, you can be creative and put each one on top of the other; I like this because it gives me more control over how to plot missing values. Let me create another spatial element, this time using the coordinates I have on the donor location. As you know, the data frame contriWAsub has columns with coordinates, which represent a point on a map:

```
> contriWAsub[,c(9:10)]%>% head()
```

```
        Lat       Lon
1 47.78220 -122.0626
2 47.42512 -120.3399
3 47.63716 -122.2765
4 47.72272 -122.3513
5 47.52707 -122.0466
6 47.26280 -122.5228
```

Let's use those columns to create a spatial point data frame, while making sure it has the same coordinate system as our map:

```
> WApoints= st_as_sf(contriWAsub,
+                    coords = c("Lon", "Lat"), #in that order
+                    remove = FALSE,
+                    crs = st_crs(allZip)$epsg)
```

The `WApoints` object is now a *spatial points* data frame:

```
> class(WApoints)
```

```
[1] "sf"        "data.frame"
```

You can achieve the same in **Python** with with this code:

```
WApoints = gpd.GeoDataFrame(contriWASub,
               geometry=gpd.points_from_xy(contriWASub.Lon,
                                           contriWASub.Lat))
WApoints.crs = wazipMap.crs
```

Let me create a map with the polygons that have missing values in the column `total`:

```
> allZipNA=allZip[!complete.cases(allZip$total),]
```

That was easy. It is also easy in Python:

```
allZipNA=allZip[allZip.total.isnull()].copy()
```

Let me use some objects I already have:

- the **border** of Washington State: `waBorder`
- the **zips** with missing information: `allZipNA`
- the **location** of the contributors: `WApoints`.

If we have more than one spatial object, we need layering:

```
> #layers respect the order:
> layerBorder=ggplot(data=waBorder) + theme_void() +
+                                     geom_sf(fill=NA)
> layerMissing=layerBorder + geom_sf(data = allZipNA,
```

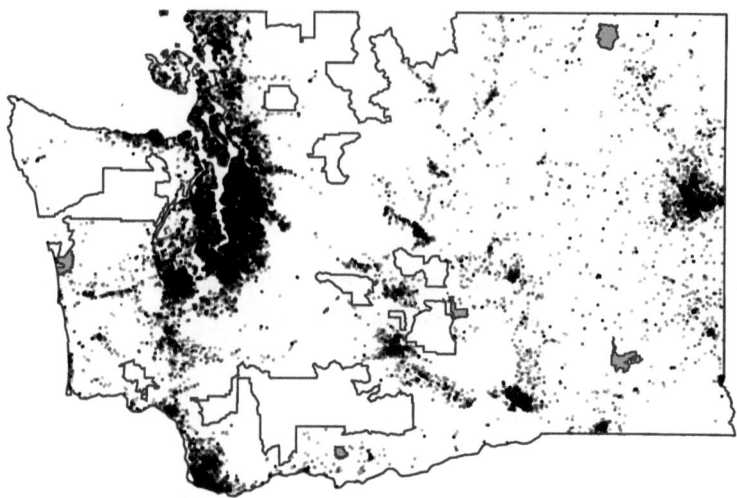

Figure 7.13 Layers

The plot shows a set of points as a layer on top of the border map of Washington State. The original shapefile was downloaded from the Office of Financial Management from Washington State; and the data on contributions were obtained from Washington State portal for open data.

```
+                                    fill='grey')
> layerPoint= layerMissing + geom_sf(data = WApoints,
+                                    size = 0.1,
+                                    color='black',
+                                    alpha=0.1) #transparency
```

As you can see in Figure 7.13, you have a map that combines the information from every layer.

Python with *geopandas* uses the same approach: layering respecting the order of the code:

```
layerBorder= waBorder.plot(edgecolor='grey',color='white')

layerMissing=allZipNA.plot(edgecolor='grey',color='grey',
                           ax=layerBorder)
WApoints.plot(color='black',
              markersize=0.1,alpha=0.1,
              ax=layerBorder) # on top of!)
```

Notice that the argument **ax** is the one which each map uses as the base map. That argument is also used in *geoplot*:

```
layerBorder = gplt.polyplot(waBorder,
                            edgecolor='grey',
                            facecolor='white')
layerMissing = gplt.polyplot(allZipNA,
```

```
                             edgecolor='grey',
                             facecolor='grey',
                             ax=layerBorder)
gplt.pointplot(WApoints,
               color='black',
               s=0.1,#size of point
               alpha=0.1,
               ax=layerBorder)# on top of!
```

7.3.4 Layers and Map Reprojection

Keep in mind that the objects allZipNA and waBorder are "children" of
the original map contriWA, so all of them share the same projection, and
since we used that projection to create the object WApoints, our layered map
layerPoint was perfect. You can get far from perfect results if your layers
do not share the same projection (by default the projection assumed is the one
from the first or base layer). Let me show you how to set or change a projection
on the fly.

In **R**, you only need to add the element coord_sf(), indicating the
projection needed (*Mercator* (Osborne, 2013) in the code below):

```
> layerPointRP= layerPoint +  coord_sf(crs = "+proj=merc")
```

If you know the EPSG, you can alternatively write:

```
> layerPointRP= layerPoint +  coord_sf(crs = st_crs(3857))
```

You can see the result of this reprojection in Figure 7.14.
Geopandas does not offer a simpler alternative, you just need to reproject
every map:

```
layerBorder= waBorder.to_crs("EPSG:3395").plot(edgecolor='grey',
                                               color='white')

layerMissing=allZipNA.to_crs("EPSG:3395").plot(edgecolor='grey',
                                               color='grey',
                                               ax=layerBorder)

WApoints.to_crs("EPSG:3395").plot(color='black',
                                  markersize=0.1,
                                  alpha=0.1,
                                  ax=layerBorder)
```

Geoplot has a simpler way of reprojecting, as it only requires you to
reproject the base layer. See how I do that next, and notice I need the activation
of geoplot.crs first:

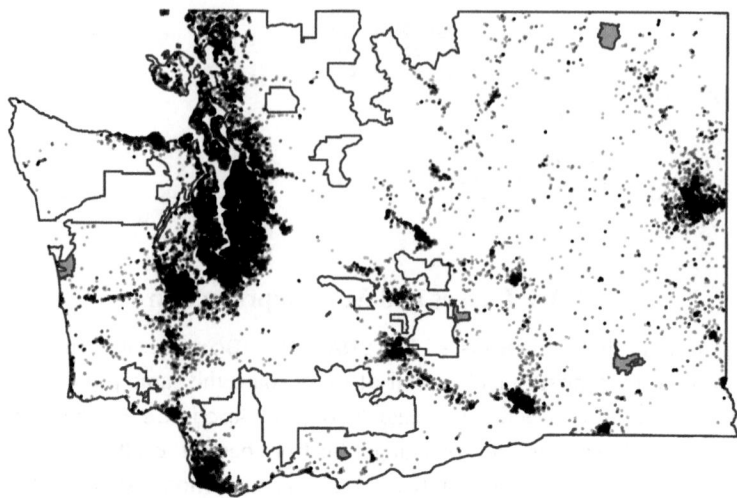

Figure 7.14 Layers reprojected

This is a reprojected representation of Figure 7.13 using the *Mercator* projection. The original shapefile was downloaded from the Office of Financial Management from Washington State; and the data on contributions were obtained from Washington State portal for open data.

```
import geoplot.crs as gcrs #activating!

layerBorder = gplt.polyplot(waBorder,
                            projection=gcrs.Mercator(),#HERE!
                            edgecolor='grey',
                            facecolor='white')

layerMissing = gplt.polyplot(allZipNA,
                             edgecolor='grey',
                             facecolor='grey',
                             ax=layerBorder)
layerPoint= gplt.pointplot(WApoints,
                           color='black',
                           s=0.1,
                           alpha=0.1,
                           ax=layerBorder)# on top of!
```

Notice that the reprojected map got rid of the axis values, so it will be a harder job for the basic user to zoom the reprojected map. Let me talk about this next.

7.3.5 Fixing Projection in Layers

Let me use another map. I have this map of the county borders from Washington State from the *Washington Department of Natural Resource GIS Open Data*. After I downloaded the shapefile from that address, I transformed

```
Simple feature collection with 39 features and 1 field
geometry type:  POLYGON
dimension:      XY
bbox:           xmin: -13899440 ymin: 5707530 xmax: -13014940 ymax: 6275274
epsg (SRID):    4326
proj4string:    +proj=longlat +datum=WGS84 +no_defs
# A tibble: 39 x 2
   JURISDIC_2                                                        geometry
   <chr>                                                       <POLYGON [°]>
 1 Grant       ((-13244144 6097477, -13244380 6097576, -13244493 6097651, -132446…
 2 Lincoln     ((-13173695 6089301, -13173818 6089081, -13173992 6088770, -131741…
 3 Whitman     ((-13028820 5984497, -13029142 5984496, -13029471 5984515, -130308…
```

Figure 7.15 Problem with projected geojson

Original shapefile from the Washington Department of Natural Resource GIS Open Data.

those files into a *geojson* map using *mapshaper* as I had done before. Let me open that version currently in the *GitHub* from this book:

```
> myGit="https://github.com/resourcesbookvisual/data/"
> myGeo2="raw/master/WA_County_Boundaries.json"
> mapLink2=paste0(myGit,myGeo2)
> waCounties=read_sf(mapLink2)
> waCounties[,c("JURISDIC_2")]
```

The previous command should have given you the information shown in Figure 7.15, which tells you the *espg* is the same as we have been using for our previous maps. However, you can clearly see a big problem: the values in the geometries are not right. The previous map used a projection with latitude and longitude coordinates; and, you may know, latitude can take values between 0 and 90 (positive or negative), while longitude can take values between 0 and 180 (positive or negative). As the metadata of the file are corrupt, this will not allow you to use this map with the other ones, even though they are illustrating the same geography.

There may be several sources for this problem in Figure 7.15, but the fact is that the *geojson* file I created from the original shapefile using *mapshaper* has no information on what projection to use, as you can see in Figure 7.16.

When no projection is found, **R** and **Python** will assign the EPSG **4326**. I need to tell **R** the right projection, then I advise a couple of things: You can try a program like *QGIS* (QGIS.org, 2020), which may recognize the geometry and choose the right projection; alternatively, you can check the original website and see some extra information, in my case I checked *metadata* and *source*. I did both things, and found out the EPSG was **3857**, so I reloaded the file using that value:

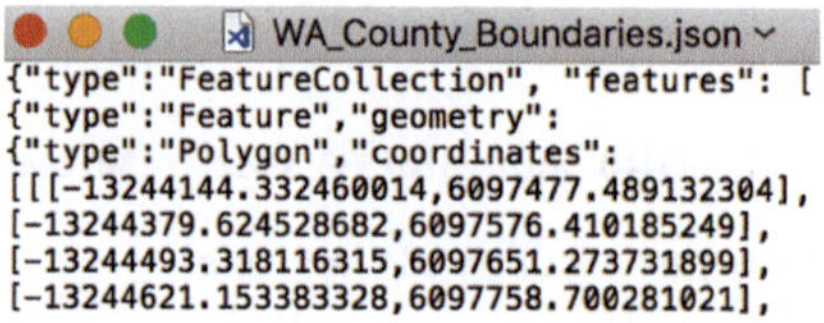

```
●  ●  ●      ⊠  WA_County_Boundaries.json  ⌄
{"type":"FeatureCollection", "features": [
{"type":"Feature","geometry":
{"type":"Polygon","coordinates":
[[[-13244144.332460014,6097477.489132304],
[-13244379.624528682,6097576.410185249],
[-13244493.318116315,6097651.273731899],
[-13244621.153383328,6097758.700281021],
```

Figure 7.16 Contents of geojson file without projection information

Using a simple text editor I opened and found the contents shown, where I confirm no information on projection is given. The original shapefile was downloaded from the Washington Department of Natural Resource GIS Open Data and converted to *geojson* using mapshaper website.

```
> waCounties=read_sf(mapLink2,crs=3857)
```

The previous code worked very well; I got the data in the right projection (pseudo mercator). However, I need to transform this map of counties into the right projection. Let me do that next:

```
> waCounties=st_transform(waCounties, crs=4326)
```

Python will have the same problem, so I will save the reprojected object in **R**, and I will call this file later in **Python** (I will upload a file named waCountiesfromR into the book's *GitHub* and read it from there in Python):

```
> # extension "geojson" is used instead of "json"
> # so the driver for the conversion can be easily assigned.
> st_write(waCounties, "waCountiesfromR.geojson")
```

You may have chosen to keep looking for a map with the right projection, or you can even alter the original geojson file by adding whatever was missing. You can see the reprojected contents of the geojson file in Figure 7.17.

7.4 Focusing on Map Zones

One important operation in any mapping project is zooming. I have some previous maps but now I have the need to focus in a particular area. My intention now is to focus on King County. Since I have the right map, I will keep that county:

```
> kingMap=waCounties[waCounties$JURISDIC_2=="King",]
```

```
● ● ●                    ▨ waCountiesfromR.geojson ⌄
{
"type": "FeatureCollection",
"crs": { "type": "name", "properties": { "name": "urn:ogc:def:crs:OGC:1.3:CRS84" } },
"features": [
{ "type": "Feature", "properties": { "OBJECTID": 2480, "JURISDICT_": 25, "JURISDIC_1":
4, "JURISDIC_2": "Grant", "JURISDIC_3": "Grant County", "JURISDIC_4": 13, "JURISDIC_5":
53025, "JURISDIC_6": "", "EDIT_DATE": "2018/03\14 00:00:00+00", "EDIT_STATU": 1,
"EDIT_WHO": "TSTE490" }, "geometry": { "type": "Polygon", "coordinates":
[ [ [ -118.974172789337629, 47.943602893987752 ], [ -118.97628645395281,
47.944198145095157 ], [ -118.977307780827559, 47.944648627140772 ],
[ -118.978456144569648, 47.945295046129559 ], [ -118.979268314852789,
47.945855190052626 ], [ -118.980329709493873, 47.94675986658887 ],
[ -118.980441581886723, 47.946842866719095 ], [[ -118.980515602977263,
47.946897975348271 ], [ -118.9816420972559, 47.947736641907568 ],
```

Figure 7.17 Contents of geojson file with projection information

Using a simple text editor I opened and found the contents shown, where I confirm the information on projection is given. The original shapefile was downloaded from the Washington Department of Natural Resource GIS Open Data and converted to *geojson* using mapshaper website, the map was then reprojected in **R**.

Remember I did not solve the reprojection in **Python**, so I will use **Python** to call the improved map file I saved in **R**, and keep King County:

```
myGit="https://github.com/resourcesbookvisual/data/"
myGeo2="raw/master/waCountiesfromR.geojson"
mapLink2=myGit + myGeo2

waCounties= gpd.read_file(mapLink2)

kingMap=waCounties[waCounties.JURISDIC_2=="King"]
```

The easiest way to zoom in is to know the limits of the area of interest, also known as the *bounding box*. You can get the bounding box of our King County map with this code:

```
> st_bbox(kingMap)

     xmin        ymin        xmax        ymax
-122.54166   47.08435  -121.06595   47.78058
```

The values above give you coordinates of the diagonal of the box, I will now use those values to zoom in a particular zone of my map in Figure 7.14. Notice that I need to select the right the zoom area using the right indices:

```
> # zooming area:
> forX=st_bbox(kingMap)[c(1,3)] # recovering X range
> forY=st_bbox(kingMap)[c(2,4)] # recovering Y range
> # maps of WASHINGTON
> Border=ggplot(data=waBorder) + theme_classic() +
+                     geom_sf(fill='white')
> Zips=Border + geom_sf(data = wazipMap,fill='grey90')
> Points= Zips + geom_sf(data = WApoints,size = 0.1,color='black',
+                     alpha=0.1) #transparency
> # ZOOMING IN:
> zoomedMap=Points + coord_sf(xlim=forX,ylim = forY)
```

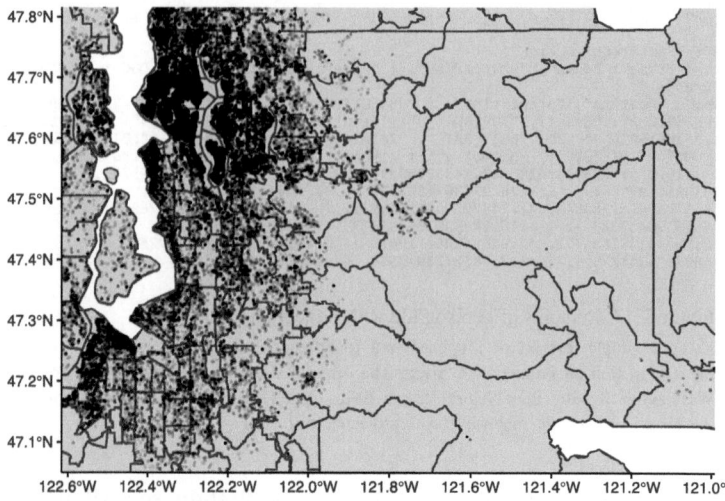

Figure 7.18 Zooming in
The bounding box of one polygon (King County) was used to set the zoom box. The original map of zip codes from Washington State was downloaded from the Office of Financial Management from Washington State, the original map of counties was downloaded from the Washington Department of Natural Resource GIS Open Data and converted to *geojson* using mapshaper website, the map was then reprojected in **R**.

The object `zoomedMap` has zoomed in the information of three map layers, the result is shown in Figure 7.18.

Python needs to use *matplotlib* to produce a zoomed map in an easy way. The alternative in *geopandas* is shown next. Notice I also show you, as a comment, how to alter the size. An important piece of code is the use of `total_bounds` to get the bounding box.

```
import matplotlib.pyplot as plt

fig, ax = plt.subplots() #plt.subplots(figsize=(10,6))
# zooming area:
ax.set_xlim(kingMap.total_bounds[0:4:2]) #recovering indices
ax.set_ylim(kingMap.total_bounds[1:5:2]) #recovering indices
# maps of WASHINGTON
Border= waBorder.plot(edgecolor='grey',color='white',ax=ax)
Zips=wazipMap.plot(edgecolor='silver',color='whitesmoke',ax=Border)
# ZOOMING IN:
WApoints.plot(color='black',markersize=0.1,alpha=0.1,ax=Border)
plt.show()
```

You are now aware of certain spatial operations that help you merge data and maps, and combine maps by layering. These are operations that novice user of spatial information will find easy. Going deeper into these matters will require more formal training on these subjects. Let me now start using the numerical or categorical information in our maps.

7.5 Customizing Color and Size

Let me use the map `allZip`, which already has information from Washington State contributions for the year 2012. I will make a couple of maps using the money contributed. Let me remind you that the map `allZip` has some missing values in columns describing contributions:

```
> sum(is.na(allZip$total))
```

```
[1] 15
```

All those polygons made up the map `allZipNA` which was previously created. Let me subset `allZip` without missing data:

```
> allZip=allZip[complete.cases(allZip$total),]
```

The **Python** version is very similar:

```
allZip=allZip[~allZip.total.isnull()]
```

Let me prepare a couple of maps:

- The first map will represent the amount of money given to Democrat campaigns (see Figure 7.19 panel a) by color intensity:

```
> base =ggplot(data=waBorder) + geom_sf(fill='red') + theme_void()
> forDems =base + geom_sf(data=allZip,aes(fill=DEMOCRAT),color=NA)
> forDems =forDems + guides(fill=FALSE) # no legend
```

The **Python** code in *geopandas* looks like this:

```
Border= waBorder.plot(edgecolor='grey',color='red')
allZip.plot(column='DEMOCRAT',ax=Border)
```

The **Python** code using *geoplot* looks like this:

```
Border = gplt.polyplot(waBorder,
                       edgecolor='grey',
                       facecolor='red')
gplt.choropleth(allZip, hue='DEMOCRAT',ax=Border)
```

- The second map will represent the amount of money given to campaigns in general (see Figure 7.19 panel b) by color intensity:

```
> forALL = base + geom_sf(data=allZip,aes(fill=total),color=NA) +
+                  guides(fill=FALSE)
```

The *geopandas* version can be:

```
Border= waBorder.plot(edgecolor='grey',color='red')
allZip.plot(column='total',ax=Border)
```

A *geoplot* version follows:

```
Border = gplt.polyplot(waBorder,
                       edgecolor='grey',
                       facecolor='red')
gplt.choropleth(allZip, hue='total',ax=Border)
```

Figure 7.19 shows you the result for both of the previous objects.

Notice a couple of things when comparing Figure 7.19 panel a and 7.19 panel b. First, I have used the border map in red, so that you can identify the polygons with missing values; second, and most important, both maps are not very different. They show you "absolute" amounts that are clearly influenced by the size of the population. That is why the coloring of maps requires some thinking in order to produce a **choropleth** map, which represents relative values instead. Let me produce a map of the contributions to Democrats relative to the the total contribution in the zip code (see Figure 7.20):

```
> #new variable:
> allZip$DemChoro=allZip$DEMOCRAT/allZip$total
> #plotting new variable
> choro1 = base + geom_sf(data=allZip,aes(fill = DemChoro),color=NA)
```

The object `choro1` is shown in Figure 7.20. Notice I keep using the same base map, but the coloring is very different.

The code for the object `choro1`in *geopandas* should look familiar:

```
Border= waBorder.plot(edgecolor='grey',color='red')
allZip['DemChoro'] = allZip.DEMOCRAT / allZip.total
allZip.plot(column='DemChoro',legend=True,ax=Border,
            legend_kwds={'shrink': 0.6}) #shrink legend size
```

Notice that the legend for the continuous variable was located off the map. However, the size of the legend may be a little bigger, so I showed you how to resize it using the argument `'shrink'` inside the dictionary `legend_kwds`, which allows further settings for the legend. If you prefer to use *geoplot* in **Python**, you can do this (I will leave the default legend size):

```
Border = gplt.polyplot(waBorder,
                       edgecolor='grey',
                       facecolor='red')
gplt.choropleth(allZip, hue='DemChoro',ax=Border, legend=True)
```

Notice that the process to represent missing values in **Python** was easier than when we tried this on page 207. Also, you should realize by now that while **R** can keep using the `Border` map, once *geopandas* or *geoplot* have used it you need to call it again.

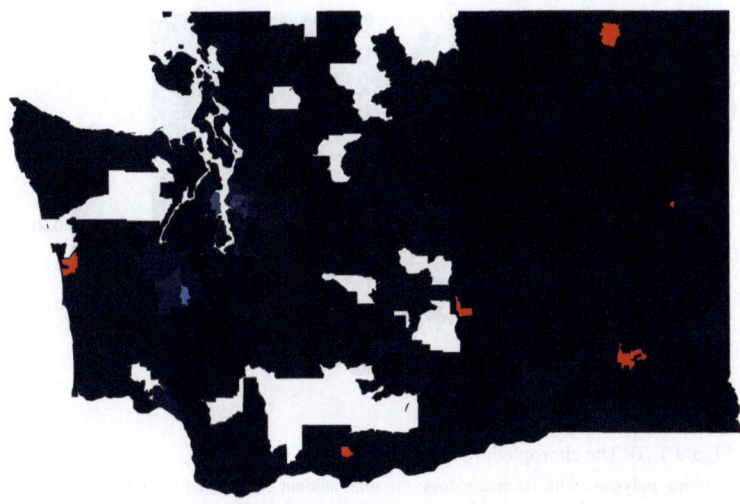

(a) Coloring contributions to democrats

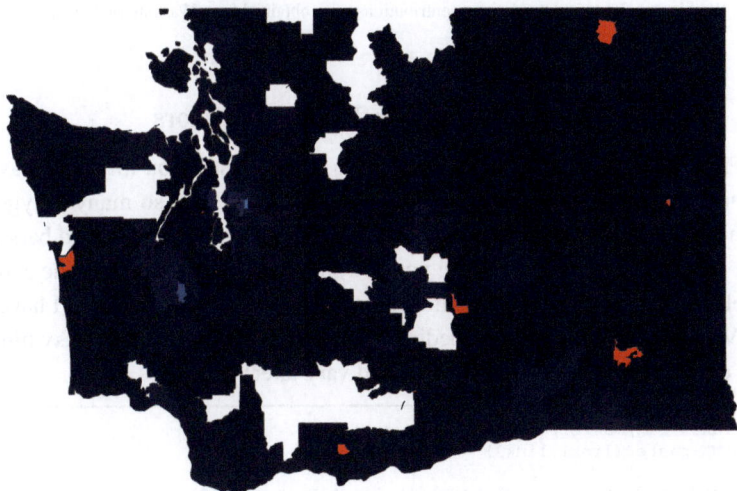

(b) Coloring total contributions

Figure 7.19 Coloring polygons with absolute values

The total amount contributed in the zip code. Polygons with missing information are colored in *red*. The original shapefile was downloaded from the Office of Financial Management from Washington State; and the data on contributions were obtained from Washington State portal for open data

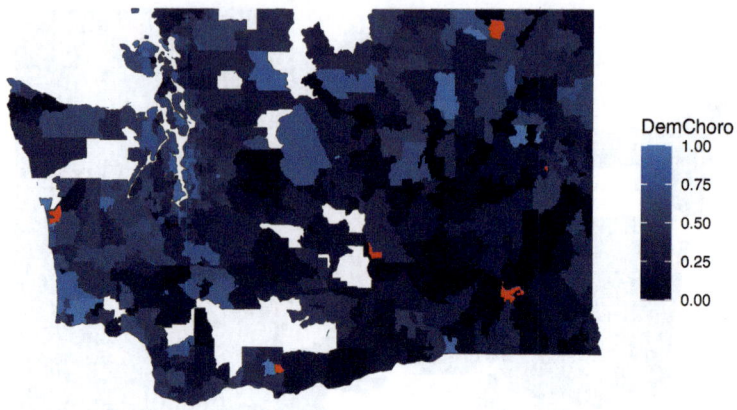

Figure 7.20 The choropleth map

Coloring polygons with relative values: the total amount contributed to Democrats by the total amount contributed in the zip code. Polygons with missing information are colored in *red*. The original shapefile was downloaded from the Office of Financial Management from Washington State; and the data on contributions were obtained from Washington State portal for open data.

7.5.1 Discretizing Values for Colors

In Figure 7.20, we used relative values to plot, but still you might be having a hard time displaying the information because you have so many polygons, with different sizes. This situation is similar to depicting five hundred bars in a plot (maybe harder). Let me take you to a simpler set of polygons at the county level. I am going to add some information to the current county map I have on COVID from wikipedia (Wikipedia, 2020), which I have saved in a csv file for this example (as the data structure could vary later).

```
> link3='raw/master/covidCountyWA.csv'
> LINK=paste0(link1,link3)
> #getting the data TABLE from the file in the cloud:
> covid=read.csv(file=url(LINK),stringsAsFactors = F)
> #first rows:
> head(covid)
```

```
   County Cases Deaths Recov Population CasesPer100k
1   Adams   134      0    45      19983        650.6
2  Asotin    21      2    NA      22582         93.0
3  Benton  1731     82    NA     204390        824.9
4  Chelan   330      6    NA      77200        408.0
5 Clallam    36      0    19      77331         46.6
6   Clark   731     30    NA     488241        142.8
```

As you see, the column candidate to be colored in the next choropleth is `CasesPer100k`. First let me do the merge:

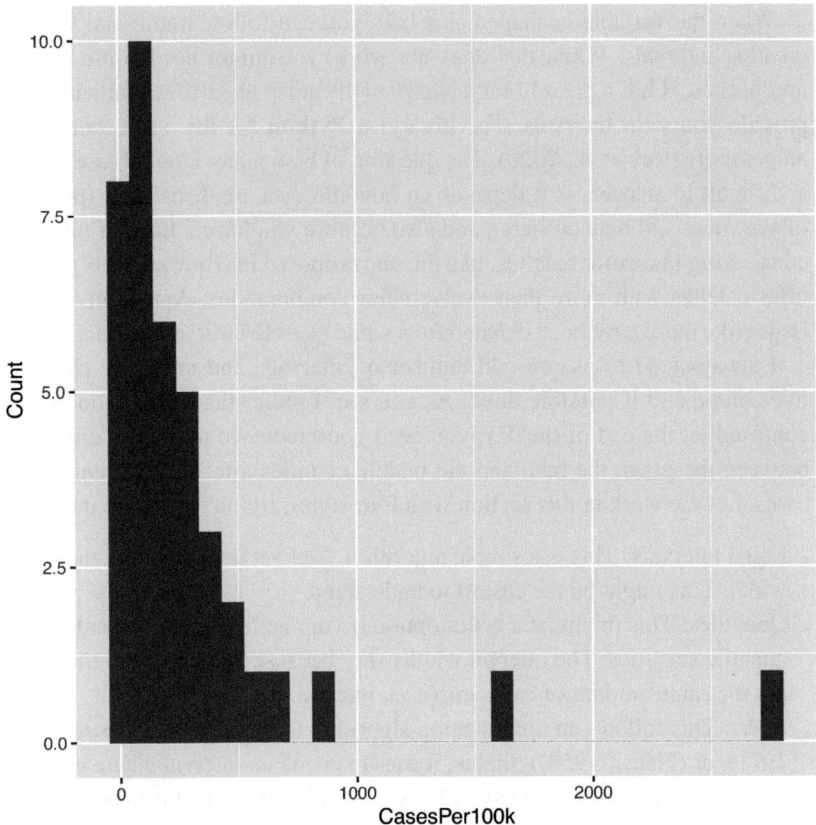

Figure 7.21 Exploring the distribution of cases per one hundred thousand people
This is needed to decide the way intervals will be created. The original data comes from (Wikipedia, 2020).

```
> covidMap=merge(waCounties[,c("JURISDIC_2")],covid,
+                by.x="JURISDIC_2",by.y="County")
```

When preparing Figure 7.20, I did not customize the colors or the amount of intervals. The first step in this process is to explore the variable to plot. With this simple code, I can produce a histogram.

```
> explore1=ggplot(covidMap,aes(CasesPer100k)) + geom_histogram()
```

The object `explore1` can be seen in Figure 7.21. Notice that it is positively skewed.

When the variable is shaped as a bell, you can follow traditional ways of creating intervals. When this does not work, you might need some modern approaches. **R** has a great library, *classInt* (Bivand et al., 2020), that will easily provide you with intervals. The library in **Python** for this same purpose is *mapclassify* (Rey et al., 2020). The question of how many intervals are needed is difficult to answer, as it depends on how the data are distributed (presence of skewness and data outliers), and also because you have a limit of intervals, considering that color palettes, like the one proposed in (Brewer, 1999), do not offer palettes with more than twelve color combinations. Apparently simple issues like these have been debated for a while (see (Brewer and Pickle, 2002)).

I always tend to use an odd number of intervals, and my usual choice is five colors, and if possible three. As you see, I prefer that readers do not get confused; at the end of the day, you need your audience to see the difference between the good, the bad, and the middle counties affected by a number of cases. Let me work in this section with four styles, trying to get five intervals:

- Equal intervals: This is a simple algorithm. You get intervals with the same width. This might be the easiest to understand.
- Quantiles: This might be a better option if your audience understands quantile statistics. The interval widths vary because the algorithm tries to put the same amount of cases into each interval.
- Jenks: This follows an optimization algorithm (see (Jenks and Caspall, 1971), or (Fisher, 1958)); that is, it tries to create an interval where it considers there is more density of cases, so it looks for an intrinsic grouping.
- Head-Tails: This is also an optimization algorithm, but it is more suitable for distributions with long tails (Jiang, 2013). In this style, you do not have to request the amount of intervals, the algorithm decides that.

Let me show you the steps for the *equal* style in **R**, which will be similar for the others:

1. Select variable:

```
> varToPlot=covidMap$CasesPer100k
```

2. Activate the library, and get the break points using the selected *style*. Notice that I need to request **brks** at the end here:

```
> library(classInt)
> cutEqual=classIntervals(varToPlot,n = 5,style = "equal")$brks
```

3. Create a categorical variable from numeric variable. The previous step will allow you to get the break points, which will be used to cut the numeric

variable. Notice I have selected, obviously for this case, that the output is an ordinal variable:

```
> covidMap$cases_Equal=cut(varToPlot, breaks = cutEqual,
+                          dig.lab=5, # digits to use in legend
+                          include.lowest = T,ordered_result = T)
```

4. By default, the function `cut` will write the values in each interval separated by a comma, here I change it to a dash and spaces:

```
> levels(covidMap$cases_Equal)=gsub(",", " - ", #substituting
+                                   levels(covidMap$cases_Equal))
```

5. The ordinal palettes can be divergent or sequential, as discussed in Section 3.1.3 (read from page 36). Let me choose a sequential one:

```
> colorPal="OrRd"
```

6. Prepare the object to plot:

```
> base= ggplot(covidMap) + theme_light()
> choro2=base + geom_sf(aes(fill=cases_Equal))
> choro2=choro2+scale_fill_brewer(palette = colorPal,direction=1)
```

The variable `rate_Equal` is ready. You will soon realize that, as it can happen in the *equal* style, one interval has no cases. Now let me follow the same steps to get the intervals using the quantile style:

```
> # get intervals
> cutQuant=classIntervals(varToPlot,n = 5,style = "quantile")$brks
> #create variable
> covidMap$cases_Quant=cut(varToPlot, cutQuant,dig.lab=5,
+                          include.lowest = T,ordered_result = T)
> #change separator
> levels(covidMap$cases_Quant)=gsub(",", " - ",
+                                   levels(covidMap$cases_Quant))
> #prepare object
> base= ggplot(covidMap) + theme_light()
> choro3=base + geom_sf(aes(fill=cases_Quant))
> choro3=choro3+scale_fill_brewer(palette = colorPal,direction=1)
```

You can see the objects `choro2` and `choro3` in Figure 7.22.

In **Python**, *geopandas* is connected to the `mapclassify` library, so once it is loaded, the steps are simple, as you just need to fill in the parameters requested by the function, without the need to create new columns as I did in **R**.[7]

---

[7] Notice that the legend requested appears on top of the plot, I will show you how to improve that in Subsection 7.5.2.

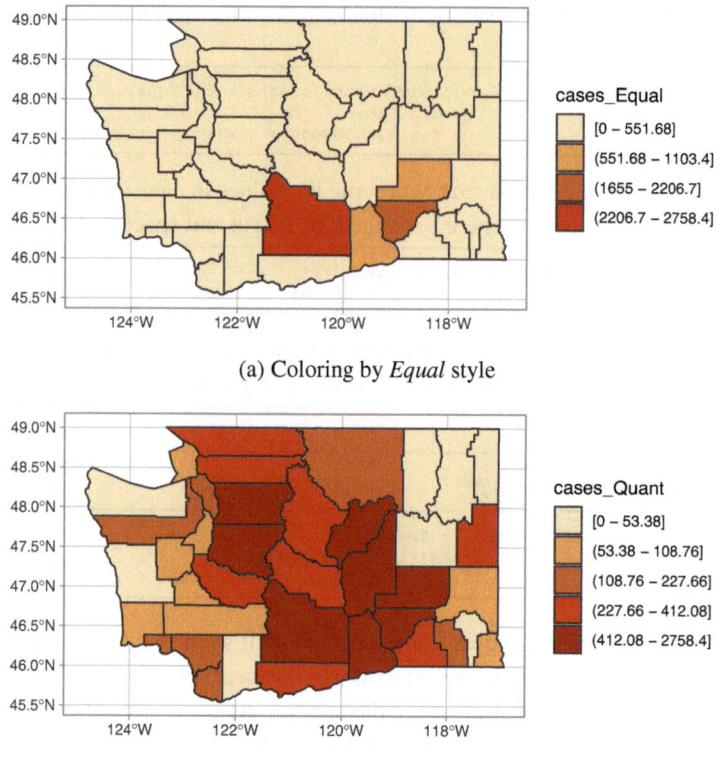

(a) Coloring by *Equal* style

(b) Coloring by *Quantile* style

Figure 7.22 Coloring polygons with traditional styles

The variable used has been rate of Covid positives per 100,000 habitants. Five intervals were
requested, but the **equal** option produced only four, because one interval had zero cases. The
palette used is sequential and named as *OrRd*. The palette has been recommended (Brewer,
1999); the map was downloaded from the Washington Department of Natural Resource GIS
Open Data, and includes the data on COVID from (Wikipedia, 2020).

```
import mapclassify as mc

#well-known styles
#geopandas for Equal intervals
covidMap.plot(column='CasesPer100k',
              scheme='EqualInterval',
              k=5,
              cmap='OrRd',
              legend=True)
#%%
#geopandas for Quantiles
covidMap.plot(column='CasesPer100k',
              scheme='Quantiles',
              k=5,
              cmap='OrRd',
              legend=True)
```

You can also use *geoplot*, which also reads the `mapclassify` output, but it does require you to call it explicitly (like using `mc.EqualInterval` where you also indicate how many cuts are needed).

```
#well-known styles
#geoplot for Equal intervals
gplt.choropleth(covidMap,
                hue='CasesPer100k',
                scheme=mc.EqualInterval(covidMap.CasesPer100k,k=5),
                cmap='OrRd',
                legend=True)
#%%
#geoplot for Quantiles
gplt.choropleth(covidMap,
                hue='CasesPer100k',
                scheme=mc.Quantiles(covidMap.CasesPer100k, k=5),
                cmap='OrRd',
                legend=True)
```

Remember that once you know which color palette is the right one, you can reverse the color if needed. In **R**, you need to change from 1 to -1 in the `direction` argument of `scale_fill_brewer`; while in **Python**, you just append `_r`, for example, the palettes previously used can be reversed if you just write `OrRd_r` instead.

Let me prepare the plots with the intervals created using the optimization alternatives. Let me create the variables first:

```
> # get intervals
> cutJenks=classIntervals(varToPlot,n = 5,style = "jenks")$brks
> cutHT=classIntervals(varToPlot,style = "headtails")$brks
> #create variable
> covidMap$cases_Jenks=cut(varToPlot, cutJenks,dig.lab=5,
+                     include.lowest = T,ordered_result = T)
> covidMap$cases_HT=cut(varToPlot, cutHT,dig.lab=5,
+                     include.lowest = T,ordered_result = T)
> #change separator of intervals (better legend)
> levels(covidMap$cases_Jenks)=gsub(","," - ",
+                                 levels(covidMap$cases_Jenks))
> levels(covidMap$cases_HT)=gsub(","," - ",
+                                 levels(covidMap$cases_HT))
```

Now let me plot both variables (see the result in Figure 7.23):

```
> #prepare object to plot
> base= ggplot(covidMap) + theme_light()
> #for Jenks
> choro4=base + geom_sf(aes(fill=cases_Jenks))
> choro4=choro4+scale_fill_brewer(palette = colorPal,direction=1)
> #for Head-Tails
> choro5=base + geom_sf(aes(fill=cases_HT))
> choro5=choro5+scale_fill_brewer(palette = colorPal,direction=1)
```

The **Python** alternative follows in *geopandas*, simply using *mapclassify* as before:

```
#optimization styles in geopandas
covidMap.plot(column='CasesPer100k',
```

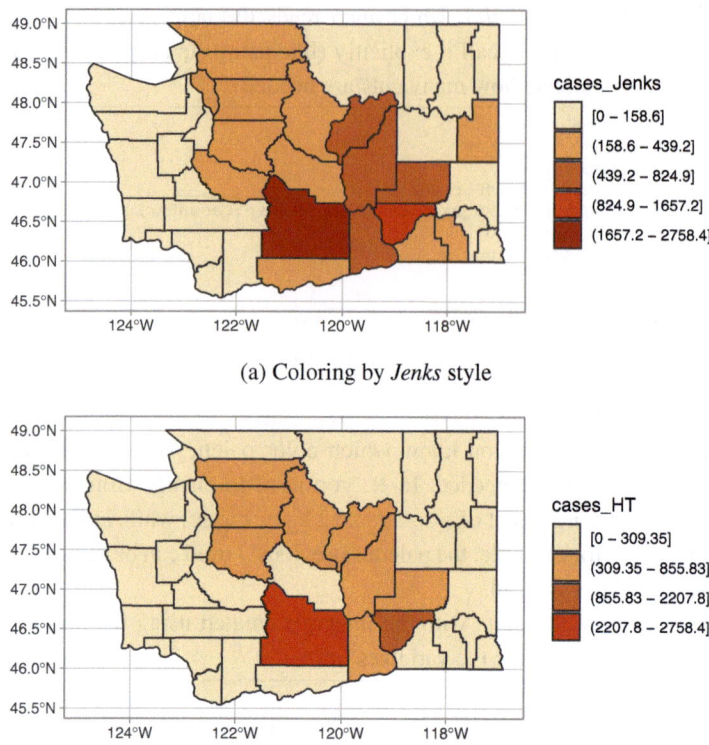

(a) Coloring by *Jenks* style

(b) Coloring by *Head-Tail* style

Figure 7.23 Coloring polygons with optimization styles

The variable used has been rate of Covid positives per 100,000 habitants. The palette used is sequential and named as *OrRd*. The palette has been recommended (Brewer, 1999); the map was downloaded from the Washington Department of Natural Resource GIS Open Data, and includes the data on COVID from (Wikipedia, 2020).

```
                scheme='FisherJenks',
                k=5,
                cmap='OrRd',
                legend=True)
#%%
covidMap.plot(column='CasesPer100k',
                scheme='HeadTailBreaks',
                cmap='OrRd',
                legend=True)
```

Similarly, this is the alternative version using *geoplot*:

```
#optimization styles in geoplot
gplt.choropleth(covidMap,
                hue='CasesPer100k',
                scheme=mc.FisherJenks(covidMap.CasesPer100k, k=5),
```

```
                        cmap='OrRd',
                        legend=True)
#%%
gplt.choropleth(covidMap,
                        hue='CasesPer100k',
                        scheme=mc.HeadTailBreaks(covidMap.CasesPer100k),
                        cmap='OrRd',
                        legend=True)
```

So far, I have used one variable. The next logical step would be a two-variable approach.

7.5.2 Color and Area

Color and area are not the best way to encode information. However, maps are a familiar visual whose readers are expect to see color, so the material covered in this section should be useful. Size is not a familiar attribute people expect, beyond experts familiar with this.

A first condition for resizing the polygon that might not seem obvious, is making sure you have a projected map. If your map is in latitude/longitude projection, it is actually unprojected. It is your task to look for a suitable projection to the map you have. In this case, I will turn my lon-lat into mercator again:

```
> library(sf)
> covidMap_reprj=st_transform(covidMap,3857) #mercator
```

Let me create a variable based on deaths and population:

```
> newDeathVals=100000*(covidMap_reprj$Deaths/covidMap_reprj$Population)
> covidMap_reprj$DeathsPer100k=newDeathVals
> varToCut=covidMap_reprj$DeathsPer100k
> cutEqualDeath=classIntervals(varToCut,
+                              n = 3,
+                              style = "equal")$brks
> #create variable
> covidMap_reprj$death_equal=cut(varToCut,
+                                cutEqualDeath,dig.lab=5,
+                                include.lowest = T,
+                                ordered_result = T)
> #change separator
> levels(covidMap_reprj$death_equal)=gsub(","," - ",
+                                levels(covidMap_reprj$death_equal))
```

In **Python**, I will simply create the new variable.

```
#new variable
valuesNew=100000*(covidMap.Deaths/covidMap.Population)
covidMap['DeathsPer100k']=valuesNew
```

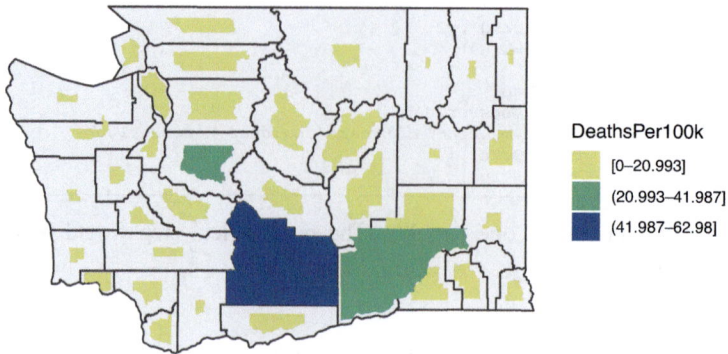

Figure 7.24 Changing polygon sizes via cartogram

The size of the polygon depends on the rate of cases per 100,000 habitants, and the color represents the rate of deaths per one-hundred thousand habitants. The original data comes from (Wikipedia, 2020).

Then, I will first use the variable `CasesPer100k` to alter the area of the polygon, while ensuring that the biggest value in the data should keep the same size with `k=1`. This new visual will be known as *cartogram*:

```
> library(cartogram)
> cartoCases=cartogram_ncont(covidMap_reprj,
+                            weight = "CasesPer100k", #var for resize
+                            k=1) #expansion limit
```

Let me use the object `covidMap_reprj` to plot my two variables, `DeathsPer100k` and `CasesPer100k`, represented by color and size, respectively:

```
> border=ggplot(covidMap_reprj) + geom_sf(fill="grey95") +
+        theme_void()
> cartogram=border+ geom_sf(data=cartoCases, #size
+                          aes(fill=death_equal),
+                          color=NA) #no border
> cartogram=cartogram+scale_fill_brewer(palette='YlGnBu',
+                                        direction=1,
+                                        name="DeathsPer100k")
```

The object `cartogram` will be shown in Figure 7.24.

In **Python**, *geoplot* can produce cartograms while reprojecting at the same time:

```
import geoplot.crs as gcrs #activating!

#border
border=gplt.polyplot(df=covidMap,
                     projection=gcrs.Mercator(), #reproject
```

```
                    edgecolor='gray', #border
                    facecolor='gainsboro') #fill of polygon
#area and color
gplt.cartogram(df=covidMap, #map
               scheme=mc.EqualInterval(covidMap.DeathsPer100k,k=3),
               cmap=plt.get_cmap('YlGnBu',3),#palette
               hue="DeathsPer100k", #var for color
               scale='CasesPer100k',#var for resize
               limits=(0.3, 1),  #limits cartogram polygons
               edgecolor='None', #no border
               legend=True,
               legend_var='hue', #legend of what
               legend_kwargs={'bbox_to_anchor': (0.1, 0.4),#location
                              'frameon': True, #with frame?
                              'markeredgecolor':'k',
                              'title':"DeathsPer100k"},
               ax=border)
```

The code in **Python** plots the cartogram on top of the basic map (unaltered). I am using more arguments for the legend this time so it looks better than in previous plots. When I requested legend for the plots with intervals, legends were drawn on the plot, covering some areas of the map. *Geoplot* has the argument `legend_kwargs` that allows you to move the legend around. For that, it uses a dictionary to set up several values; where the most important for this case is `bbox_to_anchor`. If you want the legend at the bottom to the left you use the tuple (0,0), and if you want the legend at the top to the left you use the tuple (1,1); of course, you can vary those values to move it around.

If you want to combine area and color, you do not need to use a cartogram but a simple option such as a symbol, like a dot, to represent size and color. I do not have a spatial point for my current map of counties, but I will get a point for each by calculating the *centroid* in each polygon. In **R**, you use `st_centroid()` to get the centroids. See the code:

```
> base=ggplot(covidMap_reprj) +
+       geom_sf(color='grey50') + theme_void()
> pointSize=base + geom_sf(data=st_centroid(covidMap_reprj),
+                          aes(fill=death_equal, #color
+                              size=CasesPer100k), #size
+                          pch=21) #shape of dot
> pointSize=pointSize+scale_color_brewer(palette='YlGnBu',
+                                        direction=1,
+                                        name="DeathsPer100k")
```

Figure 7.25 might be an easier visual to digest than a cartogram.

I can get a similar result in **Python**, but *geoplot* does not offer an option to plot two legends; you have to choose what the only legend possible represents using the argument `legend_var`. *Geoplot* needs two steps to plot the centroids. First, you need to create a column with the centroids, and then you set that column as the geometry of the map:

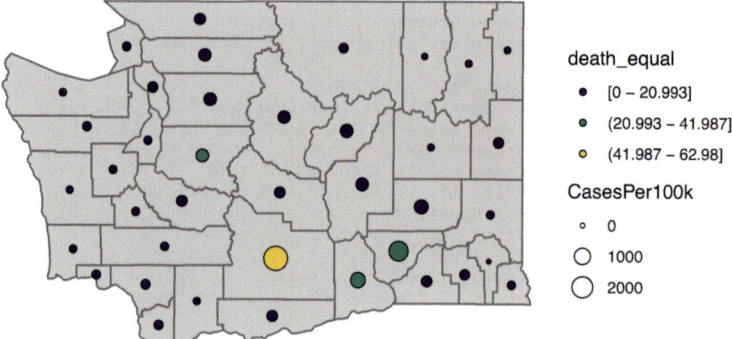

Figure 7.25 Changing polygon sizes via cartogram

Exploring the distribution on cases per one hundred thousand people. The original data comes from (Wikipedia, 2020).

```
import geoplot.crs as gcrs #activating!

#borders
countyBorders = gplt.polyplot(df=covidMap,
                        projection=gcrs.Mercator(),#HERE!
                        edgecolor='grey',
                        facecolor='gainsboro')

#points scaled
covidMap['centroid']=covidMap.centroid #compute centroids
gplt.pointplot(df=covidMap.set_geometry('centroid'), #set geometry
            scheme=mc.EqualInterval(covidMap.DeathsPer100k,k=3),
            cmap='YlGnBu',#palette
            hue="DeathsPer100k",
            scale='CasesPer100k', #sizes of points
            limits=(4, 40), #range for sizes of points
            legend=True,
            legend_var='hue',
            legend_kwargs={'bbox_to_anchor': (1, 1),
                        'frameon': True,
                        'markeredgecolor':'k',
                        'title':"DeathsPer100k"},
            extent = covidMap.total_bounds,
            ax=countyBorders)
plt.show()
```

Notice I have added the argument extent. This is important for this particular case to make sure both maps fit well together by setting the extent of the map with the value total_bounds, an attribute of covidMap.

You can also use color and shapes to identify where a set of points are denser than in other places, which also receives the name of *heatmap*; we have previously created those using frequency tables. Let me use the spatial points I have for the people contributing to campaigns to show you this. A simple and direct version can be:

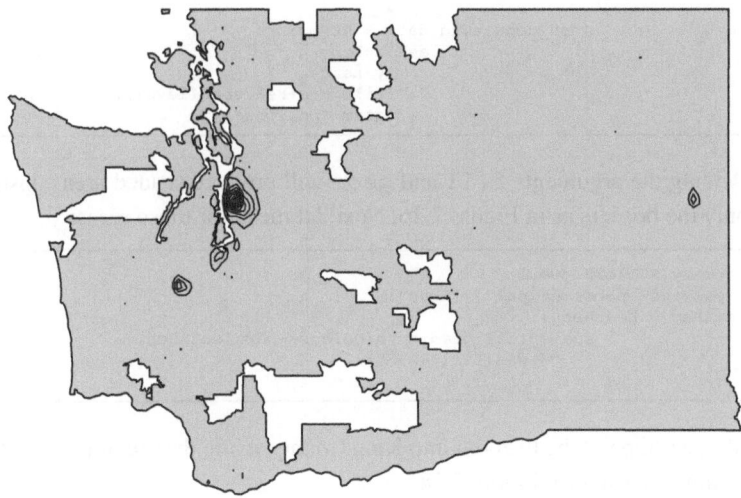

Figure 7.26 Basic spatial heatmap

Exploring the distribution of contributions to political campaign of the year 2012. The data on contributions was obtained from Washington State portal for open data.

```
> border=ggplot(data = waBorder) + geom_sf() + theme_void()
> heat=border+geom_density_2d(data = WApoints,
+                                   aes(x=Lon,y=Lat))
```

The object `heat` is represented in Figure 7.26.

The code for **Python** to obtain a similar result may look like this:

```
counties=gplt.polyplot(waCounties,edgecolor= 'silver')

gplt.kdeplot(WApoints,
             shade=False,
             shade_lowest=False,
             ax=counties)
```

Let me try several things using my points on contributors. First, let me split my points by party:

```
> REPpoints=WApoints[WApoints$party=="REPUBLICAN",]
> DEMpoints=WApoints[WApoints$party=="DEMOCRAT",]
```

Let me prepare a similar plot to Figure 7.26, but only for the contributions to Republicans:

```
> base= ggplot(data = waCounties) + theme_void()
> counties = base + geom_sf(fill=NA)
> heatRep = counties +
```

```
+                stat_density2d(data = REPpoints,
+                               aes(x=Lon,
+                                    y=Lat,
+                                    fill = after_stat(level)),
+                               geom="polygon")
```

Adding the arguments `fill` and `geom` will produce shaded areas, instead of only the borders as in Figure 7.26. Next, let me color those areas:

```
> library(RColorBrewer)
> kdpaletteRep=brewer.pal(7,"Reds")
> heatRep = heatRep +
+            scale_fill_gradientn(colours=kdpaletteRep) +
+              guides(fill=FALSE)
>
```

My last step will be to zoom into King County, using the previous bounding box limits we used for Figure 7.18:

```
> heatRepKing = heatRep + coord_sf(xlim=forX, ylim = forY)
```

I can use the same steps to produce the map of contributors for the Democrat Party campaign:

```
> #colors
> kdpaletteDem=brewer.pal(7,"Blues")
> heatDem = counties +
+            stat_density2d(data = DEMpoints,
+                           aes(x=Lon,
+                                y=Lat,
+                                fill = after_stat(level)),
+                           geom="polygon")
> heatDem= heatDem +
+            scale_fill_gradientn(colours=kdpaletteDem) +
+              guides(fill=FALSE)
> heatDemKing = heatDem + coord_sf(xlim=forX, ylim = forY)
```

The maps `heatDemKing` and `heatRepKing` are shown in Figure 7.27. The code to produce the `heatRepKing` in **Python** follows:

```
counties=gplt.polyplot(waCounties,edgecolor= 'black',
                       projection=gcrs.Mercator())#reproject)

gplt.kdeplot(WApoints[WApoints.party=='REPUBLICAN'], #subset
             shade=True,
             cmap='Reds',
             shade_lowest=False,
             ax=counties,
             extent=kingMap.total_bounds)
```

And, the code to produce the `heatDemKing` in **Python** follows:

```
counties=gplt.polyplot(waCounties,edgecolor= 'black',
                       projection=gcrs.Mercator())#reproject)
```

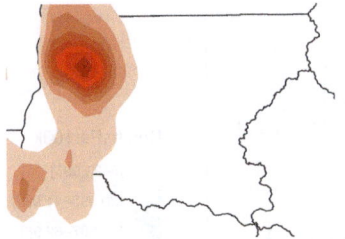

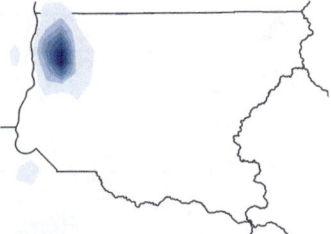

(a) Heatplot-Contributions to Republicans.

(b) Heatplot-Contributions to Democrats.

Figure 7.27 Heatplots

```
gplt.kdeplot(WApoints[WApoints.party=='DEMOCRAT'], #subset
             shade=True,
             cmap='Blues',
             shade_lowest=False,
             ax=counties,
             extent=kingMap.total_bounds)
```

7.5.3 Final Touches

Let me pick the Figure 7.24. You have the map and the legend, but it is good practice to add some elements when mapping. First, you should consider adding caption explaining the projection you used:

```
> creditsText="EPSG:3857\nProj=Mercator"
> cartoCap=cartogram + labs(caption = creditsText)
```

Another element you should include is the *scalebar*. The easy way to add one is by using the library *ggspatial* (Dunnington, 2020).

```
> library(ggspatial)
> cartoCapSca=cartoCap +
+           annotation_scale(location = "bl", #'tr', etc.
+                            width_hint = 0.2,#size related ti plot
+                            plot_unit = 'mi',#or: 'km','ft', etc.
+                            unit_category='imperial', #or 'metric'
+                            style='ticks') # or 'bar'
```

I added familiar alternatives to the scale bar next to each argument of the function. Notice that for location you can combine *bottom* or *top* with *left* or *right* (no "middle" option) using the first letter of each word. A final element to include should be the *north arrow*, which is also facilitated by *ggspatial*:

```
> cartoCapScaNorth=cartoCapSca +
+           annotation_north_arrow(location = "tl",
```

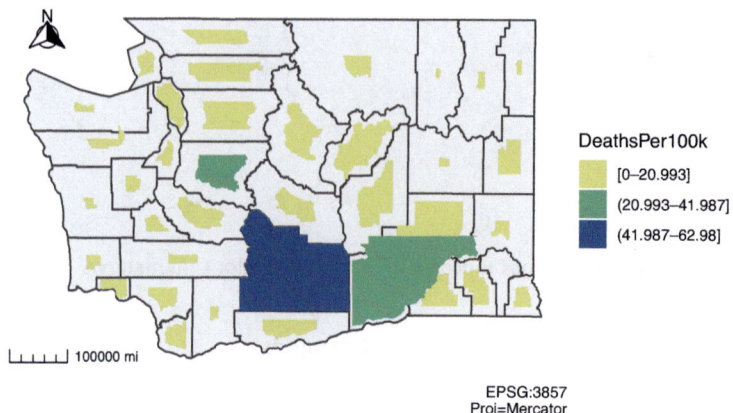

Figure 7.28 Map and its elements
Based on Figure 7.24, this plot is adding other elements: information about projections, scalebar, and north arrow. The elements were added using *ggspatial* (Dunnington, 2020). The original data comes from (Wikipedia, 2020).

```
+                        style = north_arrow_fancy_orienteering,
+                        height = unit(0.3, "in"))
```

The style of the north arrow requires a function to draw it, so do not write the style in quotations (the other basic option can be `north_arrow_minimal`; a more decorative can be `north_arrow_nautical`; you also have `north_arrow_orienteering`). You can see the final result, the object `cartoCapScaNorth`, in Figure 7.28.

In **Python**, neither *geopandas* nor *geoplot* offer simple ways to add the north arrow or the scale bar, but it is a feature suggested in their online forums. The discussion on how to do this just using *matplotlib* is directed to people with more expertise on geography. If you are an advanced user, you may try exploring how to add a scale bar by installing and using *matplotlib-scalebar* (Pinard, 2020), or by exploring the `AnchoredSizeBar` in *matplotlib*. For the north arrow, you can try the annotate function from *matplotlib*:

```
fig, ax = plt.subplots(figsize=(10, 10))
gplt.choropleth(covidMap,
            hue='CasesPer100k',
            scheme=mc.HeadTailBreaks(covidMap.CasesPer100k),
            cmap='OrRd',
            legend=True,
            legend_kwargs={'bbox_to_anchor': (1, 1),
                          'frameon': True,
                          'markeredgecolor':'k',
                          'title':"DeathsPer100k"},
            extent = covidMap.total_bounds,
```

```
                    ax=ax)

x, y, arrow_length = 0, 0.3, 0.3
ax.annotate('N', xy=(x, y),
            xytext=(x, y-arrow_length),
            arrowprops=dict(facecolor='black',
                            width=5,
                            headwidth=15),
            ha='center', va='center', fontsize=20,
            xycoords=ax.transAxes)
plt.show()
```

8

Data from the Social Network

In this final chapter, I will briefly pay attention to the social network. I am sorry for using this term to attract your attention, as it might mean several things to you, such as online news, Twitter, Facebook, YouTube, and the like. The fact is that each of these services has a particular policy to grant access to the data. I will not deal with this variety, as there are interesting and detailed books to guide you on this process, such as Russell and Klassen (2019).

For the sake of simplicity, or oversimplicity, let me use Twitter data to discuss the visualizations in this case. Twitter similar steps to other to allow you access to the data they keep:

- Create a developer account. You will need to apply for this and get approved. This permission may take some time (minutes, or even days).
- Register an **APP**lication that will access the Twitter data.
- Get the credentials that allow your code to interact with Twitter.

The creation of the process is documented by Twitter[1], and the steps are the same if you are in **R** or **Python**. However, there is more than one library in those languages to carry out this interaction, so I had to decide which one to use in my code. In **R**, I have used **rtweet** (Kearney et al., 2020); and for **Python**, I have used **tweepy** (Hill and Roesslein, 2020).

Every time you want to get information from a particular social web application, you may need to do some research and decide which library is more reliable and active. You may need to be very careful at this point, as the policies to access data change from time to time in these services, and some examples you could find while surfing the web might not work any more. The libraries I have chosen to collect the data are currently active (as of mid-2020),

[1] https://cran.r-project.org/web/packages/rtweet/vignettes/auth.html

but if something is not working by the time you read this book might be due to changes in the policies in Twitter, for this case.

8.1 Getting Access

If your account as developer was approved, then you can simply copy and paste the *credentials* of your application. When using `rtweet` in **R**, you can use this code to create a token (a file) in your computer that will always be read by the `rtweet` functions:

```
> library(rtweet)
> # your credential in quotations:
> api_key = "write__yours__here"
> api_secret_key = "write__yours__here"
> access_token = "write__yours__here"
> access_token_secret = "write__yours__here"
> # creating the token (this creates a file in your computer)
> token = create_token(app = "bookVisual",
+                       consumer_key = api_key,
+                       consumer_secret = api_secret_key,
+                       access_token = access_token,
+                       access_secret = access_token_secret,)
```

In **Python**, I decided a different strategy. I created a text file with my access information formatted as a dict, then I just read the file and use the information there:

```
import json
import tweepy

# your credentials as a dictionary in a text file:
keysAPI = json.load(open('keysAPI.txt','r'))
api_key = keysAPI['consumer_key']
api_secret_key = keysAPI['consumer_secret']
access_token = keysAPI['access_token']
access_token_secret = keysAPI['access_token_secret']

# authorizing your application:
auth = tweepy.OAuthHandler(api_key, api_secret_key)
auth.set_access_token(access_token, access_token_secret)

# some extra attributes
api=tweepy.API(auth,
               retry_count=3,
               timeout=600,
               wait_on_rate_limit=True,
               wait_on_rate_limit_notify=True,
               parser=tweepy.parsers.JSONParser())
```

The **Python** option has similar code, but it has a piece of code at the end specifying what to do when you reach the time limit Twitter gives you. Also, you tell your API to collect the data into a dict structure in the `parser` option (via `JSONParser()`). The library `rtweet` does work like this, the "waiting" capability is available only in some functions (you will need to create more code for "waiting"). Remember that `rtweet` will return a data frame, as dicts are not supported in **R**, while you will get a dictionary in **Python**.

I have previously taken the time to organise a data frame with the Twitter accounts of the presidents or heads of government/state of the Americas (North, Central, South and the Caribbean), take a look:

```
> link1="https://github.com/resourcesbookvisual/data"
> link2="/raw/master/PresidentsTwitter.xlsx"
> LINK=paste0(link1,link2)
> library(rio)
> twusers=import(LINK)
> # check first two columns
> head(twusers[,c(1,2)])
```

```
          twitter                    country
1 MartinVizcarraC                    Per\'{u}
2 realDonaldTrump United States of America
3   JustinTrudeau                     Canada
4        SkerritR                   Dominica
5     chansantokhi                    Surinam
6   DrKeithRowley        Trinidad y Tobago
```

I can also upload the file in **Python**:

```
import pandas as pd

link1="https://github.com/resourcesbookvisual/data"
link2="/raw/master/PresidentsTwitter.xlsx"
LINK=link1 + link2

twusers=pd.read_excel(LINK)
```

You may need a different list when you read this book, but the strategy will be the same.

8.2 Getting Texts

Using the data from `twusers`, let me get the *Tweets* from *Donald Trump*.

```
> library(rtweet)
> trumpTweets = get_timeline("realDonaldTrump", n = 2)
```

The function `get_timeline` will bring at most two hundred recent tweets. You will get a *tibble* which I will just turn into a basic data frame. You will get several columns, but I will just select some:

```
> selection=c("created_at",
+             "text",
+             "is_retweet",
+             "favorite_count",
+             "retweet_count")
> trumpDF=as.data.frame(trumpTweets[,selection])
```

The column `created_at` includes *date* and *time*; if you want to create separate fields for this column, you can consider doing that with the help of *lubridate* (Grolemund and Wickham, 2011). Notice that using `wday()` function as it is will assign Sunday as the number **1** and Saturday as number **7**:[2]

```
> library(lubridate)
> trumpDF$Date=date(trumpDF$created_at)
> trumpDF$Hour=hour(trumpDF$created_at)
> trumpDF$Day=wday(trumpDF$created_at)
> #saving the selected info:
> write.csv(trumpDF,"trumps.csv",row.names = F)
```

Python will load its `trumpTweets` as a dict, which follows a structure similar to a tweet. Let me turn my dict into a data frame, so I will get the the data frame `trumpDF` like I did in R[3]:

```
# get timeline
who='realDonaldTrump'
trumpTweets = api.user_timeline(screen_name = who,
                                count = 2,
                                tweet_mode="extended")
# create data frame
dates=[t['created_at'] for t in trumpTweets]
text=[t['full_text'] for t in trumpTweets]
likes=[t['favorite_count'] for t in trumpTweets]
rts=[t['retweet_count'] for t in trumpTweets]

trumpDF=pd.DataFrame({'created_at':dates,
                      'text':text,
                      'retweet_count':rts,
                      'favorite_count':likes})
```

Now, let me create the columns with date, hour and day of the week, as well as the columns flagging which text is a re tweet:

```
from datetime import datetime as dt

trumpDF['created_at']=pd.to_datetime(trumpDF['created_at'],
                                     infer_datetime_format=True)
trumpDF['Date']=[dt.date(d) for d in trumpDF['created_at']]
trumpDF['Day']=[dt.date(d).isoweekday() for d in trumpDF['created_at']]
trumpDF['Hour'] = [dt.time(d).hour for d in trumpDF['created_at']]

# a column for flagging a retweet.
trumpDF['is_retweet'] = trumpDF.text.str.startswith('RT')

# saving the file (commented just to avoid rewriting it)
#trumpDF.to_csv("trumps.csv",index=False)
```

---

[2] If you need Monday to be the *first* day of the week, just add `week_start = 1`.
[3] Notice that using `isoweekday` will assign Monday as number **1** and Sunday as number **7**.

As you have seen, I saved the data in the file `trumps.csv` (I did not do it in **Python** to avoid overwriting the file I created in **R**), I will not collect tweets again, and I will only use the ones in that file for the next section.

8.3 Visuals Based on Text

Twitter, like other social data services, collects messages. Let me open the file I saved on *GitHub* and keep the texts that are not retweets:

```
> link3="/raw/master/trumps.csv"
> trumpLink=paste0(link1,link3)
> allTweets=read.csv(trumpLink,stringsAsFactors = F)
> DTtweets=allTweets[allTweets$is_retweet==FALSE,] #no retweets
> row.names(DTtweets)=NULL
```

Let me do the same in **Python**:

```
#loading
link3="/raw/master/trumps.csv"
trumpLink=link1 + link3
allTweets=pd.read_csv(trumpLink)

#no retweets
DTtweets=allTweets[~allTweets.is_retweet]
DTtweets.reset_index(drop=True,inplace=True)
```

The column `text` has the tweet messages. These messages are not yet ready to be turned into a visual. This is one of them:

```
> DTtweets$text[49]
```

```
[1] "Big Stock Market Numbers!"
```

Twitter texts are full of characters that are not needed by the researcher; but researchers are the ones who decide what is relevant or not. In general, you need at this point to get rid of what you consider not relevant. Generally, you should remove characters using some regular expressions:

- Emoticons. People use emoticons in their Tweets. Unless you translate their meaning, these are not to be analyzed. Use this code to get rid of them:[4]

  ```
  > DTtweets$text=gsub("[^\x01-\x7F]", "", DTtweets$text)
  ```

Some **R** users have some strategies to translate emoticons (Peterka-Bonetta, 2017, 2019). **Python** has a package that also offers translation of the emoticons (Kim, 2015).

---

[4] Unfortunately, I can guarantee this code will erase every emoji, as there are more complex emojis and similar ornamental symbols appearing every now and then.

- URLs. Generally, you do not need the URLs.

```
> DTtweets$text=gsub("http\\S+\\s*","",  DTtweets$text)
```

- Special characters. Pay attention to symbols like &, >, or <, which may need to be replaced or eliminated like this:

```
> DTtweets$text=gsub("&amp;", "and", DTtweets$text) #replaced
> DTtweets$text=gsub("&lt;|&gt;", "", DTtweets$text) #eliminated
```

- Optional elements. There are some optional cleaning techniques that might be needed:

  - Users. You can delete references to other Twitter users, if you believe they do not matter:

```
> DTtweets$text=gsub("@\\w+", "", DTtweets$text)
```

  - Hashtags. You can delete the hashtags, if you believe they do not matter:

```
> DTtweets$text=gsub("#\\w+", "", DTtweets$text)
```

The previous steps for preparing the text can be done in **Python** like this:

```
# just readability
dirtyVar=DTtweets.text

# cleaning steps
DTtweets.loc[:,['text']]=dirtyVar.str.replace('[^\x01-\x7F]','')
DTtweets.loc[:,['text']]=dirtyVar.str.replace('http\\S+\\s*','')
DTtweets.loc[:,['text']]=dirtyVar.str.replace('&amp;','and')
DTtweets.loc[:,['text']]=dirtyVar.str.replace('&lt;|&gt;','')

### optional steps
#DTtweets['text']=dirtyVar.str.replace('@\\w+','')
#DTtweets['text']=dirtyVar.str.replace('#\\w+','')
```

You may decide you need users or hashtags; if so, keep them. In this example, I decided not to remove them (the @ and # symbols will be removed in a later step, but not the text after them).

8.3.1 Text as Clouds

Clouds of words, or *wordclouds*, are a very common visual to inform you about the text present in your messages. They are not meant as a precise visual to explain what the conversation in Twitter is about, or any collection of texts from other social media, but as always, they complement other visuals. The main strength of wordclouds is their ease of use for describing (similar to a barplot). They do not require the audience to know math or statistics. However, clouds can be frustrating if you do not see what you expect; or confusing if no patterns appear, or the default configuration does not help reveal those patterns.

I need to follow a couple of steps before I produce my cloud for the Twitter text. Let me deal with word cases and punctuation. I need every word to be in upper or lower case, while getting rid of punctuation symbols. That is easily achieved with one function `unnest_tokens` from *tidytext* (Queiroz et al., 2020):[5]

```
> library(tidytext)
> library(magrittr)
> DTtweets_Words = DTtweets %>%
+                  unnest_tokens(output=EachWord,  # for DTtweets_Words
+                                input=text,       # from DTtweets
+                                token="words")    # for tokenization
> # result
> head(DTtweets_Words[,-c(1,2)],10)
```

	favorite_count	retweet_count	Hour	Day	Date	EachWord
1	18714	5305	23	5	2020-08-13	donyoungak
1.1	18714	5305	23	5	2020-08-13	really
1.2	18714	5305	23	5	2020-08-13	produces
1.3	18714	5305	23	5	2020-08-13	for
1.4	18714	5305	23	5	2020-08-13	alaska
1.5	18714	5305	23	5	2020-08-13	he
1.6	18714	5305	23	5	2020-08-13	is
1.7	18714	5305	23	5	2020-08-13	an
1.8	18714	5305	23	5	2020-08-13	incredible
1.9	18714	5305	23	5	2020-08-13	congressman

As you see above, `DTtweets_Words` has the same columns as `DTtweets` but it has been greatly modified. The new column `EachWord` has one row for each word in the tweets, as I requested *tokenization* as words. Keep in mind that words can repeat as they are generated per tweet. Notice they all are in lower case and punctuation symbols have been deleted. Let me keep using regular expression, basic string functions, and *Pandas* in **Python**:

```
# punctuation
import string
PUNCs=string.punctuation # '!"#$%&\'()*+,-./:;<>?@[\\]^_`{|}~'
DTtweets.loc[:,['text']]=dirtyVar.str.replace('['+PUNCs+']', '')

# to lower case
DTtweets.loc[:,['text']]=dirtyVar.str.lower()
```

Python has done the cleaning in the tweet column, now let me tokenize the tweets:

```
#tokenize into a list
DTwordsList = " ".join(DTtweets.text).split()
```

---

[5] Notice that I got rid of some special characters before using this function, as they will not be properly erased.

I have tokenized the whole text into a list, so **Python** has not modified `DTtweets` as **R** did. Notice that you can alter the order of these steps, and you might get different amounts of tokens. In **Python**, I got twelve elements less; that difference occurs when you replace punctuation symbols, for example **R** will split `9:00` into `9` and `00`, while my **Python** code will simply turn `9:00` into `900`.

I am not finished yet. Another common step is removing the stop words. These are words that are not needed for common analysis, like pronouns, prepositions, interjections, etc. The library *tidytext*, recently loaded, has a file for that:

```
> # calling the file
> data(stop_words)
> # seeing some rows
> head(stop_words)
```

```
# A tibble: 6 x 2
  word      lexicon
  <chr>     <chr>
1 a         SMART
2 a's       SMART
3 able      SMART
4 about     SMART
5 above     SMART
6 according SMART
```

So, the logical step here is simply to keep the words in `DTtweets_Words` that are *not* in the *stop_words*.[6] The function `anti_join` from *dplyr* (Wickham et al., 2020a) will be helpful:

```
> library(dplyr)
> # The column 'word' from 'stop_words' will be compared
> # to the column 'EachWord' in 'DTtweets_Words'
> DTtweets_Words = DTtweets_Words %>%
+    anti_join(stop_words,
+              by = c("EachWord" = "word"))
```

The data frame `DTtweets_Words` has reduced its previous version, and I will use its updated column `EachWord` to produce a frequency table of the words it contains.

```
> FTtrump = DTtweets_Words %>%
+    dplyr::count(EachWord, sort = TRUE)
```

The object `FTtrump` is a data frame representing a frequency table, which you can use to make barplots or any other visual mentioned in Chapter 4:

[6] The *stop_words* from *tidytext* is a *data frame*, so you can add elements to it as needed, using *rbind* or similar.

```
> head(FTtrump)

          EachWord  n
1              bus  20
2           people  18
3            usdot  17
4   infrastructure  14
5          service  14
6          support  13
```

I already have a list in **Python** (DTwordsList) with the tokens I will use for my wordcloud. I just need to remove the stop words and create the frequency table of words. Let me do the first step using the *nltk* library (Bird et al., 2009):[7]

```
from nltk.corpus import stopwords
STOPS = stopwords.words('english')
DTwordsList=[word for word in DTwordsList if word not in STOPS]
```

The last step may create discrepancies, as the stop words need not be the same across libraries in **R** or **Python**. Now let me create the frequency table:

```
FTtrump={word:DTwordsList.count(word) for word in DTwordsList}
```

The frequency table in **Python** is a dictionary, where the key is the word token, and the item value is the frequency of that token.

Let me first use the frequency table FTtrump from **R** to produce the code for our cloud. Before that, make sure you have installed the library *wordcloud2* (Lang and Chien, 2018), this time directly from its *GitHub* repository:

```
> library(devtools) # needed for "install_github()"
> install_github("lchiffon/wordcloud2")
```

Now, the code for the word cloud:

```
> library(wordcloud2)
> # option for shape are:
> # cardioid,diamond,triangle-forward,triangle,pentagon or star.
>
> wc1=wordcloud2(data=FTtrump,
+               size=1,
+               minSize = 0,
+               fontFamily = 'Arial',
+               color='random-light',
+               backgroundColor = "white",
+               shape = 'circle')
```

The cloud wc1 can be seen in Figure 8.1.

---

[7] The *stop.words* from *nltk* is a *list*, so you can add elements to it as needed using the *append* function or similar.

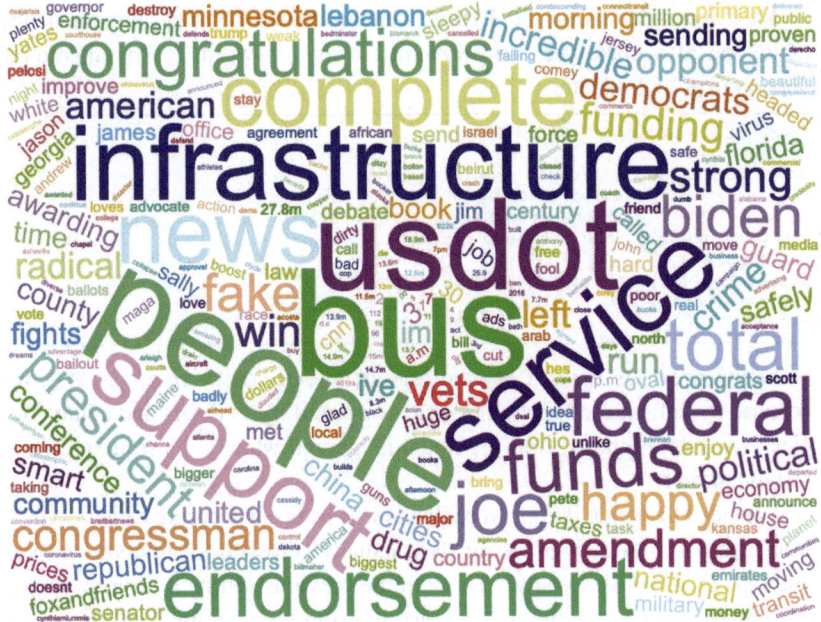

Figure 8.1 Wordcloud of all acceptable words from the last 200 tweets from Donald Trump's public account (from August 18 to August 14, 2020) collected using get_timeline from *rtweet*. (Kearney et al., 2020).

Let me use now the dictionary we created in **Python**, also named FTtrump, to create my cloud using the *wordcloud* library (Mueller, 2018):

```
import matplotlib.pyplot as plt
from wordcloud import WordCloud

wc1 = WordCloud(background_color='white')
wc1.generate_from_frequencies(frequencies=FTtrump)
plt.figure()
plt.imshow(wc1, interpolation="bilinear")
plt.axis("off")
plt.show()
```

Notice the use of interpolation in the code above. You might need this as the image you want to show may need to have its quality adjusted if scaled up or down.[8]

---

[8] In https://matplotlib.org/3.3.1/gallery/images_contours_and_fields/interpolation_methods.html you can find further details.

Most examples using the **Python** version do not compute the frequency table, and also make use of *wordcloud*'s own stop words.[9] This alternative version may look like this:

```
from wordcloud import STOPWORDS

wc1 = WordCloud(background_color='white',
                stopwords=STOPWORDS, #its own list
                collocations=False) # no bigrams
wc1.generate(" ".join(DTtweets.text))
plt.figure()
plt.imshow(wc1, interpolation="bilinear")
plt.axis("off")
plt.show()
```

In the previous code, I set the argument `collocations` as `False`; because by default the function `WordCloud` will try to detect and count couples of words (bigrams) (this argument is ignored when you use frequencies, as I did at first).

You need to decide if your wordclouds will be just a decorative piece, which in fact they can effectively be, or they actually help you to support decision-making. That requires you to play with the previous setting a little. A couple of things to try are subsetting `FTtrump` to avoid least common words, and/or choosing a different color combination. Let me prepare a code to keep only the words which have a frequency higher than four, and let me color the words using different levels of red.

```
> library(RColorBrewer)
> #subsetting
> FTsub=FTtrump[FTtrump$n>4,]
> colorQuant = length(unique(FTsub$n))
> #new colors
> newColors=brewer.pal(9,"Reds")
> palette = colorRampPalette(newColors)(colorQuant)[FTsub$n]
> #new version
> wc2=wordcloud2(FTsub, color=palette)
```

The cloud `wc2`, with less words and the *Reds* sequential color palette (Brewer, 2009), can be seen in Figure 8.2. Notice that I have chosen 9 for the color palette because that is the top value accepted.

I will offer two strategies to replicate 8.2 in **Python**. The first one will simply subset the dictionary with same condition (counts greater than 4), requesting the *Reds* color palette.

---

[9] The *STOPWORDS* from *wordcloud* is a *set*, so you can add elements to it as needed using the *update* function or similar.

Figure 8.2 Wordcloud of words whose frequency is greater than four from the last 200 tweets from Donald Trump's public account (from August 18 to August 14, 2020) collected using get_timeline from *rtweet* (Kearney et al., 2020)

Colors from *Reds* brewer palette (Brewer, 2009).

```
#subsetting
FTsub={k:v for k, v in FTtrump.items() if v>4}

#replotting
wc2 = WordCloud(background_color='white',
                colormap="Reds")
wc2.generate_from_frequencies(frequencies=FTsub)
plt.figure()
plt.imshow(wc2, interpolation="bilinear")
plt.axis("off")
plt.show()
```

The previous code will not give you what you might expect. The previous code will assign color randomly to the words, so it will not give you what you see in Figure 8.2. If you need to correlate color intensity with word frequency you need to use this function:

```
#recoloring function
def myColor_func(word, **kwargs):
    # key of max value
    kMax=max(FTsub.items(), key=operator.itemgetter(1))[0]
    # 0 for red /  120 for green / 240 for blue
    return "hsl(0, 100%%, %d%%)" % (5*FTsub[kMax]/FTsub[word])
```

As you see above, you need to create colors using an *hsl* format (hue, saturation, and lightness). The *hue* goes from *0* to *360*, where *0* is red, *120* is green, *240* is blue; *saturation* is a percentage value where *100 percent* is the full color, and any decrease will add some shade of gray (*0* will turn any color to gray); *lightness* is also a value from *0 percent* (black) to *100 percent* (white). In my function, you need to include a value for the *hue* (I chose *0* for red), the 100 percent saturation will keep the full *hue*, and the lightness will vary according to the frequency of the word (I wrote a simple function, you may try a different one). Let me use the function myColor_func in the color_func argument of the WordCloud function.

```
#replotting
wc3 = WordCloud(background_color='white',
                color_func=myColor_func)
wc3.generate_from_frequencies(frequencies=FTsub)
plt.figure()
plt.imshow(wc3, interpolation="bilinear")
plt.axis("off")
plt.show()
```

It requires some time to produce an informative wordcloud, I just recommend using it wisely, as different people may notice different patterns (which may not help while you are presenting).

8.3.2 Text as Network

A good complement to a wordcloud can be a network of words. The basic idea is that a network, or graph, connects words that appear one after the other. This adjacency is the focus of the visual exploration.

Let me use the DTtweets data frame I used when I started the previous subsection which was already cleaned. From that point, let's go to every clean text and get every *two* adjacent words, or *bigrams*:

```
> DTtweets_2g = DTtweets %>%
+               unnest_tokens(output=pairWords,
+                             input=text,
+                             token = "ngrams", n = 2) # 2-grams
```

In the previous code, I used unnest_tokens again, but this time I requested bigrams instead of simple words. The bigrams are in the column pairWords in the DTtweets_2g data frame:

```
> head(DTtweets_2g$pairWords)
```

```
[1] "great meeting"    "meeting today"    "today with"    "with the"
[5] "the coronavirus"  "coronavirus task"
```

Let me get the bigrams in **Python**. I will only use the column `text` from the data frame:

```
#bigrams per twitter (per cell)
from nltk import bigrams

theBigrams=[bigrams(eachTW.split()) for eachTW in DTtweets.text]


# list of all bigrams
from itertools import chain

pairWords = list(chain(*theBigrams))
```

I followed a couple of steps to get something similar to `pairWords` as I did in **R**. First, using the `bigrams` function from *nltk*, I got the bigrams from every tweet. The function `bigrams` will turn the input into consecutive pairs; so you need to input the right structure. If you input a string, it will turn the string into pairs of characters, that is, `bigrams("Hi Jim")` will be: [('H', 'i'), ('i', ' '),(' ', 'J'), ('J', 'i'),('i', 'm')]).

You do not want the previous outcome, so I input a list of words into `bigrams`. I got the lists of words by tokenizing each tweet text using `split`. This process creates lists each with a *generator*[10] of tuples. After that, I needed to visit every element of `theBigrams`, and make a list containing all the tuples from those lists. Since I need a simple list for my word cloud (and not a list of tuples) I had to flatten the object `pairWords`.[11] I easily did that with the function `chain` from the library *itertools*.[12]

You have bigrams as two-word strings in **R**, and as a tuple in **Python**, so far. The next step is to get the frequency table of the bigrams. Let me first show you the steps in **R**:

- Split the column `pairWords` into different columns. I will use `separate` from *tidyr* (Wickham et al., 2020b) for splitting it into columns named `word1` and `word2`; then I use `select` from *dplyr* to keep the new columns:

```
> library(tidyr)
> DTtweets_2g_only=DTtweets_2g %>%
+               separate(pairWords, #source column
+                        c("word1", "word2"), #new columns
+                        sep = " ") %>% # split by
```

---

[10] This is a function from *nltk* that creates a generator, which actually can produce an iterator of tuples. It is a fine way to avoid populating the memory with all the tuples, which will only be created when requested.

[11] Turning a list of tuples (or other structure) into a simple list is called *flattening*.

[12] The function of `chain` is turning something like
`list(chain([(1,2),(3,4)],[(5,6)]))` into [(1, 2), (3, 4), (5, 6)].
As in this case, `theBigrams` receive a list (several arguments as a list); you use the asterisk before its name.

```
+                   select(c("word1", "word2"))  # keep these
>
```

Now, I have every pair of words in two columns in the
`DTtweets_2g_only` data frame.

- Make the frequency table of bigrams:

```
> FT_DT_2g = DTtweets_2g_only %>%
+            dplyr::count(word1, word2, sort = TRUE)
> #take a look
> head(FT_DT_2g)

    word1    word2   n
1   <NA>     <NA>   22
2   will       be   19
3     of      the   18
4    for      the   14
5     in      the   13
6    bus  service   12
```

- My data frame `FT_trump_2g` is almost ready, I just need to get rid of the
  missing values:

```
> FT_DT_2g=FT_DT_2g[complete.cases(FT_DT_2g),]
```

- Next, I should remove the "stop words":

```
> FT_DT_2g = FT_DT_2g %>%
+              filter(!word1 %in% stop_words$word) %>%
+              filter(!word2 %in% stop_words$word)
```

Let me create the frequency table `FT_DT_2g_dict` in **Python** (and turn
it into a data frame):

```
# frequency of DTrump bigrams
from collections import Counter

FT_DT_2g_dict = Counter(pairWords) #generate counter

# Turn FT_DT_2g_dict  into dataframe, naming columns
FT_DT_2g = pd.DataFrame(FT_DT_2g_dict.most_common(),
                        columns=['theBigram', 'count'])
```

I used the function `Counter` from *collections* to create the frequency
table (`FT_DT_2g_dict`) which returns a dictionary. This dict will have the
bigram tuple as the key and its frequency as the value. When you have the dict
produced by `Counter`, it allows you to apply the function `most_common`[13]
to it, and you get a list as a result. *Pandas* easily turned that list into a data
frame while giving names to the columns.

---

[13] I used this function without arguments to get all the pairs.

Python requires another step to turn the column `theBigram` (it has the tuples) into two columns (`word1` and `word2`). I will use those two new columns to filter the rows with stop words:

```
# Turn column of tuples into separate columns
FT_DT_2g['word1'], FT_DT_2g['word2'] = FT_DT_2g.theBigram.str

# Getting rid of stopwords:
FT_DT_2g=FT_DT_2g[~FT_DT_2g['word1'].isin(STOPS)]
FT_DT_2g=FT_DT_2g[~FT_DT_2g['word2'].isin(STOPS)]
```

I hope the bigrams in each row make some sense to you. Of course, you can not synthesize much just by looking the bigram texts. The proposal here is to show how all bigrams tell you something. However, if I use a wordcloud, you may see repeated words. Then, if I want to *connect* words that are part of a bigram, a suitable option is a graph. For that, let me first install and use *igraph* (Csardi and Nepusz, 2006):

```
> library(igraph)
> DT_2g_net=graph_from_data_frame(FT_DT_2g)
```

The function `graph_from_data_frame` just read the first two columns of the data frame `FT_DT_2g` and created the graph, translating the first column as the *source* (from) and the second as the *target* (to). Then, the object `DT_2g_net` is your graph where each *node* is a word, and words connected via a *link* indicate they are a bigram in the text. I can show you that using *ggraph* (Pedersen and RStudio, 2020), an extension for *ggplot*.

```
> library(ggraph)
> # graph layout: 'ggraph' will decide this time
> layout = ggraph(DT_2g_net) + theme_void()
> # draw nodes (words) in a position based on layout
> nodes= layout + geom_node_point()
> # draw links to connect nodes
> net1 = nodes + geom_edge_link()
> # customize some text in node
> net1= net1+ geom_node_text(aes(label = name),
+                                   vjust = 1,
+                                   hjust = 1,
+                                   size=2)
```

The graph `DT_2g_net` is now the visual object `net1`. You can see the plot in Figure 8.3. Notice that the variable `name` in the aesthetics of `geom_node_text` is referring to the node name attribute of the graph created by default. Also, notice that the position of nodes was automatically picked by `ggraph`.

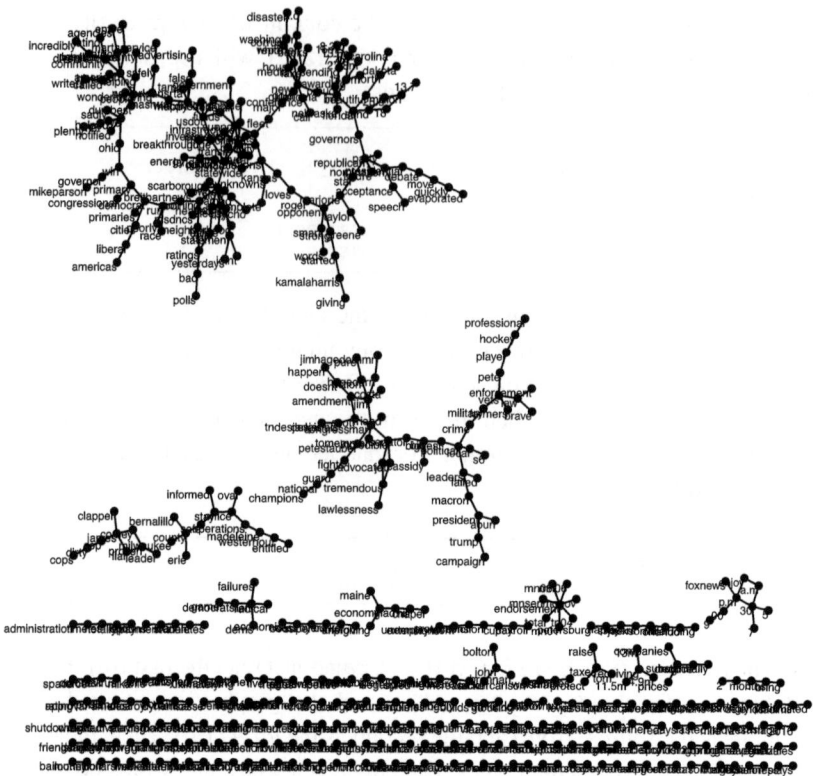

Figure 8.3 Graph of Bigrams

The graph represents all the bigrams from the last 200 tweets from Donald Trump's public
account (from August 18 to August 14, 2020) collected using `get_timeline` from *rtweet*
(Kearney et al., 2020). The position of the nodes was automatically picked by the function
`ggraph` (*stress* algorithm (Gansner et al., 2005)).

Let me prepare my version of **Python** using *networkx* (Hagberg et al.,
2020). *Networkx* can easily turn the `FT_DT_2g` data frame into a graph with
its function `from_pandas_edgelist`:[14]

```
import networkx as nx

# from data frame to graph
DT_2g_net=nx.from_pandas_edgelist(df=FT_DT_2g,
                                  source='word1',
                                  target='word2')
# plotting graph (default layout)
nx.draw_networkx(DT_2g_net,
```

---

[14] The function `from_pandas_edgelist` requires that you indicate what columns are the
source and the target, unless you had named the columns with those labels.

```
          font_size=7,
          edge_color='red',
          node_color='yellow',
          node_size=100,
          alpha=0.9,
          with_labels = True)
```

In the previous code, I created the *DT_2g_net* graph and used the function `draw_networkx` to create the plot. *Networkx* was not meant to be a package for beautiful plotting, it recommends using more specialized software for that, such as Cytoscape (Cytoscape Consortium, 2020) or Gephi (Bastian et al., 2009). You should not expect to get the same layout as shown in Figure 8.3, which was chosen by *igraph* in **R**; in this case, the default layout will be *spring* (Fruchterman and Reingold, 1991).

If you do not see clear labels, you can try moving them on the horizontal or vertical axis; for that, you need to use :

```
#setting size
fig, ax = plt.subplots(figsize=(10,10))

#saving layout positions
pos = nx.spring_layout(DT_2g_net)

# Plot networks
nx.draw_networkx(DT_2g_net,
                 pos,   #layout
                 edge_color='red',
                 node_color='yellow',
                 node_size=100,
                 with_labels = False,
                 ax=ax) # for matplotlib ax

# labels away from node
for word, freq in pos.items():
    x, y = freq[0]+.01, freq[1]+.01 # new pos values
    ax.text(x, y, #new positions
            s=word, #label
            horizontalalignment='center',
            fontsize=7, rotation=30)

plt.show()
```

Notice that in the previous code, I needed to save the actual positions of the nodes first, so that I could alter them later.

Let's come back to **R**. Figure 8.3 included all the data available; that may have not been the best choice. Let me create the graph `DT_2g_net3`, which will only include bigrams with a frequency higher than or equal to three:

```
> #subsetting
> FT_DT_2g3=FT_DT_2g[FT_DT_2g$n≥3,]
> DT_2g_net_sub=graph_from_data_frame(FT_DT_2g3)
> #new plot
> layout2 = ggraph(DT_2g_net_sub) + theme_void()
```

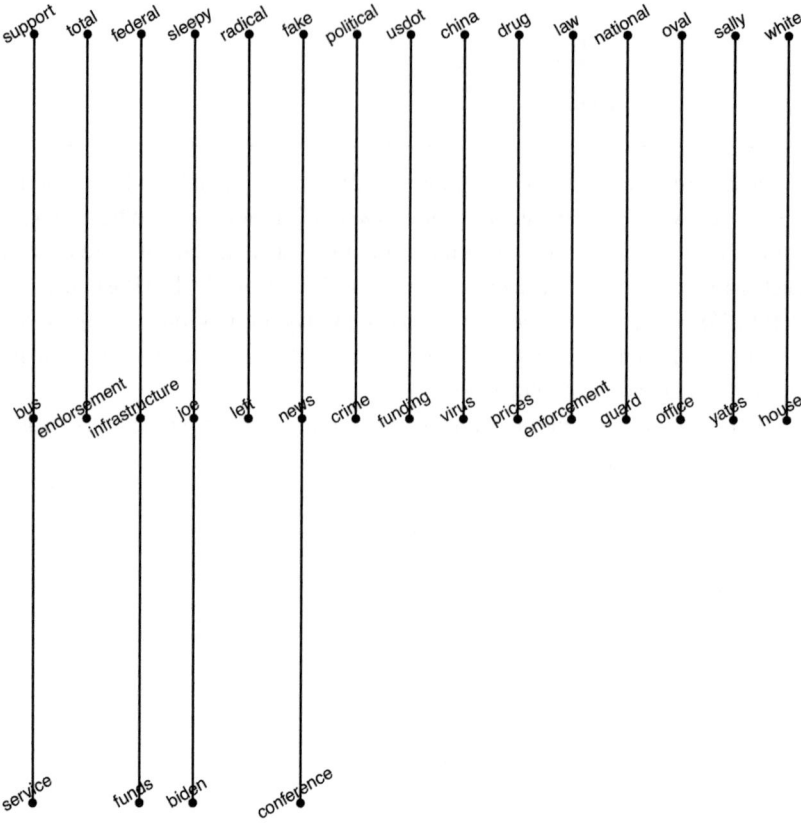

Figure 8.4 Graph of Bigrams with frequency greater than two

Bigrams from the last 200 tweets from Donald Trump's public account (from August 18 to August 14, 2020) collected using get_timeline from *rtweet* (Kearney et al., 2020). The position of the nodes is automatically picked by the function ggraph.

```
> nodes =layout2 +  geom_node_point()
> net2 = nodes +  geom_edge_link()
> net2 = net2 +  geom_node_text(aes(label = name),
+                               vjust = -0.5,
+                               hjust = 0.5,angle=30,
+                               size=3)
```

The visual object net2 can be seen in Figure 8.4. Notice that the position of the nodes was again automatically picked by ggraph, here the *tree* layout was chosen (Pedersen, 2020).

You can redraw net2 in **Python** using this code:

```
#subsetting
FT_DT_2g3=FT_DT_2g[FT_DT_2g['count']≥3]

DT_2g_net_sub=nx.from_pandas_edgelist(FT_DT_2g3,'word1','word2')

#plotting
fig, ax = plt.subplots(figsize=(6, 6))
pos = nx.spring_layout(DT_2g_net_sub)

# Plot networks
nx.draw_networkx(DT_2g_net_sub, pos,
                 edge_color='red',node_color='yellow',
                 node_size=100,with_labels = False,ax=ax)

# labels away from node
for word, freq in pos.items():
    x, y = freq[0]+.05, freq[1]+.03
    ax.text(x, y,s=word,horizontalalignment='center',
            fontsize=13,rotation=30)

plt.show()
```

I will now now focus on the relationships among network actors in this last section of the book.

8.4 Visuals Based on Actors

The previous section served as a quick introduction to a fascinating area of analysis: networks. A network is a familiar term used in science, engineering, humanities, and social sciences. If you have a network structure, composed of nodes (vertices) and links (edges) you can make several computations supported by the mathematics of graph theory, but the plotting of the network is a different story, with many algorithms competing to help you find some pattern in the complexity of networks (please read this discussion by Tarawaneh et al. (2012)). If you are interested in this topic, you should be aware that it is difficult to get a good layout when your nodes reach amounts pass the hundreds. However, let me guide you in the basic steps of organizing your network information and the steps required to get a plot.

8.4.1 Actors

Using the noun actor, instead of simply using "node" or "vertex", in social and policy research contexts may be a good idea. I think this can help you focus on the role of computational social science (Cioffi-Revilla, 2014), while allowing you to be a step away from introducing yourself into agent-based modeling (Railsback and Grimm, 2012), a topic I have not dealt with in this book.

The social media network is a great source of information about actors. In the data I presented at the beginning of this chapter, the presidents or heads of government/states of the Americas are the actors. Actors can have variables or attributes – in this case, the country they belong to. You can decide that the country is the actor, and while it can be more abstract you might have a good reason for that; however, that may change the kind of relationship that is suitable among the actors.

8.4.2 Relationships

Similarly, I prefer using the noun "relationship" instead of "edge" or "link". As mentioned in the previous paragraph, the nature of the actor allows for some kinds of relationships. In general, they can be *directed* or *undirected*. A relationship is undirected when once it exists both actors have the same kind of connection; a great example of this is for our data on the Americas is *be neighbor of*, because if Bolivia is a neighbor of Brazil, Brazil can not avoid having the same relationship with Bolivia. On the other hand, when a relationship is directed, it is not always possible to have the same relationship reflected back. The directed relationship *supplies natural gas* may be one-directional; while the relationship *supplies workforce* may be two-directional.[15]

If the actors are people, like the political leaders we have, they might not have a neighborly relationship if they live in different countries (unless some have different places to live in). Since we have the Twitter accounts of each for these leaders, we could think of relationship *follower of*. This is an example of directed relationship which may not be a two-way one. This particular fact is very interesting in political terms, as it may reveal presidents whose tweets are of interest to some, or not. Of course, you need to be careful when you consider this as a general rule, as a political actor need not be a follower on Twitter to actually be following some other actor.

8.4.3 Making the Network

Making the network requires nodes and the connections among them. In Section 8.2, the data I collected using **R** and **Python** is not helpful in preparing a network, as it does not indicate who follows who. I need a different way to

---

[15] This is possible using the term workforce in a very general way, but digging further into it may make the relationships look more one-way.

get connections from Twitter, and only then I will use the functions to prepare a network, something similar to what I did with the bigrams in Section 8.3.2.

Finding Relationships

In **R**, the library *rtweet* has a function `lookup_friendships`.[16] It can tell you who follows who, given a pair of users. You can use the function like this:

```
> relationship= lookup_friendships(source='user1',target='user2')
```

If I input every possible pair[17] into that function, I can get the relationships that exist among them. You can use the function combn (from *utils*) to get all pairs:[18]

```
> pairs=combn(twusers$twitter,2,simplify = F)
```

Using both previous functions, I will verify the existing relationships, and I will keep the actual connections. I have organized those relationships into a data frame:

```
> link4="/raw/master/edgesAmericas.csv"
> linkEdges=paste0(link1,link4)
> relationships=read.csv(linkEdges,stringsAsFactors = F)
> head(relationships)
```

```
        source          target
1      alferdez      nayibbukele
2      alferdez    JustinTrudeau
3   JeanineAnez       IvanDuque
4   JeanineAnez  realDonaldTrump
5 jairbolsonaro  sebastianpinera
6 jairbolsonaro            Lenin
```

The data frame `relationships` has the edges showing who follows who; then I need a directed network:

```
> library(igraph)
> set.seed(123)
> net = graph_from_data_frame(d=relationships, #data frame
+                             vertices=twusers, #data frame
+                             directed=T)
```

---

[16] Your alternative in *tweepy* is `show_friendship`.
[17] If you do not have premium developer account, I recommend that you split these pairs into smaller chunks, both in **R** and **Python**, as the Twitter restrictions may cause your code execution to fail.
[18] In **Python**, you can use the `combinations` function from the library *itertools*.

The function `graph_from_data_frame` used a couple of data frames, one with the *relationships* and one with the information about the *actors*. It is of course a directed network. Let me see what I have:

```
> summary(net)
```

```
IGRAPH fbfc7b1 DN-- 34 168 --
+ attr: name (v/c), country (v/c), president (v/c), region (v/c), sex
| (v/c)
```

The summary presents several interesting facts. After a seven-character code (not relevant for any purpose), you see a **D** because the network is directed (the other option is *U*), and the **N** because you have vertex "names" (it is using the data frame). It is also telling you that you have 34 actors and there are 168 relationships. You see several attributes, all of them including **v/c**, which means that they are attributes of the actor (vertex) and the data type it holds, in this case a "character" (other options are **n**umeric, **l**ogical, and **x** for other)[19].

Let me create the same network using **Python**:

```
#get relationships data
link4="/raw/master/edgesAmericas.csv"
LINK=link1 + link4
relationships=pd.read_csv(LINK)

# build network
import networkx as nx
net=nx.from_pandas_edgelist(relationships,create_using=nx.DiGraph())

# make sure isolates are in the network
net.add_nodes_from(twusers.twitter)

#add attributes from data frame
### data frame as dictionary
attributes=twusers.set_index('twitter').to_dict('index')
### add attributes of nodes to network
nx.set_node_attributes(net, attributes)
```

The `net` object created using *networkx* was also created from the data frame `relationships`. The problem is that the data frame might not have some actors. The network from *igraph* in **R** included all the actor nodes because you also added the actors data frame. Then, I needed to use `add_nodes_from` to add the missing nodes. Once I had all the nodes, I added the attributes. Notice that the attributes should be input as a dictionary, that is why I used `to_dict` to convert the data frame into a dict where each row is a dict item. Since the user name in that data frame will be the key to

---

[19] For further details on these metadata, check the documentation of the function `print.igraph`.

each row, I needed to set the column `twitter`, where the user names are, as the index; let me show a portion of this dict:

```
In [8]: twusers.set_index('twitter').to_dict('index')
Out[8]:
{'MartinVizcarraC': {'country': 'Perú',
   'president': 'VIZCARRA, Martín',
   'region': 'SouthAmerica',
   'sex': 'male'},
 'realDonaldTrump': {'country': 'United States of America',
   'president': 'TRUMP, Donald',
   'region': 'NorthAmerica',
   'sex': 'male'},
 'JustinTrudeau': {'country': 'Canada',
   'president': 'TRUDEAU, Justin',
   'region': 'NorthAmerica',
   'sex': 'male'},
```

You do not have a function to summarize the `net` object from *networkx*, but you can find out about nodes and edges with other functions. If you use `net.nodes(data=True)` [20] you will get all the information available for every node; similarly, you can use `net.edges(data=True)` [21] to see what edges you have and their attributes.

8.4.4 Network Layout

Let me start with a basic plot using what we learned in Section 8.3.2.

```
> library(ggraph)
> layoutPresi = ggraph(net) + theme_void()
> nodesPresi= layoutPresi + geom_node_point()
> netPresi = nodesPresi + geom_edge_link()
> netPresi= netPresi+ geom_node_text(aes(label = name))
```

You can see a plot for the network `netPresi` in Figure 8.5. Remember that *ggraph* picks a layout automatically if you do not select one.[22]

Networkx has limited capabilities for drawing networks, and it recommends[23] exporting the network to be used for other more specialized programs, as mentioned before. If you decide to leave **Python** and use another type of drawing software, as recommended by itself, a good option is saving this *networkx* object as *graphml* file (Brandes et al., 2002):

```
nx.write_graphml_lxml(net, "presiAmericas.graphml")
```

---

[20] In **R**, you can check each actor using `V(net)`.
[21] In **R**, you can check each relationship using `E(net)`.
[22] The library *ggraph* can use the layouts available in *igraph*.
[23] https://networkx.github.io/documentation/stable/reference/drawing.html

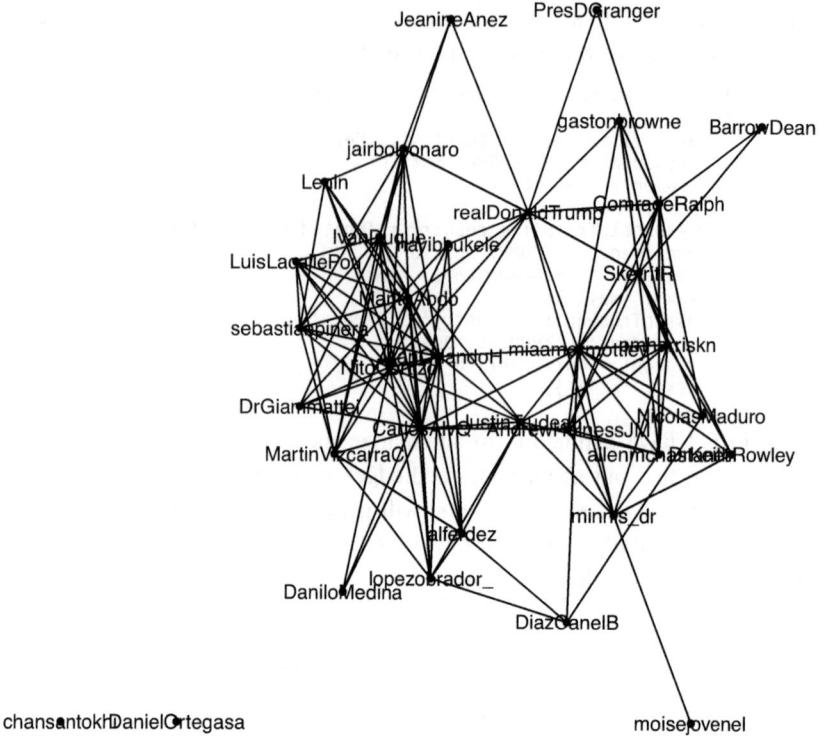

Figure 8.5 Network of Presidents of the Americas

The graph shows which president follows another president. The position of the nodes was automatically picked by the function ggraph (*stress* algorithm (Gansner et al., 2005)).

Let me continue in **Python**, and as you know, this is the most basic command:

```
nx.draw_networkx(net)
```

The previous plot could be improved if you manage[24] to use *graphviz* functionalities (Ellson et al., 2003). For that, you will need to install the libraries *pydot* (Carrera, 2018) and *graphviz* (Bank, 2020). This code will give you different results:

```
pos = nx.nx_pydot.graphviz_layout(net)
nx.draw_networkx(net,pos=pos)
```

---

[24] I have only tested this on Mac OS, so I will not use this capability again.

The result of the previous code will not look as nice as Figure 8.5. However, the default layout, *neato* (North, 2004),[25] will give a better result than the basic option. You can make some adjustments using *matplotlib* and some parameters in *networkx*:

```
import matplotlib.pyplot as plt

pos = nx.nx_pydot.graphviz_layout(net)
plt.figure(figsize=(8, 8))
plt.axis('off')
nx.draw_networkx(net,
                 pos=pos,
                 with_labels=True,
                 node_size=25,
                 edge_color='b')
plt.show()
```

Layouts depend on algorithms that decide the position of the nodes (as coordinates). They seek to position the node to avoid the overlapping of links while trying to reveal some structural pattern. There are several layout algorithms that network scientists use; some are available in **Python** and some in **R**.

8.4.5 Coloring Actors and Relationships

Once a layout has been chosen, you may want to use color to help see some patterns. You need to use some attribute for coloring the nodes. My original data frame had the attribute *region*, and it is part of the net object.

```
> nodesPresi2= layoutPresi + geom_node_point(aes(colour=region),
+                                            size=3)
> netPresi2= nodesPresi2 + geom_edge_link(color='grey90')
> netPresi2=netPresi2+ geom_node_text(aes(label = president),
+                                     size=3,
+                                     color="gray50",
+                                     repel=T)
> netPresi2=netPresi2 + scale_color_brewer(name="Region",
+                                          type = 'qual',
+                                          palette ="Set1")
```

You can see the visual for netPresi2 in Figure 8.6. I have changed the color saturation by turning the black links into light gray. I have also shortened the actor names. Since the attribute region is an aesthetics, I used color as an aesthetics.

Drawing networks is pretty easy using *ggraph* if you are already familiar with *ggplot*. An alternative code in **Python** would need much more work. That

---

[25] Other options available are 'dot', 'twopi', 'fdp', 'sfdp', 'circo'.

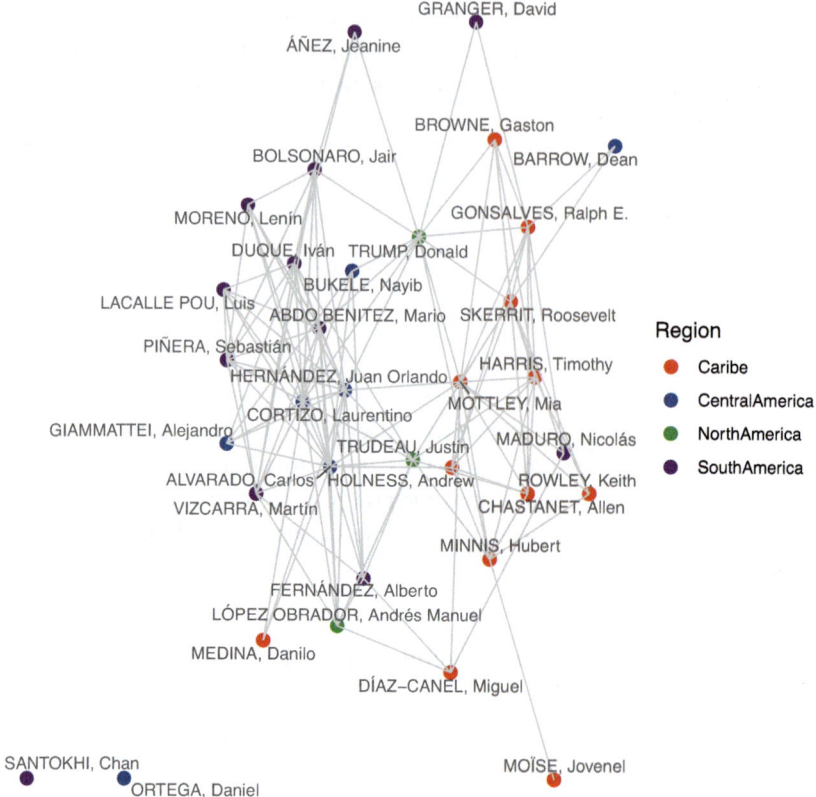

Figure 8.6 Network of Presidents of the Americas colored by region in the Americas

The graph shows which president follows another president. The position of the nodes was automatically picked by the function ggraph (*stress* algorithm (Gansner et al., 2005)).

amount of work requires you abandon the function `draw_networkx` and draw the nodes, the links, and the labels separately. Take a look:

```
from matplotlib.colors import rgb2hex
import matplotlib.pyplot as plt

plt.figure(figsize=(10,10))

#layout
pos=nx.spring_layout(net,k=1) #higher k gives more spread of nodes.
#prepare coloring by region
allValues=[n[1]['region'] for n in net.nodes(data=True)]
levels=pd.unique(allValues).tolist()
palette = plt.get_cmap("Set2") #palette

#drawing nodes - coloring nodes per attribute
```

```
for categoryChosen in levels:
    #presidents of the same region
    nodesChosen=[node[0] for node in net.nodes(data=True)
                    if node[1]['region'] in categoryChosen]
    #choosing color for these nodes
    colorChosen=rgb2hex(palette(levels.index(categoryChosen)))
    # draw chosen nodes
    nx.draw_networkx_nodes(net,pos=pos,node_size=100,
                            node_color=colorChosen,
                            nodelist=nodesChosen,
                            label=categoryChosen) # for legend!
#draw edges
nx.draw_networkx_edges(net,pos=pos,edge_color="silver")

#draw labels for nodes
#using President name (not Twitter username)
newLabels = {n[0]:n[1]['president'] for n in net.nodes(data=True)}
nx.draw_networkx_labels(net,pos=pos,font_size=8,
                        font_color='grey',
                        font_weight='bold',
                        labels=newLabels)

# requesting legend (needs "label" in nodes above)
plt.legend(markerscale=1, loc="best")
plt.show()
```

The code in **Python** required more steps than in **R**. Particularly, it needed a loop structure to code the nodes based on an attribute. Also, the code above required using the function `rgb2hex()` to get the right color code from the palette.[26] Notice also the use of `label` while drawing the nodes. That is not to label the nodes, but to create the legend. Also, notice that I changed the default labels using the dictionary `newLabels`. The keys of the dictionary are the node names and the values are the new label. If you just want to keep the node names, do not use the argument `labels` when drawing the labels.

8.4.6 Using Size Attributes

I will explore how I can use size in the network nodes. I do not have a quantitative attributes in my data, so I need to add some.

Centrality, a qualitative characteristic that tries to reveal the importance of network actors based on their relationships, has several quantitative ways to be computed, each highlighting a particular centrality concept.[27] Let me compute degree centrality with both of its variations for a directed network:

```
> # measure of being followed
> indeg = degree(net, mode="in",normalized = T)
> V(net)$indegree = indeg
> # measure of being a follower
> outdeg = degree(net, mode="out",normalized = T)
```

---

[26] You need hexadecimal, but you get RGB from `plt.get_cmap()`.
[27] The most common are *closeness*, *betweenness*, and *degree*.

```
> V(net)$outdegree = outdeg
> # reloading the network (new attributes)
> layoutPresi=ggraph(net) + theme_void()
>
```

Let me also update the *networkx* object:

```
nx.set_node_attributes(G=net,
                       values=nx.in_degree_centrality(net),
                       name='indegree')

nx.set_node_attributes(G=net,
                       values=nx.out_degree_centrality(net),
```

I will use that new attribute to vary the size of the nodes in **R**:

```
> sizeNodesIn=layoutPresi + geom_edge_link(color='grey90')
> sizeNodesIn=sizeNodesIn + geom_node_point(aes(size=(1+indegree)^10,
+                                     color=region)) +
+                           labs(size="In Degree") #legend title
> sizeNodesIn=sizeNodesIn + geom_node_text(aes(label = president),
+                                     color="gray50",
+                                     repel=T)
> sizeNodesIn=sizeNodesIn + scale_color_brewer(name="Region",
+                                     type = 'qual',
+                                     palette ="Set1")
```

The object `sizeNodesIn` is represented in Figure 8.7. Notice that in the size aesthetics of `geom_node_point` I added 1 to the actual value, since some nodes may have a zero value.

Notice that Figure 8.7 has two legends. The one for sizes may be confusing; besides the default legend name, the numeric values are not the real measurement values. Also, notice that, in contrast to Figure 8.6, I have plotted the links before the nodes, which prevents them covering the node.

Let me try **Python**, using the Kamada-Kawai algorithm for the layout (Kamada and Kawai, 1989). I would need several more lines of code to reproduce Figure 8.7. I will reuse some of the code I used to replicate Figure 8.6, adding a code inside the loop to get the `indegree` values which will alter the node sizes.

```
from matplotlib.colors import rgb2hex

plt.figure(figsize=(8,8))
pos=nx.kamada_kawai_layout(net) #layout
#prepare coloring by region
allValues=[n[1]['region'] for n in net.nodes(data=True)]
levels=pd.unique(allValues).tolist()
palette = plt.get_cmap("Set2")

for categoryChosen in levels:
    nodesChosen=[node[0] for node in net.nodes(data=True)
                 if node[1]['region'] == categoryChosen]
```

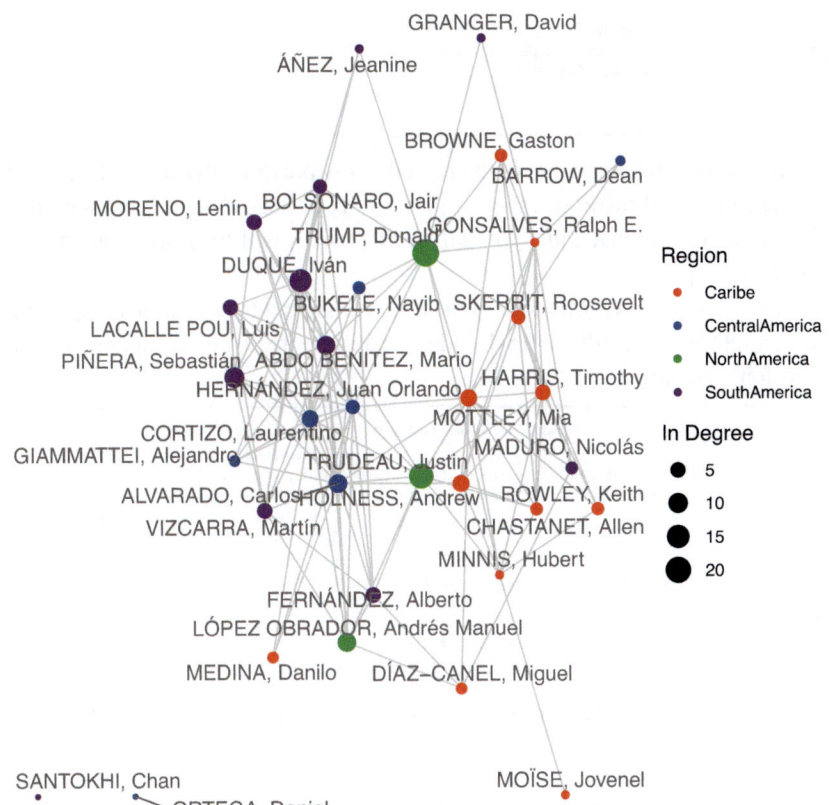

Figure 8.7 Network of Presidents of the Americas

Node sizes are based on in-degree centrality; nodes are colored by region in the Americas. The bigger the node, the more that president is followed. The position of the nodes was automatically picked by the function ggraph (*stress* algorithm (Gansner et al., 2005)).

```
colorChosen=rgb2hex(palette(levels.index(categoryChosen)))
#chosing sizes of the actors (in a list)
sizesChosen=[(1+x[1]['indegree'])**20
            for x in net.nodes(data=True)
            if x[0] in list(nodesChosen)]
# drawing the NODES
nx.draw_networkx_nodes(net,pos=pos,
                       node_size=sizesChosen, #vector of sizes
                       node_color=colorChosen,
                       nodelist=nodesChosen,
                       label=categoryChosen)
#drawing edges and labels
nx.draw_networkx_edges(net,pos=pos,edge_color="silver")
nx.draw_networkx_labels(net,pos=pos,font_size=8,font_color='grey')

# customizing legend
```

```
MyLegend = plt.legend(loc="best")
for handle in MyLegend.legendHandles:
    handle.set_sizes([20.0])

plt.show()
```

Notice the customization of the legend in my previous **Python** code, almost at the end. I used `handle.set_sizes` to fix the size of the legend symbols; if you do not use that code, you will see that sizes will be proportional to the sizes in the plot.

The decision to vary the size of the nodes might not look as well as expected, as it might become difficult to decode variability effectively. So, let me use the text font size instead:

```
> nodesPresiIn=layoutPresi + geom_node_point(aes(color=region),
+                                            size=4)
> netPresiIn=nodesPresiIn + geom_edge_link(color='grey90')
> netPresiIn=netPresiIn + geom_node_text(aes(label=country,
+                                            size=(1+indegree)^10),
+                                         color="gray50",
+                                         repel=T)
> netPresiIn=netPresiIn + scale_color_brewer(name="Region",
+                                             type = 'qual',
+                                             palette ="Set1")
> netPresiIn=netPresiIn + guides(size=F) #NO legend for size
```

As we have a directed network, let me use also the column *outdegree* `netPresiOut`.

```
> netPresiOut=layoutPresi + geom_node_point(aes(color=region),
+                                            size=4)
> netPresiOut=netPresiOut + geom_edge_link(color='grey90')
> netPresiOut=netPresiOut + geom_node_text(aes(label = country,
+                                            size=(1+outdegree)^10),
+                                         color="gray50",
+                                         repel=T)
> netPresiOut=netPresiOut + scale_color_brewer(name="Region",
+                                               type = 'qual',
+                                               palette ="Set1")
> netPresiOut=netPresiOut + guides(size=F) #NO legend for size
```

You can see the object `netPresiOut` in Figure 8.9.

Let me use an alternative **Python** version of Figure 8.8:

```
from matplotlib.colors import rgb2hex
import matplotlib.pyplot as plt

plt.figure(figsize=(8,8))

#setting layout and palette
pos=nx.kamada_kawai_layout(net)
allValues=[n[1]['region'] for n in net.nodes(data=True)]
levels=pd.unique(allValues).tolist()
palette = plt.get_cmap("Set2")

#drawing nodes and edges
```

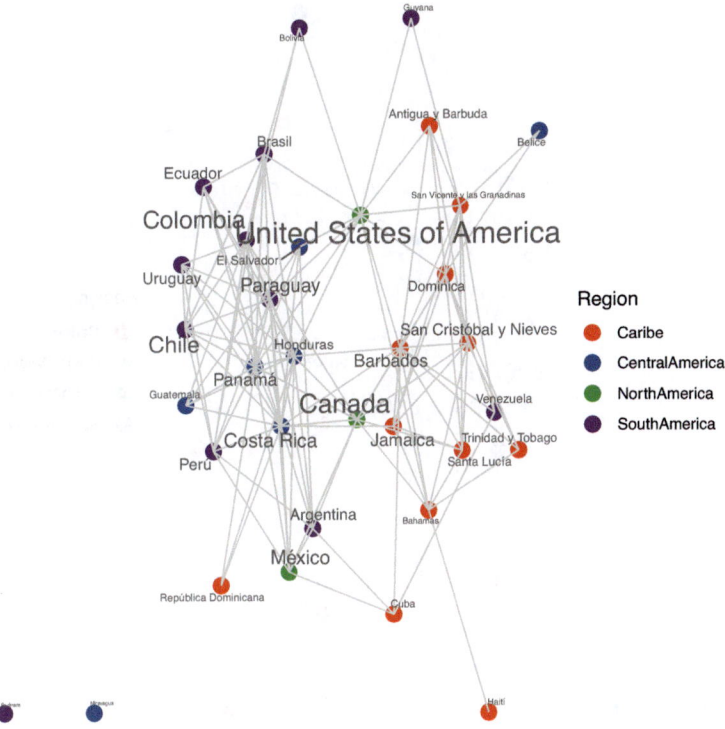

Figure 8.8 Network of Presidents of the Americas

Sizes are based on in-degree centrality; nodes are colored by region in the Americas. The bigger the text, the more that president is followed. The position of the nodes is based on *stress* algorithm (Gansner et al., 2005).

```
for categoryChosen in levels:
    nodesChosen=[node[0] for node in net.nodes(data=True)
                if node[1]['region'] == categoryChosen]
    colorChosen=rgb2hex(palette(levels.index(categoryChosen)))
    nx.draw_networkx_nodes(net,pos=pos,node_size=100,
                           node_color=colorChosen,
                           nodelist=nodesChosen,
                           label=categoryChosen)
nx.draw_networkx_edges(net,pos=pos,edge_color="silver")

#drawing each node label - SIZE by indegree!!
for user in net.nodes():
    sizeLabel=net.nodes(data=True)[user]['indegree']+1
    nodeLabel=net.nodes(data=True)[user]['country']
    nx.draw_networkx_labels(net, pos=pos,
                            labels={user:nodeLabel},
                            font_size=sizeLabel**8) #varying sizes
# requesting legend
# marker in legend same size as actor node
plt.legend(markerscale=1, loc="best")
plt.show()
```

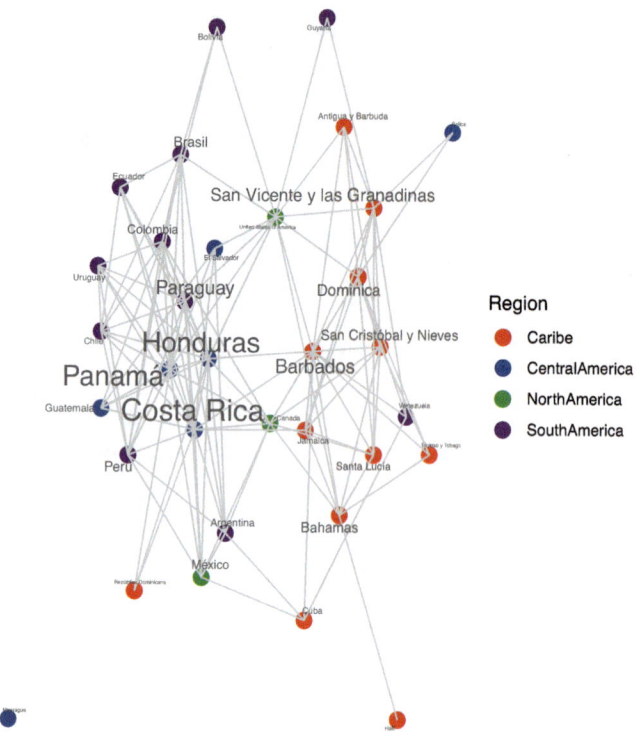

Figure 8.9 Network of Presidents of the Americas Sizes are based on out-degree centrality; nodes are colored by region in the Americas

The bigger the text, the more that president is a follower. The position of the nodes is based on *stress* algorithm (Gansner et al., 2005).

Similarly, an alternative **Python** version of Figure 8.9 follows:

```
from matplotlib.colors import rgb2hex
import matplotlib.pyplot as plt #513


plt.figure(figsize=(8,8))
#setting layout and palette
pos=nx.kamada_kawai_layout(net)
allValues=[n[1]['region'] for n in net.nodes(data=True)]
levels=pd.unique(allValues).tolist()
palette = plt.get_cmap("Set2")

#drawing nodes and edges
for categoryChosen in levels:
    nodesChosen=[node[0] for node in net.nodes(data=True)
                 if node[1]['region'] == categoryChosen]
    colorChosen=rgb2hex(palette(levels.index(categoryChosen)))
    nx.draw_networkx_nodes(net,pos=pos,node_size=100,
                           node_color=colorChosen,
                           nodelist=nodesChosen,
                           label=categoryChosen)
nx.draw_networkx_edges(net,pos=pos,edge_color="silver")
```

```
#drawing each node label - SIZE by outdegree!!
for user in net.nodes():
    sizeLabel=net.nodes(data=True)[user]['outdegree']+1
    nodeLabel=net.nodes(data=True)[user]['country']
    nx.draw_networkx_labels(net,pos=pos,
                            labels={user:nodeLabel},
                            font_size=sizeLabel**8)

plt.legend(markerscale=1, loc="best")
plt.show()
```

8.4.7 Highlighting Communities

The fact that actors belong to a particular neighbourhood does not mean that they are closely following or being followed by their neighbours. In networks, you speak of communities when you find that a set of actors is densely connected so as to differentiate itself from other set of actors, also densely connected. There are several algorithms for this, but their performance depends on how large the network is. If you are facing less than a thousand nodes, you may find that most algorithms can be chosen, but if you are speaking of thousands of nodes you need to carry out detailed research on this topic (see Fortunato (2010) and Yang et al. (2016)), and consider partnering with a network scientist.

Our data are very simple so it will be very easy to show you how this works. However, we have a directed network and most well-known algorithms can not work with directed edges. In some cases, the algorithm ignores the direction; in other cases it returns an error. Now, let me create an undirected version of my network:

```
> unet ← as.undirected(net, mode="mutual")
```

The object unet is an undirected network, but I have just kept the nodes that have a mutual relationship, using the 'mutual' option in mode. At this point, I have several nodes that are totally disconnected from the rest. If I do not do anything else, each *isolate* node will be a community of its own. So, let me get rid of the isolates:

```
> unet=delete.vertices(graph=unet, #input
+                      v=which(degree(unet)==0)) #what to remove
```

Let me do the same thing in **Python**:

```
# to indirected
unet=net.to_undirected(reciprocal=True)
# removing isolates
unet.remove_nodes_from(list(nx.isolates(unet)))
```

At this point, I am ready to find some communities in my network unet. Let me first use an algorithm based on *modularity maximization*; that is, modularity is an index that describes how well a set of nodes is connected, so those algorithms try optimize this index. Keep in mind that this family is not suitable for large networks (Clauset et al., 2004). In **R**, I can use the cluster_fast_greedy function to find the communities.

```
> modularityResult = cluster_fast_greedy(unet)
> # creating a new node attribute
> V(unet)$modCommunity = as.character(modularityResult$membership)
> # you get:
> V(unet)$modCommunity
```

```
 [1] "2" "1" "4" "3" "4" "3" "5" "6" "1" "3" "5" "1" "4" "4" "1" "2" "2"
     "6" "1"
[20] "4" "4" "2" "1" "2"
```

The new column modCommunity in the network unet tells you to what community a particular president belongs, so it is now very simple to prepare a plot:

```
> #layout
> layoutModu=ggraph(unet, layout="graphopt") + theme_void()
> #links
> moduLinks=layoutModu + geom_edge_link()
> #points
> moduNodes=moduLinks + geom_node_point(aes(colour=modCommunity),
+                                        size=5)
> #labels
> moduText=moduNodes+ geom_node_text(aes(label = name),
+                                     size=3,
+                                     color="black",
+                                     repel=T,
+                                     check_overlap = T)
> #final details
> moduVisual=moduText+scale_color_brewer(type = 'qual',
+                                         palette ="Set1")
> moduVisual=moduVisual + guides(color=FALSE)
```

The moduVisual object is drawn in Figure 8.10. This time, I have not allowed *ggraph* to choose the layout, I am explicitly requesting the use of the graphopt layout algorithm (Schmul, 2003).

Networkx has several algorithms to find communities, but I will use the external package *cdlib* (Rossetti, 2020) that works with *networkx* objects. Let me compute the communities following the same algorithm (modularity maximization):

```
# bring algorithm
from cdlib import algorithms

# Find the communities
modCommunity = algorithms.greedy_modularity(unet).communities
```

The result is saved in modCommunity, which I recovered after using .communities. If you check the contents of modCommunity you will see that the nodes have been organized into lists, like this:

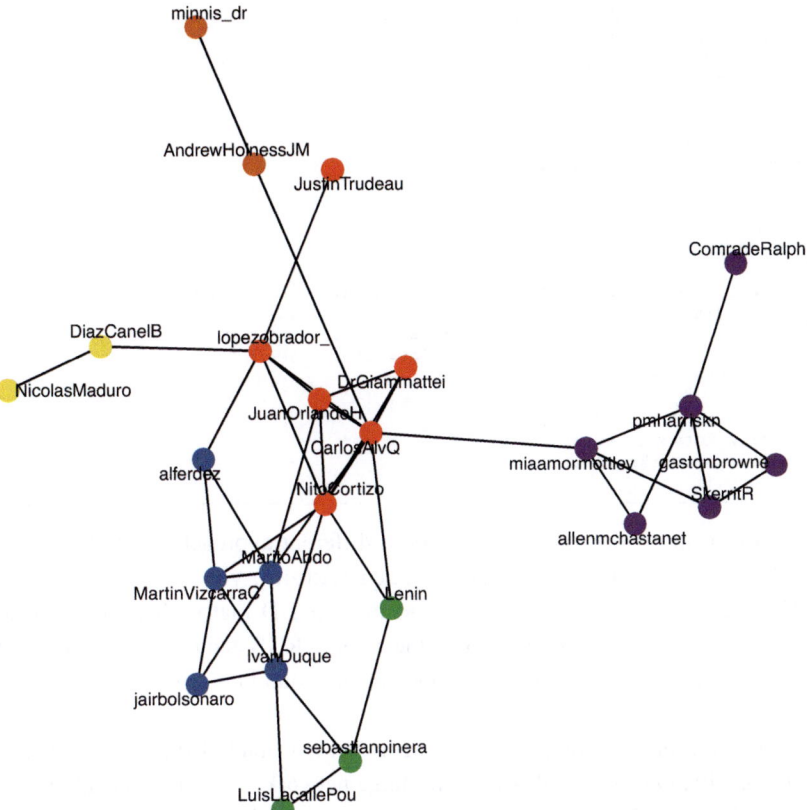

Figure 8.10 Network of Presidents of the Americas partitioned into communities
Color represents a particular community as detected following the Clauset et al. (2004) algorithm. The position of the nodes was computed using *graphopt* algorithm (Schmul, 2003).

```
[['ComradeRalph',
  'pmharriskn',
  'SkerritR',
  'miaamormottley',
  'gastonbrowne',
  'allenmchastanet'],
 ['JustinTrudeau',
  'CarlosAlvQ',
  'JuanOrlandoH',
  'lopezobrador_',
  'DrGiammattei',
  'NitoCortizo'],
 ['alferdez', 'MaritoAbdo', 'IvanDuque', 'MartinVizcarraC', 'jairbolsonaro'],
 ['LuisLacallePou', 'Lenin', 'sebastianpinera'],
 ['minnis_dr', 'AndrewHolnessJM'],
 ['DiazCanelB', 'NicolasMaduro']]
```

Once you know that the communities are identified, you can produce a result similar to Figure 8.10 like this:

```
import numpy as np
import matplotlib.pyplot as plt
from matplotlib.colors import rgb2hex

palette = plt.get_cmap("Set1")

pos=nx.kamada_kawai_layout(unet)
# for each community
colorIndex=0
for community in modCommunity:
    # INSTEAD of rgb to hexadecimal: repeating list
    colorChosen=np.tile(palette(colorIndex), (len(community), 1))
    nx.draw_networkx_nodes(unet,pos,
                         nodelist=community, #nodes chosen
                         node_color=colorChosen)
    colorIndex+=1 #increase index

#edges and labels (default values)
nx.draw_networkx_edges(unet, pos)
nx.draw_networkx_labels(unet,pos)
plt.show()
```

Notice that I decided to show you a different approach to producing the colors. If you just use `palette(colorIndex)`, you will get a warning. The warning also recommends you to input a 2-D matrix. That is what the `np.tile()` function does. It takes the color in RGB and repeats it in a matrix with as many rows as there are nodes in the community. I will not use this again.

As mentioned before, not every algorithm is suitable for networks of high complexity. One very well known for large networks is the Louvain algorithm (Blondel et al., 2008). Let me show you how easy it is to use it in **R**:

```
> louvainResult = cluster_louvain(unet)
> # creating a new node attribute
> V(unet)$louvainCommunity = as.character(louvainResult$membership)
> # as before:
> layoutLouv=ggraph(unet, layout="graphopt") + theme_void()
> louvLinks=layoutLouv + geom_edge_link()
> louvNodes=louvLinks + geom_node_point(aes(colour=louvainCommunity),
+                                       size=5)
> louvLabels=louvNodes+ geom_node_text(aes(label = name),
+                                       size=3,
+                                       color="black",
+                                       repel=T,
+                                       check_overlap = T)
> louvVisual=louvLabels+scale_color_brewer(type = 'qual',
+                                       palette ="Set1")
> louvVisual=louvVisual + guides(color=FALSE)
>
```

The `louvVisual` object is drawn in Figure 8.11.

The **Python** alternative for detecting a community using the Louvain method follows:

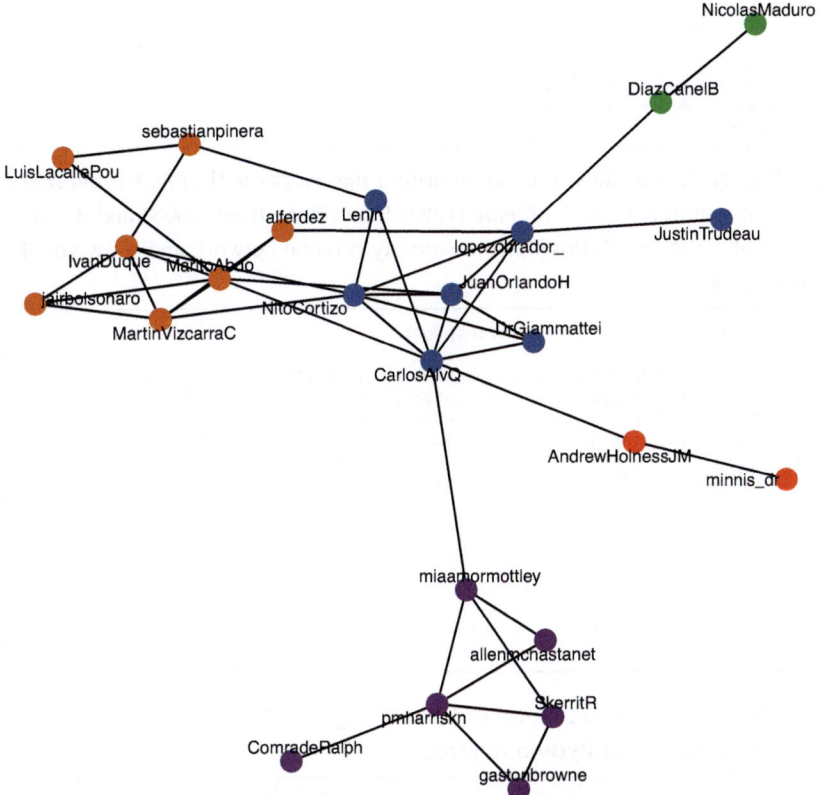

Figure 8.11 Network of Presidents of the Americas partitioned into communities

Color represents a particular community as detected following the Louvain algorithm (Blondel et al., 2008) The position of the nodes was computed using *graphopt* algorithm (Schmul, 2003).

```
louvainCommunity = algorithms.louvain(unet).communities

import matplotlib.pyplot as plt
from matplotlib.colors import rgb2hex

palette = plt.get_cmap("Set1")
pos=nx.kamada_kawai_layout(unet)

# for each community
colorIndex=0
for community in louvainCommunity:
    # from rgb to hexadecimal
    chosenColor=rgb2hex(palette(colorIndex))
    nx.draw_networkx_nodes(unet,pos,
                           nodelist=community, #nodes chosen
                           node_color=chosenColor)
```

```
      colorIndex+=1 #increase index
#edges and labels (default values)
nx.draw_networkx_edges(unet, pos)
nx.draw_networkx_labels(unet,pos)
plt.show()
```

Finally, let me show you an algorithm that works with *directed networks*. The algorithm is named *infomap* (Rosvall and Bergstrom, 2008) and it is also available in **R** and **Python**. Let me use my original network and show you the result in **R**:

```
> infomapResult = cluster_infomap(net)
> # creating a new node attribute
> V(net)$infmpCommunity = as.character(infomapResult$membership)
> layoutInfmp=ggraph(net, layout="graphopt") + theme_void()
> infmpLinks=layoutInfmp + geom_edge_link()
> infmpNodes=infmpLinks + geom_node_point(aes(colour=infmpCommunity),
+                                         size=5)
> infmpLabels=infmpNodes+ geom_node_text(aes(label = name),
+                                         size=3,
+                                         color="black",
+                                         repel=T,
+                                         check_overlap = T)
> infmpVisual=infmpLabels+scale_color_brewer(type = 'qual',
+                                         palette ="Set1")
> infmpVisual=infmpVisual + guides(color=FALSE)
>
```

The `infmpVisual` object is drawn in Figure 8.12.

The alternative in **Python** follows:

```
infmpCommunity = algorithms.infomap(net).communities

import matplotlib.pyplot as plt
from matplotlib.colors import rgb2hex

palette = plt.get_cmap("Set1")
pos=nx.kamada_kawai_layout(net)

# for each group
colorIndex=0
for community in infmpCommunity:
    # from rgb to hexadecimal
    chosenColor=rgb2hex(palette(colorIndex))
    nx.draw_networkx_nodes(net,pos,
                    nodelist=community, #nodes chosen
                    node_color=chosenColor)
    colorIndex+=1 #increase index

#edges and labels (default values)
nx.draw_networkx_edges(net, pos)
nx.draw_networkx_labels(net,pos)
plt.show()
```

There is so much more research on network science, but I think with these visual aids you can make a case whenever you have data suitable for this kind of work.

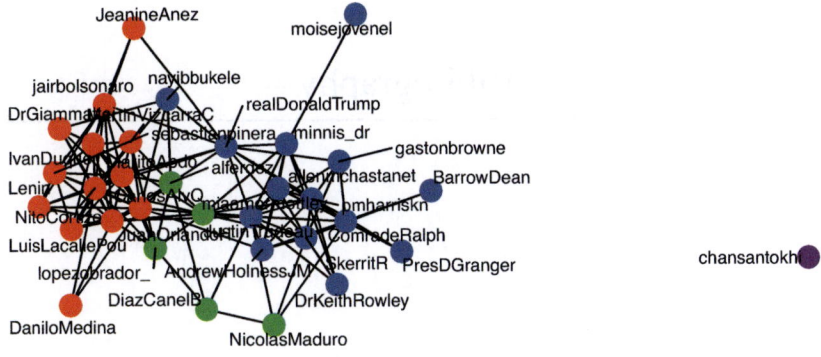

Figure 8.12 Network of Presidents of the Americas partitioned into communities

Color represents a particular community as detected following the Infomap algorithm (Rosvall and Bergstrom, 2008) The position of the nodes was computed using *graphopt* algorithm (Schmul, 2003).

Bibliography

Alvo, Mayer, and Yu, Philip. 2018. *A Parametric Approach to Nonparametric Statistics.* New York: Springer Science+Business Media.

American Psychological Association (ed). 2010. *Publication Manual of the American Psychological Association.* 6th ed. Washington, DC: American Psychological Association.

Arnold, Jeffrey B., Daroczi, Gergely, Werth, Bo, et al. 2019 (May). *ggthemes: Extra Themes, Scales and Geoms for 'ggplot2'.*

Babbie, Earl R. 2013. *The Practice of Social Research.* 13th edn. Belmont, CA: Wadsworth Cengage Learning. OCLC: ocn759584631.

Bank, Sebastian. 2020 (July). *graphviz: Simple Python interface for Graphviz.*

Barnier, Julien, Briatte, François, and Larmarange, Joseph. 2018 (Nov.). *questionr: Functions to Make Surveys Processing Easier.*

Bastian, Mathieu, Heymann, Sebastien, and Jacomy, Mathieu. 2009 (Mar.). Gephi: An Open Source Software for Exploring and Manipulating Networks. In: *Third International AAAI Conference on Weblogs and Social Media.*

Bilogur, Aleksey, Karve, Aneesh, Marsano, Luis, and Fleischmann, Martin. 2019 (Nov.). *geoplot.*

Bird, Steven, Klein, Ewan, and Loper, Edward. 2009. *Natural Language Processing with Python.* 1st ed. Beijing; Cambridge, MA: O'Reilly. OCLC: ocn301885973.

Bivand, Roger, Ono, Hisaji, Dunlap, Richard, Stigler, Matthieu, Denney, Bill, and Hernangómez, Diego. 2020 (Apr.). *classInt: Choose Univariate Class Intervals.*

Blondel, Vincent D., Guillaume, Jean-Loup, Lambiotte, Renaud, and Lefebvre, Etienne. 2008. Fast Unfolding of Communities in Large Networks. *Journal of Statistical Mechanics: Theory and Experiment,* (**10**), P10008. arXiv: 0803.0476.

Brandes, Ulrik, Eiglsperger, Markus, Herman, Ivan, Himsolt, Michael, and Marshall, M. Scott. 2002. GraphML Progress Report Structural Layer Proposal. Pages 501–512 of: Mutzel, Petra, Jünger, Michael, and Leipert, Sebastian (eds), *Graph Drawing.* Berlin, Heidelberg: Springer Berlin Heidelberg.

Brewer, Cynthia. 1999. Color Use Guidelines for Data Representation. In: *Proceedings of the Section on Statistical Graphics.* Alexandria, VA: American Statistical Association.

Brewer, Cynthia. 2009. *ColorBrewer: Color Advice for Maps.*

Brewer, Cynthia A., and Pickle, Linda. 2002. Evaluation of Methods for Classifying Epidemiological Data on Choropleth Maps in Series. *Annals of the Association of American Geographers*, **92**(4), 662–681.

Butler, H., Daly, M., Doyle, A., Gillies, S., Hagen, S., and Schaub, T. 2016 (Aug.). *The GeoJSON Format*. Tech. rept. RFC7946. RFC Editor.

Carrera, Ero. 2018 (Dec.). *pydot: Python interface to Graphviz's Dot*.

Caswell, Thomas A., Droettboom, Michael, Hunter, John et al. 2019 (July). *matplotlib*.

Chen, J. J. 2018 (Feb.). *gglorenz: Plotting Lorenz Curve with the Blessing of 'ggplot2'*.

Cioffi-Revilla, Claudio A. 2014. *Introduction to Computational Social Science: Principles and Applications*. London: Springer Verlag.

City of Seattle. 2019 (Dec.). *Crime Data/City of Seattle Open Data portal*.

Clauset, Aaron, Newman, M. E. J., and Moore, Cristopher. 2004. Finding Community Structure in Very Large Networks. *Physical Review E*, **70**(6).

Clayton, Mike. 2018 (May). *The Pareto Principle/The 80-20 Rule*.

Cleveland, William S., and McGill, Robert. 1984. Graphical Perception: Theory, Experimentation, and Application to the Development of Graphical methods. *Journal of the American Statistical Association*, **79**(387), 531.

Cook, R. Dennis. 1979. Influential Observations in Linear Regression. *Journal of the American Statistical Association*, **74**(365), 169.

Csardi, Gabor, and Nepusz, Tamas. 2006. The igraph software package for complex network research. *InterJournal* **9**.

Cytoscape Consortium. 2020 (Sept.). *cytoscape/cytoscape*. original-date: 2013-01-16T22:12:17Z.

Dorin, Federico, Perrotti, Daniel, and Goldszier, Patricia. 2020. *Index numbers and their relationship with the economy*. OCLC: 1191896788.

Dunnington, Dewey. 2020 (Sept.). *ggspatial*. original-date: 2016-07-11T21:06:12Z.

Ellson, John, Gansner, Emden R., Koutsofios, Eleftherios, North, Stephen C., and Woodhull, Gordon. 2003. Graphviz and dynagraph - static and dynamic graph drawing tools. Pages 127–148 of: *Graph Drawing Software*. Springer-Verlag.

Environmental Systems Research Institute. 1998. ESRI Shapefile Technical Description. July, 34.

Fisher, Walter D. 1958. On Grouping for Maximum Homogeneity. *Journal of the American Statistical Association*, **53**(284), 789–798.

Flyamer, Ilya. 2019 (Aug.). *adjustText*. original-date: 2016-01-10T02:11:06Z.

Fortunato, Santo. 2010. Community detection in graphs. *Physics Reports*, **486**(3–5), 75–174.

Fox, John, and Weisberg, Sanford. 2019. Appendix -Nonparametric Regression in R. Page 17 of: *An R companion to applied regression*, 3rd ed. Los Angeles, CA: SAGE.

Fruchterman, Thomas M. J., and Reingold, Edward M. 1991. Graph Drawing by Force-Directed Placement. *Software: Practice and Experience*, **21**(11), 1129–1164.

Gansner, Emden R., Koren, Yehuda, and North, Stephen. 2005. Graph drawing by stress majorization. Pages 239–250 of: Pach, János (ed.), *Graph Drawing*. Berlin, Heidelberg: Springer Berlin Heidelberg.

Gini, Corrado. 1912. *Variabilità e mutabilità: contributo allo studio delle distribuzioni e delle relazioni statistiche*. Tipogr. di P. Cuppini. Google-Books-ID: fqjaBP-MxB9kC.

Gini, Corrado. 1921. Measurement of Inequality of Incomes. *The Economic Journal*, **31**(121), 124.

Grey, Kenith. 2018 (Dec.). *ggQC: Quality Control Charts for 'ggplot'*.

Grolemund, Garrett, and Wickham, Hadley. 2011. Dates and Times Made Easy with lubridate. *Journal of Statistical Software*, **40**(3).

Hagberg, Aric, Schult, Dan, and Swart, Pieter. 2020 (Aug.). *networkx/networkx*. original-date: 2010-09-06T00:53:44Z.

Hickey, Walt. 2013 (June). *The Worst chart in the world*.

Hill, Aaron, and Roesslein, Joshua. 2020 (July). *tweepy/tweepy: Twitter for Python!*

Hunter, John D. 2007. Matplotlib: A 2D Graphics Environment. *Computing in Science & Engineering*, **9**(3), 90–95.

Jenks, George F., and Caspall, Fred C. 1971. Error on Choroplethic Maps: Definition, Measurement, Reduction. *Annals of the Association of American Geographers*, **61**(2), 217–244.

Jesus, Rogerio Prado de. 2019 (June). *rogeriopradoj-paretochart - Fork from @tintrinh*.

Jiang, Bin. 2013. Head/Tail Breaks: A New Classification Scheme for Data with a Heavy-Tailed Distribution. *The Professional Geographer*, **65**(3), 482–494.

Jordahl, Kelsey, Bossche, Joris Van Den, Wasserman, et al. 2020 (Feb.). *geopandas/geopandas: v0.7.0*.

Juran. 2019 (Mar.). *Pareto Principle (80/20 Rule) & Pareto Analysis Guide*.

Kabacoff, Robert. 2017. *Graphical Parameters*.

Kamada, Tomihisa, and Kawai, Satoru. 1989. An Algorithm for Drawing General Undirected Graphs. *Information Processing Letters*, **31**(1), 7–15.

Kearney, Michael W., Heiss, Andrew, and Briatte, Francois. 2020 (Jan.). *rtweet: Collecting Twitter Data*.

Kibirige, Hassan. 2019 (Nov.). *plotnine*. original-date: 2017-04-24T19:00:44Z.

Kibirige, Hassan. 2020a (Jan.). *mizani*. original-date: 2016-06-30T15:02:41Z.

Kibirige, Hassan. 2020b (Jan.). *scikit-misc*. original-date: 2016-10-12T01:40:36Z.

Kim, Taehoon. 2015 (May). *carpedm20/emoji*. original-date: 2014-08-18T02:55:59Z.

Kroulek, Alison. 2016 (Dec.). *International Marketing Cheat Sheet: Color Meanings Around the World*.

Laakso, Markku, and Taagepera, Rein. 1979. Effective Number of Parties: A Measure with Application to West Europe. *Comparative Political Studies*, **12**(1), 3–27.

Lang, Dawei, and Chien, Guan-tin. 2018 (Jan.). *wordcloud2: Create Word Cloud by 'htmlwidget'*.

Lee, Abraham. 2013 (Sept.). *paretochart: Pareto chart for python (similar to Matlab's, but much more flexible)*.

Lorenz, M. O. 1905. Methods of Measuring the Concentration of Wealth. *Publications of the American Statistical Association*, **9**(70), 209.

Mackinlay, Jock. 1986. Automating the design of graphical presentations of relational information. *ACM Transactions on Graphics*, **5**(2), 110–141.

Magallanes Reyes, Jose Manuel. 2017. *Introduction to Data Science for Social and Policy Research: Collecting to Organizing Data with R and Python*. Cambridge, United Kingdom; New York, USA; Port Melbourne, Australia; Delhi, India; Singapore: Cambridge University Press. OCLC: 998518603.

McKinney, Wes. 2010. Data Structures for Statistical Computing in Python. Pages 51–56 of: van der Walt, Stéfan, and Millman, Jarrod (eds), *Proceedings of the 9th Python in Science Conference*.

Mueller, Andreas. 2018 (July). *amueller/word_cloud*. original-date: 2012-11-04T22:57:59Z.

NCES National Center for Education Statistics. (2019). *Common Core of Data*. https://nces.ed.gov/ccd/schoolsearch/

North, Stephen. 2004. Drawing graphs with NEATO. Jan.

OECD, European Union, and Joint Research Centre – European Commission. 2008. *Handbook on Constructing Composite Indicators: Methodology and User Guide*. Paris: OECD Publishing.

Osborne, Peter. 2013. *The Mercator Projections*. Zenodo, Zenodo. https://doi.org/10.5281/zenodo.35392.

Pebesma, Edzer. 2018. Simple Features for R: Standardized Support for Spatial Vector Data. *The R Journal*, **10**(1), 439.

Pedersen, Thomas Lin. 2020 (May). *Layouts*.

Pedersen, Thomas Lin, and RStudio. 2020 (May). *ggraph: An Implementation of Grammar of Graphics for Graphs and Networks*.

Peterka-Bonetta, Jessica. 2017 (Mar.). *Emojis Analysis in R*.

Peterka-Bonetta, Jessica. 2019 (Nov.). *today-is-a-good-day/emojis*. original-date: 2015-09-10T10:16:25Z.

Pinard, Philippe. 2020 (Sept.). *ppinard/matplotlib-scalebar*. original-date: 2015-12-29T20:12:43Z.

Plotly Technologies Inc. 2015. *Plotly Python Graphing Library*. Library Catalog: plotly.com.

Pons, Odile. 2014. *Statistical Tests of Nonparametric Hypotheses: Asymptotic Theory*. [Hackensack] New Jersey: World Scientific.

QGIS.org. 2020. *QGIS Geographic Information System*.

Queiroz, Gabriela De, Fay, Colin, Hvitfeldt, Emil, Keyes et al. 2020 (July). *tidytext: Text Mining using 'dplyr', 'ggplot2', and Other Tidy Tools*.

Railsback, Steven F, and Grimm, Volker. 2012. *Agent-Based and Individual-Based Modeling: A practical introduction*. Princeton, NJ: Princeton University Press.

Rey, Sergio, Kang, Wei, Wolf, Levi John et al. 2020 (June). *pysal/mapclassify: mapclassify 2.3.0*.

Rossetti, Giulio. 2020 (Sept.). *GiulioRossetti/cdlib*. original-date: 2018-12-01T12:56:29Z.

Rosvall, M., and Bergstrom, C. T. 2008. Maps of Random Walks on Complex Networks Reveal Community Structure. *Proceedings of the National Academy of Sciences*, **105**(4), 1118–1123.

Russell, Matthew A., and Klassen, Mikhail. 2019. *Mining the Social Web: Data Mining Facebook, Twitter, Linkedin, Instagram, Github, and More*. 3rd edn. Sebastopol, CA: O'Reilly Media Inc. OCLC: 1059465439.

Saveljev, Vladimir, Kim, Sung-Kyu, and Kim, Jaisoon. 2018. Moiré Effect in Displays: A Tutorial. *Optical Engineering*, **57**(03), 1.

Schmul, Michael. 2003. *Graphopt layout algorithm*.

Seabold, Skipper, and Perktold, Josef. 2010. Statsmodels: Econometric and Statistical
   Modeling with Python. Page 5 of: *9th Python in Science Conference*.

Seeger, Marc. 2009. Key-Value stores: a practical overview. *Medien Informatik*,
   Sept., 21.

Signorell, Andri, Aho, Ken, Alfons, Andreas et al. 2019 (Dec.). *DescTools: Tools for
   Descriptive Statistics*.

Simpson, E. H. 1949. Measurement of Diversity. *Nature*, **163**(4148), 688.

Slowikowski, Kamil, Schep, Alicia, Hughes, Sean et al. 2020 (Mar.). *ggrepel: Automatically Position Non-Overlapping Text Labels with 'ggplot2'*.

Spear, Mary Eleanor. 1969. *Practical Charting Techniques*. New York; Maidenhead:
   McGraw-Hill. OCLC: 924909765.

Stevens, Stanley S. 1946. On the Theory of Scales of Measurement. *Science*, **103**(2684),
   677–680.

Tarawaneh, Raga'ad M., Keller, Patric, and Ebert, Achim. 2012. A General Introduction
   To Graph Visualization Techniques. 14 pages. Artwork Size: 14 pages Medium:
   application/pdf Publisher: Schloss Dagstuhl - Leibniz-Zentrum fuer Informatik
   GmbH, Wadern/Saarbruecken, Germany.

Teucher, Andy (support), Kenton Russell (JavaScript, and library), Matthew Bloch
   (mapshaper Javascript. 2020 (Apr.). *rmapshaper: Client for 'mapshaper' for
   'Geospatial' Operations*.

The Economist Intelligence Unit. 2017. *Safe Cities Index 2017*. Tech. rept. *The
   Economist*, London, UK.

The Economist Intelligence Unit. 2019 (Nov.). *Democracy Index*. Page Version ID:
   925222937.

Tufte, Edward R. 2001. *The Visual Display of Quantitative Information*. 2nd ed.
   Cheshire, CT: Graphics Press. OCLC: 248364903.

Tukey, John Wilder. 1977. *Exploratory data analysis*. Addison-Wesley series in
   behavioral science. Reading, MA: Addison-Wesley Pub. Co.

Washington State Legislature. 2019 (Aug.). *House of Representatives*.

Wickham, Hadley. 2014a. Tidy Data. *Journal of Statistical Software*, **59**(10).

Wickham, Hadley. 2016. *ggplot2: elegant graphics for data analysis*. 2nd ed. UseR!
   Cham: Springer. OCLC: 958058958.

Wickham, Hadley. 2018 (Oct.). *reshape: Flexibly Reshape Data*.

Wickham, Hadley, Chang, Winston, Henry, Lionel, Pedersen, Thomas Lin, Takahashi,
   Kohske, Wilke, Claus, Woo, Kara, Yutani, Hiroaki, and RStudio. 2019a (Aug.).
   ggplot2: Create Elegant Data Visualisations Using the Grammar of Graphics.

Wickham, Hadley, Seidel, Dana, and RStudio. 2019b (Nov.). *scales: Scale Functions
   for Visualization*.

Wickham, Hadley, François, Romain, Henry, Lionel, Müller, Kirill, and RStudio. 2020a
   (Mar.). *dplyr: A Grammar of Data Manipulation*.

Wickham, Hadley, Henry, Lionel, and RStudio. 2020b (July). *tidyr: Tidy Messy Data*.

Wickham, Hadley and Bache, Stefan Milton. 2014b (Nov.). *magrittr: A Forward-Pipe
   Operator for R*.

Wikimedia Foundation. 2019 (Oct.). *List of cities and towns in Washington*. Page
   Version ID: 923633362.

Wikipedia. 2020 (June). *COVID-19 pandemic in Washington (state)*.

Wilkinson, Leland. 2006. Revising the Pareto Chart. *The American Statistician*, **60**(4), 332–334.

Woerheide, W. 1993. An Index of Portfolio Diversification. *Financial Services Review*, **2**(2), 73–85.

Yang, Zhao, Algesheimer, René, and Tessone, Claudio J. 2016. A Comparative Analysis of Community Detection Algorithms on Artificial Networks. *Scientific Reports*, **6**(1), 30750. Number: 1 Publisher: Nature Publishing Group.

Index